Like A

Sydney C. Grier

Alpha Editions

This edition published in 2022

ISBN : 9789356891845

Design and Setting By
Alpha Editions
www.alphaedis.com
Email - info@alphaedis.com

Contents

CHAPTER I.
THE REFLECTIONS OF A YOUNG LADY ON GOING OUT INTO THE WORLD.

ROYAL OAK INN, DEAL, *Nov. ye* 26*th*, 1754.

THE hour so long dreaded is at length almost arrived, my Amelia, and your Sylvia weeps to remember that this is her last night on British soil. To-morrow, in the company of strangers, she leaves the only home she has ever known, her native land and all its dear inhabitants—and who is the best beloved of them, her sweet girl knows well—for an unfamiliar region, parents hitherto unseen, and a new manner of life. Ill would it become her to consecrate these last precious moments to anything but the duties of friendship, and in fulfilment of the promise that her latest thoughts on quitting England should be her dearest friend's, she takes the opportunity to begin this letter. It will reach you, as she understands, from about the neighbourhood of the Isle of Wight, since she expects to finish it on board the Orford, in time to entrust its posting to the pilot who steers the ship down the Channel.

But how, you will ask, has your friend contrived to learn so soon these particulars of her journey? The answer to that question, my Amelia, belongs to the history of the day's travelling, of which you saw only the heartrending commencement. Sure no young creature ever left Holly-tree House with a heart so heavy as mine! When I had kissed the hands of our venerable instructresses, and had received Mrs Eustacia's warning against neglecting the polite accomplishments, in the practice of which (she was good enough to say) I had gained so considerable a proficiency, and Mrs Abigail had begged of me not to read romances and to beware of listening to the flatteries of men, the worst was still to come. Was it not enough to encounter the tearful farewells of all the dear Misses, that I must experience the crowning grief of beholding my Amelia fallen into a fit,[01] and carried away by Mrs Abigail and the governess, thus depriving me of the last fond glance I had anticipated? Oh, my dearest Miss Turnor, when the good Rector stopped me on the footpath as I was hurrying to hide my tears in the chaise, and bade God bless me, and wished me an obliging spouse and a great fortune (hateful word!), I was hard put to it not to burst out sobbing in his face. Once seated in the chaise, however, the polite concern and surprised countenances of Mrs Hamlin and her niece assisted me to restrain my tears, and we drove off in the genteelest style imaginable, with Miss Hamlin's brother, the lieutenant of dragoons, riding beside the chaise.

As soon as she saw me a little more composed, Miss Hamlin began to rally me on the grief I displayed to quit my school, and charged me with leaving a dear friend behind me there. "And I'm certain," says she, "that I have discovered this friend. Pray, miss, wasn't it the handsome young lady in the blue lustring nightgown[02] who was so overcome by her feelings that she fainted away? Sure you must have observed her, brother?"

"That I did," says Mr Hamlin; "and a monstrous fine girl she was, too."

More to this effect was said, and my Amelia will guess how these compliments to my friend warmed my heart, and placed me on the best of terms with Mr and Miss Hamlin, while their aunt, who seems a very agreeable, good sort of a woman, did her best to set your timid Sylvia at her ease. As often as the thoughts natural to my situation threatened to overcome my composure, the ladies were ready to divert my mind to some fresh topic, the elder with infinite good humour, and her niece with the greatest archness in the world. My Amelia must not imagine herself in the smallest degree forgot when I tell her that I am persuaded I shall find Miss Hamlin a vastly agreeable companion, in spite of the difference between her constitution and mine. At midday we abated our journey at an inn, where we found the advantage of Mr Hamlin's company, since every one was agog to serve him. No sooner had he entered the place in his laced scarlet coat, with the King's ribbon[03] in his hat, than there was all manner of rushing hither and thither, and it was, "What does your honour please to desire?" and "What will the noble Captain[04] take?" on every side.

Miss Hamlin rallied her brother very pleasantly on the matter during the meal, and I was thankful that she was thus engaged, since I could scarce eat a morsel. On returning to the post-chaise, Mrs Hamlin fell asleep, and her niece confided to me in whispers many points of extraordinary interest touching the clothes she is taking out to Bengal with her—confidences which I did my best to return, although I can't hope to rival them. We reached Deal about four in the afternoon, and Mrs Hamlin ordered tea immediately in the private parlour she had engaged beforehand, whither we repaired. Presently up comes Mr Hamlin, who had been seeing our trunks brought in, and acquainted his aunt that there were lodging in the inn two young gentlemen of whom he had some slight knowledge, and who were to be our fellow-passengers to India on board the Orford, adding that if we could come to an agreement with them to share a boat on the morrow, we might reach our vessel at far less cost.

"Well thought of!" cries Mrs Hamlin. "Pray, Henry, request the gentlemen to step upstairs and drink a dish of tea with us here."

"With all my heart, madam," says the Captain, and down he goes, returning quickly with the two gentlemen, who differed considerably from each other in appearance. The first, whom Mr Hamlin presented to his aunt as Lieutenant Colvin Fraser, of his Majesty's ship Tyger, was tall and very well made, but a degree too thin for his height, his complexion ruddy, his eyes grey, his hair, which was his own, of a reddish colour. He wore the King's ribbon, but a plain fustian suit of a dark blue. The other gentleman, who was of a smaller and slighter figure and a dark complexion, and with whom Mr Hamlin had a much better acquaintance than with Lieutenant Fraser, was introduced as Mr Ensign Ranger, of the Hon. Company's Bengall European Regiment. The gentlemen were presented to us severally, and both entered into conversation in a very genteel manner, modest without being bashful, although it seemed to me that Mr Ranger was the more assured, and Lieutenant Fraser the more cautious.

"Come, gentlemen," says Mrs Hamlin at last, "since we are to be fellow-travellers for so long, let us begin, like the personages in the romances, by telling each other our histories. As for myself, you will have guessed that I am sailing to rejoin my spouse, who was until lately head of the Company's house at Ballisore, and that during the journey I have the charge of Miss Freyne, whose papa is a member of Council at Calcutta, as well as of my niece, who will reside with her uncle and me when we reach Bengall."

"And questionless you'll also have guessed that both ladies are sailing to seek their fortunes—with spouses attached to 'em," says Mr Hamlin.

"Oh, fie, brother!" cries Miss Hamlin. "See how Miss Freyne is out of countenance for your freedom. Pray, miss, don't heed the Captain. He has no delicacy of mind."

"And pray, miss, why are you going, if not in the hope of getting married?" demanded Mr Hamlin. "How silly must these gentlemen think it in you to be so nice in denying what's the truth!"

Before Miss Hamlin could reply, Lieutenant Fraser took up the dispute with great warmth, saying that for his part, not only would he not venture to suggest to a lady the terms she should employ in speaking, but he thought that man a sad coxcomb who would presume to do so, more especially in a matter of such delicacy as had just been touched upon. Mr Hamlin, though astounded by this outburst, was about to reply warmly, when his aunt interfered, reproved both disputants for the heat they were displaying, and desired them to return to the topic on which she had requested information.

"You, Lieutenant Fraser," she said, "shall be the first to recount to us your history. How is it, pray, that we find a King's officer taking passage in an Indiaman?"

"Indeed, madam," says he, fetching a heavy sigh, "my situation can't appear stranger to you than it did irksome to myself until a few minutes ago. Sure you see before you the victim of a series of the cruellest misfortunes that ever baulked a man of his most reasonable desires. You'll be already aware, questionless, that in February the King despatched Admiral Watson to the East Indies with the Kent and Salisbury and others of his Majesty's ships, in the anticipation that when war next breaks out with France, much will hang upon the situation in the Decan, where our nation and the French have been so continually at strife of late years. You will be at no loss to imagine that the recent exploits and successes of Colonel Clive have stirred up such a spirit of emulation in both the sea and land services that the Admiral might have had his pick of the whole nation either as officers or volunteers on board of his ships, but it so happened that having been fortunate enough to gain his approbation when serving with him before (for I was bred up under him from my earliest youth at sea), I had his promise to take me with him if he could in any way compass it. But now, madam, came in the first of the distressing accidents I have mentioned. Not only did I find my applications continually set aside in favour of gentlemen who possessed greater interest than I could boast, but Mr Watson's own desires were thwarted with a like persistence. And all this was in spite of the many signal services rendered by my father to the Government in the rising of the Highlands nine years back, so true is the saying that good offices are seldom remembered unless their repetition is looked for."

"Pray, sir," cries the Captain, "stick to your tale, and don't weary the ladies with pieces of musty wisdom that you've picked up from some long-winded divine."

"Pray, nephew Henry," says Mrs Hamlin, seeing that Lieutenant Fraser, although out of countenance by reason of the interruption, was looking very fierce; "don't break into the gentleman's history, which we all love to hear him tell in his own style. Sure you ought to know that though you fine London sparks may make a boast of your ignorance, every Scottish gentleman prides himself on possessing a store of polite learning and reflections, and if Mr Fraser is good enough to display his for our entertainment, he is to be commended, and not blamed. Pray, sir, continue."

"I'll do my best not to be tedious, madam," says the Lieutenant, with a bow. "You may conceive then my mortification when the squadron set sail without me, although I was a little comforted by the Admiral's assuring me that he had left my case in the hands of a friend of his that had interest at the India House, and would see that my name was brought before the Admiralty if there were any question of sending out reinforcements to him. If my distress had been extreme at the rude blasting of my hopes, it was equalled by my delight when in the month of May I received my commission as fourth lieutenant of the Tyger. You may not, madam, have heard at the time that Admiral Watson met with such severe weather in the Channel that he was forced to send back part of his fleet disabled from Kingsale, where he had put in for the purpose of taking on board Colonel Adlercron's regiment of foot[05] for service in the Carnatic. On hearing of this disaster the Government determined to fit out and despatch immediately the Tyger and the Cumberland, which might take on board the remainder of the soldiers, and endeavour to overtake Mr Watson, who had continued his voyage without regarding the smallness of his force. No words can paint my delight on receiving this news, but making the best of my way to join my ship at Plymouth, I was so unfortunate as to spend the night at an inn where a man lay sick of the small-pox. Although I did not approach him, as you may well guess, it seems that the air of the place must have carried the infection, for I was seized with the malady the day before that on which the Tyger and her consort were to sail. The disorder of my mind, on seeing my hopes again overthrown, aggravated my sufferings to such a degree that I barely escaped with my life, and only left the hospital after an extraordinary long bout of sickness. As soon as I was fairly recovered, I made haste to open my affairs to the Admiralty, who, compassionating my hard case, gave me leave to proceed at my own costs to the East Indies, where, if I find my post aboard the Tyger filled up, I must even offer my services as a volunteer."

"Unless your ill-fortune should pursue you so far as to prevent your sailing with us to-morrow, sir," says Mrs Hamlin.

"Sure, madam, in the company in which I now am no ill fortune can prevail to touch me."

"I protest, sir, you are too flattering. Pray, sir," and Mrs Hamlin looked towards the second gentleman, "tell us your history now."

"Alas, madam!" says Mr Ranger, heaving a prodigious sigh, in extravagant imitation of that with which his friend had commenced his recital; "I have no tale to tell that will bring the moisture of compassion to the eye of beauty, as that of Mr Fraser has been happy enough to do. My sufferings are of too ordinary a nature to do more than excite the tribute of a pitying glance. I can but say that I had the honour to serve his Majesty in the regiment which your nephew, my esteemed friend here, so justly adorns, and that the modest fortune I inherited proved insufficient to support the dignity with which I desired to invest my situation. I need not wound the tender hearts of the young ladies by describing the disagreeable results of this unfortunate disproportion; it is enough to remark that I was thankful to accept the offer of my uncle, who is an India director, to make interest to obtain for me a pair of colours in the Bengall Regiment."

"Indeed, sir, you en't in no way to be pitied," says Mrs Hamlin, with some coldness. "Are you aware how many worthy young gentlemen, each of whom has spent several years as a private man in the Company's forces, carrying a musket and mounting guard in the Select Piquet,[06] will be disobliged by this placing you over their heads?"

"No, indeed, madam," said he; "and for the sake of my own peace of mind, I'll beg you won't acquaint me of their exact number. I'll assure you that I have a very feeling heart, and to wound it would in no way advantage these unfortunate gentlemen, while it would be prodigiously disagreeable to me. To conclude my story, madam; I fell in with Lieutenant Fraser in Leadenhall Street, and learning that we were travelling by the same vessel, we agreed to post to Dover in company, by which means I enjoy the happiness of being at your service to-night."

This whimsical reply, delivered with infinite good humour, to her reproof, put Mrs Hamlin into some difficulty not to laugh, and turning again to Mr Fraser, she enquired of him how soon our vessel was likely to sail?

"I heard but an hour back, madam," he answered, "that those on board were much concerned to lose so much of this fair wind—as indeed I would be, in their case—and that the passengers should all be in their places by eleven o'clock to-morrow, when the captain, who is posting from town, is looked for."

"La!" says Miss Hamlin, with the most engaging vivacity, "what a pity to waste time in this way! I'm all anxiety to be well on my way to India."

"Because you know nothing about it, child," says her brother. "Ask my aunt whether she finds a voyage as agreeable as you think. I'll lay you a guinea you'll be in a fine pickle before you reach Bengall, with no chance of getting at your 'things,' as you call 'em, to divert yourself with."

"Brother, you're a sad bear," said Miss Hamlin very gravely. "Gentlemen, now that we have drank our tea, I have been waiting in vain for one of you to suggest a promenade. Must I make the proposal myself?"

"Pray permit me to wait on you out of doors, madam," said both the strange gentlemen in a breath.

"Well, indeed," says Mrs Hamlin, "I think we shan't do wrong in hiring a boat to take us on board to-morrow, since our time is like to be so short, and though it be dark already, the lights on the water afford a vastly agreeable prospect if we take a short stroll. You'll accompany us, Miss Freyne?"

But I excused myself on the plea of fatigue, and sat down to begin this letter, which diverted Miss Hamlin excessively when she came back into the parlour in her capuchin[07] to look for her muff.

"I protest, miss, you're quite an author!" she cried. "Sure you must be emulating the practice of the divine Clarissa?"

"You're right, miss," said I. "Like Miss Harlowe, I am writing to the best of friends."

She went away laughing, and I employed myself all the time of their absence in writing these pages, which would not be so many had I not desired to fulfil my promise of making my Amelia acquainted with the companions of our voyage. This shocking scribble that follows is wrote in my chamber before going to rest, for I must tell you of some droll things that Mrs Hamlin has been saying. She is, my dear, the oddest kind of woman! Coming in with her niece about half-an-hour before supper, leaving the gentlemen downstairs, she sat down upon the settee, and requested me to spare her a moment. You may be sure I lost no time in complying, more especially since I catched a very whimsical glance from Miss Hamlin as I shook the sand over my paper.

"I don't doubt but you was a good deal surprised, miss," says Mrs Hamlin, motioning me to take my place in the window-seat opposite her, "by my admitting those two young gentlemen to our company?"

"Indeed, madam," said I, "I never ventured——"

"You thought I was a good easy body, questionless, and no prude, and you passed remarks upon my discretion in your mind, perhaps?" I had no chance to answer, Amelia, for she went on without stopping: "Then I would have you know, miss, that you was mistaken. My complaisant behaviour is dictated altogether by policy, and I will go so far as to open to you my mind in the matter, the more so since I am persuaded you are a young woman of sense."

"I shall hope to deserve your good opinion, madam."

"As for my niece Hamlin," continued the good lady, "she has been bred up by her grandmamma, who was a toast in her youth, and even in her genteel retirement has not forgot the manners of the great world, so that she has, questionless, furnished her granddaughter with a whole battery of defensive arts. You han't enjoyed this advantage, miss, but I don't doubt the respectable gentlewomen who instructed you have warned you against the ways of Men?"

"Indeed, madam, they have spoke to me of little else for some months past, and their very last words——"

"Why, that's very well," says she, "for I must think better of you than to imagine that after such sedulous care you, any more than my Charlotte, could fall a prey to the wiles of the designing creatures. Pray, miss, what do you think was my intention in presenting the gentlemen to you two young women to-day?"

"Indeed, madam, I don't know," for what dark political meaning there could be in so natural an act, I could not imagine.

"Why, then," says Mrs Hamlin, "I desired to provide you both with agreeable cavaliers for the voyage, without the fear of falling in love on either side."

"Sure, madam, you're very kind," Miss Hamlin puts in.

Mrs Hamlin. Don't be pert, miss. I observed just now, Miss Freyne, that you was put out of countenance by a foolish remark of my nephew's, which his sister very properly reproved. Such sensibility does you honour, but I would have you learn to take such sayings in good part, since, though it be true that a man of fine manners would not allude to the fact so freely, 'tis yet undeniable that both you and my niece are going to Bengall to be married, as my poor Henry said.

Sylvia. Sure, madam, 'tis but the action of a woman of spirit to protest against such a view, and endeavour to discredit it?

Mrs H. I see, miss, that, like other romancical young ladies, you cherish the notion that you would prefer to lead a single life. I don't fancy you would remain long in that mind in Britain—since we en't Papists, and if I may say so to your face, you are reasonable well-looking—but in India such a resolution could not hold for a single day. When you have seen, as I have, the numerous crowds of gentlemen in respectable, if not in affluent circumstances, that will hasten to the *Gott*[08] to see the European ladies disembark, and rush to hand you out of your *palanqueen* and into church on Sunday, you will perceive that no woman could be so cruel as to keep so many worthy persons pining in suspense. I have known a young lady—and she not a creature of any figure—who was married, within two hours of her landing, to a gentleman she had never seen before.

Sylvia. I hope, madam, you don't anticipate such a fate for me?

Mrs H. I don't doubt, miss, but you'll consider your punctilio demands a longer time for choice. But if you'll reflect for a moment, you'll see that there's no forwardness, as you seem to imply, but rather the truest kindness on the part of their parents and guardians, in this sending out young ladies to find spouses. The Company's service is for life, and a gentleman can't come home to seek a suitable wife for himself. Imagine, then, his joy and gratitude when an agreeable match presents itself, and the assiduous complaisance with which he will behave to the lady who has done him the honour of selecting him out of so many suitors! I hope, miss, that you'll do credit to your bringing-up in the choice you make, and that the gentleman's fortune will be worthy of the advantages you bring him.

Sylvia (*smiling*). I have studied my 'Spectator,' dear madam, too closely to be ignorant that an honest life and an obliging temper are more to be regarded in the marriage state than a great fortune.

Mrs H. The 'Spectator,' miss? Sure he's the person that tells a tale of some old Roman,[09] who said he had rather marry his daughter to a man without an estate than to a great estate without a man. The good gentleman was certainly mad. Such a marriage as that would be the happiest that could befall most young women. But, indeed, miss, I would have you look at the whole matter from a judicious standpoint. There's some prudes that affect horror when they hear of a young lady's doing well for herself, not considering that she has but placed out her capital, which is herself, to the best advantage. Think of your good papa. He has sunk a great sum of money in sending you home to be brought up, and he'll look for a handsome return on his investment. You'll have a tolerable fortune—unless, indeed, it be true, as I heard said on my voyage home, that your papa has made such large settlements on the present Mrs Freyne as leaves but little for you. She was a Quinion—one of the Quinions of Madrass, and they have a sharp eye in money matters, and would get all they could from Mr Freyne.

Sylvia. Oh, pray, madam, don't use these terms of my papa. Sure he has every right to please himself in the disposition of his own property.

Mrs H. Very true, miss, but all the same it's fortunate for you that gentlemen in India ask less in the way of fortune with their wives than in England. I can but hope that you'll marry a man of wealth sufficient to give Mr Freyne a solid return upon his expenditure. And that brings me to the question on which I had purposed to speak to you. You may have heard a silly jest to the effect that young ladies sent out to India by their parents to marry great fortunes commonly disappoint their anticipations by entering into engagements of marriage with such young cadets and writers as may have pleased their fancy on the voyage out.

Sylvia. I had not heard it, madam.

Mrs H. You will, questionless, hear it often in the future. Well, miss, this unfortunate state of affairs is due, in my mind, to the injudicious severity of the ladies who have the charge of these young women. By forbidding them to converse with, or even to glance at, any of the gentlemen about them, they force them to appear either shy or uncivil, while by engaging the authority of the captain on their side they deliver a direct challenge to the young gentlemen to evade their prohibitions, so that it becomes the dearest wish of the young people to make each other's acquaintance, and this they'll succeed in doing by foul means, if not by fair. Ah! I could tell you of some sad unhappy marriages that have come about in this way, and also of many cases in which the young lady has seen her folly, and wedded the person selected for her by her guardians, after infinite trouble and foolish behaviour on the part of the suitor she has abandoned! Now I design to place no restriction upon you and my Charlotte, Miss Freyne. I have treated you as reasonable creatures, and I look to you to requite my kindness, mixing with these gentlemen, and any others I may introduce to your notice while on board, as young women of sense should do, and giving them no cause for presumption, nor others for talk. I leave the matter with your own consciences, requesting you to consider the pains taken with your bringing-up, and to remember that you would be actually robbing your relatives if you married below the rank they have a right to expect.

Sylvia. Pray, madam, would it be impossible for us to confine ourselves chiefly to female society, while conversing with these gentlemen so far as civility demands?

Miss Hamlin. La, miss! would you have an Indiaman a floating nunnery?

Mrs H. Your suggestion, miss, is extremely proper, but 'twould be impossible to carry it out on board ship. You'll find it almost necessary to have a gentleman at hand who will run your errands, and wait upon you on deck when the weather is fresh. But I can rely upon you to let the acquaintance go no further, and to preserve in your carriage such a distance as may keep your cavalier on the humble footing that becomes him.

It appeared to me, my Amelia, that there was scant tenderness shown for the feelings of the gentlemen in this device, but indeed I am so confused with all I have heard that I can scarce be sure my pity en't chiefly for myself. How humbling is it to a young creature's pride (I had almost said, how wounding to her delicacy), to find herself regarded in the light of a bale of merchandise, to be knocked down to the highest bidder! And why do our instructors recommend to our perusal the mild counsels of the excellent Mr Addison, if the most important action of our future life is to give them the lie in every particular? But Mrs Abigail would say that I was passing judgment on my elders; I will cease, therefore, and only hope that my papa may be of a different spirit from Mrs Hamlin.

The gentlemen joined us at supper, and Lieutenant Hamlin demanded of his sister to give him some music afterwards—a request that was very heartily seconded by both the others—but on Mrs Hamlin's declaring that she was dog-tired, and would fain be early a-bed, the company broke up. Miss Hamlin very good-naturedly waited upon me to my chamber, and when she had set down the candlestick, I thought would have taken her leave, but to my surprise she shut the door, saying—

"Pray, miss, what is your opinion of my aunt's great piece of policy?"

"Sure I'm grateful to be treated as a reasonable creature, miss," said I.

"And for that," says she, "you may thank my aunt's love of ease. She is desirous to pass her time agreeably in playing whisk[10] and brag with her friends, reading romances, or slandering her neighbours—not in looking after two young women that happen to be placed in her charge."

"Indeed, miss, you make vastly free with your aunt's name."

"And therefore," Miss Hamlin went on without heeding me, "she throws the burden on the young women themselves, and thinks she has done all her duty when she has placed it on their consciences. Pray, miss, was you born with a heart?"

"Sure I don't understand you, miss," said I, staggered, as they say, by so sudden and particular[11] a question.

"Because I was not," said this strange girl; "or if I were, it has been bred out of me—without it be like the coquette's heart at the dissection of which your dear 'Spectator' says he attended. But you, miss, if I don't mistake, are burdened with this useless and improper possession. Pray understand that by the time you reach Bengall it must be gone, and replaced either by a purse of gold or a chest of toys and laces, or else the determination to outshine your neighbours, if you are ever to cut a figure in Calcutta. The voyage is your opportunity of practising for its removal."

"Indeed, miss——" said I, bewildered, but she interrupted me.

"I have pointed out to you your work for the next eight or nine months, miss, and I shall hope to see you fashionably heartless when we land in India. But for the present, which of the two gentlemen that have been designated as our bond-slaves for the voyage will you attach to your service?"

"Oh, pray, miss, oblige me by choosing first," said I.

"Then I choose Mr Ranger," said she, quickly.

"I'm quite content to take Mr Fraser," said I, well pleased.

"That's as I should have guessed. I have chose Mr Ranger because he is the more entertaining to me, but if I were acting the part of a true friend by you, miss, I should have taken the Lieutenant."

"Indeed, miss, I'll assure you he pleases me vastly the better of the two."

"So I foresaw. A witty blade like Mr Ranger would have no charms for you, miss, but this Scottish gentleman, with his tags of philosophy and his turn for relating his troubles in a moving style, is a dangerous person to meet a young lady that possesses a heart and has but just left her boarding-school."

"I hope, miss, you wasn't intending a sneer at my bringing-up?"

"Not for the world, though I will say that my grandmamma is a better instructor for adventurers like you and me than the venerable ladies I saw this morning. But tell me, miss, do you purpose to inform your Fraser of the terms on which he is permitted the honour of your acquaintance—that he is to run your errands and not fall in love with you?"

"Pray, miss, do you look for me to suggest to the gentleman that I expect him to do any such thing?"

"But you'll allow that such a thing is at least possible? Come, miss, prudence should lead you to anticipate calamities, you know. What is to happen if Mr Fraser should have the presumption to lay his heart at your feet, or even—an extraordinary wild supposition, I grant you—if your heart should betray you, and you fall in love with him?"

My Amelia will guess I was so horridly confused by these remarks that I was at a loss how to answer Miss Hamlin, but at last I got out something to the effect that I hoped I should do my duty in any case.

"But will you break the poor fellow's heart as well as your own, miss?" persisted my tormentor.

"I trust, miss," said I, "that there'll be no question of such an unhappy event. I give you free leave to warn me, and Mr Fraser also, if you will, if you think either of us to be in danger."

"I promise you I will," says she; "and finely you'll hate me when 'tis done."

With that she left me, and I sat up to write this. But here I must cease, for my candle is burning low in its socket, and Miss Hamlin has just tapped again at my door to ask me whether I desire to make my last night in Britain memorable by setting the inn afire.

Hon. Co.'s Ship Orford, off HASTINGS, *Nov. ye* 28*th.*

I am adding these few last lines in lead pencil to my great pacquet in haste, since Mr Fraser assures me that once past Beachy Head we shall find ourselves in rough water. I can't at present call myself indisposed, though I am not quite at my ease, as I ought to be, since Mr Fraser says the wind is so light as to be almost a calm. The space on board is very much confined, particularly since the decks are still lumbered up with all kinds of packages, but I learn that these will before long be stowed away below. Pray, my dear friend, pardon these seaman's phrases. My head is too confused to remember the correct terms. You would smile to see how we are all lodged here, the gentlemen in the great cabin, on shelves like those in a draper's shop, and only large enough to hold a small mattress, and we in another apartment, similarly furnished. There are two ladies on board besides ourselves, but neither of them young, and both married, and about a dozen gentlemen. I had intended to write something of the day and a half since we left Deal, but find that the end of my paper is all but reached. You shall receive a long letter by the first opportunity that offers of sending one. Adieu, my dearest, dearest Emily.[12] Rest assured that you was ever in my thoughts from the moment of our parting.

CHAPTER II.
IN WHICH IS SET FORTH THE INCONSTANCY OF MAN.

Hon. Co.'s Ship Orford, FONCHIAL[01] HARBOUR, *Dec. ye* 31*st.*

Since despatching my first letter to my Amelia by the hands of the pilot, I have passed through such an experience as I should not care to repeat. Ah, my dear, we thought it at school a simple thing to hear that Britain is an island, but 'tis a fact one learns to appreciate when it is being fixed in one's mind by a sea-voyage. For over three weeks, my dearest friend, was your Sylvia pent up in the narrow floating prison which is called the ladies' cabin, enduring, for the greater part of the time, such protracted torments as she could not have dreamed the human frame would be able to support. You may smile to hear that I had willingly relinquished all the future glories of Bengall, and even the hope of a meeting with my papa, for the sake of a grave on dry land, where, at least, there would be no more shaking and tumbling, but had the exchange been offered me, I don't dare say that I would not have accepted it gladly. Imagine, my Amelia, your unfortunate friend confined with four other females in a narrow chamber lighted only by a ship's lantern (for the weather was so bad that the ports, by which is signified the small windows of the vessel, were forced to be closed), each extended on a wooden shelf about the size, so I should think, of a coffin. To the sufferings caused by illness, add the terrors of a storm, when the hatches were battened down, as they say (this means that heavy coverings were fastened over the only openings by which light and air can visit the lower decks, lest they should admit water as well), and the howling of the wind and roaring of the waves as they dashed over the ship was attempted to be drowned by the hoarse shouting of the seamen. I'll assure you that I never expected to see dry land again, and as I have said, I was glad to think so. But how, you'll say, did my companions support the trials which were so painful to your Sylvia? Truly, my dear, they supported them with as bad a grace as I did. Miss Hamlin, indeed, never lost her sprightly humour, and diverted herself, even in the extremity of our sufferings, by rallying the other ladies on the dangers they apprehended, but her aunt had no spirit to do more than lie upon her shelf and groan, which she did in the most moving style. As for the other two ladies, whose husbands were on board, they seemed to consider that the bad weather was to be laid to the fault of their spouses. These unfortunate gentlemen had betaken themselves to their shelves in the great cabin (as, indeed, had all the male passengers, with the exception I shall presently mention), and lay there as miserable as ourselves, but their ladies were persuaded that they were employing themselves in drinking and playing high with the officers of the ship, and many were the messages of rebuke sent to them through the steward. This was a stout fellow, of the most unfeeling temper, who brought in our broth or tea when the black women that Mrs Hamlin and the other ladies are taking back to India with them were too ill to move, and never failed to assure us that we should find ourselves quite recovered if we would but pluck up courage to put on our clothes and go on deck.

We did not, as my Amelia will imagine, follow the advice of this odious person, but when the storm had ceased, and we were able to rest on our shelves without holding perpetually by the edges, he brought a message from Mr Fraser, asking if he might have the honour of waiting upon any of the ladies on deck. Now the Lieutenant, who was the exception I have mentioned to the general rule of illness among the gentlemen, had shown great consideration for us poor women during the storm, coming frequently to the door of the cabin to assure us that all was well, and had gone so far as to promise that he would bring us instant warning if any grave danger threatened the vessel, so that I thought it only civil to make some effort to respond to his politeness.

"Pray, miss," I said to Miss Hamlin, "have you any fancy to rise? Shall we ask the gentleman to attend us both?"

"Why, no, miss," says she. "'Tis your fellow sends the invitation, not mine. Pray beg the Lieutenant to inform Mr Ranger that I am dependent upon his civilities, and that I look to him to attend me on deck to-morrow."

"But you would not have me go on deck alone?" I said.

"No, miss, I would have you go with Mr Fraser. Sure the poor man must be pining for a sight of your face after so long a deprivation of it."

This sly hint made me so angry that I was about to say I would not go, but being unwilling to allow Miss Hamlin so much power over me as this would imply, I made shift to dress myself with infinite trouble (although I did not attempt to appear in anything but an undress, as you may imagine), and with my hair huddled into a mob[02] under my capuchin, tottered out into the passage, where I found Mr Fraser awaiting me. He expressed great concern at my altered looks (for you may guess that one's face is not at its best after three weeks of such misery as we have been enduring), and gave me his hand on deck. There, while I stood holding to a rail, scarce able to keep my feet, he devised a seat for me in a corner sheltered from the wind, and having placed me there covered with a great watch-coat of his own, stood looking at me very kindly, and asked me how I did? I was so much overcome by the sudden return to air and daylight that I could hardly answer him, and perceiving this, he began to point out to me the different parts of the vessel, and tell me their names. The bales and cases which had encumbered the deck when I had last seen it were now removed, and the ship, though her upper works had suffered in places from the violence of the waves, had a much more spacious and agreeable air.

"But pray, sir," said I, when I had recovered my intellects, "tell me whether you was ever in so terrible a storm in all your life hitherto?"

"So terrible a storm, madam?" says he, as if surprised. "What storm?"

"Why, the storm that is but just subsided, sir?"

"There was no storm, madam. We met with some dirty weather in the Bay, but every seaman looks for that."

"Dirty weather!" said I. "In what way could a storm be worse, sir?"

Before Mr Fraser could answer, a person who had been walking up and down the deck paused in front of us. He wore a watch-coat and an oil-skin cover to his hat, and carried a marine glass under his arm.

"So, young gentleman!" he said; "dancing attendance on the ladies, hey? More likely work for a King's officer than soiling his hands with horrid tarry ropes, en't it? Your servant, madam. Trust a navy gentleman to know a pretty face when he sees one, but when you get tired of your present convoy, you hoist signals, and I'll find you a fresh consort in no time."

"Sir," says Mr Fraser (I was so confounded by this address that I knew not how to reply), "I would think better of you if you kept your insults for company in which I could resent 'em on the spot."

"I vow, sir, you're right!" cried the stranger, with an oath. "It en't pretty behaviour to seek to lower a man in the eyes of a lady he desires to stand well with, and you show a proper spirit in rebuking it. Don't be afraid that I'll try to cut out the little craft from under your guns. King's officer or Company's, a gentleman should have his fair chance where the ladies are concerned."

"Pray, sir," said I, as this person departed with a very ceremonious bow, "who is the gentleman, and what's the meaning of his talk?"

"Why, madam," says Mr Fraser, "I regret to say that your being in company with me has exposed you to a share of the ill humour with which I am regarded on board here."

"But how have you aroused this gentleman's resentment, sir?"

"I have the honour to wear the King's uniform, madam."

"But is that a cause for subjecting you to insult, sir?"

"Unfortunately, madam, it is—at least among the low-bred persons that are placed in authority on board such vessels as this. You may not know that among merchant seamen there's always a certain jealousy of us who belong to his Majesty's service, and they take a pleasure in gratifying their dislike at the expense of any navy officer that comes in their way."

"And this disagreeable humour is entirely unprovoked?" said I. "You, sir, would entertain no objection to meet the captain of a merchant-vessel on board of a ship of war?"

"Madam," says Mr Fraser with great haughtiness, "if such a person were by any chance to find himself aboard one of his Majesty's ships, he would be entirely beneath my notice."

I was forced to hold my fan before my face to hide a smile, for it seemed to me that the merchant-captain was not altogether without cause of complaint, but lest the Lieutenant should think I was laughing at him, I made haste to say, "I fear, sir, your life has been but a disagreeable one since we left Deal?"

"Say rather, madam, since we passed Beachy Head, and you went below," he replied. (Was it not neatly put, Amelia?) "The worst point in my situation was that I could do nothing to please. When during the rough weather I offered my services to help in cutting away the wreck, or otherwise endeavoured to make myself of use, I was bid by the mate there not to thrust my nose in where I was not wanted, while if I stood back, I was cursed for a lazy lubber and a long-legged Scotch loon, with many other insulting terms."

"I marvel, sir, that you was able to leave such rudeness unresented," I could not help saying, remembering Mr Fraser's readiness to take offence at a word while we were at the inn. His face reddened somewhat.

"I owe my meekness to you, madam. Every captain has supreme authority on his own ship, but I fear that even that reflection would not have restrained me had I not remembered that if I gave Mr Wallis occasion to put me in irons as a mutineer, which he had gladly done, I would have little hope of being of any service to you afterwards."

"Indeed, sir," I said, "I'm happy to have been of use to you."

At this point the steward came to announce that dinner was served, and Mr Fraser asked if he might attend me to the cuddy.[03] But this I refused, both because I had no desire to be the only lady at table, and because I felt little inclination for food, and remaining where I was, I dined sumptuously on some broth and toasted bread which the Lieutenant was so obliging as to bring me. I stayed on deck during the greater part of the afternoon, and the next day Miss Hamlin joined me, on receiving assurances that Mr Ranger would count it an honour to hold himself at her service. Since then there has been but one day when we were forced by rough weather to remain below, and even Mrs Hamlin and the other ladies are now sufficiently recovered to come on deck. As for the rest of the gentlemen, they nearly all made their appearance the day after Mr Ranger, and have done their best to prove themselves an agreeable set of fellows. The weather is grown continually hotter. Miss Hamlin and I were not long in exchanging our capuchins for beaver bonnets and short cloaks, but today we have taken to wearing gipsy hats and India scarves, though it is midwinter! But when we reach Bengall, so Mrs Hamlin says, we shall find that none of the ladies wear either hats or hoods when they ride abroad, but only lace caps trimmed with ribbons and flowers, as we do in the evening, and that one don't need so much as to throw a handkerchief over one's shoulders out of doors. Sure either the heat must be far greater than we can imagine, or the constitution of these ladies must be extremely hardy.

While I pen these lines to my Amelia, our ship is lying in the Bay of Fonchial, in the Madeiras, where we remain for a week to take in water and fresh provisions, and also to give us poor passengers an opportunity of remembering that there is such a blessed thing as firm ground. Each morning we visit the land in a boat from the shore, which is constructed, so Mr Fraser informs me, in a special manner on account of the force of the waves, and ride up the beach in the oddest fashion. What do you say to a frame of boards, like the sledges of which we read in Sweden and Poland, and drawn by oxen? Two or three of the gentlemen (you'll guess that the Lieutenant is one) refuse to ride in this machine, as a slight to their dignity, and prefer to crawl up the beach in the stifling heat. Arrived in the town, which has many very genteel houses, we spend some time on the Parade, which is here called the Praza. To me it recalls memories of the time I spent with my Amelia at Tunbridge Wells, but the trees here are orange-trees, and the company, though very polite, is nothing near so elegant as that we used to watch. Later in the day the gentlemen devise some party of pleasure, to which they invite the ladies, generally in some garden near the town, where the time passes agreeably enough, and we return to the Orford by moonlight.

Yesterday we visited a certain convent, which is considered (why, I don't know) to be one of the sights of the place. The appearance of the nuns, who are nearly all ladies of a discreet age, was vastly disappointing to the gentlemen, and Mr Ranger declared roundly that they had certainly immured themselves from necessity rather than choice. These religious persons occupy their leisure in making small articles, such as cockades and sword-knots, of silk and gold thread, which they are permitted to sell to visitors, passing them through the double grating by means of a cleft stick. Among these toys was a handsome fan-girdle, which I coveted for my Amelia, very neatly made with tassels, but my purse refused to allow me the pleasure of purchasing it. I had contented myself with a plainer sort, which I handed to Mr Fraser to carry for me, but when we sat down under the trees on the Parade to look over our purchases, what was my surprise when he presented me with the girdle I had first admired! Assuring the Lieutenant that there was some mistake, he told me that 'twas not so, but he had made bold to secure for me the article I desired. 'Twas a civil thought, was it not? and I could have found it in my heart to wish it were possible to accept the poor man's courtesy, but I desired him very seriously to restore me my own property. He was very highly offended, but I persisted in my demand, with which at last he complied, though with an excessively bad grace. The plain girdle I am sending to my dearest friend with this letter. I could wish it had been t'other, but I know my Amelia Turnor will prefer a smaller gift to a greater purchased at the sacrifice of her Sylvia's punctilio.

At Mynheer Brouncker's House, CAPE TOWN, *April ye 8th*, 1755.

Behold me now, my dear, with the half part of my journey passed, spending with delight a few days on shore in Holland—yet at the furthest extremity of the African continent. This is a sweet pretty place, the houses flat-roofed, and painted white or some bright colour, and the streets prodigiously regular and crossing one another at right angles with the most surprising neatness, and in the middle of the town a fine handsome square. Along each street are planted rows of trees, vastly symmetrical, and beside them are water-courses or small canals fed from springs, which are very agreeable for their coolness. This house (belonging to a private person who, like most of the better sort here, is glad to lodge and board us English for a rix-dollar a-day apiece, so that the sight of a British vessel entering the harbour is hailed with the most extravagant demonstrations of joy), though not what we in England should count luxurious, is almost incredible in its cleanliness, all the chamber-maids and servants being blacks. These people are called Hottentots, and the Dutch *boors*, which seems not to be understood here as a term of contempt. Our windows command a charming prospect of the great mountain overlooking the town, which from its flatness is called the Table. At times one sees the clouds descend and spread themselves upon its summit, and this, Mr Fraser tells me, is called by seamen, "the devil laying his table-cloth." Seamen are droll creatures, en't they, Amelia? And this reminds me to say that Messieurs Fraser and Ranger, with several other gentlemen from the Orford, are lodged in the same house as ourselves.

But you'll demand some account of our voyage since I last put pen to paper in the Madeiras. Alas, my Amelia, your Sylvia is a sad lazy girl! And yet, how could it engage your interest to hear that for so many days we lay becalmed off the coasts of Guinea, and at other times met baffling winds that threw us out of our course, and on a very few occasions found ourselves making good progress with the aid of a favouring breeze? or that we touched at Ascension Island, and waited there while the seamen catched twenty great turtles for us to take on board—horrid sprawling creatures, and their fat *green* when it is cooked? But all these delays, you'll say, afforded me only the more time for writing to you. True, my dear, but what should be the subject? My beloved girl knows that I love her, and to waste paper in repeating assurances of that would be to outdo even a lover's folly. When the history of one day is told, you have 'em all. Know then that the mornings have been spent seated under the awning on deck, we ladies with our embroidery at hand, to give us a decent semblance of industry, but really occupied in watching for distant sails, or the sight of land, or flying-fishes, or a change of wind, or any of the important nothings that appear of so much moment to the traveller on board ship. The gentlemen, meanwhile, busy themselves in fishing for creatures with such odd names as albacores, bonitoes, and doradoes, catching the smaller ones with hooks and lines, and the larger with fish-gigs or harpoons, in the casting of which Mr Fraser is particularly skilful. There are also many birds which venture near enough to the vessel to be caught, as albatrosses (but these the seamen protect, through some sentiment of superstition), tropic-birds, which are about the size of a hawk, with one extravagantly long feather in the tail, and booties and noddies, whose names (so Mr Fraser says, but I'm sure I can't see how) express their natural foolishness. The afternoon is passed like the morning, unless one of the gentlemen be so obliging as to deprive himself of the excitement of fishing in order to read aloud to us females as we work. Then comes the evening, when there's really nothing in the world to do (owing to the dimness of the lights provided for us below), but remain on deck and watch the sea, which indeed shows the strangest and most extraordinary fiery ripples and waves, unless the captain think fit to call up one of the seamen that plays the fiddle, and bid us set to for a dance. But this is rarely more than once a-week, and we call such occasions our assembly nights, when we dress ourselves with more attention than at other times, and the gentlemen wear their wigs, or have their hair curled and powdered.

But in general, as I have said, there's nothing to do but talk, and I can't pretend that the style of the conversation is altogether as ceremonious as the venerable Mrs Eustacia would desire. For instead of the ladies all sitting in a circle, with the gentlemen standing behind their chairs, and each endeavouring to contribute some piece of wit or information for the advantage of all, the passengers seem naturally to divide themselves into small groups, often, I must confess, containing as few as two persons. At least, this is my experience. Nay, I'll go so far as to say (for I see my Amelia's eyes asking the question), that I am not much in the habit of changing my companion on these occasions. 'Tis very seldom that my cavalier is not Mr Fraser, and this not only because I find his discourse always modest and agreeable, but because I am in continual alarm lest he should involve himself in some quarrel when he is not with me. You may have observed that this gentleman is of a somewhat fiery temper, and since the officers of the ship continue to treat him in the same offensive manner as I have already described to you, I am kept in a perpetual fear. Not that he is altogether without self-command, as I remarked one day when I looked to him to take the part of one of the crew who was knocked down and kicked by the second mate. These unfortunate seamen, who are kidnapped or inveigled by the Hon. Co. on board of their ships, and there forced to serve without hope of release, are handled with the most shocking barbarity by those in authority, and sometimes injured in a horrible manner. Knowing that Mr Fraser, as he had told me, had learned from his former commander, Mr Watson, to behave with justice and humanity to those serving under him,[04] I was not surprised to see him step forward with his hand raised, as though about to lay the wretch on the deck by the side of his victim. But dropping his hand and returning to my side, he said, in answer to my mute expostulation, "Pray, madam, pardon my disobliging you, but I have learnt by this time that my interference on behalf of these poor wretches only serves to ensure them a worse treatment, if not the being placed in irons forthwith."

Pleased with this care of his for the unfortunate seamen, I ceased to expect Mr Fraser to interpose himself on such occasions, and you may imagine that I take none the less pleasure in conversing with him. He has told me that he is the third son of a Scots gentleman of quality, who was granted the confiscated estate of a cousin that was a rebel in consideration of his services to the Government in the affair of the '15, services which he repeated in the rebellion nine years ago, but for which, as I understand, no recompense has as yet been awarded him. You'll be surprised to hear that a son of the cousin who was thus dispossessed is serving in the Company's army at Bengall, and that Mr Fraser declares it his purpose to seek him out if he can obtain leave to visit Calcutta. This seems to me conduct scarce to be expected from a delicate mind, but Mr Fraser laughed when I hinted as much.

"Any port in a storm," says he; "and after all, madam, blood is thicker than water."

Hon. Co.'s Ship Orford, MADRASS ROAD, *Aug. ye 20th.*

I must be content to permit my Amelia to scold me as she will, for not only have I allowed a long time to pass without adding to my bulky pacquet, but I confess freely that I had not sat down to write to-day had I been able to find anything else to do. In fine, my dear, I have the vapours very badly, and know not whether it be more disagreeable to look forward to arriving at Bengall or to look back upon our voyage. But how? why? what? you'll cry; I can see you trembling with eagerness to unfold this puzzle. Must I acknowledge that I have felt tempted to allow my letter to end with that part I writ at the Cape, and to shroud in oblivion all that has happened since? But I picture my Amelia reading the long sheets through with a face full of suspicion. "What's this?" she cries; "Mr Fraser here, Mr Fraser there, and again Mr Fraser, and all at once he disappears as though he had never been!" I could not resolve to sacrifice the pages wrote at so much trouble, and telling, moreover, of such quiet happiness as I can't look to see again; but be sure, my dearest friend, that nothing but the memory of the dreadful compact by which I bound myself to my Amelia, promising never to conceal from her any point soever, even the most intricate or delicate, of any transaction in which I should chance to engage, would lead me to disclose even to you the history of the past two months. I see you, when you read this, shake your head wisely, and cry, "Ah, I knew it—the old story, a devoted lover, a dutiful daughter, a hated elderly suitor in the background. Sure there's nothing new nor strange here!" By no means, Amelia, but wait until you hear what I have to say.

After leaving the Cape of Good Hope, everything continued in the same agreeable course as before until we were past the island of St Johanne.[05] We had taken in water early in the day, and weighed anchor in good time, in order to avoid the dangerous reefs guarding the harbour, and in the evening we were sailing on an agreeable breeze which was sufficient to fill the sails, without making the ship heel over. (Pardon these nautical terms, my dear. They will come to my pen, even now.) Mr Fraser and I were sitting near the binnacle (which is an odd sort of stand on which the mariner's compass is placed), and the Lieutenant was reckoning out very seriously how much time must elapse before he might decently ask for leave to visit his cousin at Calcutta, supposing that he found his ship in harbour when we arrived at Madrass, and was permitted to rejoin her. Having satisfied (or perhaps I should rather say dissatisfied) himself on this head, he asked whether he might have the honour of paying his respects to me at my papa's house. To this I could say nothing but that it wasn't for me to dictate to Mr Freyne what persons he should repulse from his doors; but Mr Fraser, seeming not to be content with this, seized my hand suddenly, and was vastly urgent with me to say whether it would cause me any pleasure should he come. The more warmly he demanded an answer, the more rigidly I refused one (for you know one can't always yield to these fellows, my dear; their conceit is already so enormous), and he was going on to denounce me as a cruel coquette that lived but to torment him, when Miss Hamlin, who had been sitting upon the steps of the poop, drew near with Mr Ranger. I won't deny that I considered her coming unnecessary, but I had no heart to think of that when once she began to speak.

"You was assisting Mr Fraser to reckon up the time that must pass before he visits Bengall, miss, was you not?" said she. "Now I would prophesy that the gentleman will arrive in Calcutta just in time for the wedding-day of the lovely and accomplished daughter of Henry Freyne, Esq."

I would have given worlds not to blush, my Amelia; but the words were accompanied with so provoking and malicious a glance that I felt the traitorous red rise all over my face and neck. Miss Hamlin, marking it, smiled, and addressed herself to Mr Fraser.

"I fear, sir," she said, "that Miss Freyne han't exhibited to you the full merit of her conduct in undertaking this voyage to the Indies. You must know that she and I are not bent upon seeking pleasure for ourselves, but on laying out what my aunt Hamlin calls our fortunes to the best advantage. Our parents (or guardians) intend—and we are fully determined to second their efforts—to marry us to a couple of frightful old Nabobs, each with a face as yellow as his guineas, and a liver as large as his money-bags. Now pray, miss," turning suddenly to me, "shriek out and fall into a fit at the indelicacy of my language; pray do!"

I was ready enough to faint, though not for that reason; but meeting her eye, I forced a smile, and she went on:—

"Sure you don't know, sir, that Miss Freyne is of so provident a constitution that she has even brought her wedding clothes with her, like myself. Her wedding-suit is of silver tissue, and the dear creature has embroidered it with her own fair hands in wreaths of violets. Thus, you see, her native modesty exhibits itself in a transaction against which both her heart and her punctilio must revolt. Now my gown is of a light pink, worked so stiff (but not by my fingers, oh no!) with gold flowers that it would stand up of itself."

"Pray, miss, how will these clothes interest Mr Fraser?" I asked, though I felt as if my lips and throat were parched with thirst.

"You should allow the gentleman to declare his want of interest for himself, miss. Shall we see you as bride-man at that wedding, sir? I would claim you as my partner if I were to be bride-maid; but Miss Freyne and I are resolved to deny ourselves that pleasure, since both could not enjoy it, and neither of us would be favoured at the expense of the other, and therefore we are to be married on the same day. You look pale, Mr Fraser. I fear I have wearied you. Perhaps, after all, you won't be at the wedding? But you will—you must—be present when the happy pair first show themselves in church on the Sunday after. 'Twill be a sight not to be missed. Pray figure to yourself the fortunate spouse—shall we call him Mr Solmes, miss?—in his new laced clothes, making him look yellower than ever, handing in his lady, in the largest hoop and the richest lace and the finest diamonds in Calcutta! And Madam will pretend to hide her blushes with a fan painted all over with cupids, while the entire time she will be watching through the sticks to see what effect her clothes are producing on the other ladies of the congregation. Did you speak, miss?"

I think I had cried out to her to stop. I know I tried to rise, but she put her hand on my shoulder and kept me down. "Hold your tongue, miss," she said in a whisper; "if you have to endure it, what harm can there be in speaking of it beforehand?"

I sat down again, but I had dropped my fan, and Mr Fraser restored it to me. His hand as it touched mine was cold, and he moved further away from me before he spoke, with difficulty, as it seemed to me.

"Sure, madam," he said, "the friends of a lady of Miss Freyne's high merits need have no fear as to her future course. If she'll follow the dictates of her own heart, they will be found to be those of reason and virtue."

"By no means, sir," says Miss Hamlin, quickly. "The dictates of reason and virtue will be found to be those of Miss Freyne's papa. Sure you are forgetting, as was pointed out to Miss Freyne and me before we embarked on this adventure, the huge sums of money which have been spent on our education, and which must be proved to have been put out at good interest. No, no, sir; we have the sad history of the divine Clarissa to warn us of the fate of an undutiful daughter, even though she behave so from the highest motives. The Lovelaces don't have it all their own way nowadays. Miss Freyne will marry her Solmes, and with the air of a martyr will feel that she has done her duty."

She laughed again, and beckoning to Mr Ranger with her fan, tripped away. I would have accompanied her, if I had found strength to rise. I seemed so strangely tired, Amelia. But Mr Fraser, who had been leaning against the mast, turned suddenly towards me, and said hastily, though with some measure of hesitation, like a man who takes a resolution at the moment—

"I would not, madam, have presumed to touch on such delicate matters as Miss Hamlin has thought fit to introduce; but since that has been done, I'll make bold to enlist your sympathy on behalf of a lady who is in a like case with yourself—that is, she is the daughter of wealthy parents at Bengall, who will, questionless, desire to make up a good marriage for her."

I felt myself grow cold all over, though I had thought I was cold already. "You—you cherish an interest in this lady, sir?"

"Madam, I adore her. My whole life and endeavour—saving only my duty to his Majesty—had gone to make her happy, if she would have permitted it."

"And she refuses to accept of your devotion, sir? But in what way can I assist you? Is it likely I shall meet the lady?"

"I imagine you'll often be in company with her, madam."

"And what is her name, sir?"

"Her surname, madam, I think 'twould be scarce delicate in me to reveal, even to a lady of your discernment. Her given name I don't know, but to me she'll always be the peerless Araminta."

"But how am I to plead your cause with her, sir, if you won't tell me her name?" I may have laughed, Amelia, but I felt as though I had died an hour ago.

"I'll hope to plead my own cause, madam, when I make that journey to Calcutta to visit my cousin of which we have been talking. I was rather desirous to engage your help for myself, and during the remainder of our voyage here. I can't help, madam, being conscious that I am a sadly rough and clumsy creature to pretend to the hand of so fine a lady as my Araminta, and you have shown me so much kindness that I would venture to ask you to assist me in rendering myself less unfit to approach her."

"I hope you'll command me, sir." I could not help being struck with the oddity of the notion, and the coolness of the young gentleman, even at such a moment.

"Why, madam, if you'd be so good, I would entreat you to take—in so far as may be—the part of my Araminta, so long as our voyage lasts. She is still unaware of my passion, but I understand there's many ways in which a lover may recommend himself to the object of his respectful adoration, even before he presume to declare his devotion by word of mouth. If Miss Freyne would condescend to suffer my awkward attempts to serve her, and would do me the favour of suggesting any improvement in my carriage that she might think called for, 'twould set my mind more at ease when I come at last to face the lovely and awful presence of my charmer. Am I asking too much, madam?"

"Why, no, sir; only it seems to me I have been doing what you ask all the voyage already."

"Precisely, madam. It did not strike me until to-night that perhaps I ought to have revealed to you earlier the existence of my Araminta."

"Indeed, sir, I don't desire to pry into your private concerns." I spoke with much severity, but seeing the Lieutenant's visage fall, I called up a smile, and giving him my hand, promised heartily to render him all the service in my power. Could I have said less, Amelia? Had I displayed any reluctance to oblige him, he might have thought—well, who can tell what the fellow might have thought?

Going below to the ladies' cabin, I found Miss Hamlin there alone. She came to meet me with a face full of curiosity.

"Well, miss, and don't you hate me now?" she said.

"Why should I hate you, miss? You desired to spoil the pleasure you saw me take in Mr Fraser's company, and you've done it, but it don't advantage you in any way that I can see."

"You don't add that you yourself gave me permission to do it if I found it necessary, miss, but you did. I was sorry that I had no time to prepare you, but I saw that if I waited any longer Fraser would have declared his passion, and laid his heart at your feet."

"Indeed, miss, you was mistaken, then. Mr Fraser worships at the shrine of another lady."

"Impossible, miss! Who has put such a notion into your head?"

"Mr Fraser himself, miss;" I told her what he had said.

"It sounds likely enough," she said, "but I must question him. If it be true, I shall recommend to the other lady to look after him better. There's just the possibility——" she shook her head and looked wise. "But pray, miss, where did you get that book?" She pointed to the first volume of Mr Henry Fielding's 'History of Amelia,' which I had seen Mr Fraser reading, and had taken up from the table of the cuddy as I passed. "Have you read much of it?"

"Only the first chapter," I said. "I was charmed by the title, which recalled to me my dear Miss Turnor."

She said no more, but after she had left the cabin again I missed the book. When she returned, I had climbed to my shelf, and was, I fear, feigning sleep, but she came and whispered to me—

"I have asked your Fraser about the divine Araminta, and he confesses to the truth. But such a sweet pretty name! Why did you not tell it me, miss? And how do you like the thought of playing Araminta to Araminta's humble adorer? 'Twill be as good as a play for us who look on."

With that she left me, and I won't grieve my Amelia's tender heart by telling her how I spent the hours of that night. But I must close this huge letter, and tell you more of my misfortunes in the next.

CHAPTER III.
IN WHICH MISS FREYNE ENTERS CALCUTTA, BUT NOT IN TRIUMPH.

Hon. Co.'s Ship Orford, HOOGLY RIVER, *Sept. ye 2nd.*

My last letter to my Amelia was finished writing in the roadstead of Madrass, where our vessel was lying, but now I am got so far in my voyage that I can date this almost within sight of Culpee,[01] at which place all we passengers leave the Orford, and embark in smaller boats to perform the concluding stage of our journey. But remembering where I left off, I know that my dearest friend will be in the most cruel anxiety for her Sylvia's peace of mind, and I hasten, now that we have fairly left the ocean behind us, to satisfy her concern, although I have but little to say that's agreeable.

Awaking from a troubled sleep on the morning after the shock I have described to you, Amelia, it seemed to me at first that 'twould be well to plead indisposition, and remain below, thus avoiding the performance of the hard task Mr Fraser had laid upon me. But I feared lest he should believe my illness caused by anything he had said, and rose determined to preserve my punctilio jealously, and carry the matter off with a bold face.

"You're rightly punished, miss," said I to myself, as I combed my hair. "You have pleased yourself imagining that the gentleman sought your company for your own sake, and now you find that he regarded you but as in some sort a picture of his Araminta. You was a silly creature to be so taken in, and I hope you'll be wiser in the future. Pray, miss," I said to Miss Hamlin, who was watching me from her shelf, "what have you done with my book?"

"Why, miss, I didn't know 'twas yours. I took it up to look at, and finding it prodigiously dull, carried it back to Mr Fraser. I'm sure I thought it was his."

"Oh, that's quite right," said I, but I made up my mind to ask the Lieutenant for the book again. This I did later in the day, but he met me with so many excuses that I was tired at last. It seemed as though every gentleman on board of the vessel had been promised to read 'Amelia' before I might so much as see it again.

"Indeed, sir," I said to Mr Fraser, before retiring to the ladies' cabin that night, "I should be failing in my duty to the lovely Araminta if I put up with this discourtesy any longer. I don't care what you say to the gentlemen, but if you can't place the book at my service in the morning you'll please be good enough to keep out of my sight," and I refused to hear a word from him.

"Well, sir, where's the book?" I asked my disobliging cavalier in the morning.

He seemed distressed. "Alas, madam——" he began.

"No more, sir," said I. "If my wishes—say rather those of your Araminta—have so little weight with you, they shall by all means cease to be imposed upon you."

"Indeed, madam, you wrong me. I had recovered the book from the person to whom I lent it, but while the decks were being washed before the ladies were risen, I happened to be skylarking, as we call it on board ship, with Mr Ranger, and the first volume, as it chanced, fell overboard and sunk. The others are at your service."

"And all the gentlemen to whom it was promised?"

"Why, madam, I fear they must bear the loss."

"Sir, you threw that book overboard of set purpose, knowing that I wished to read it."

"I am not saying you are wrong, madam."

"Do you venture to confess that you desired to disoblige me, sir?"

"Well, no, madam, I was seeking to oblige myself."

"Then you desired I should not see that part of the book? I vow, sir, your assurance is prodigious! Pray, who bid you direct my reading?"

"Indeed, dear madam, I would not presume so far."

"You have presumed too far already, sir. No, pray leave me alone. I don't desire your company."

"Ah, madam, if you knew how that majestic air recalls my Araminta to me!"

I started as if I had been stung. Araminta had been forgotten, but now I recollected my determination. If I persisted in banishing the Lieutenant, he would questionless (these men have so horridly high a conceit of themselves) have imagined that I was moved by pique owing to the announcement of the night before.

"Have you anything to urge in your defence, sir?"

"Nothing, madam. It was the impulse of a mad moment, and I acted upon it. I throw myself upon the mercy of the court."

"Do you desire to offer any promise of amendment, sir?"

"Questionless, madam. The crime won't be repeated (unless upon the same provocation), and if there be a copy of the book in India, I'll hope to lay it at your feet in due time."

"When your purpose has been served, sir?"

"Pray, madam, don't try to drive me into confessing the deed to have been premeditated. A prisoner can't be forced to criminate himself."

And in this foolish posture I was constrained to leave the matter. But I desire to charge my Amelia to procure the book, and to read it carefully, as she values her Sylvia's friendship, and to tell her what there is in it that could have any bearing upon the present complexion of affairs. True, this relief can't reach me for fifteen, perhaps even eighteen months, but at least I shall know it to be on the way, and some means may offer to make use of it. This gentleman appears to me to be what they call a wag; I would have him see for once how it feels to have a joke played on himself.

I have little more to tell you about the voyage, Amelia. My very fear lest Mr Fraser should suspect any change in me if I altered my carriage towards him forced me to continue in the old ways, so that by times I even forgot what had happened, but only to awake again to the bitter remembrance. I can't tell why it should be so disagreeable to me to do those things in the character, so to speak, of Araminta, which I had had no thought of doing for any advantage of my own, but so it was, though I'll confess that my pupil was an apt one. You must not imagine that in advancing his conversation (as Sir R. Steele phrases it in the 'Guardian') I was in the habit of pointing out Mr Fraser's faults in any vulgar or scolding manner. When I observed any awkwardness in his address, I would get out the 'Spectator' from my trunk, and request my scholar to be so good as to read a certain number aloud for the entertainment of the ladies. In this way he learned to see what was wrong and to correct it, and I never found it necessary to repeat the lesson. Whether he learned to expect a covert reproof whenever he saw me bring out the 'Spectator' I don't know, but at least the plan was successful. Sometimes I fancied that he was a good deal diverted by my care of him, but between my own discomfort and my fear of his penetration I had no time to think of that. It seemed to me, however, that as we neared Madrass his air became noticeably more serious, and that he appeared to desire to say something to me, which yet he could not compass. I had it in my head that he was determined to reveal to me the real name of his Araminta, and to bespeak my friendship for her, and I must confess I did my best to avoid the disclosure, for indeed, my dear Miss Turnor, I have no curiosity to know who the lady is. But as we sat on the poop-steps the night before reaching Madrass, I felt a sudden impulse to say—

"I hope, sir, that the amiable Araminta won't despise the result of my efforts when she beholds you again. Pray contrive some means of letting me know whether she observe any change in you."

"Indeed, madam, if I am so happy as to reach Calcutta, you'll hear all that I can tell you of myself."

"Oh, pardon me, sir. That privilege belongs to your Araminta. I desire but to hear the lady's opinion, if she'll be so good as to permit you to acquaint me of it."

I could not hear what Mr Fraser said, but I believed that he cursed Araminta under his breath, and this made me vastly angry. Was it not enough that the fellow should break my—I mean, should pester me for so long about his Araminta, that he should suddenly turn traitor to her name?

"Oh, sir, I fear you're unworthy of the lady's regard. Perhaps you'll permit me to observe, without swearing at me, that whether she have remained constant to you or not, she surely merits your highest respect."

"Madam, I protest you're right. Whether she be mine or not, my charmer will always be as far above me as an angel. But, madam, I——"

"Pray, sir and madam, why this heat?" says Miss Hamlin. "En't the weather hot enough for you? Here have Mr Ranger and I felt constrained to cross the deck to prevent your falling to blows."

"Sure I saw no danger of that, miss," said I.

"Who should expect you to, miss? You're too close to the thunderstorm to perceive its force. But pray continue your quarrelling. Mr Ranger and I will see fair, and rescue you if it be needful."

"Oh, madam," says Mr Ranger, "Miss Freyne is too nice to quarrel in a public place."

"Pray, sir, what do you know of Miss Freyne? En't you aware that she writes down all the events of every day to send to her dear friend in England? You see we are all living in public, so to speak, so that none of us need be squeamish about quarrelling before others. Look you there now, how dainty a chronicle must that be which the admirable Miss Turnor receives from her adored Sylvia—all the scandal of the ship set down in the finest hand imaginable!"

"I'll thank you, miss, not to make so free with my name," said I.

"So your name is Sylvia, madam?" says Mr Fraser.

"And what if it be, sir?" cried Miss Hamlin. "Han't you just heard Miss Freyne rebuke me for taking the sacred word on my lips? Pray understand that it en't for you and me to take liberties with the lady's Christian name."

She appeared so much offended by my hasty remark that I forbore to ask her pardon, in the hope that she and her humble servant would leave us again; but this they refused to do, so that I could never discover what it was that Mr Fraser had been about to say to me. The next day we entered the Madrass Road, and found several great ships lying at anchor, which when Mr Fraser saw, "Here's the fleet, then!" he cried; but I thought his voice was not altogether joyful. Yet I could not be sure of this, for he began at once to be very busy in pointing out to us which was his own ship, the Tyger, and which was the Kent, on which Admiral Watson wore his flag, and so on. Then when we came to an anchor, he went below to change his dress, saying that he must go on board at once to report himself, and so left our vessel, making a very fine figure in a blue uniform faced with white. He returned about an hour later, when we were all in a bustle with making ready to go on shore, and had but time to tell us that both Captain Latham and the Admiral had received him very kindly, promising to restore him to his post on board the Tyger, since the gentleman who had supplied his place had failed to fulfil its requirements, and he was bid to get to his ship at once. He parted from us on the deck, promising to come and pay his respects before the Orford left Madrass, and we had little leisure to think of anything but transporting ourselves to the shore, for this was only to be accomplished by means of one of the country boats, called *mussoulas*, which pass in the most incredible manner over the surf which breaks on the beach. When we were once landed, after a passage that I scarce venture to look back upon, we found ourselves welcomed by a gentleman of Mrs Hamlin's acquaintance, who was come by desire of his wife to invite us to lie at their house so long as the Orford continued in the roadstead. This we did; and such a time of merry-making it was as I had scarce imagined possible. Every sort of party of pleasure was devised, either by the officers of his Majesty's ships or by the gentlemen of the factory, and every one that had any pretensions to gentility might be sure of finding himself elegantly entertained every day. In all this, however, we saw Mr Fraser very little, for having been so long absent from his ship, it fell naturally to him to relieve the rest of the officers of a good part of their duties; while the ladies were again so few in number compared with the gentlemen, that only the officers of the highest rank were able to enjoy the honour of handing one of us.

We had spent near a week at Madrass when it was suggested that we should make a party to St Thomas's Mount, which lies about three miles from Fort St George, and at its foot the Company has a very fine garden.

Here is the Company's garden-house, which we in England should call a mansion standing in its own grounds, and likewise the garden-houses of the gentlemen of the greatest figure in the factory, and the proposition was that we should lie a night at the Mount, and return to Madrass in the cool of the morning. 'Twas an agreeable jaunt enough, and the general enjoyment was not marred but by the anxiety of the navy gentlemen, to whom the Admiral had only granted leave to be present on the condition that they returned at once should they hear a cannon fired as a signal of recall. This seemed to most of us only a pleasant jest on Mr Watson's part, to tease his officers by reminding them of the insecure foundation of their present joys; but before it was light in the morning we were all awaked by the sound of a great gun, and on jumping out of bed and peering through the *checks*[02] (which are a sort of blind made of slips of wood), we saw the gentlemen all rushing together from the different summer-houses where they had been lodged, calling for their servants, and shouting for their horses or palanqueens. How they managed it I can't pretend to say, but all the officers were equipped and gone in a quarter of an hour, leaving the garden as quiet as it had but just now been full of noise. Some two hours later, when the young lady who shared my room was taking with me the slight meal which is served here on rising, we heard another gun.

"Sure that will be to call in the stragglers," says my companion. "The fleet must be going out with the morning tide."

A horrid sinking feeling seized me on hearing this, and I need not hide from my Amelia that it was caused by the thought that Mr Fraser, who had not been of the party to visit the Mount, should be departing without ever being able to tell me what he had desired to make known. But calling to mind the tales I had heard of the Admiral's jesting humour, I reflected that he was, questionless, only trying the obedience of his officers by this sudden summons, and that we should find the fleet still at anchor when we reached Madrass. But when we were in the act of returning, and I looked out of my palanqueen towards the roadstead, there were no vessels there save the Orford and a few country ships, while far out at sea was a disappearing sail or two. Forcing myself not to manifest my discomposure, I waited impatiently until I could take leave of my companion at the steps of the house where we were staying, and run indoors to find Miss Hamlin, who had remained in Madrass by her own request to keep our hostess company. I found her reclined in the *varanda*, on an odd sort of Chinese couch made of the bamboo reed, and would you believe it, my dear, the provoking creature would do nothing but ask questions, such as whether we had danced all night, and whether the *notch*[03] with which Mr President had entertained us was a fine one.

"Pray, miss," I cried at last, "do you know the fleet has sailed?"

"Oh, the fleet has sailed, has it? I guessed as much."

"How, miss? You knew of Mr Watson's design?"

"Well, two nights back, when he was my partner at Government House, he let drop a hint, which he did his best immediately to conceal."

"And you never told me, miss?"

"Pray, miss, would you have me betray a State secret learnt in such a manner?"

"Then you stayed behind here on purpose when we went to the Mount?"

"I did, miss. I thought it was better I should stay than you."

"I—I don't understand you, miss," I stammered.

"I stayed here," said Miss Hamlin, looking at the wall, "because I believed that Mr Fraser would come to pay his respects, and I desired to see him."

"And—and did he come?"

"He did come, miss—soon after daybreak. I had expected that, and was dressed to receive him. He desired his most humble thanks to you for all your kindness to him."

"And that was all, miss?"

"That was all, miss. I refused to charge myself with any more."

"But did he purpose saying more? That message—What have you there, miss?" I had discerned a slip of paper that had catched in the robings of her gown, and seized it. It was part of a torn letter, and there was "To Mrs Sylvia Freyne" wrote upon it.

"Oh, dear! I thought I had got rid of it all," says Miss Hamlin, with the calmest air in the world.

"You destroyed Mr Fraser's letter to me, miss?"

"I tore it up in his presence, miss, and defied him to send you another. And in that I was your true friend."

"Sure it could only have been some message that he desired me to deliver to his Araminta," I said, half unwillingly.

"And for whose sake would you have kept it, miss—for Araminta's or your own?"

"There's no reason why I shouldn't receive a letter designed to reach me, miss."

"Yes, miss, there is, if it come from Fraser. As I said, I have stood your friend in this. Perhaps you have forgot the plans which your parents have for you, and the good nature with which my aunt, before our voyage began, left it with you to remember 'em. You're a young woman of prudence and good sense, though you know nothing of the world but what a boarding school can teach—which is vastly little, and that topsy-turvy—and you'll accept this escape of yours with thankfulness when you think upon it calmly. Fraser has behaved to you in a monstrous cavalier fashion—leading all around you to believe that he had laid his heart at your feet, when he was enamoured the entire time of another lady. You remember, miss, your tenderness for the fellow's feelings when my aunt first presented him to you as your humble servant for the voyage; pray, will you have people say that you are fallen into the trap yourself while he's escaped?"

I saw the justice of her contention, but I have been very low-spirited ever since that morning, so much so that after leaving Madrass I kept my cabin for two or three days, suffering from a serious enough indisposition, from which I am now recovered, though still unhappy in mind. Yet I don't know what I could have expected had I been able to bid Mr Fraser farewell. He could have said nothing to bring me any complacence, since had he even desired to transfer his allegiance from Araminta to myself, what answer could I have made to such a perjured lover? No, my Amelia knows enough of her Sylvia's heart to be sure she would never entertain a thought in favour of one who could act in so base a manner. Ah, my dear Miss Turnor, I am rightly punished. I am a very wicked girl, for though Miss Hamlin thought I had forgot my parents' designs for me, they came often to my mind in the first part of our voyage, until I had contrived to drive them away, resolving to enjoy while I had it the pleasure of Mr Fraser's company. And now I will answer the question which I see trembling on my dearest friend's lips. Do I confess, then, you'll say, that my heart is engaged on this gentleman's behalf? and to this I can answer, No. How could either my heart or my judgment take sides with one who could act, as I can't help perceiving, with so much unkindness—I had almost added, so much duplicity—both towards the amiable Araminta and myself? But this I'll acknowledge, that had matters been otherwise, had he been the honest man I thought him, I could have loved him.

So there, Amelia, you have the worst of it—the dreadful, the humiliating confession—and I'll beg you won't mention the subject again, as I shall hope to let this be the last page of my writing on which Mr Fraser's name appears. Miss Hamlin has used me kindly enough, yet with the contemptuous kindness that says nothing better could be expected from a boarding-school miss, and I must do my best to find happiness in the future in a strict obedience to the commands of my dear papa. But oh, Amelia, if only Mr Freyne were a Papist, as Mrs Hamlin once said! Sure you'll think I am gone mad, but I mean that in that case he might suffer me to follow my own inclinations, and lead a single life. Why is it that parents will never allow their daughters in this mode of life? We hear continually of the difficulty of making up good marriages, and of the monstrous fortunes demanded with brides, and yet no young woman of our quality is permitted to remain single, even if she desire it. Or if she be afflicted with such a want of looks that no one will take her, even for the sake of her guineas, how hardly do her parents give up their search! How many proposals of marriage sent to the friends of reluctant gentlemen, how many treaties broken off when all but arranged, before she can be allowed to follow her own inclinations!

At Mr Freyne's house in the Cross-road, CALCUTTA, *Sept. ye* 12*th.*

At last I am able to address my Amelia from my papa's house, if only to describe the disconcerting adventures I met with in reaching it. Sure, my dear, your Sylvia is the most unlucky girl alive, so extraordinary are the mortifications that assail her! But to take up my history from the point where I left off. In twelve days after sailing from Madrass, for at this time of the year the winds are favourable to those approaching Bengall, we came to the factory at Ballisore, where we expected to find Mr Hamlin waiting for us, but learned that business had kept him at Fort William, and that he would await us at Culpee. Taking on board a pilot (these persons are provided by the Hon. Company for the better navigation of their vessels in these dangerous channels), we entered the Hoogly River, passing the island called Sawgers.[04] Here Mr Marchant, the chief mate, whom I believe I have mentioned before, chanced to be entertaining Miss Hamlin and me with tales of his travels, and told us that this island is much pestered with tygers, as indeed are all in this neighbourhood; but that it is considered a place of great sanctity by the pagans, insomuch that in the months of November and December very many *Gioghis*,[05] which is a name given to holy men among the Gentoos,[06] go there on pilgrimage. This they do that they may wash themselves in the salt water, and Mr Marchant declared that an incredible number of them perish in the performance of this fancied duty. More times than he could tell, he said, had he beheld a great tyger crouching on the shore and licking his lips, while he watched one of these poor wretches in the water as a cat watches a mouse. 'Twas in vain that the unfortunate should seek to escape; if he would not be drowned he must return to the shore, and there the beast met him. I was expressing my horror on hearing this, and asking Mr Marchant why he had not made haste to kill the tyger and so save the poor Indian, when Miss Hamlin nudged me smartly with her elbow, and when the mate was gone, told me that he was merely rallying me. I was very angry, as you may conceive, at this piece of presumption on the part of such a person, and when he next spoke to us, asserting that the great danger to our ship in sailing up the river arose from the fact that the shoals and currents, nay, the very banks themselves, were continually changing their shape and direction, I allowed him to perceive the disbelief I accorded to his words. But this time, so Miss Hamlin assures me, he was telling nothing but the truth, so that I had been credulous and incredulous at the wrong times. Is not that hard, Amelia?

At Culpee, which overlooks a broad reach of the river, the Orford was met by a huge number of boats, variously called, as I learned, *budgeroes*, *wollacks*, and *ponsways*. The budgeroes are like our state barges, but far exceeding them in neatness and magnificence, the rowers, who are called *dandies*, and the *mangee* or helmsman, all dressed in white, with sashes and ribbons of the colour of their masters' liveries. Mrs Hamlin had assured me that my papa's budgero would come to meet me here, and my dearest friend won't be at a loss to imagine with what turmoil of heart I looked at all the gentlemen on board the barges, hoping and yet dreading to find that each one of them was Mr Freyne. But I could perceive no one that I could guess to be my papa, nor did any of them appear to recognise me, so that at last I turned back to Mrs Hamlin, with whom was now standing her spouse, a somewhat stout and red-faced gentleman, but agreeable enough, in a suit of white clothes.

"Here's a pretty to-do!" says Mrs Hamlin, as soon as she sees me. "My dear Miss Freyne, your good papa, hearing we could not be in before to-morrow, has taken his journey to Dacca on the Company's occasions, and won't return until to-night, and Mrs Freyne han't thought fit to send to meet you."

"Why no, my dear," says Mr Hamlin, "sure you forget what I just told you, that Mrs Freyne desired to use the budgero herself to-day, and asked me to give Miss Freyne a passage in ours as far as the Gott, where she will find a palanqueen waiting for her. You wasn't grudging the young lady a seat in the boat?"

"No, sir," says Mrs Hamlin, "and Miss Freyne knows me better than to think so. I am vexed that the lady should treat her daughter's punctilio so lightly as to deny her their boat, while she goes off on some jaunt of her own."

"Oh fie, my dear! You're too hard on a little innocent gaiety. Pray, Miss Freyne, can you tell me why ladies are always so severe when there's a handsome woman in the case?"

"I don't know, sir. Are they so?"

"Oh, come, madam, han't you found it so?" And the man bowed so that I might not fail to perceive he had intended a compliment.

"When you are ready, Mr Hamlin," said his spouse, "we'll go into the budgero."

"Quite so, my dear. Have you bestowed all your *buxies*[07] on the steward and his mates? Does our Miss Freyne know that word yet? If she don't, she will soon. Buxies, madam, is a gift of money, made by a man that don't desire to give it, to a set of rascals that don't deserve it. No Indian will work that can help it, so that he needs buxie money to enable him to live."

Talking in this way, so fast that I could scarce understand him, Mr Hamlin accompanied us to wait upon the captain, whom he thanked very genteelly for his care of us during the voyage, and bade visit him at his garden-house on the way to Surmans[08] as often as he should be in Calcutta. Having bid farewell to the mates of the ship and our fellow-passengers, and avoided the importunities of the extraordinary great number of gentlemen that had come aboard in their budgeroes, and would have had Mr Hamlin present them to us, he replying that they should wait till Sunday, we descended into our boat, and so set out with great magnificence. During this second short voyage, Mr Hamlin showed himself very obliging in pointing out to us the places we passed by, as Fultah, where the Dutch have a factory, seated on the most unhealthy spot in the country, and Buzbudgia,[09] which is a fortress belonging to the Moors,[10] as also is the place called Tanners,[11] on the opposite bank. When we were past Tanners, Mr Hamlin bade us look alive, for we should soon find ourselves on British soil, and coming to a piece of water called Govindpoor's Reach,[12] he showed us on the shore a little pyramid in stonework, which, said he, marked the boundary of the Company's territory. My dearest friend will comprehend how fast my heart beat at this spectacle. Now at last, Sylvia (I said to myself), thou art to find a parent and a home. But Mr Hamlin, seeing how much I was moved, refused to give me any leisure for meditation, and went on pointing out all the objects we passed, now the garden called Surmans, and the garden-houses of the Company's servants beyond it, then the Company's docks and the garden of the Armenians on t'other side of the river, and lastly the town itself, with Fort William and the church. On our exclaiming at the odd aspect of the sacred edifice, which seemed to have lost its upper parts, Mr Hamlin told us that in a great storm near twenty years ago[13] the whole of the steeple, which was of the most elegant proportions imaginable, was blown down by a frightful gust of wind, and driven fifteen feet or so into the earth without breaking. But this I have since seen reason to doubt, for in such a case, sure the gentlemen of the factory would have restored the steeple to its place, or at least have preserved it where it lay, on account of the strangeness of its fate, but there's no sign of it, wherefore I believe that when it reached the ground 'twas in ruins, and fell speedily into decay. Of the Fort, Mr Hamlin bade us mark the crumbling state of the walls, and the many fine cannons that lay on the ground, without their carriages and useless, outside them, observing that we might now see the trust entertained by the gentlemen of the Presidency in the innocency of their lives and the justice of the Soubah (this was all Greek to me, but I'll tell you the explanation later).

"We have the felicity, madam and niece Charlotte," said the good gentleman, "to live under a President that would not with his goodwill hurt a fly. Nay, if a wasp should sting him, he would sooner beseech it to depart than kill it in an angry fit. Sure he should by rights have been born a Quaker, which is the name by which he is known here, for all his tastes lie that way."[14]

We were now fast approaching the steps of the Gott, which is to say the landing-stage, and became aware of a second great crowd of gentlemen, who flocked out of the Fort and from the streets near, some to greet friends that were landing from other budgeroes that had arrived before our own, and others to stare and whisper at us two poor girls as we were handed ashore. Miss Hamlin looked at me with a malicious smile, and whispered me to make my choice, for all the young sparks of Fort William were there paraded before me.

"Nay, miss," said I, not to be outdone; "you first, if you please."

"Why, then, I choose the respectable person there at the Fort gate," she said, pointing with her fan; and we both laughed, for although the gentleman she indicated was somewhat advanced in years, his coat of yellow silk was richly laced, and he seemed to take no small pride in his appearance. "A man that has such care for his own dress would not be niggardly over that of his spouse," says Miss Hamlin; but just then her uncle, who had pushed on through the press, came posting back to us, apparently in some disturbance of mind.

"I fear, madam," says he to me, "you'll have but a poor opinion of our Calcutta manners, or at least of our memories, for I can't perceive your papa's servants anywhere, and the gentlemen tell me they han't seen his liveries to-day, and how you are to get home I don't know."

"What did I tell you, sir?" asked Mrs Hamlin, with an air of triumph.

"Pray, sir," said I, "don't trouble yourself about me. If Miss will be so good as to let me share her palanqueen, sure I can be dropped at Mr Freyne's door without incommoding anybody."

"Why, so you could, madam," says he, "but for the little trifling fact that Mr Freyne's house lies out Chitpore way, which is in the opposite direction from Surmans."

"Oh pray, sir," I said in great uneasiness, "let me hire a coach or a chair, and so relieve you of the charge of me."

"There en't no such things here, miss," says Mrs Hamlin. "No, you must please to take my niece's palanqueen to go home in, and we'll wait here in the sun until you're done with it."

By this time, Amelia, I was ready to cry, for the good lady's tone was sharp enough, and indeed the sun was hot, though I hadn't perceived it before; but I had no time to bewail my misfortunes, for Mrs Hamlin cried out suddenly—

"As I live, there's Captain Colquhoun! Pray, Mr Hamlin, go and fetch him hither. He'll take Miss off your hands."

As Mr Hamlin hurried to obey her, she whispered to me, "Pray observe, miss, how careful I am of your punctilio. I wouldn't for the world place you under an obligation to any of these young gentlemen here, that are all on fire to offer their services in any way; but Captain Colquhoun is your papa's closest friend, and would take it most unkind if we didn't appeal to him."

"Sure the gentleman bows for all the world like a ramrod breaking in two!" says Miss Hamlin in my ear, as we watched Mr Hamlin press through the crowd a second time and accost a person in a military dress that had paused on the outskirts to watch the landing. I could not forbear smiling, though the tears had been at my eyes the moment before, for not only did Captain Colquhoun hold himself like a ramrod, but he moved as stiffly as if his limbs were worked by springs, like those of a Dutch baby.[15] His face was burnt red with the sun, and was so rough and hard in its features that it might have been cut out of a block of wood, and his dress was as plain as his rank would allow, without any of that foppery about the sword-knot and cockade that so many military officers affect.

"Why don't the gentleman ride in his palanqueen, since he has it with him?" I whispered back to Miss Hamlin, pointing to it as I spoke.

"Why, that's the Calcutta punctilio, miss. To be without a palanqueen argues you to be a person of no figure, and therefore, even if a gentleman don't ride in his, it must be carried after him."

"'Tis all the better for me," I said, just as Mrs Hamlin brought up the captain, who bowed so low that I could almost fancy I heard the springs creaking.

"Now, what could be more charming than this?" the good lady was saying "Miss Freyne, you took pleasure in the company of our good Lieutenant Fraser, I know, and you won't feel strange with Captain Colquhoun when you learn that he's his cousin. Questionless, Mr Fraser has often mentioned him to you?"

That dreadful name again, when I thought I was done with it for ever! I was ready to sink into the ground, but the Captain relieved me by saying—

"The young lady need not burden her conscience with fibs for my sake, madam. My cousin had questionless far more agreeable matters to discuss, and at best he knows as little of me as I of him. Difference of politics has separated our families for many years."

This was little enough to say, when one remembers that Mr Fraser's father holds the estates that should by right be Captain Colquhoun's, and I was ashamed to recollect how lightly Mr Fraser had spoken of demanding his cousin's hospitality should he visit Calcutta. But Mrs Hamlin was speaking again.

"We won't talk of these disagreeable matters, Captain. Your friendship with Miss Freyne's papa is a stronger claim on your kindness than her acquaintance with your relation. Our good Captain Colquhoun is so kind as to offer you the use of his palanqueen to convey you home, miss, and he will himself be your cavalier. I'll wish you a happy meeting with your papa and Mrs Freyne."

"We shall meet on Sunday, miss!" says Miss Hamlin with her drollest air, as we curtseyed; and then Captain Colquhoun lent me his hand to lead me to the palanqueen, which was of a kind common in Calcutta, though I had not met with it before—like an armchair supported on poles, with a roof over it, and not like a covered bed, such as those I had seen at Madrass. I was forced to let down the checks to keep out the afternoon sun, but I could hear Captain Colquhoun walking stiffly beside me, and reproving the bearers when they stumbled. Then the machine was carried in at a gateway and set down, and the Captain raised the blind for me.

"Permit me, madam, to bid you welcome to your home!" said he.

CHAPTER IV.
SHOWING HOW MISS FREYNE BECOMES ACQUAINTED WITH HER SURROUNDINGS.

CALCUTTA, *September ye* 14*th.*

I looked round with great eagerness when Captain Colquhoun handed me out of the palanqueen, but discovered nothing in my home that was different from other houses in East India. It is of two storeys, with a flat roof, and surrounded with a varanda, which is a sort of penthouse shelter supported on poles, and all closed in with long checks, like what we call Venetian blinds. There is a handsome flight of stone steps leading to the front door, but the house itself is built of *pucca*, which is a sort of cement made of dust and lime mixed with molasses and chopped-up hemp. A whole parcel of servants came gliding from all quarters as we mounted the steps, and the Captain addressed them in English.

"Where's the Beebee?"[01] he said.

One of the servants, who seemed the chief, made some answer in his own language, which I understood to signify that the Beebee was out.

"What's the meaning of this?" cried the Captain, very angry. "Here's the *chuta Beebee*" (this means young lady, Amelia), "your master's daughter, just arrived off her journey, and no one to receive her! What's that you say?" for the servant had proposed something in a very humble style. "Yes, send for her *iya*[02] by all means."

I knew that *iya* meant maid-servant, and I looked on with great curiosity as the servant brought back with him a yellow-faced woman in gay clothes.

"Here, Bowanny," said Captain Colquhoun, but stopped suddenly. "Sure you en't the woman that was to come to wait on Miss Freyne with my Lady Russell's good word?"

"No, sir," says the woman, and I observed that she did not say *saeb*,[03] like the other servants. "Me Madam's servant before, but when she see Bowanny, she choose her, and set me to wait on Missy."

"And what do you call yourself?"

"Me Marianna da Souza, sir—good Portugal blood."

"Indeed!" says the Captain, somewhat rudely, as I thought. "Well, madam," turning to me, "this person is your attendant, you'll perceive. I trust you'll find her obliging and obedient. For your comfort I may say that Mrs Freyne has always been counted the best dressed woman in Calcutta. And now, unless I can serve you further, I'll take my leave. Your cabin trunks will arrive shortly. I placed 'em in charge of a couple of *cooleys*."

"Oh, pray, sir," said I, "permit me to express the deep obligation you have laid me under by your kindness——" but he was departing.

"I am promised to sup with Mr Freyne to-night, madam," he said on the steps, "and I'll hope to find you recovered from your fatigues."

Indeed, my Amelia, I felt ready to drop as I followed the woman into the house, which seemed dark and hot instead of bright and hot like the air outside. Marianna desired to show me the chamber where I should lie, and to bring me a dish of tea there, and you may guess I did not refuse it. The chamber to which she led me was large enough, and would have been airy had there been any air moving. There was but little furniture, and that of Chinese make, in quaint and pleasing shapes fashioned out of the bamboo. But the bed—ah, there was a disappointment for me! To understand my feelings, you must know that during all these weary months on shipboard I have comforted myself perpetually for the bare and narrow shelves of the cabin with the prospect of finding at my papa's house such a bed as we should consider good in England. And, indeed, the bedstead was sufficiently genteel, the posts elegantly carved and inlaid with ivory, but instead of the feather-bed and pillows I had pictured to myself, there was only a meagre mattress and cushion such as we had used on board ship. And the curtains! no substantial woollen stuff—such as those within whose ample shade my Amelia and I have often exchanged confidences far into the night, holding our breath while Mrs Abigail prowled about outside, lest she should discover our wakefulness and peer in upon us with, "Pray, young ladies, are you asleep?" (Do you remember, Amelia, that once I innocently answered, "Oh yes, indeed, madam, we are"?)—the curtains, I say, were not of this sort, but a flimsy kind of muslin or fine netting, apt enough to keep out the *musketoes*, but admitting freely every current of air. I was the more disturbed to observe this, since the windows were defended only by screens of woven reeds, and not by glass.

"Sure," I said to Marianna, "it must be vastly dangerous to the health to admit the night air so freely?"

"If Missy not have air in Bengall, Missy die," was her answer, and this in as smiling and complaisant a tone as if she had uttered the most charming prophecy imaginable.

"With what cheerfulness and philosophy do these poor people contemplate death!" I reflected, somewhat ashamed to have exhibited my apprehensions before her, as she went to fetch my tea, but since I did not choose that my first night at Bengall should also be my last, I resigned myself to this outlandish style of sleeping. Before I had drunk my dish of tea my trunks arrived, and I was able to change my clothes and put on a silk nightgown instead of my travelling-suit, which was a huge refreshment. And after that I am ashamed to say that I dozed on my couch, while Marianna unpacked my clothes, moving about the chamber with the lightest tread in the world, until I was awakened by the noise of palanqueens' setting down in the courtyard, and presently a message came that Mrs Freyne desired me to attend her in the saloon. My dearest Miss Turnor will be at no loss to imagine my apprehension as I followed Marianna, and will guess that my heart was in my mouth when I stepped into the saloon, where three ladies were seated enjoying an elegant collation of fruits and sweetmeats. I divined at once which was Mrs Freyne, and at the first glance I determined that my stepmother was a very beautiful young woman, but this opinion did not last. My Amelia won't think me censorious, for I experienced a feeling of disappointment that a face which seemed at first sight extraordinary handsome should come so far short of beauty. There's a general *something*, that I can't express, which spoils it. No one feature is bad, but none is quite good. The eyes are a little too small and far apart, and of a blue a little too light, as the hair is of somewhat too pale a golden; the nose is a little too short, the lips a little too thin, and the chin a little too much pointed. Such trifles as all these are, yet they spoil the face. For her clothes, my stepmother was wearing a very fine nightgown of white gauze striped with gold, and a Brussels mob trimmed with French flowers, and this dress was well designed to show off the air of great elegance and languor which I observe to be the peculiar[04] of all the Calcutta ladies.

"So you're arrived, miss!" she said to me. "Had you a short voyage?"

"A monstrous long one, madam. Near ten months."

"It don't seem to have done you no harm. I see you've brought a pair of red cheeks with you, which is thought vastly ungenteel in Bengall."

My cheeks were red at that moment, Amelia, I'll assure you, and I was grateful to one of the other ladies, who seemed a good-natured sort of body, and made room for me on the settee beside her. There I sat, like a good little Miss out of the nursery, to be seen and not heard, and listened to all that was said, while nobody spoke to me, until Miss Dorman, the lady next me, turned and said—

"Have you unpacked your gowns yet, miss? All Calcutta will be agog to see 'em, I'll assure you."

"Oh, indeed," says Mrs Freyne, in a great to-do, "Miss is only just off her journey, and too tired to go showing her clothes this evening. I won't hear of it. You shall see 'em in good time, miss, I promise you."

Miss Dorman smiled in rather a droll fashion as she rose to take her leave.

"Pray, miss," says my stepmother to me, "attend the ladies to their palanqueens," and I obeyed her.

"Don't let Madam frighten you, dear Miss," whispered Miss Dorman to me in the hall. "An English colour is excessively admired in Calcutta, I can tell you, and the plainest woman will pass for a beauty so long as she keeps it. I did, so I know."

I was sorry for her as she offered me this kind consolation, for sure she's no beauty now, though well enough, and I began to perceive why young ladies going to Bengall should be in such haste to get married. Not that this consideration changed my feelings on the matter, for indeed I would get rid of my English colour to-morrow, if that would serve me as a protection. Well, I saw the ladies into their palanqueens, and then returned to the parlour, where I looked at Mrs Freyne, and she at me.

"I would have you know, miss," said she, "that I don't purpose to put myself out for you in any way. If Mr Freyne had been guided by me, he would have instructed his friends in England to set on foot a treaty of marriage for you with some respectable person there, instead of dragging you half round the world to find a spouse. But since he has chose to bring you out here, pray understand that I won't carry you at my apron-string to every party of pleasure I may attend."

"Indeed, madam," I said, "I don't doubt but I shall be able to make myself happy at home when you don't please to take me out with you. I hope I shall always be ready to oblige my mamma in any way I can." I was resolved to get the word out (though I hated to utter it), both because I was anxious to do my duty, and because I hoped it might render her better inclined towards me. But this was not the case.

"Never let me hear you call me that again, miss!" she said. "En't it enough to have to take about with me a great creature near as old as I am and half a head taller, without her insulting me by making out she's my daughter? You must know that I would never have married Mr Freyne if I had thought he would insist on bringing you out, so it behoves you to be as meek as possible."

"I'll do my best to oblige you, madam," I said.

"Well, I must change my dress for supper," she said, as a black woman came and stood silently at the door. "Your nightgown and mob will do well enough, miss, so don't change 'em. We are only a small company to-night."

She went out, and I sat aghast for a moment, then looked round for some diversion, for in fact, my dearest friend, I was too great a coward not to seek to occupy my mind. I durst not think. There were two books on a table near me, and I took them up. One was a French novel, which did not please me, the other a volume of Archbishop Tillotson's sermons, but with half the leaves torn out, and the rest all singed with curling-tongs. I was turning them over, wondering who could have so misused such a book, when I heard voices, and jumped up all in a fright, for the one voice was Captain Colquhoun's, and I could not doubt but the other was my papa's. If I had been disturbed at the prospect of meeting my stepmother, what was the state of my feelings now? My heart swelled, and was thumping fit to burst, as a fine portly gentleman came in at the door, following the Captain.

"Why, who's this?" he cried.

"Your daughter, sir," says Captain Colquhoun, and hearing my doubts resolved, I could forbear no longer, but ran across the room and threw myself at my papa's feet, seizing his hand and bedewing it with my tears. I fear my agitation must have disturbed Mr Freyne, for all he could say was, "Hey, Sylvy? hey, my girl?" touching my hair with his other hand.

"Oh, won't my papa bestow his blessing on his child?" I sobbed, looking up at him with eyes streaming with tears. He failed to understand what I said.

"Hang me if I know what the girl would be at!" he said, gruffly.

"I believe, sir, that Miss is entreating your blessing," says Captain Colquhoun, with his stiffest air.

"There, there, child! God bless you!" says my papa. "Get up, and don't cry. I want to have a look at my girl."

I rose as he bade me, and dried my eyes as well as I could, and he led me to the window, to look into my face with the aid of the wax candles which were now set alight under glass shades on the varanda. "The living image of my lost charmer!" he said, kissing me kindly. "Han't my girl got a kiss for her old father?"

I put my arms about his neck, and was bold enough to kiss him two or three times, but it did not seem to displease him, for he blessed me again, and I think there was tears in his eyes. "I could believe that I saw your mother alive again, child," he said. "But there's no need to let Madam know that. 'Twould vex her sorely, poor woman, and we should never hear the end of it. Your coming out has been a sad trial to her, miss."

Captain Colquhoun coughed somewhat loudly, and Mr Freyne remembered his presence. "Come in, Captain, come in," he cried. "I want to present you to my daughter."

"I have had the honour already of meeting Miss, sir, and of offering her some slight service in a sufficiently disagreeable situation, for she was landed at the Gott from Mr Hamlin's budgero with no means of getting here."

"What! wasn't my budgero sent for her, nor so much as a palanqueen to the Gott?" cried my papa, and turned upon Mrs Freyne, who came into the parlour very fine, as I saw to my surprise, in a dressed suit and a fly cap.[05] "Pray, madam, how is it you showed such neglect towards my daughter? Must I be at the pain of giving all my orders myself when I leave home for three or four days? Wasn't it understood when I married you that you was to relieve me of all these points of ceremony? What else did I do it for?"

I took the words as a jest, though they seemed to me harsh enough to hear even then, but Mrs Freyne shut her fan with a snap that bade fair to break the sticks, and said, "Indeed, sir, I can't guess, no more than I can tell why I married you."

"Oh yes, madam, you can," says my papa, "or your clothes and jewels would tell it for you." He seemed about to continue, but I catched his hand boldly.

"Oh, pray, sir, dear sir, don't let me be a cause of dissension between you and Mrs Freyne," I said, and I think my face must have exhibited to him the agony I felt.

"Don't be a fool, child," he said, but not roughly. "When you are married, you'll know better than think every hasty word a tragedy. But sure you don't look to get a husband if you come to supper in an undress? We'll pardon a nightgown and mob this first evening, but the Calcutta ladies go very fine, and I don't want my girl to fall behind them."

"O' my conscience, sir, you are on monstrous familiar terms with your daughter already," said Mrs Freyne. "Perhaps you'll forgive my asking who it is you expect to supper?"

"Why, two or three fine gentlemen that all chanced to have business at this end of the town, and to be passing just at the time I came home, madam. They had never heard that I had a handsome daughter just landed from England, of course—hey, Miss Sylvy? And as I came through the town I met the *Zemindar* and the *Padra*, and asked them in."

"Which Padra?" asked Mrs Freyne. (This is the name by which all clergymen are known here, Amelia.)

"Why, the old Padra, madam, our good Mr Bellamy."

"That man!" cried Mrs Freyne. "I do think, Mr Freyne, that if you must invite a divine, you might oblige me so far as to let it be Mr Mapletoft."

"But I don't think so, madam. Be sure Parson Mapletoft is far better in the bosom of his family than rustling about here in his best cassock, and flourishing his white hands to show off his fine lace and his diamond ring."

"The *chuta Padra* is a person of taste and spirit," says Mrs Freyne. "Mr Bellamy is no better than any of the gentlemen of the place."

"I am thankful if I'm no worse than Mr Bellamy, madam," says my papa, and some of the guests arriving, we moved into the dining-parlour. Mr Bellamy, who is the senior chaplain of the factory, a cheerful and respectable person, handed Mrs Freyne, and I found myself taken in by Mr Holwell, whom every one called the Zemindar, a gentleman of a serious and somewhat troubled aspect. He spoke little to me, but I found abundant entertainment in listening to the general conversation, although there was much that I could not understand. But as you know, my dear, your Sylvia is afflicted with an invincible desire to know all that there is to be known, and as soon as supper was over, and we were gone out on the varanda, where the checks were drawn up, so that we could see the stars, I seized upon Captain Colquhoun. "Pray, sir," I said, "be so good as to tell me the meaning of all those words I hear the gentlemen use."

"*All* of them, madam? Are they so many, then?"

"Why, yes, sir. I can think of nothing but the letter with which the East India officer confounded the pedant in the last volume of 'Sir Charles Grandison.' Pray, sir, who is Mohabut Jing, and the *Chuta Nabob*, and what is a Zemindar and a Go-master? I know what Moors and Gentoos are, but what are To-passes and Fringys? What are *hummums* and *soosies*, and *seersuchers* and *kenchees*, and by what names are all these tribes of servants called that I see everywhere?"

"Why, madam, you have set me a task indeed. To tell you the offices of all your servants alone would take me pretty near the whole night. There's your papa's *mohurry*, who is his clerk for the Company's business, and his *banyan*, who is both his private clerk and his chief servant. There's his *secar*, who keeps his money and pays the wages; and his *compidore*, who goes a-marketing and helps the banyan; and the *kissmagar*, that stands behind his master's chair and looks after his clothes. There's the *consummer*, who in England would be called the butler; and the *peon*, who guards his master and beats the other servants. There's the *mussall chye*, that runs before the palanqueen o' nights; and the *pyke*, that watches in the varanda and lets no robbers in but his own friends. And there's a whole parcel more, down to the sweeper and the *harry*, which is the wench that brings water, but sure a longer list will but incommode you at present."[06]

"I'll do my best to make sure of these, sir, and then I'll ask you for more." And I am setting the names down here, both to assist me in remembering them, and also that my Amelia may learn them too. For I foresee that before I have been long at Bengall, I shall use these outlandish words without thinking of them, as do the ladies and gentlemen here, and I had as lief not puzzle my dearest friend more than I can help. "But, pray, sir," I continued, "tell me some of the other words I asked you."

"Why, indeed, madam, as for *soosies* and *kenchees* and the like, they are different kinds of cloths made in this country, of which I en't merchant enough to give you a particular account. The To-passes (called so because they wear *topees* or hats) are the country-born Portuguese, like your serving-wench yonder; and Fringys[07] is a vulgar Moorish name for Frenchmen and other Europeans, and also the Armenians. Then I fancy you desired to know what is a Zemindar, such as our good friend Mr Holwell. He is both Judge of the Court of Cutcherry, which decides all matters in dispute among the Indians in the Company's bounds, and he collects the taxes on merchandises and articles manufactured in the Presidency. A Go-master is an Indian agent, who is sent into the country to buy the cloth for the Company from the brokers, who buy it from those who weave it. Until five or six years back this business was done by other Indians working on their own account, called Dadney merchants, who should have dealt honestly with the Company, and did not, to their own damage, for the work was put under European superintendence, just as the corruption and dishonesty of the former black Zemindar led to his being deprived of his office, to the great advantage of the place. Was there anything more you desired to know, madam?"

"Why, yes, sir. About the persons with the strange names, to be sure."

"I ask your pardon for my negligence, madam. Mohabut Jing, whom some call Ally Verdy Cawn, is the Nabob of Bengall, and dwells at Muxadavad,[08] a great city lying close to our factory of Cossimbuzar.[09] The term Nabob signifies a deputy, or what the Portuguese call a viceroy, and Mohabut Jing affects to consider the Mogul Emperor of Delly[10] his master, though in reality he rules for himself alone. Having attained his present situation by violence, he has held it with a strong hand, though unable to resist the encroachments of the Morattoes,[11] a fierce pagan nation from the Decan. These came so far as to invade Bengall some thirteen years ago, at which time the Indian inhabitants of the Company's territory sought leave, in a panic, to dig a great ditch all round the place at their own charges. Three miles of this fortification was made, and then stopped as unnecessary, for the Nabob came to an accommodation with the Morattoes, giving up to them the province of Orixa,[12] and consenting to pay them a tribute, which they call *chout*, for sparing Bengall. This he did, fearing lest the European factories would take the side of the Morattoes, and so drive him out; for he goes very much in fear of us, and desired to have leisure to humble our pride. And this he has done by forbidding any hostilities in Bengall when there was war at home, and also in the Carnatic, between Britain and France—a prohibition which was, as you may guess, the most irksome thing in the world to us. 'Tis his aim to reduce our trade to the level of that of the Armenians, which is carried on merely on sufferance, whereas we are here in virtue of the *phirmaunds* and *husbulhookums*[13] granted to us by several of the emperors."

"But sure, sir, Britons would never submit to such a spoliation?"

"I am not saying they would, madam. But Ally Verdy en't our worst enemy, for he's a man of sense and of some honour, if I may speak so of a Moor. But he has lately raised to the *musnet*,[14] or as we would say, adopted as his heir, his grandson, a youth of the vilest disposition, called Surajah Dowlah, and from him we have little better to hope than we would from a tyger. He is the *Chuta Nabob* concerning whom you was pleased to inquire."

"But pray, sir, tell me more of this person."

"Why, madam, what little I could tell you would be as displeasing for you to hear as for me to relate."

I went as red as fire, I am sure. "Oh, sir, pray pardon me if I have trespassed on your patience. I know I'm a sad creature for asking questions, and I fear you'll think I'm intruding into matters too high for a young woman to concern herself with."

For I remembered, Amelia (how can I ever forget it?), that dreadful day at Holly-tree House, when the Rector brought his brother, the Admiral, to wait on our instructresses. You'll know with what spirit the dear good gentleman described the last fleet action in which he had taken part, and how I was carried away by my excitements, and asked him all sorts of questions about the ships and their disposition. He saluted me at parting, you'll remember, and said to Mrs Eustacia, "I dare be bound, madam, this pretty little Miss could write as fair an account of the fight as any clerk I ever had on board ship," which piece of kindness puffed me up not a little. But when he was gone away with his brother, I was sent for to Mrs Eustacia, and chidden for meddling in matters with which I had no concern. There was nothing, said the good lady, that was so much disliked by gentlemen as the affectation of masculine knowledge in a young woman, and if I was so unhappy as to be cursed with a taste for severe learning, it behoved me to conceal it as I would the plague. And so I have always strove to do, aided by the kind condescension that prompts most gentlemen to turn the answer to a lady's question into a compliment to her eyes or her smile, but this inquisitive spirit of mine (what am I to do with it, my dear?) is perpetually leading me wrong. But Captain Colquhoun was more tender to my fault than Mrs Eustacia had been.

"Indeed, madam," he said, "I could wish there was more of our ladies here with your laudable desire of knowledge. If they took these things into account, there might be less of that grasping and grinding for money, which is making us (saving your presence) to stink in the nostrils of the Indians. But when every one is seeking to outshine her neighbours, and luxury is come to such a pitch among us that Rome herself can't scarce have been worse, what wonder that money is sought by the sale of *dussticks*[15] and in other irregular ways, to the great damage of the Nabob and our eternal discredit?"

"Then you look for a judgment upon this place, sir?"

"I look for an invasion sooner or later of our territory on the part of the Chuta Nabob, madam, unless heaven should interpose and raise one of the other claimants to the *soubahship*[16] in his place. And when that invasion comes, here are we, with the Fort all tumbling to pieces, the guns useless, no powder, and a militia that don't know one end of their muskets from t'other."

"And is this the fault of the Company, sir?"

"No, madam. The Company sent out orders for the drilling of the militia by the Godolphin four years ago, and this year they have ordered positively the repair of the fortifications on two separate occasions, chiefly on account of the threatened war with France. But Colonel Scott, who prepared the complete plan of defence which was ordered to be carried out, is dead, and Mr Drake and the gentlemen of the Presidency won't listen to any one of less responsible station. So the work is hung up, as the lawyers say, and when the place is plunged in one common ruin, all will suffer alike, though with different deserts."

This and some further conversation to the same effect has made me (as I may without shame confess to my Amelia) almost afraid to sleep in my bed, lest I should find myself aroused at midnight by the terrors of a Moorish invasion. Here, where there's no Whigs nor Tories, I am become as strong a party-woman, to use Mr Addison's phrase, as any of the ladies of whom he wrote; and should the fashion arise, as in his days, of wearing hoods differing in colour according to the politics of the wearers, I should be among the first to adopt it. Let me see: our side would choose red, I suppose, as signifying our desire for warlike preparations, while the ladies of Mr Drake's party would wear the Quaker gray. I think our party would have the best of it, Amelia; don't you?

CALCUTTA, *September ye* 21*st.*

'Tis time, indeed, that I brought this letter to a close; but there's one or two things I must first put down, though at the risque of my dear girl's thinking me a sad tedious scribbler. I have found the way, Amelia, into my stepmother's favour—a thing that would be altogether charming, were it not that the means thereto are such as, to borrow a phrase from our great but neglected British poet, would leave me poor indeed. But you shall hear. On Saturday, then, my trunks, which had been in the hold of the Orford, were brought to the house, and I was extraordinary well pleased, for I had feared to be forced to stay from church the next day for want of a suitable gown. Mrs Freyne was to the full as glad as I, and shut herself up with me in my chamber to see the trunks unpacked, telling the banyan, who performs such services of ceremony here, to deny her to her visitants, using the phrase "The door is shut," which is so understood by everybody. Well, as Marianna unfolded and laid out one gown after another, I could see that Mrs Freyne became less and less contented, and at last she burst out with—

"I vow, miss, you have a prodigious great store of clothes. Pray how much did Mr Freyne send home for providing you with 'em?"

"I don't know, madam," I said, and I was thankful to be able to say so. "The gentlewomen at Holly-tree House were bid to provide them, and account to Mr Freyne, within a certain sum."

"You might have been coming out as a married woman," says my stepmother, smoothing the satin of my white quilted petticoat. "I never saw a young Miss so absurdly well provided. Look you there now; you have three—four—silk night-gowns, and questionless a dozen or two of muslin ones."

"No, madam, I have none of muslin. Mrs Abigail said they would be made cheaper here, and the limit of the money not exceeded."

Mrs Freyne's countenance cleared. "Why then," she said, "I'll show you what's to be done. You shall give me two of these silk night-gowns, and I'll have half a dozen muslin ones made for you from stuff that I have lying by, and so you'll be properly dressed and not over-furnished."

"As you please, madam," said I. But I was glad she left me the white damask and the yellow lustring, and took the blue and the green, which, as you know, I was not so pleased with. But I trembled when I saw her considering my blush-coloured paduasoy with the silver lace. If she had laid hands on it, I must have ventured to suggest to her that the hue was not becoming to ladies of such a delicate complexion as hers, but only to brown girls with a high colour, like your Sylvia. But she passed it over, and after requesting of me such trifles as an apron or two and a French necklace,[17] came to my head-clothes.

"Indeed you're not badly off for lace!" she said. "Three heads,[18] as I'm alive—two Brussels and a Mechlin. I'm sure you can't want this Brussels mob, miss."

"Oh, pray, madam," I said in a great taking, "you are welcome to the other two, but leave me that one."

"I think it's very ill-natured in you, miss, to say that when you know I have set my heart on it. How can you be so unamiable? I like to see a young woman facetious[19] to those about her."

"Indeed I can't give it you, madam," I said, "for the lace was my mother's, but if you'll accept of the loan of it——"

"I see you en't so disobliging as I thought," said she graciously, and carried off the cap, though I would have given almost any of my other clothes to have kept it. But she has treated me much more obligingly since, and now that I know the way into her good graces, I shan't forget the lesson, though to practise it might cost me all my favourite gowns, even to my mother's white brocade flowered with gold. But no, I had forgot. She won't want that, though she was mightily taken with the fashion of it (it was made over after the pattern of the Princess Emily's gown for the last Birth-night,[20] my dearest friend will remember), for she said the stuff might have come out of Noah's Ark.

The next day we went to church in state, all of us in our palanqueens, with the peon marching before, and boys with fans and so on following behind. I was wearing my paduasoy, with the ribbons to match in my cap, and before we started my papa was so very kind as to place round my neck a collar of pearls, so large and white and fine that a queen might wear them, and I could scarce believe they were really designed for me. Mrs Freyne wore a very fine flowered satin, with the embroidered apron she had from me, and her diamonds made me wink to look at them. Forgive me, my dear, for entering into such particulars on such an occasion. I can't tell why it should be that the Calcutta people should make such a show and parade of one's first appearance at church, any more than why we in England should do the same on the Sunday after a wedding, but it is to them as important as an appearance at Court. I must tell you that I had devised a little plan with Miss Hamlin, which she succeeded in carrying out with the greatest exactness imaginable. Our respective processions (I can't find any other word for it) approaching from opposite directions, we reached the church *compound* (which means an enclosure) at the same time, but at different gates, so that the gentlemen who were waiting to catch sight of the newly-arrived ladies were drawn two ways at once, and divided their forces. Still, there were enough of them to cause me great uneasiness, as they all pressed round to help me from the palanqueen, desiring to be allowed to hand me into church, or to carry a prayer-book, a fan, or even a handkerchief. I was so pressed and pestered that I didn't know what to do, and suddenly catching sight of Captain Colquhoun on the outskirts of the crowd, I beckoned to him with my fan (I hope it wasn't very forward in me), and he came and lent me his hand into the church. As we entered, in came Miss Hamlin at the opposite door, and handing her was the very gentleman we had seen standing in the gateway of the Fort on our arrival. We made our honours to each other as we passed to our pews, and there, with the Indian boys flapping us with feather fans, and the eyes of half the congregation fixed on one whenever the time came to stand up, I did my best to compose my thoughts suitably to the solemnity of the service. I am ashamed to say that I never found it so hard in my life.

After an excellent discourse from good Mr Bellamy (I had now commanded my thoughts sufficiently to be able to listen to it with attention), we passed out into the church porch, and there was such a bowing and curtseying and whispering and staring as you never saw. Every moment it was, "Pray, sir, present me to your lovely daughter," or, "Do, dear madam, make me acquainted with this charming Miss," and kind things enough said to confuse a London beauty, much more a poor girl just fresh from her boarding-school, as Miss Hamlin has so great a fancy for reminding me. And, indeed, Amelia, I was so flurried and flustered with trying to curtsey all ways at once, and with saying, "Sir, you're most obliging"—"Madam, you are too good"—"Dear sir, you overpower me"—"Pray, madam, don't make me blush with your kindness" (though I think it far from kind, and quite barbarous, to praise a young creature's looks to her very face, till she don't know whither to turn her eyes),—that I don't know what would have happened if it had not been for Miss Hamlin. This extraordinary young lady had been receiving the compliments of the gentlemen with all the composure of a queen, though now and then she would lift her eyes and reply with a witty sentiment that set all but one of her admirers laughing at that one; but now, when we were both beset by some twenty importunate persons, all crying, "Madam, permit me the honour"—"Allow me, madam"—"Madam, your most obedient," desiring to hand us to our palanqueens, she stepped across suddenly to me, and, seizing my hand, led me down the steps. "We can't allow you all the pleasure and the honour, gentlemen," she said, holding up her fan to shelter her from the sun. "Sure you won't none of you grudge a little of it to Miss Freyne and me?"

I heard the gentlemen shout with laughter at the whimsical drollery of her tone, and I laughed myself, though I made sure we should not find our palanqueens among those at the foot of the steps, and should be forced to beg one of the gentlemen we had scorned to go in search of them. But there, to my surprise, they were, and Miss Hamlin handed me in with the most graceful air in the world.

"Oh dear, miss," said I, "what should we have done if this had not happened so pat?"

"Happened?" says she. "I had it happen, sweet innocence. I gave my uncle's peon his orders before church, and let me tell you, miss, that if that blackfellow think it safe to disobey any one's orders at our house, it en't those of the Chuta Beebee."

"But shan't we discommode Mr and Mrs Hamlin by bringing 'em to this door, miss?"

"No, indeed, miss. Why, we are all coming to *tiffing* at your papa's, and our elders ought to thank me for ridding 'em so soon of the gentlemen."

But we were not yet rid of the gentlemen, for they came down the steps in a body, headed by our fellow-passenger, Mr Ranger, and by Mr Ensign Bellamy, the Padra's son, and with much raillery about the rival beauties, and the pretence of devoted friendship to deceive the looker-on, proceeded to *escorte* us home, marching before and behind our palanqueens, which they insisted should be carried exactly abreast. On reaching the house, we were handed out with great ceremony by our chief cavaliers, the rest of the gentlemen standing and bowing, and my papa, who had reached home by a shorter way, invited them all into the varanda to drink our healths. For indeed he was pleased to be charmed, not only with the honour the gentlemen had done us, as they considered it, but with Miss Hamlin's action on the church-steps, and said afterwards that she was a fine, handsome, sprightly girl, and he would not be sorry to see me with a touch of her spirit, but my stepmother called her a bold-faced slut.

The things I have mentioned all happened the day before yesterday, and last evening, finding Mrs Freyne about to set forth to an assembly at my Lady Russell's house in the Rope-walk, I wondered whether she would bid me attend her there, since I was now introduced into the world of Calcutta. But she said nothing of taking me with her, and started alone, while I sat down and wrote these sheets to my Amelia, since my papa was gone to sup with the Governor at the Company's house on the other side of the Fort. To my surprise, however, he returned home early in the evening, and testifying some vexation on finding me alone, offered to carry me for an airing in the budgero on the water in the moonlight. You'll guess that I accepted his kindness with transports of gratitude, and sure the occasion had been a charming one, even if it had not brought the added pleasure of his dear company. But as it fell out, he was good enough to speak to me in so tender and affecting a manner as I could describe to no one but my dearest friend.

"Has any one here remarked to you that you are like your mother, miss?" he asked me.

"No, sir; no one but yourself."

Mr Freyne. And yet to me every turn of your head, every motion of your arm, recalls her to mind. But I suppose few would remember her.

Sylvia. It must be near eighteen years since she left Fort William, sir.

Mr F. True, my girl, and our generations are but short ones in Bengall. Yet it seems to me, seeing you, only yesterday that I took leave of my Sally on the deck of the Sunderland (for I had accompanied her out to sea as far as I might go). The iya stood behind her, holding her infant (that was you, miss), christened by the Padra in haste that very day. Your mother would have you named Sylvia, saying that her own name was so ugly she would choose a sweet pretty one for her baby, and 'twas as much for your sake as her own that she embarked upon that voyage to the Cape of Good Hope which the physician said would save both your lives, for that season was a prodigious unhealthy one at Fort William. The Company's rule forbids its servants to leave their posts unless sent on business by the Council here, and I durst not throw up the Service if I did not wish us all to starve. So I went back to my work, and managed to scrape together a sufficiency of money to enable me to hire the house we now have from Omy Chund, the Gentoo *shroff*[21] that owns half Calcutta. 'Twas an agreeable place enough, and cooler than my old quarters in the Fort, and I watched for the coming of the ships from home, which should bring my Sally back to me from the Cape. Instead of that, the first that arrived brought me the news of her death. She had died at sea, and the child was gone on to England with its nurse, to be bred up, as its mother had desired, by the two French gentlewomen who had instructed herself. Does my girl recollect anything of that voyage?

Sylvia (*weeping*). Nothing, sir. I was barely a year old when I reached Holly-tree House.

Mr F. And you knew as little of your papa as he of you. In mourning my lost charmer I forgot the sweet little pledge of our loves which she had left me. Was there anything to remind you that you possessed a living parent, child?

Sylvia. Indeed, dear sir, there was not much. The other young Misses could talk of their papas' kindness to them in their holidays, but all times were the same to me. Once or twice you were good enough to say in your letters to Mrs Eustacia, "I hope Miss is a good girl, and minds her book," and I'll assure you the school could scarce contain me, I was so proud to be remembered so far away.

Mr F. At times I could almost wish that I had left the Service five years ago, and gone home to settle down somewhere with my girl. But, no; I had not money enough, and must make more. And make it I did, and am making it every day more and more—for Madam to spend.

Sylvia. Sure, sir, Mrs Freyne lays it out with great elegance.

Mr F. Questionless, miss. But I had as lief the money and the elegance had been some other man's. There's a pleasing quality of your sex, that they can't endure for any one to be indifferent towards 'em. When Miss Harriet Quinion from Madrass came to visit her relations here, and had the whole place at her feet, sure 'twas more than kind in her to take no satisfaction in the admiration she received because there was one old fellow that had no part in it. I dare avouch that Henry Freyne's coldness piqued her more than all her conquests pleased her. At any rate, she was determined to overcome it, and brought all her feminine artillery to bear on the man that was still wedded to the memory of a wife dead these fifteen years. All the ladies gave her their assistance, of course—they love to hunt down one that they believe a contemner of their sex—and you don't need telling what the event was, which gave me the honour of keeping Mrs Freyne in gowns and equipages, and blessed you, miss, with the tender care of a stepmother, for which I don't doubt you have often thanked me with tears.

Sylvia. Oh pray, dear sir, don't think I have ventured to cavil at anything you may choose to do. En't it your right to please yourself?

Mr F. To please myself! Quite so, and I did it, you would say, miss? But it did not please Madam to have you out here at all, not knowing your dutiful inclinations towards her. Indeed, I was almost resolved, for your own sake, to request your instructresses to see you married at home, with no question of coming out, but Madam over-reached herself there. Knowing nothing of my intentions, she kept up such a clamour at me about you, that hearing Mrs Hamlin was to bring out her niece this year, I took a sudden determination, and wrote that you should come with her.

Sylvia. How can I ever thank you enough, dear sir?

Mr F. What, you were glad to come? But how long am I to keep you, miss, pray? Are you to be married to-morrow or the day after?

Sylvia (*trembling*). Oh, dear sir, if I might venture to entreat——

Mr F. (*roughly*). Out with it, miss. Are you married already?

Sylvia. Oh no, no, sir. All I desired was to ask that I might be permitted to lead a single life for the present, and devote myself to my dear papa, of whom I have seen so little.

Mr F. (*looking stern*). This means, miss, that you're entertaining some lover whom you don't dare present to me.

Sylvia. Forgive me, dear sir, but you wrong me. My papa will believe me when I assure him that there's no one I could marry sooner than another.

Mr F. Then pray, miss, what does all this mean that Madam has been telling me, having heard it from Mrs Hamlin, about some nephew of Captain Colquhoun's?

Sylvia. I don't know, sir, I'm sure, what you may have heard from Mrs Freyne, but the only relative of the Captain with whom I am acquainted is the humble servant of another lady.

Mr F. It en't an unheard-of thing for a lover to change his divinity.

Sylvia. Indeed, sir, I can assure you that the very last time I saw him the gentleman protested to me his unaltered devotion to his original charmer.

Mr F. Then Madam has been trying to make mischief, curse me if she hasn't! Give me a kiss, my girl. You deserve something for answering with so much sense and calmness questions over which most young Misses would have fallen into fits, and you shan't be drove into any marriage to please her. You may have this coming cold weather to look about you and decide whom you'll have. But mind you, there's to be no coquetting first with one and then with another. The first sign I see of that, I vow I'll marry you off next day to the oldest and ugliest gentleman of my acquaintance. I won't have half the young sparks of Calcutta killing t'other half in duels about my daughter.

Sylvia. 'Twill be no hardship to me to obey you, sir. I believe I prefer the elder gentlemen to the younger. If you choose, I'll adopt Captain Colquhoun as my cavalier whenever he's present.

Mr F. As you did yesterday? By all means, miss. But you're not to set yourself to break the poor Captain's heart because you think him old and ugly. He's the most respectable person in Calcutta, save Padra Bellamy and one or two more, and also the most foolish and the worst treated.

Sylvia. You surprise me, sir.

Mr F. He's the most foolish because, in company with Captain Jones of the Train,[22] he persists in running his head against a stone wall. Only last week they were told not to come troubling the Council with their nonsense, having been pressing them for the hundredth time to put the place into a state of defence. And he's also foolish because, when he might have been transferred two years ago to the Carnatic he refused to go, lest he should seem to be running away from his enemies here, and you won't wonder that he's ill-treated after what I have told you.

This, my Amelia, ended our conversation, which has filled me with a hundred grateful thoughts of my dear papa. One thing only troubles me, but surely I am not called upon to confess my foolishness in the matter of Mr Fraser? To admit that he gave me cause to think him my lover would mean that my papa would insist upon quarrelling with him, while surely the poor man en't to blame if a silly girl took his undoubted kindness to mean other than it did. No, the history of my mistake shall still be confided only to the faithful bosom of my Amelia, and I'll hope more fervently than ever that winds and tides and the public service may combine to keep the Tyger, and in especial her fourth lieutenant, away from Bengall. My deepest love and gratitude are owed to my dear papa for his goodness, which is beyond what I had dared to hope, and will enable me to triumph over Miss Hamlin, whose prophecies have been so signally belied.

CHAPTER V.
IN WHICH DESPATCHES FROM ADMIRAL WATSON REACH CALCUTTA.

CALCUTTA, *March ye* 10*th*, 1756.

What! (I think I hear my Amelia cry, when her eye lights upon the date of this letter,) no word for close upon six months, and this from the friend who swore that her most secret thoughts should lie open to me? Indeed, I must confess that I have been sadly remiss in writing to my dear girl, and what's worse, I have no valid excuse for't, but only two or three weak ones. For whether I plead that I have begun a letter two or three times over, and torn it up because it seemed that there was nothing but trifles to tell, or that at another time I delayed because I thought that I could describe the life of this place better when I had had more experience of it, it but goes to prove that I deserve no pardon. Nevertheless, I can satisfy my Amelia in one thing. My idleness en't due to any alteration in my friendship for her, nor yet to any change in my own condition. Your friend is Sylvia Freyne still. But oh, my dear, prepare for a surprise; your Sylvia is become a toast! Now, indeed, you'll laugh, and well you may. When the gentlemen come thronging about me, 'tis as much as I can do not to cry out to them, "Good sirs, you are pleased to commend me so highly, I wonder what you would say if I could exhibit my Miss Turnor to you?" 'Tis all my English colour, Amelia; my stepmother has told me so again and again (although, as you'll remember, she was of the contrary opinion at first), and when that's gone, as it will go in this coming hot weather, I shan't be able so much as to find a gentleman that will hand me to my chair. But this I don't believe, for young women are sufficiently scarce in Calcutta to receive polite attention however plain they be, and for this cold season, at any rate, I have had my fill of homage.

Don't charge me with boasting when I tell you, merely in order to exhibit the absurdity of the whole affair, that I am now quite accustomed to be guarded home at night from a ball or assembly by a troop of gentlemen with drawn swords, who force every European they meet to uncover and stand humbly aside, and every Indian to take off his shoes and bow himself to the ground before my palanqueen. Day after day, too, I find my dressing-table covered with *chitts* (which are small notes or billets) and *salams* (by which is meant nosegays of flowers, and other tributes of admiration), all of which Marianna sweeps aside with the greatest coolness in the world, as though she had not accepted a rupee (and I'm much mistaken if it was not a *sicca*[01] one) for placing each of them there. Sure, my dear, these things are enough to make one feel silly, and indeed I thought myself the greatest fool imaginable at first, but by this time I have learnt to practise the carriage which becomes a Calcutta beauty. Why, Amelia, I would not lift a finger to brush a fly from my dress if there was a gentleman (or at the worst a servant) within call to do it for me; and as for taking the trouble to fan myself—! No, your Sylvia has learned the lesson of elegant languor which befits these climates, and even Miss Hamlin would hardly call her a boarding-school Miss now. The gentlemen say, I am told, that your friend has the coldest heart (and the finest eyes, they are pleased to add) in Calcutta, and they choose to resent my preference for a single life so fiercely that they have bound themselves together against me, all agreeing to support any one of their number who can show that he possesses good hopes of capturing the fortress. Now en't this a quantity of silly stuff for a young creature to write that piques herself on her good sense? Forgive me, Amelia; your Sylvia's head en't quite turned, though it has often bid fair to be with all this violent admiration.

But what, you'll say, of Miss Hamlin? Is she married yet? No, my dear, she is not, and all because, as she says, she won't allow herself to be outdone by a chit of a girl like your friend. If Miss Freyne has sufficient strength of mind to refuse to be made a slave of before she choose, so has she. But she has promised her suitors (and they are many) that her wedding, when it comes, shall be like none that was ever solemnised in Calcutta before, so that the mere honour of being present shall be sufficient consolation to every man but the bridegroom. "And as for him," says she, "if he be so adventurous as to marry Charlotte Hamlin, he will deserve the punishment he'll get." This piece of pleasantry was repeated all over Calcutta before it had been two hours uttered, but none of the gentlemen appeared to be deterred by it from continuing to press his suit. For if your Sylvia be a toast, Miss Hamlin is a queen, and the more sternly she rules, the more eagerly do her subjects crowd forward to place themselves under her yoke. This strange girl and I have never quarrelled, in spite of constant provocations. We differ in opinion fifty times in an hour, we bicker and squabble as often as we meet, and yet, next to my Amelia, there's no female friend I would sooner find at my side in trouble than Miss Hamlin.

But now to let you know something of the course of my life here. I rise early, as does all the world, and take a light breakfast with my papa in the varanda. My Amelia will understand how agreeable these morning hours, spent in the company of the most venerable of men, are to me. I should never have dared to offer myself as Mr Freyne's companion, but it so happened that one day he asked me why I never came near him in the mornings, although he heard me moving about the house.

"Indeed, dear sir," I said, "I was afraid to interrupt your conversations with Mrs Freyne."

"Pray, miss," said my papa, with much displeasure, "don't be pert. You wasn't used to be when you landed."

"Pardon me, sir, but indeed I feared to intrude."

"If Mrs Freyne were to do me the honour to leave her bed and sit opposite me, miss, I should see nothing but a dirty wrapper and the point of my wife's nose, covered in with five or six nightcaps. But she don't."

"Then may I really attend you at breakfast, sir?"

"You may, miss. I'll be hanged if I know why I should be deprived of my girl's company for the sake of Madam's punctilio."

And thus it has happened that all this cold weather I have enjoyed the advantage of listening to my dear papa's conversation, which he has been good enough to direct especially to my improvement, encouraging me to ask questions, and rewarding my inquisitiveness (which you'll say needed no such spur) with an infinity of curious information. After the remark he was pleased to pass on Mrs Freyne's morning undress, you may guess how careful I am never to wait upon him in a wrapper, far less in a bedgown[02] and petticoat, such as is worn by some of our ladies here as late as the middle of the day. When my Amelia and I entered into a resolve to emulate the example of the excellent Clarissa, and never appear outside our chambers unless fully dressed for the day, we did not think that I should have so much reason to be grateful for the forming of this good habit in a climate where it's only too easy to fall into idle ways.

Well, when my papa has finished his breakfast, which he takes at his ease in his nightcap and gown and slippers, he returns to his chamber to dress, while I go into the garden and give directions to the *molly*[03] or gardener, who don't understand half I say, and never by any chance obeys what he does understand. My papa comes down the steps while I am speaking, and tells the man in Moors[04] what I want, when the rascal bows to the ground and says, "Very good, master," but obeys his master no more than he does me. The garden is very neatly laid out in our English style, with alleys of brick and statues and pavilions, not like most of the gardens here, which are sad untidy places, and Mr Freyne and I explore the entire extent of it every morning, in order to admire the ingenious manner in which the gardener has contrived to disobey his orders of the day before. In these airings we have sometimes the company of Captain Colquhoun, who comes in after his morning parade, in which he is the exactest person I ever saw, and far more punctual in his duties than any of the other captains here. Then my papa goes away to his *dufter-conna*,[05] or place of business, at the

Fort, and I occupy myself in reading or needlework. Captain Colquhoun is good enough to lend me books from his library, which treat chiefly of wars and sieges, but must tend admirably to the improving of the mind, and good Padra Bellamy has promised to extend to me the same favour when the Captain's store shall have come to an end. As for my needlework, I had so many new gowns when I arrived that it seemed absurd to set to work on any more clothes for myself, but I had the happy thought to embroider a set of robings for Mrs Freyne as a present at the New Year, and she was so vastly pleased that I was well content, though it took me all my time. I am at work now on another set that I design for Miss Hamlin, but as she don't intend to marry yet, there's no hurry about it.

Did I mention to you in my first letter from this place, my dear, that none of the Calcutta ladies take any oversight of their households? The servants manage everything, under the orders of the banyan, and the mistress knows nothing of the œconomy of her dwelling. It grieved me so deeply to see that Mrs Freyne did not so much as wash her own best China tea-dishes herself, but left them to the servants, that I begged my papa to inform her I would gladly take upon myself any household duties that she found too much for her; but he laughed very heartily, and told me that European ladies had no household duties in Bengall.

"But sure, sir," said I, "their households must go to ruin."

"And if they do, miss, their spouses pay the bill. Why, en't it sufficient honour for us that while we climb the pagoda-tree, the ladies are good enough to recline in the shade on couches of shawls and permit us to shake the gold *mohrs* into their laps? Would you have us make slaves of the lovely creatures in this climate? Go to, miss; you're a traitor to your sex."

My dear papa is so droll!

At nine o'clock is the late breakfast, to which Mr Freyne returns with a boy holding over his head a great umbrella called a *kittesan*, and at which every one appears in an elegant undress of white muslin, and you may wear a mob or not, as you please. When my papa is returned to his business, and Mrs Freyne to her chamber, where she looks over her jewels, or devises with her iya new fashions of garments, or, it may be, receives her intimates, I turn to my music or drawing, accomplishments which are both very highly regarded here. At noon comes tiffing, which is a cold luncheon (sure it must seem that we do nothing but eat, but indeed, my dear, one has no great appetite in Bengall), and after that all those who have been long in the country retire to rest; while silly persons like your Sylvia, who can't reconcile themselves to sleeping in the middle of the day, lie down in their cool chambers and look out at the heat in the garden and think of Britain. They tell me that in the hot weather I shan't be able to endure even to draw aside a corner of the blind; but perhaps I shall have learned to sleep at midday by that time.

Dinner is at three, and for this meal every one is dressed with all the exactness imaginable, for 'tis the rarest thing in the world for us to take it alone. One must pay special attention to one's hair, for in this matter the Calcutta ladies are very punctilious; and I can't tell you how grateful I am for the present simple and elegant mode of wearing it. Should it be, as you'll remember we heard was to be the case, that the cumbrous style of head-dress which is rallied so often in the 'Spectator' were to come again into vogue, these ladies would adopt it without a moment's delay, I'm positive, and suffer the torments of martyrs owing to its weight and heat. The gentlemen, all wearing white jackets, have an air of the most agreeable coolness, and behind all our chairs stand boys with flappers or fans,—so that, in spite of the excessive seasoning of the food (the favourite dish being meat or vegetables dressed in a *currey* with spices), we suffer less from the heat than might be expected. But then, as I am perpetually being told, this is only the cold weather yet.

After a second short rest comes the season for going abroad. One may go fishing or fowling on the river, walk in the park called the Loll Baug,[06] and listen to the band of music that plays beside the great tank or pond, ride out in a chaise or a palanqueen, or take the air in a budgero; and there's continual parties made to spend the evening in some garden at a little distance from the town, whether that of the Armenians, or Surman's, or those of two rich Gentoos, called Omy Chund and Govinderam Metre, close to the Morattoe-ditch. Sometimes I am called to attend Mrs Freyne to an outcry, which in Britain would be styled a sale by auction, either of the goods of some deceased person or of a parcel of toys which have been brought from China or the great islands by some gentleman travelling on the Company's occasions. This last is what pleases me best, for it seems to me sadly unfeeling to go bidding for the possessions of a person to whom you may have been talking two days before without a thought of sickness, far less death; but every one here cares infinitely more for the commonest Europe goods than for the most delicate toys from the East. This I could not understand; but one day Miss Dorman came to visit me, and found me setting up in my chamber the things I had bought with a handful of rupees which my papa was so good as to throw into my lap, knowing that I could not bring myself to write a chitt for the value, as is always done in Calcutta.

"What do you think of my toys, miss?" I said to the young lady.

"Vastly pretty," she said. "But do you really care for 'em, miss?"

"Sure they're prodigious delicate and strange," said I.

"Why, yes; but they are all country-made," she said. "I used to be pleased with such things once, but in the hot weather I longed to throw 'em all away, and put up the commonest English stuff in their place; and at last I bid my iya take them somewhere so that I should never see them again."

Do you think I shall be like that soon, Amelia? How melancholy must life appear when one can take no delight in such beauties as are to be observed around one, and all for thinking of those upon which one placed but little value when one possessed 'em! But sure the whole polite world, and not only the unhappy exiles that, like myself, have most probably bid farewell to Britain for ever, would cry shame on me for comparing the poor barbarous works of the pagans here with the handiwork of Europe.

But to my day, which bids fair to be as long as some of those of which our Clarissa or Miss Byron write. It sometimes happens that neither Mr nor Mrs Freyne desire my attendance in the evenings, and on these occasions I call for my palanqueen (I have plenty of assurance now, you see), and go to pass the time with Miss Hamlin, who has desired me always to visit her when I have nothing better to do, since the gentlemen are then able to wait upon us both at the same time, and are not torn in two by an anxiety to rush away to the further side of Calcutta. 'Tis seldom, indeed, that we are left alone for long—but oh, my dear, I must tell you of the adventure that befell me the first time that I rid out in a palanqueen by myself. I had given the peon (which is the servant that walks before you with a silver-headed stick) the direction of Mr Hamlin's house, and as he speaks English, I thought myself safely embarked. But scarcely had my equipage left my papa's door, when I became conscious that the bearers were uttering the most affecting groans and sighs imaginable. At first I paid no attention, thinking that this might be only their way at starting, as I have heard say of the camel; but on the continuance of the sounds, I could not resist putting my head out of the palanqueen and calling to the peon to know what ailed his fellows.

"These *gwallers*[07] poor weak men, Beebee," said he, speaking English after his fashion; "not got enough to eat."

"I'm sure I'm sorry to hear it," said I; "but what ails them in particular just now?"

"Beebee too much heavy," replied the wretch. Was it not mortifying, my dear? You know I was never used to be counted a great weight, and I could not believe that the voyage had changed me much in this respect, but since I had plunged into the discussion of these men's misfortunes, I could not well do less than request the peon to hire an extra bearer or two. But this wasn't what he wanted.

"If Beebee give buxie money," he said, "gwallers buy good supper to-night; carry Beebee all right to-morrow."

"But how will that help them now?" I asked, taking out with hesitation one of my rupees.

"Beebee give me the buxies, I show the gwallers, and keep it till we go home. Then gwallers so pleased, not cry any more."

"Pray try it," said I, "for these noises are most distressing."

His fingers closed upon the rupee, but he made no effort to display it to the bearers. Instead he laid about him heavily with his rattan, reviling the rest, so far as I could judge, for their idleness, and menacing them with Mr Freyne's displeasure; and all this to such good purpose that they shouldered their poles and went on again without any more groans. But I have never been able, my dear Miss Turnor, to divest my mind of the persuasion that the abandoned wretch kept the rupee for himself, and made the poor creatures believe that I had paid it to him for his assiduity in beating them. This suspicion I have not dared to unfold even to my papa, for fear he would never cease laughing at me; but it has long haunted me, and now I share the horrid thing with my Amelia.

Well, after all this, our days commonly end with either an assembly or a ball. Such a thing as a small party is unknown, and would indeed have but a mean appearance in these vast saloons. There's a good deal of music and singing (some of it, if I may be censorious in my Amelia's hearing, not of the very best), and an extraordinary quantity of cards. Of this amusement Mrs Freyne is passionately fond, but play runs so high in Calcutta that my papa has forbid her to go beyond rupee points in his house. In this he is considered vastly singular, as also in forbidding my stepmother and me to accept shawls or other presents offered us by the Indians with whom he has to do in his business—a means by which some of our ladies here have amassed incredible numbers of these beautiful fabrics; but he lays no restraint upon Mrs Freyne's doings abroad, and 'twould not surprise me if she takes her revenge there. There's a certain set of persons with whom she plays very commonly, and of one of them I am horridly afraid my Amelia will hear more in the future. This gentleman is a Mr Menotti, a Genoese by birth, but settled here so long that he speaks English like ourselves, who does your Sylvia the honour to regard her with favour, and who has got Mrs Freyne upon his side. Secure in the justice and complaisance of my good papa, I could look upon this odious person with contempt, were it not that he's perpetually forcing himself upon me, and seems to regard my displeasure as an object worth living for.

But enough of this detestable subject. There's one thing I must tell you about the balls here that will surprise you. The first of these to which I attended my stepmother was before the end of the hot weather, and I was apprehensive lest I should expire of discomfort in my stiff brocade and monstrous hoop. I knew there would be no rest for me so long as I remained in the ballroom; for all persons of fashion in Calcutta are prodigiously addicted to dancing, and there are so few ladies in proportion to the gentlemen that they are scarce allowed even time for dessert.[08] Mrs Freyne did not offer to relieve my apprehensions; but after the ball had been opened very ceremoniously with a minuet, I was surprised to see all the ladies preparing to depart. "Come," thought I, "this is better than I had hoped," but I found that the object of this interval was to allow the ladies to change their clothes. Disencumbered of our hoops and dressed suits, we returned to the ballroom wearing muslin nightgowns elegantly trimmed with lace and ribbons, and danced until we were as tired as—oh, my dear, I am sure I have never been so tired in my life, nor so consumed with the heat.

There's my day for you, Amelia, ending ordinarily at midnight, but sometimes not till three in the morning, which is, indeed, another day. Now you will find it possible at any hour to imagine just what your Sylvia is doing, not forgetting always to think of her especially on rising, as she does of you. I have writ this long tale in several parts, but the greatest piece of it this evening, when, my papa fearing an attack of fever, I entreated to be permitted to stay at home with him, and so denied myself to visitors. I had hoped to try and cheer him by singing or by reading aloud some entertaining book; but Captain Colquhoun dropping in, I perceived how much Mr Freyne must prefer his solid conversation to his girl's foolish chatter, and so withdrew into a corner to write, though remaining within earshot in case I should be called. So far as I can discover, the two dear gentlemen have been occupied with but one topic the entire time, to the discussion of which they have, as usual, brought despair on the Captain's part, and an easy confidence on my papa's. Did I tell you that I was once saucy enough to ask Captain Colquhoun how he could be so friendly with Mr Freyne when they agreed so badly? "Madam," says he very solemnly, "your father has one fault, an extravagant hopefulness, and of that 'tis the business of my life to cure him."

Well, but to this mighty matter. I told you once, I'm sure, of the Nabob of Bengall, Mohabut Jing, and of the apprehensions felt here by many as to his successor. The venerable potentate is in but poor health of late, and requires the utmost assiduity and watchfulness on the part of Mr Forth, the surgeon of our Cossimbuzar factory, who is admitted to attend him. Thanks to the care of this humane gentleman, there seems at present no reason for anticipating a fatal issue to the Nabob's illness, but there is great excitement in his Court. It seems that there are two possible claimants of the Soubahship besides the infamous young rake who has been designated the old Nabob's successor, and these are Surajah Dowlah's cousin Sucajunk, the Phousdar of Purranea,[09] and Moradda Dowlett,[10] the son of his deceased brother Pachacoolly Cawn, who has been adopted by his great-aunt, the Nabob's daughter, a widow lady named Gosseta or Gauzeetee, who is commonly called the Chuta Begum. Of these, the Purranea Nabob, they say, has no hope of success; but if Gosseta Begum play her cards well, she may look to place her adopted son on the *musnet*, since she is very rich and of a most intrepid spirit. But what, you will say, has this to do with the Presidency? Why, this, my dear, that we English have much more to hope for from the Chuta Begum than from the Chuta Nabob, and that Mr Watts, the head of the Cossimbuzar factory, reports that she has made overtures of friendship through him to the Company. More than this, it seems that the lady's servants are desirous to avail themselves already of our protection, since Mr Watts asks leave for one of them, the son of Radjbullubdass, her *duan*, or high steward, to tarry some days in Calcutta. This son of the *duan*, Kissendasseat by name, had started to sail down the river on a pilgrimage to the pagoda of Juggernaut, which is a pagan idol worshipped somewhere in Orixa. Notwithstanding his pious object, the gentleman don't seem to travel light, for he brings with him a vast quantity of treasure in several boats, and his father's entire seraglio, which the Gentoos call *ginanah*.[11] One of the women was taken ill on the journey, which is the reason for their stay here; though why they brought her so far when they were able at the commencement of their voyage to obtain Mr Watts' letter asking shelter on her account, I don't know. The whole train arrived after dusk this evening, and Captain Colquhoun had seen them disembark.

"Fifty-three sacks of gold and jewels alone, sir!" said he to Mr Freyne.

"Kissendass is a lucky dog, then," says my papa.

"Kissendass is an—eternal schemer, sir. Can you be so blind as not to see through the trickery of the whole affair?"

"You would have me infer that the treasure belongs to the Chuta Begum, and is brought to us on her account?"

"Brought to us, sir? No. But brought within our bounds to embroil us with the Chuta Nabob, yes. 'Tis no more Gosseta Begum's doing than mine."

"Then you would say, Captain, that the admirable Kissendass is making off with his mistress's property? They say his father. has never rendered any accounts since he first got his *duanny*, and he may think it well not to risque his gains, whatever the Begum may choose to do."

"My papa thinks this Gentoo is like a rat that forsakes a sinking ship," I put in, using a saying I had picked up from Mr Fraser[12]—I mean, I had heard it from some one.

"Oho, saucebox, are you listening?" says Mr Freyne.

"With all respect to Miss and to you, sir," says the Captain, "the matter, I opine, is worse than you think. Whether Radjbullubdass is seeking to place his ill-gotten gains in safety, or whether the Chuta Begum is providing against a possible reverse of fortune, don't concern us now. Whichever it be, Kissendass had no need to come here, recommended by a letter from Mr Watts, and bringing with him the treasure he is ostentatiously removing out of Surajah Dowlah's reach. The thing is a deep-laid plot. Who met the fellow at the wharf? Omy Chund's banyan. Who settled him in a convenient house belonging to himself? Omy Chund. And who was dismissed from his service as the contractor for cloth to the Company, after forty years of cheating? Omy Chund again. He and his friend Govinderam Metre, who also has his grudge against Mr Holwell for turning him out of the *zemindary* he had enjoyed for so many years, have long been watching to catch us tripping, and now they have found their chance. Mark my words, sir, this plausible scoundrel Kissendass will yet prove our ruin."

"The ruin won't be unexpected, then," said my papa. "Why did you not warn the Presidency, Captain?"

"I'm the right man to warn them, en't I, sir? Finely they have listened to my warnings in the past! But even so, the President was down at Ballisore when Mr Watts' letter arrived, and Mr Manningham in authority, all agog to curry favour with the Chuta Begum and make himself a friend at Dacca. This evening Holwell's people at the waterside send to ask whether Kissendass and his troop are to be admitted, and Mr Warehouse-keeper Manningham sends to meet 'em with open arms almost. Could anything I might hope to say avail to turn him from his dreams of sharing in those sacks of treasure?"

"Gently, Captain. It en't well to speak evil of those in high places before Miss Pert here, for she notes down all she hears as sharp as any shorthand writer, and sends it home to her dearest friend, in letters long enough to reach from here to the Downs. Don't you, miss?"

"'Twill serve all the better to prove the truth of my words when my prophecy of ill is come to pass," says the Captain, bowing to me.

"True, man, so it will. And my saucy girl shall gather your prophecies into a book, and call 'em the 'Sayings of the Cassandra of Fort William.' Such a pother about a set of blackfellows and their wenches!"

CALCUTTA, *April ye 9th.*

Oh, my beloved Amelia, what a hateful misfortune has occurred to your friend since she began this letter to you! On what a sea of troubles is she now embarked! I am all of a tremble, my dear. I can't sleep; I can't even lie down quietly. Like the heroine of a novel I am employing in writing the hours that should be sacred to sleep, but alas! I know only too well that my behaviour has not been that of a heroine, but of a foolish, untaught girl.

But I shall alarm my Amelia. Be still, my throbbing heart, and allow me to recount in order the history of my misfortunes, of which twelve hours ago I had not the smallest anticipation. This evening was the occasion of an entertainment given by Mr President in the Fort, for some reason that I have forgot, when we were diverted, as at all state ceremonies here, with a *notch.* I say diverted, because the exhibition is designed to be diverting, although some have chose to find it improper. But my Amelia may take my word for it, there's nothing improper in the affair, but only the most infinite dulness that it's possible to experience. Well, after this, we all departed in our palanqueens to the Company's gardens, not far off, which are prettily laid out with trees and shrubs brought from the most distant regions, as well as with such flowers as flourish in this climate. Entering at the gate, my papa was so good as to hand me out of my machine, since Mrs Freyne was already attended by Lieutenant Bentinck, a young gentleman who affects her company pretty frequently, and as he did so, up comes Captain Colquhoun.

"Mr Holwell tells me that the Indians in the Buzars[13] are saying the Soubah is dead, sir," says he.

"So they have been saying every other day for these two years," said Mr Freyne. "When do they pretend the event happened?"

"To-day," said the Captain.

"And you believe that the news could have reached Calcutta by this time? Why, my good sir, 'tis a two days' journey from Muxadavad, even when the messengers are hastened by every conceivable means. This is but another piece of Buzar lying."

"The Indians have ways of conveying news that we en't acquainted with, sir. I fear the curtain has rose upon a tragedy for the English in Bengall."

"What, Captain, still croaking?" says Mr Eyre, my papa's chief friend in the Council, a very cheerful and sprightly gentleman, coming up. "It's well for you that public affairs go so contrary, for otherwise you'd have nothing to do. But come, sir, come, Mr Freyne, the President has just received important despatches from Bombay, and would have us wait on him to hear 'em read. You must hand your lovely Miss over to one of the young fellows, Mr Freyne. I vow you'll have no difficulty in finding her a cavalier."

Ensign Bellamy, who was the nearest gentleman, sprang forward to offer me his hand, and conducted me to a raised seat in one of the illuminated pavilions, where I sat like a queen, and the crowd of gentlemen (without whom your vain Sylvia would scarce know herself nowadays) gathered round. One of them had catched some hint of the contents of the despatches, and told me that they were from the hand of Admiral Watson, to inform Mr Drake that his ships, acting in concert with the forces of Colonel Clive, had captured a town named Gyria,[14] the stronghold of some robber or pirate-chief. I'll confess to my dearest girl that my thoughts did stray to the only person on board of Mr Watson's fleet that I had much concern with, and I wondered whether he had shared in this feat of arms, and even whether he had been wounded, but as I live, Amelia, I went no further than that. Judge, then, my dear, of my feelings when two gentlemen advanced through the crowd that filled the place, and I saw that one of them was Mr Fraser, wearing the blue and white dress in which I had seen him last at Madrass. Pity me, Amelia, despise me if you will—you can't think more meanly of me than I think of myself—a great wave seemed to sweep over me, there was a singing in my ears, and—oh, my dear, I could beat myself when I remember it, if that would do any good—for a moment I leaned back against the column behind me, quite faint. I did not fall into a fit—for that at least I may be thankful—and as all the gentlemen were looking towards Mr Fraser, my indisposition might have escaped notice, had it not been for the odious Mr Menotti, who had brought him to the place.

"Sure Miss is ill!" cried the wretch, springing forward in the most officious manner. "Sweetest madam," such was his presumptuous address, "what may I do for you?"

"Nothing, I thank you, sir," I said, finding all the gentlemen regarding me with great concern. "I was never better in my life." You will think this a horrid fib, Amelia, but I vow I was as hot now as I had been cold the moment before, and conscious of a strange rising of the spirits. "Pray, Mr Fraser," I cried, beckoning to him with my fan, "don't remain at such a distance. We have met one another before."

"Indeed, madam, I was scarcely daring to hope you'd remember it," said he, with an air of finding something to displease him in what he saw. There was that in his carriage which made me angry.

"Have you yet paid your respects to the fair Araminta, sir?" said I.

"I have seen her, madam."

"I hope you found her in good spirits, sir?"

"I had been better pleased, madam, to have found her in worse."

"For shame, sir! Come, gentlemen," I turned to those around, "Araminta is the poetical name of the lady to whom Mr Fraser's allegiance is vowed. What do you think of the lover that can coldly declare he had preferred to find his mistress's health—it may be even her looks—impaired by reason of his long absence, instead of rejoicing to behold her in good spirits?"

"Why, madam," says Ensign Bellamy, "we're all relieved to hear that the gentleman worships at another altar than Miss Freyne's. Now we can welcome him to our company without fearing to find another added to the band of adorers who must one day be made miserable for life—all but one. Since this is secured, we must in gratitude leave him to settle his quarrels with his mistress as he will."

"Nay," said another young gentleman, Mr Fisherton. "Mr Fraser is questionless guilty of a treason against love. Here's his mistress, as we can't doubt, surrounded by other suitors, each importuning her to grant him her favours. She's steadfast in refusing 'em; but what lady in such a situation would find her spirits fail? Her entire existence is a series of triumphs."

"Yet Penelope suffered from melancholy in the absence of Ulysses," says Mr Fraser.

"Oh, sir," says Ensign Bellamy, "she was persuaded that her spouse was living. There was no merit in resisting her suitors; 'twas a necessity."

"And Ulysses came back to her from sea," says Mr Menotti, in his mincing style, as though he spoke without thinking, but looking from Mr Fraser to me and back again. All the gentlemen smiled. As for me, I rose and allowed my hoop to spread itself with great exactness, watching it over my shoulder as though I had no other care.

"Come, gentlemen," I said, when my gown satisfied me, "let us take a turn in the gardens, if you please. Mr Fraser shall conduct me, because he's the greatest stranger, if his Araminta don't require his presence, and we'll request him to be so good as to give us some account of this great victory he has brought us intelligence of."

Perhaps I was a little cruel, Amelia, for I gave Mr Fraser no chance for half an hour or more of speaking of anything but the capture of Gyria, and the gentlemen seconded me to the best of their ability, continually pouring in fresh questions when he seemed to have come to the end of all he had to tell. But he took his revenge upon me, for when we were in that part of the garden which is laid out in knots,[15] he succeeded in distancing our companions, and turning into another path. So apprehensive was I on finding myself alone with him, that I conceived my sole hope to lie in setting the tone of the conversation myself.

"And how is it you're able to visit Calcutta, sir?" I asked him.

"Why, madam, it so happened that I had a chance to pleasure Admiral Watson, and he asked me afterwards how he might serve me. Miss Freyne won't pretend to be ignorant what my request was, and that it was granted is shown by my presence here."

"Indeed, sir, I should have looked to find you elsewhere, I'll assure you."

"Perhaps, madam, you had been better pleased so?"

"I protest, sir, I don't understand you. You'll allow me to say that you have used me to-night in a style for which I have given you no warrant."

"Questionless, madam, that is so. 'Tis no affair of mine that I find you surrounded with a crowd of chattering fools, that think themselves at liberty to prate of the favour in which they stand with a lady who, when I had the honour of meeting her first, could not hear the word love mentioned without a blush."

"I vow, sir, this outrage is too much! I have endured a vast amount from you——"

"Only from me, madam? All these gentlemen in their laced clothes, with their talk of love and favour—has any one of 'em ever laid his heart and fortune at your feet?"

"Yes, sir, every one, and some more than once." Oh, Amelia, if you could guess how I triumphed at that moment, forgetting, as I saw him stand confounded, the resolution I had taken never to boast of the honour done me by the gentlemen whose partiality I could not return. Supposing, even, that the fellow had cause to be ill-pleased with his Araminta, why should he vent his spleen on me? I drew my hand from his, and was turning away, with my head well in the air, when he hastened after me.

“Madam, dearest madam, pardon me, I was wrong; I have abused your goodness. Pray, madam, give me the chance to justify myself so far as may be. You’ll permit me to wait upon you to-morrow?”

I think he would have said more, but we were now in sight of the rest of the company. I was not minded to allow him to imagine that ’twas to him all the other gentlemen owed their ill success; and I said, very sedately—

“Mrs Freyne receives company to-morrow afternoon, sir. I don’t doubt but she’ll be pleased to see you.”

“But you’ll allow me the honour of speaking to you in private, madam?”

“No, sir, I won’t. Permit me to recommend you to spend the time in the company of the lady to whom you owe it. And now I see my papa looking for me.”

“Cruellest of charmers!” said the perfidious, taking my hand to conduct me to Mr Freyne (you may be sure, Amelia, that I gave him no more than the very tips of my fingers), “surely you must know that ’tis you alone——”

He durst not finish his sentence, for I turned upon him a glance in which I trust he read the anger and contempt that filled my soul. Was it not enough, my dear, for this person to set himself up as a schoolmaster over me, and claim the right of directing my most ordinary diversions, without going on to insult me further by protestations of an affection that he has taken pains to render incredible? ’Twas all I could do to bring my lips to pronounce his name to my papa when he desired me to present to him my new cavalier; and I could almost have cried my thankfulness aloud when, on Mr Freyne’s learning that he was Captain Colquhoun’s cousin and inviting him to tiffing on the morrow, he was forced to excuse himself on the score of having already accepted Mr President’s invitation to the Company’s house.

“So that’s the young gentleman who is the humble servant of another lady!” says Mr Freyne, when Mr Fraser had taken his leave, reproaching me with his eyes. “Was the other lady present to-night, miss?”

“I don’t know, sir. Mr Fraser told me he had seen her.”

“She’s a lady of an easy temper, en’t she, miss?”

“Really, sir, I don’t know. I have no acquaintance with her.”

“By choice or by necessity, miss?”

"Mr Fraser's friends are no concern of mine, sir. But if I'm to tell the truth, I have no notion who the lady may be."

"What, miss? Han't your heart warned you of the existence of a rival as soon as she entered your presence?"

"I know nothing of any rivalry, sir, and I could wish you would be pleased not to jest on such a topic."

"Heyday, miss, will you prescribe to your papa the subjects of his discourse?"

"Oh, dear sir, forgive me!" I cried, cut to the heart to think that I had vented my vexation upon the best of fathers. "If you only knew all the mortifications I have endured this evening——" and I burst into tears, sobbing as I clung to Mr Freyne's arm. My dear papa was infinitely disturbed.

"Come, come, my girl, don't make such a commotion about a hasty word! Dry your tears quick, and don't let Madam see 'em. What, torn your gown?" raising his voice: "that's nothing to cry about. You shall have a new one to-morrow."

"Torn your gown, miss?" cried Mrs Freyne. "You may well weep, indeed. Of all the careless and thoughtless young bodies that ever wasted their parents' money, you are the worst. I have lost patience with you."

I cared little for the loss of Mrs Freyne's patience, but the thought of my pertness to my dear papa made me miserable, and I could not go to my chamber without stealing back to catch him alone. "Dear sir," I cried, falling on my knees, "pardon your sullen girl. I'll tell you anything you are so good as to ask me." But my papa laughed at me, and bade me go to bed for a silly puss, saying that he had no wish to pry into my secrets. "When you think I can help you, Miss Sylvy," he said, "tell me anything you please, but otherwise I won't hear a word of it. Now be off with you," and he embraced me and pushed me out of the room. Oh, Amelia, what should I have done throughout the past winter but for the kind countenance of this dearest of men? I have striven to hide my real sentiments, even from my Amelia (yes, I'll confess it. When Mr Fraser's name found itself somehow in my letter to you t'other day, I stroked it out with all the art imaginable), but I can't conceal from myself the nature of the feeling I have had for—for the person I have mentioned. 'Twas not love—how could it be that after what he has done?—but if there had been any explanation of his behaviour, any real extenuation to be offered, I think it might have become even that. Alas! to what is your Sylvia Freyne sunk, when she can give utterance to such a confession on the very day that the person concerned has conducted himself in so strange, so unaccountable a manner?

CHAPTER VI.
SHOWING HOW CALCUTTA FOUND FOOD FOR TALK.

CALCUTTA, *April ye* 12*th*.

Is my Amelia anticipating a more cheerful epistle than that with which I saddened her tender heart three days ago? Alas, my dear girl! the expectation is vain. These three days have brought your Sylvia's affairs into such a coil that she, poor simpleton! can see no way of getting 'em straight again. But to begin at the beginning. Last Saturday, which was the day after my sudden meeting with Mr Fraser at the Gardens, I passed my time in fear and trembling, dreading lest the young gentleman should come to the house and force his way into my presence. For oh, Amelia, remember that Mrs Freyne knows nothing as yet of all my troubles. When she learns of them, I fancy I shall begin to think that until then I had no troubles at all. It seemed, however, that Mr Fraser was so much offended by my words to him the evening before that he would not condescend even to pay his respects to my papa, and I tried to assure myself that he would incommode me no more. We were engaged that night to attend Mrs Hamlin's assembly, and very early in the evening, before I had thought of going to dress, there came a servant bringing me a chitt from Miss Hamlin to beg that I would come early. This has happened pretty often before, chiefly when Miss Hamlin has devised a new mode of dressing her hair, or has desired to consult me as to the most elegant style of making over a gown. I hurried into my fine clothes, therefore, and started off in my palanqueen at least an hour before my papa and Mrs Freyne. Mrs Hamlin met me in her varanda, and, after saluting me in what I thought a rather conscious manner, carried me to Miss Hamlin's chamber, begging me in a whisper to do what I could to keep her niece's spirits up. I could imagine no less than that the tailor had ruined Miss's new gown in the making, or her iya spilt a bottle of pomatum over it; but on entering I found my friend, not weeping in her wrapper, as I had expected, but standing before the mirror in a gown of light peach-coloured satin, laced with gold at all the seams, the finest I have ever seen.

"Why, miss, a new gown!" said I, "and you've never showed it me."

"It's never been unpacked," says she. "What does my Miss Freyne think of it?"

"'Tis fit for a queen," said I, "or a wedding."

"Come, miss, you're sprightly to-night. It is my wedding-gown."

"La, miss! Are you going to be married? When is it to be?"

"To-night," says she, as solemn as you please.

"To-night? and you never told me? I take this very unkind in you, miss. Has Sylvia Freyne deserved it at your hands?"

"'Twas not in my power to tell you what I didn't know myself, miss. No one knows it yet. The bridegroom himself don't know it."

"Dear miss, you must have got a touch of the fever," I said, for I could no longer doubt but her intellects were disordered. "Let me help you take off that gown and assist you to bed, while someone runs for Dr Knox."

"Dear miss," said she, mimicking me, "your concern for my health en't needed, I'll assure you. I tell you solemnly that I'm to be married to-night, if the bridegroom don't desire to shame me before all Calcutta."

"But who's the gentleman?" I cried.

"Mr Hurstwood, of course," said she. Now Mr Hurstwood was the gentleman that we had seen in the gate of the Fort on our landing, and that Miss Hamlin had declared to me then and ever since to be her destined spouse, whenever I sought to discover whether her heart inclined in any particular direction, so that this fresh piece of pleasantry made me angry.

"Oh well, miss, if you choose to rally me at so solemn a moment——" said I.

"You're like the good people that refused to believe the shepherd-lad when he cried 'Wolf!' miss. All I can say is that Mr Hurstwood is to have the chance of marrying me to-night. If he won't take it, that's his fault."

"But there's been no engagement of marriage between you. You was saying just now he knew nothing about it," said I, excessively perplexed.

"Oh, pardon me, miss, I said the gentleman didn't know the time I had fixed. To tell truth, I have been testing him. He—he pestered me so with his proposals that I accepted 'em to be rid of him, but I imposed my conditions. There was to be no public announcement, and I was to have the direction of everything, and I bade him have no hope of marrying me for at least a year."

"Then he's happier than you permitted him to expect, miss?"

"He made my life a burden to me with his importunities, miss. I have never had a peaceful moment but when I was in company."

"Oh, miss," I cried, "why try to deceive your friend any longer? There was a traitor in the camp. Your heart was on the gentleman's side."

"What's all this galimatias about?" says she, but she turned her face away, and played with the lace on her sleeve. "Han't I told you long ago that I had no heart? The worst you can say of me is that I'm marrying him to please him."

"True, miss—and the best is that you're marrying him to please yourself."

"You're a piece of impudence," says she. "Do you realise that in an hour or so I shall be a married woman? I protest I'll teach you your place, Miss Sylvia Freyne. To please myself, indeed!"

But I went round softly, and, lifting her chin, looked into her face. "Don't tell me that it don't please you, miss," I said, "for your own countenance would give you the lie. There!" and I embraced her very heartily, "you have sought to deceive me long enough. Now tell me the whole truth."

"Why, what can I tell you?" says she, meekly. "You know I promised the gentlemen that my wedding should be such as had never been seen in Calcutta before (and I can tell you, miss, I would not have left you still single to triumph over me for anything less), and sure it's true, for there's not a soul knows of it but my uncle and aunt Hamlin and the Padra, and yourself."

"But not Mr Hurstwood, miss—truly?"

"Truly. 'Tis my final test for him, whether he'll marry me all on a sudden, with no time to devise a new suit of clothes for the ceremony. All he knows is that he may at any moment find himself summoned to the trial."

"But where's the wedding to be, miss?"

"In the saloon here, of course."

"Oh, miss, not in the church? These chamber-marriages seem to me to lack something—I don't know what. I can understand them in the case of persons objecting to public notice, but you've no reason for that. I should scarce feel that I was married if 'twas not done in church."

"The very arguments of the excellent Pamela, I vow!" Miss Hamlin had recovered her usual coolness. "Well, child, when you're married, I'll make it my business to see that everything be done according to your mind. I fear it's useless my offering you a share in good Mr Bellamy's services this evening?"

"Indeed, miss—" I said, and could not get out another word for the foolish tears that would come. Miss Hamlin did not perceive 'em at first.

"The Padra rejected the notion of taking the world by surprise for some time," she went on, "but consented to perform the ceremony on condition that all the dancing and jollity should be over by midnight, so as not to interfere with the Sabbath. But what, miss? Have I vexed you? I hoped—no, I can't say that I hoped—but I heard Mr Fraser was here. Han't he set things right?"

"How can he?" I cried. "Oh, dear miss, if you can tell me anything to unravel this dreadful mystery, pray relieve my mind. Is there any plea that can acquit Mr Fraser of the most unmanly behaviour?"

"Why, if there is, it en't for me to advance it," says she. "Give the gentleman a hearing, miss, if you desire him to justify himself. I never thought to offer you such advice, but my heart is foolishly soft to-night, and my dear Miss Freyne seems to have taken the affair much more hardly than I had hoped. Let him speak if he will, and if he won't, don't waste another thought on him. Has Menotti persecuted you again of late, by the way?"

"He never ceases his importunities, miss."

"So I thought. Well, should the fellow go so far as to address himself to your papa, refer Mr Freyne to me. I can tell him why Mrs Freyne supports Menotti's suit, and 'tis a reason won't commend itself to him. But now, miss, we must join the company. I look to you to support me on this trying occasion. You and Polly Dorman will be my sole bride-maids, but sure there never was a wedding with such a quantity of bride-men."

But I catched her by the sleeve. "Oh pray, miss, tell me what this secret is that you offer me as a weapon against Mr Menotti. If it be anything that would injure my papa's credit, or wound his heart, I would not use it—no, not though I were standing at the altar with the wretch."

"It en't so bad as that, though Mr Freyne will take it hard enough. Have you never wondered that your stepmother managed to play so continually without asking your papa for money, which she knows he'd refuse her?"

"I thought she was a great fortune when my papa married her."

"Only so-so. I'll be bound she costs Mr Freyne more than ever she brought with her. But as to her debts of honour, she borrows the money to pay 'em from Menotti. What consideration he is to receive you can guess as well as I."

"But this has been going on a great while, miss—before we landed."

"So it has. I hadn't thought of that." Miss Hamlin looked thoughtful. "But at least we can guess a portion of the consideration. The rest we may discover some day. At any rate, keep the secret carefully. It may help you yet. And now let us illumine the company with the splendour of our presence."

But as we passed along the varanda, Miss Hamlin slipped suddenly into a small closet where Mr Hamlin keeps his boots and whips, and sat down upon a bench that stood there.

"Come, miss," she said to me, as I looked at her in surprise, "you must be love's messenger, and fetch me Mr Hurstwood here. He shall know of the punishment in store for him, and if he show the slightest sign of hesitation, why, he shall have his *congé*, and no one the wiser."

I could not help smiling to myself to see Miss Hamlin giving way to the tremors and apprehensions natural to a young woman on such an occasion, and seeking to avoid the possibility of finding Mr Hurstwood backward in acceding to her wishes in the presence of the general company, but I went willingly enough to seek the happy man. There was a good few people already in the saloon, and Mrs Hamlin was looking excessively flurried and uneasy.

"My niece han't changed her mind, miss, has she?" she asked me, eagerly.

"Oh no, madam. She is most excellently well disposed towards Mr Hurstwood."

"I'm glad of it. The fact is, my dear miss, I felt it my duty to give the gentleman a slight hint of the happiness that might be coming his way—nothing clear, of course, but just sufficient to let him set about getting his house in order. Young creatures don't think of that sort of thing, but Charlotte would have been fairly put about without the new table equipage and the chaise and pair of horses that I hear he has been buying. After that I should never have held up my head again if she had sent him about his business."

The next person that stopped me was Mr Hamlin, who seemed—positively, Amelia, he did—ready to burst with the greatness of the secret. When I catched sight of him he was exciting the wonder of his guests with promising them a diversion of quite a new sort, and hinting, with many nods and winks, at the extraordinary great surprise they should shortly receive. When he saw me, breaking away from those who surrounded him—

"And how is our dear Charlotte, miss? I trust her spirits are pretty fair? Was you with her until just now? Did you ever hear of a young woman's behaving so strangely? Why, positively, I am forbid to speak about this—this charming event until the ceremony's over!"

Admiring the subjection to which Miss Hamlin had reduced her relations, and their efforts to release themselves from her yoke, I succeeded at last in finding Mr Hurstwood, who was standing apart from the rest of the company, and signified to him that I bore a message from Miss Hamlin. With the greatest eagerness imaginable he desired to know where he might attend me, and I led him out into the varanda, and so in at the window of the closet where Miss was sitting among her uncle's boots. You may guess, Amelia, that I was excessively gratified to remark that the splendour of her appearance so disconcerted him that he could not utter a word (for indeed, in figure and air, she is quite the finest woman I ever saw, when she chooses to assume the dignity that sits so well upon her), but only bow, with his hand on his heart.

"Pray, sir," says his mistress, striving hard for her old rallying tone, "do you know why I have sent for you this evening?"

"Why, madam," he said, finding his tongue, "I'll confess that I did experience a hope that you might be about to name the day which is to make me the happiest of men, but now that I behold you, I can but wonder at the goodness that grants me even the distant prospect of calling so lovely and majestic a creature mine."

"I see," said Miss Hamlin. "You are contented with your present situation then, sir, since the prospect is so distant?"

"No, indeed, madam. Endure it I must, since anything else would be so far beyond my deserts, but I defy any man to call me contented."

"But, sir, contentment is a virtue. Sure it would be wrong in me to deprive you of so good a chance of acquiring it?"

"Ah, madam, if there was any mercy for me in your heart when you called me here, don't do yourself such an injustice as to feign that you summoned me only to torment me."

"Why, then, I won't, sir. If you'll take me to-night, you shall have me; if not, you shan't have me at all."

"Do you look for me to hesitate, madam? Though my mind be reeling under this unexpected happiness, it is sufficiently sound not to refuse it. Dear madam, the happiest man in India is at your feet at this moment."

I was prodigiously relieved, since Miss Hamlin's heart was so much set on the matter, to see that the gentleman played his part with such dexterity, neither startling her by too extravagant expressions of delight, nor wounding her punctilio by revealing the hints he had received from her aunt. And indeed, my dear, he is a most respectable person, of a high character, and polite and easy in his manners, and entirely devoted, as one may perceive, to his whimsical mistress. Not that I think Miss will find him like wax in her hands, for though he has borne so patiently with her strange notions hitherto, I can't fancy he admires her humoursome ways, and I expect she'll lay 'em aside of her own free-will to please him.

Well, when my pair of lovers had brought things to this happy conclusion, I hurried off to whisper to Mrs Hamlin to keep Mr Bellamy under her eye, and not suffer him to wander away into the gardens and talk politics with Mr Eyre and Mr Holwell. Dear me, Amelia! how much I was occupied with politics a day or two ago, and now I have no thought of the Soubahship, or anything but love-affairs. Next I sought out Miss Dorman, and startled her nearly out of her wits by telling her the part she was to play, though she retained sense enough to lament that she had not known of the wedding in time to put on her newest gown, and we two entered the saloon from the varanda with Miss Hamlin, Mr Hurstwood going round to the door. Advancing towards his bride as he entered, he took her hand with the finest bow imaginable, and led her up the room to Mr Bellamy, who had stationed himself beside a table. Warned by Mr Hamlin's hints, the rest of the company perceived what was on foot, and came crowding round, all eagerness, although, thanks to the fierceness with which the good Padra glanced round on the assembly, the utmost decorum was preserved, as much as if the marriage had been performed in church. But never will I consent to a chamber-wedding when I am to be married, Amelia. The moment that Mr Bellamy ceased speaking, the tongues of the company began to wag, and almost before Mr Hurstwood had saluted his bride, she turned to the bystanders, and cried—

"Well, gentlemen, was I not right when I promised you such a wedding as was never seen in Calcutta before?"

"Why yes, madam," said some one. 'Twas the vile Menotti. "But saving your presence, your promise en't all fulfilled yet. We were assured that Calcutta was to be drove to desperation by beholding both its charmers wedded at one time, but Miss Freyne don't seem in any hurry to carry out her part of the compact. Sure we ought not to leave this charming spectacle uncompleted. Sooner than that, I would put myself forward as the needed bridegroom."

The horrible assurance of the man took me so entirely by surprise that I could only stare stupidly at him, but Mr Ranger was obliging enough to call out—

"Not so fast, sir! Who talks of a needed bridegroom when there en't a man in the room but would be proud to stand up with Miss Freyne before the Padra? If it be the lady's pleasure to end this surprising business in a manner still more surprising, let us draw lots for the honour of becoming her spouse, and so give every gentleman a fair chance."

My dear, I was dazed with horror. It seemed to me that in a minute or two I should find myself married to some chance bridegroom, without having a word or a will in the matter. Of course, now that I can think over it quietly, I know that Mr Bellamy would never have consented to such a course, even had my papa not been within call, but at the moment I stood staring like a fool, unable to utter a word. It was the bride who ran forward and tore from Mr Ranger's hand the piece of paper on which he was beginning to write down the gentlemen's names.

"I admire your assurance, gentlemen!" she cried. "Is it possible that you've all missed the finest point in the surprise I designed for you? En't there a solitary man that remembers a lady is privileged to change her mind? Have I permitted you all the honour of waiting upon me for six months, and yet not one of you perceives that when I say I'll wait to marry until my Miss Freyne does, 'tis only a device to steal a march upon her? Oh, I have no patience with you! No, you'll have no second wedding to-night, trust me. I don't doubt but Miss Freyne will astonish you all another day, for she's a most ingenious young lady, but when she does, she won't permit you the honour of attempting to surprise her first."

Thus was your poor trembling Sylvia saved, for the gentlemen all laughed prodigiously, saying they had feared lest Mrs Hurstwood should be in league with Mr Menotti, and they did not intend him to anticipate them in a matter which was now doubly near their hearts since Mr Hurstwood had carried off my only rival. But in such a state of apprehension was the simpleton who now writes to you, that she was forced to sit down on a couch, and suffer herself to be fanned by Captain Colquhoun, who finds himself perpetually in debt for new fans to the ladies for whom he performs this service, since he does it with all the lightness and grace of a blacksmith hammering on an anvil, though with the best will in the world. 'Twas not at first that I saw his cousin was standing behind him, close behind the couch to which I had retreated, but then I remembered that in the moment of silence after Mr Menotti's speaking I had heard some one draw a sword, which some one else had thrust back into its scabbard. How I knew that it was Mr Fraser who had drawn his sword, and Captain

Colquhoun that had forced him to put it up, I can't tell, for I durst not look at either of them, but I was certain of it, and the sick terror which had seized me gripped me tighter still all the time that the gentlemen of the company were occupied in saluting the bride, and the bridegroom the ladies present. After that I had to rise, for it was time for the dancing to begin, and I could not be too thankful that my partner was Captain Colquhoun, who with Mr Holwell were to act as bride-men to us two poor maids, even though the good man is a vile dancer, and though he found himself obliged for very shame to crush the broken remnants of my fan into his pocket and promise to bring me a new one in a day or two.

And now comes the most mortifying event of this dreadful evening. Oh, my dearest Amelia, if Providence should never see fit to place you in the high situation which my dearest girl's beauty and merits would so charmingly adorn, let me beg of you not to repine; for sure it's a terrible thing to find oneself a toast. Your talents, my dear, would questionless enable you to manage better than I, but you know what a sad bungler I am by nature, and the trials of the evening had made of me an actual idiot. Well, we went through the minuet decorously enough (though if my partner and I, he so stiff and I so much alarmed, did not move the room to laughter, it must have been that the company had other things to think of), and we ladies retired to change our dresses for the country-dances. And here I may say that I wondered the less at Miss Hamlin's strange fancy for forbidding her uncle and aunt to speak of her approaching marriage, when I heard the free talk in which Mr Hamlin was indulging with his guests. This gentleman's jests are not like my good papa's, which could never bring a blush to any the most modest cheek, and Mrs Hamlin's talk with the married ladies was no less disagreeable, although there was no jest in it, but the most solemn earnest, indeed. Sure, my dear, this habit of free conversation is a dreadful evil, and I could wish that some of our moralists would direct their attention to it. Indeed, I am not sure that if I were in England I would not write under a feigned name to the 'Gentleman's Magazine' in order that some more powerful pen might be inspired to treat the subject, as was done forty years back in the 'Spectator.' But to our country-dances. I have told you, my dear, what difficulties a lady here lies under if she wish to satisfy all the gentlemen who ask her to dance, but I'm not certain whether I mentioned that to grant a second dance to one gentleman is a proof of such high favour on her part that the happy man pretty frequently finds himself with several duels on his hands, for which reason this favour is never granted by any one that prides herself on her discretion.

Well, we had danced a long time, and I had snatched a moment's rest, deaf to the entreaties of the gentlemen that crowded round me. When at length I owned myself refreshed, every one desired to be my next partner. Among them was Mr Fraser, whom I refused with some sharpness, having danced with him already when Captain Colquhoun presented him to me. Next came Mr Menotti, with whom I was determined not to dance, for if a poor creature may not protect herself in the way she dispenses her favours, who shall help her? but not to appear too particular, I turned my head before he could speak to me, intending to satisfy the importunities of Ensign Bellamy, who I thought was at my elbow. He had been separated from me in the crush, however, and giving him my hand, as I imagined, what was my mortification to find that I had chosen Lieutenant Bentinck, to whom I had given a dance before. It was too late to tell him that I had thought him to be some one else when he had led me out, though if I could properly have done so I would, such *puppy* airs did the creature put on when he found himself, as he believed, so highly distinguished. My Amelia may be sure that I did not make this mistake a second time, though my mind was so busy and confused that I almost wonder I did not, for I was persuaded that Mr Fraser would resent my contemptuous usage of him (as it must appear), and all the rest of the evening I was apprehensive lest he should assail me with reproaches in public. This he had the grace not to do (I'll assure my dear girl that I was properly grateful for his forbearance, since I had no expectation of it), but just before midnight, when we were all waiting in the varanda to attend the bride and bridegroom home, I heard a voice behind me, very cold and haughty.

"May I presume, madam, to ask the reason of the public affront you was pleased to put upon me just now?"

"Indeed, sir, I had no design to affront you. It en't the custom here for a lady to grant more than one dance to the same gentleman."

"And therefore, madam, you took pains to show special favour to the modest and highly obliged person whom you preferred to honour with your hand?"

"There was no preference in the matter, sir. I had intended to dance with Mr Bellamy, and found Mr Bentinck at my elbow instead. I hope you'll believe that no slight was intended you, as should be proved by my offering you this explication, which you had no right to demand."

"No right, madam, when a man believes himself publicly insulted? Sure it had gone hard with Mr Fopling Bentinck if the explication had not been granted."

"I did not look for such a piece of unpoliteness from you, sir, as an attempt to bluster a lady into compliance with your unreasonable demands."

"Unreasonable, madam? Are you seeking to drive me into fighting the fool? I'll assure you that I had picked a quarrel with him in the dance itself if I hadn't feared to disoblige you. But perhaps you're one of those ladies that love to know that swords are drawn and blood shed for their sakes?"

"Now, sir, you're insulting me. If you pick a quarrel with Mr Bentinck, rest assured that you have spoken for the last time with Sylvia Freyne."

"But indeed, madam, you han't permitted me to speak with you at all as it is. If I obey you in this, may I wait upon you on Monday in the morning?"

"As you please, sir," said I, very carelessly, though I could have bit my tongue out with vexation to think of the way he had catched me, and turned away.

"Where's my Miss Freyne and my scarf?" cried the bride, coming to the door, followed by the rest of the company, who had been making her their final compliments; and remembering my duty, I went to take the scarf from Miss Dorman and throw it round Mrs Hurstwood's shoulders.

"I shall see you in church to-morrow, miss?" I said, forgetting the changes of the day until I saw every one laughing at my mistake.

"Why, I hope so," said she; "but pray understand, miss, that a married woman en't to be browbeaten by you. You may call me Charlotte, if you choose, but don't otherwise try to put me off with less than madam."

She tripped laughing down the steps to her palanqueen, followed by the bridegroom, and attended by the whole company in their own equipages. I can assure you, my dear, that I was glad Mr Hurstwood's house lay on our road home, for otherwise I think there would have been little rest for us that night. As it was, Sunday was well begun when I got to bed, only to dream over again with added discomfort the strange events of the evening.

My Amelia will guess with what joy I welcomed the Sabbath, as a pleasing respite from those cares which have agitated my mind of late. There was little at first to mark it from the former Sundays I have spent here, although it startled me at first to see my Charlotte (I must call her so, I suppose) curtseying to me from Mr Hurstwood's pew instead of her uncle's, and to observe that she was wearing the pink gown worked with gold flowers of which she had spoken to Mr Fraser on that night of our voyage when, with a kindness that seemed cruel at the time, she opened my eyes to see whither I was drifting. Her place in Mr Hamlin's pew was filled by Mr Fraser himself, and I wondered to see him there, since I had determined the night before that the mysterious Araminta who has caused me so much uneasiness could be no other than my fellow-bridemaid, Miss Dorman. Not, indeed, that I had observed Mr Fraser to be much engaged with her, but that Miss is almost the only young person of our sex unmarried in Calcutta. There he sat, however, and I was pleased to notice that he did not put himself forward to hand me into church before service, but only bowed genteelly, and without too great particularity, from his place as I entered. I was thankful indeed for the high walls of the pew during the sermon, for Mr Mapletoft, the junior chaplain, who preached it, thought fit to address us on the duties of the married state, with special reference to the event of the night before, as though he believed that the good Mr Bellamy had let slip his opportunity at the time, and I think I should have died of shame if those who knew how nearly I had been married myself had been able to see me.

It may be, however, that my timidity was unnecessary, for on coming out of church it seemed that every one had other matters to think of. Some one declared that Mr President had received letters from Muxadavad, and there was much talk on the subject, though no one could tell what they contained. 'Twas only to be expected, therefore, that the elder gentlemen should appear occupied and somewhat gloomy, but I was surprised to see that the younger, whom I have never known before to pretend any knowledge of public affairs or concern with them, seemed to be fully as much taken up. There was about them an air of mystery, and a strange absence of that rallying humour which generally distinguishes them, and which was replaced by an affectation of meeting one another with dignity, even with distance. Not that this involved any want of ceremony towards myself, for they were all even more than usually forward to offer me civility, but 'twas all done with so precise and particular an air that I could almost have found it in my heart to be alarmed, had it not been for assuring myself that the young fellows were ashamed of the freedom with which they had treated my name last night, and desired to display their penitence to me. Even Ensign Bellamy, who had taken no part in my mortification, seemed afraid to trust himself near me, and only approached in order to present to me a newcomer in the place, to wit, a young French gentleman of the name of Mons. le Beaume, who was until lately an officer at the factory of Chandernagore, belonging to that nation, but has quitted it on a point of honour, and chosen to throw in his lot with us. This gentleman had much to say of the felicity he experienced in being presented to the loveliest lady in Calcutta (so the foolish, flattering fellow phrased it, my dear), and would have had me believe that 'twas the report of my charms which had drawn him from Chandernagore hither. To this extravagant speech I returned a suitable reply, not ridiculing his words, but allowing him to see that I penetrated their excessive homage, and knew it merely for politeness, and was passing on, when I heard him cry out—

"Ah, sir, do I meet you here? What pleasure, to find in a strange place a gentleman whose face is so familiar to me."

"I beg your pardon, sir," says Mr Menotti (he was in my train, of course, the wretch!), very stiffly; "I have not the honour of your acquaintance."

"A thousand pardons!" cried the Frenchman. "But—but surely I have seen you at Chandernagore, in the company of our *directeur*?"

"Indeed, sir, when I have visited Chandernagore (which is very rarely) I han't pretended to such high company as Mons. Renault's, I'll assure you."

"Pray pardon me, sir. My eyes have played me false," says Mr le Beaume, and the matter dropped. I don't know why I have set it down, save that I am always longing for anything to happen that might relieve me from Menotti's pursuit, and that for the moment I was so uncharitable as to hope he might be proved to have been in correspondence with our natural enemies.

In the course of the afternoon we heard something of the letters from Muxadavad which had caused such a commotion, for Captain Colquhoun looked in to tell Mr Freyne that they contained no confirmation of the death of the Soubah, mentioning only his great weakness. The communication was a private one from Mr Watts to the President, but it had got abroad that he warned Mr Drake very solemnly of the unfriendliness shown towards the factory at the Court of the Nabob, where all the talk concerned only the weakness of the defences of Calcutta, and the ease with which even a small army might overcome 'em. More than this, Mr Watts declared that our town is filled with the spies of Surajah Dowlah, and that every word and motion of ours is reported at Muxadavad. He recommended Mr Drake very earnestly to make search for these persons and turn them out of our bounds, and counselled him also to get rid of the Gentoo Kissendasseat and his family, who have remained in Calcutta on one pretext or another for a whole month, and whose sheltering has given great umbrage to the Chuta Nabob. But the effect of this excellent advice the good man spoiled by mentioning that the opinion at Muxadavad seemed to be favourable to the claims of Gosseta Begum to the throne rather than those of Surajah Dowlah; for this has strengthened the Council in their resolution to wait and see what happens before taking any steps.

This news gave us a troubled Sunday, as my Amelia will readily believe; but at least we enjoyed an interval of rest from our private woes, which were to burst upon us this morning with greater violence than ever before. Surely, Amelia, I must be either a very guilty or a very unfortunate creature, for not only am I in perpetual tribulation myself, but I bring trouble upon all connected with me. I was at work with my pen and ink in the varanda after breakfast, copying to the best of my power a fine print in one of the books Mr Bellamy had lent me, when I heard at the gate the boisterous cry of "Tok! Tok!" by which the bearers of a palanqueen announce their approach. My first impulse was to fly to my chamber, for the only likely visitor I could think of was Mr Fraser; but remembering that he had not been long enough in Calcutta to insist on riding such short distances, I waited where I was, and presently ran to assist Mrs Hamlin out of her machine.

"Then it en't true!" she said, looking at me as if in surprise.

"What en't true, madam?" I asked her.

"I'll tell you, miss." She mounted the steps and sank upon a couch, unpinning her cap-strings and panting. "They said you was gone off with Mr Bentinck."

"Me, madam?" I stared at her. "With Mr Bentinck?"

"They did indeed, miss. Of course I contradicted it at once. 'Miss is much too dutiful and well brought up a young woman to do anything of the sort,' I told 'em; 'and with such a dear good papa, too, that would indulge her in anything she set her heart on, where would be the use of it?' But the duel and all that has given such an occasion for talk that you can't be surprised at 'em."

"Dear madam, you torture me!" I cried, all manner of horrors tumbling over one another in their haste to rush into my mind. "Who has fought a duel, and what was the reason of it, and what have I to do with it?"

"Why, miss, 'twas Lieutenant Bentinck and the sea officer, Captain Colquhoun's cousin, who came out with us." I gasped. "Dear me, you do look badly! Sit down, my dear miss. 'Twas my nephew Grayson that told me about it, but not hearing the quarrel itself, he could only say what others had told him, and you shall hear it just as he related it."

"But the Lieutenant, madam?" I cried in an agony. "Was any one hurt?"

"Which Lieutenant, child? They were both of 'em hurt, though not more than enough to be a lesson to them in the future; but no one was killed, which is better than they deserved. It began on Saturday night—and sorry I am that my niece Hurstwood's wedding should have such an ending—as the young gentlemen went back to their quarters. They left Mr Menotti at his house on their way to the Fort, and it was as they were bidding him good-night that the quarrel occurred. How it began I don't know, but 'twas in some dispute between Mr Bentinck and Mr Fraser about you. My nephew was told by one person who was there that 'twas because Mr Fraser had heard you promising to run off with Mr Bentinck, and declared he had a better right to you; but some one else said that Mr Bentinck was boasting of the favour you had shown him that night, and saying he had but to hold up his finger and you would marry him, for you had always rolled your eyes at him when he visited at your papa's house, and shown him by smiles and signs and tricks that you wasn't indifferent to him——"

("Rolled my eyes at him!" What a horrid vulgar phrase, Amelia! Smiles and tricks, indeed! Oh, the base slandering coxcomb! Was ever a poor creature so served by a man that called himself a gentleman?)

"But the duel, madam? the duel?"

"Why, miss, Mr Fraser contradicted t'other gentleman vastly warmly, so this second person said, and swords were drawn there and then. But Mr Menotti and Mr Fisherton and some others persuaded the two gentlemen of the impolicy of fighting at night and in a public place, and it was resolved to decide the matter at dawn this morning, and at the usual spot, the entire affair being kept a secret from Calcutta. For a set of feather-headed young fellows, they kept their secret well, I will say that for 'em; and Mr Fraser and Mr Bentinck met this morning under the trees by the race-course. They fought with swords, and while Mr Bentinck was run through the leg, Mr Fraser escaped with a scratch on his arm. It was understood, said my nephew Grayson, that Mr Bentinck withdrew in the most genteel manner whatever pretensions or remarks he had advanced; but not knowing for certain what these were, he could not be sure."

"For this at least I may be thankful, that the false accuser was confounded," I cried; "dreadful as were the means by which his vile slanders were exposed."

"La, my dear miss! you are too nice," says Mrs Hamlin. "Sure you think too much of the little innocent freedoms which were all that the poor Captain imputed to you, according to the less alarming account. There's nothing so vastly shocking in a young lady's permitting a gentleman to guess that she returns his sentiments, if it go no further than that."

"But I don't return Mr Bentinck's sentiments, madam!" I cried. "He don't cherish any sentiments towards me, that I know of, so how could I return 'em, even with the best will in the world, which I'm sure is wanting in me?"

"Pray, don't be so warm about it, miss. Sure no one will ever impute to a young lady of your delicacy more than an easy frankness, whose very innocence may render her liable to be misunderstood. Of course 'tis always a pity for a young woman to get herself talked about, and it might have been better that you was married before this, but it can't be helped, and you have in me, I'll assure you, a friend always ready to put the best construction on all you do."

What could I say, Amelia? A pretty friend, indeed, this good lady had proved herself, if I was right in discovering something of disappointment in her air when she found I was not run away; and as for her kind interpretation of my actions, what had she just done but charge me with the most culpable levity, and with allowing such freedoms as I have always believed to be quite incompatible with modesty? To tell her that I had never spoken with Lieutenant Bentinck but in a general company, and that I was as far from desiring to exchange signals of intelligence with him as he with me, would be of no avail, since she had made up her mind on the matter, and I attempted nothing more than to entreat her, as I waited on her to her palanqueen, to contradict any report she might hear of any partiality I had for him. In answer, she assured me that she was all discretion, and that I should find her constantly active in silencing any talk to my disadvantage, and so rode away, nodding and smiling at me as though we had established an understanding together. I know my dear friend would have pitied her unhappy Sylvia could she have seen me as I returned to the varanda. I tried to compose myself again to my work, but my hands were hot and cold by turns, and shook as if I was in an ague-fit, while the pen slipped about all over the paper, so that I could not draw a straight line.

"Sure the plague's in the thing!" I cried at last, speaking very loud and bold, as though to give myself courage; "or perhaps I have catched a fever. I have felt vapourish once or twice of late."

I rose to go to my chamber and fetch some hartshorn, but glancing out towards the gate I saw Mr Fraser entering. I can't tell you what a state the sight of him threw me into. My limbs trembled so frightfully that I had to sit down again, and pulling my drawing towards me I began to work so hard at it that in two minutes I had spoiled the work of weeks, while all the time my heart was beating as though it would jump up into my throat and choke me. I durst not run away even if I had been able, but I know I wished that the roof of the varanda might fall and cover me. I think I must have fallen into a fit if it had not been for a mischance that happened to Mr Fraser as he entered, announced by the banyan. Coming out of the sunlight into the shade of the varanda, and groping his way, I suppose, towards me (for I could not advance a step towards him, holding one hand on my heart to still its tumultuous beating, and supporting myself by a pillar with the other); as he approached, I say, this white figure in the distance, he was so unfortunate as to strike against my table, and down it went, the ink pouring over my drawing and on the floor. I could have found it in my heart at any other time to pity the poor young gentleman for making such an entry, but now I could only be thankful for the interruption caused by calling in the servants to wipe up the mess, and by Mr Fraser's apologies. But breaking off abruptly in his expressions of sorrow—

"Dear madam," he said, "you look sadly disturbed. I fear my clumsiness has startled you more than you'll own. Permit me to lead you to a seat."

"I thank you, sir—no, I am quite well, believe me—I'm sadly vapourish to-day—pray, sir, excuse this sorry welcome." Silly, stammering words, were they not, Amelia? but indeed I had so great an inclination to weep, coupled with so strong a resolve not to do so, that I could scarce speak at all.

"You'll pardon me, madam," says Mr Fraser, standing before me very civilly, "for forcing myself upon your retirements at such an hour, but I have no time to spare. Mr President is leaving for Ballisore this evening, and he is obliging enough to offer me a passage in his barge to that place, where I can pick up the country junk I came in from Madrass. My dearest Miss Freyne won't think me, I hope, unmannerly in pressing for an interview with her as I did, when she knows the reason of my eagerness."

Now, strangely enough, there was something in this speech that made me more inclined to cry than ever, so that 'twas the most fortunate thing in the world that I remembered I was very angry with Mr Fraser, and had every reason to be more angry still.

"I hope you have left Mr Bentinck at his ease, sir?" I said. He started.

"Had I known that his health was an object of interest to you, madam, I would have inquired about it more particularly than I did."

"Why," said I, very lightly, "when two gentlemen are so good as to make a lady's name the subject of a public brawl, sure she has some concern with the issue?"

"Pardon me, madam; my dispute with Mr Bentinck, with which you appear to be acquainted, related to the respective merits of the King's officers and the Company's, as he also will tell you if you'll ask him."

This comforted me a little at first, but I soon shook my head.

"Ah, sir, you should have settled your subject of debate earlier, if you desired to throw dust in the eyes of Calcutta. Now 'tis too late."

"Indeed, dear madam," he said, very earnestly, "I'm at a loss to know how you can have experienced the uneasiness you hint at in the few hours since my meeting with Mr Bentinck; but rest assured that my sword is at your service to fight all Calcutta if any one would breathe a word to your prejudice."

"Oh, sir, you mistake me!" I cried. "Alas that I should have to say it, your sword has done me too much harm already. Why should you, who had no reason to resent 'em, call attention to words which would never have been remarked—which would have been forgot as soon as uttered—if it had not been that your precipitancy fitted too well with the spiteful schemes of one that is ever on the watch to mortify me?"

"I vow, madam, I don't understand you. I had no right to resent Mr Bentinck's words, you say? Sure any gentleman is bound to resent a disparagement of the lady he esteems above all others?"

"Questionless, sir; but your Araminta is that lady."

"But sure you're Araminta, madam."

I thought my ears must have deceived me, as I stared at Mr Fraser, but his countenance was so full of contrition and earnestness that I was taken aback. "I am Araminta, sir?"

"Sure, madam, you must have penetrated my expedient before? So often as you have rallied me upon the subject of Araminta—you could not be in earnest?"

"Indeed, sir, I have but sought to hold you to your duty."

"My duty is owed to you, madam, and to no other lady."

"I don't understand," I said. It seemed to me, Amelia, that some one else was speaking, and not I, the voice had so strange a sound.

"Indeed, madam—" the young gentleman had the grace to look ashamed—"I fear I must ask your kind allowance, for maybe the trick wasn't altogether a fair one. When I had the honour of spending a considerable time in your company, in our voyage to Madrass, the constant intercourse with so much beauty and virtue produced upon my heart the effect that might have been anticipated——"

"Pray, sir, spare me your flattery," I said, with some impatience, I fear.

"I'll assure you, madam, I'm incapable of flattering you, even were the thing possible. But I must spin my yarn in my own style, if you please, or I will never get to the end of it. Well, madam, you must know that I became consumed with a desire to penetrate your true sentiments for me. Many and many a plot did I lay to surprise you, if possible, into some avowal that might justify me in believing that you entertained a partiality for me, but you was always at once so sprightly and so sedate, so reserved and so open, that I was in despair. Then one evening Miss Hamlin revealed the design with which you was going to Bengall—perhaps, madam, you recollect the occasion of her speaking?"

(He asked me that, Amelia, as though I could ever forget it!)

"The young lady's words troubled me inexpressibly, madam," he went on. "I have a cursed Scots pride about me" (yet I am well assured that Mr Fraser is proud of that pride, for all his calling it names), "that would not suffer the thought that I had been made a fool of. Such was the notion that came to me, madam, that you had been diverting yourself with my homage for the voyage, designing to throw me aside when 'twas over. But if the wound was bitter, the remedy was at hand. That very day I had been reading in 'Amelia' of the expedient by which Booth sought to prevent the discovery of his passion for the lady, in leading her to believe that he loved another. 'Sure,' I thought, 'if my dearest Miss Freyne have any tenderness for me in her heart she must give me some hint of it now; and if my fears are truer than my hopes, yet I will come off with no apparent loss, and she without a triumph.' The thought no sooner came to me than I acted upon it, as you, madam, know."

"And so your punctilio was saved, sir!" I cried. "Indeed, it seems a mighty serious matter to be a Scotsman."

"You wasn't intending any reflection on my country, madam, I hope? But no, my dear Miss Freyne's lips couldn't utter such an unkindness. You know best, madam, how my scheme miscarried. Whether you did entertain any partiality for me, I won't venture to say, but if so, you played your part with a cheerfulness and a spirit that left me no chance to discover it."

(Hear him, Amelia, and applaud your Sylvia's power of dissimulation!)

"In fine, madam," he went on, "it was I who found myself perplexed, since either you had discovered my plot and resented it, or you was quite indifferent to me. This perplexity caused me so much misery that I resolved to end it, but unfortunately I waited too long. Your persistency in leading the conversation around to Araminta, whenever I sought to approach the tender subject, drove me off again and again, for I believed you was rallying me, and Miss Hamlin's incessant watchfulness lost me other chances. Then I was called upon to quit Madrass suddenly, and, flying to your lodging on the wings of desperation, found only Miss Hamlin, who refused to bear any message for me. I entreated her to allow me to entrust a letter to her care, but she tore it up before my face, telling me that I had done my best to turn your heart, madam, against me, and that she was glad I had succeeded. I had no one else to whom to entrust a letter, and I dared not send one in the ordinary way, lest it might fall into the wrong hands, but I have watched for the chance, which appeared as though it would never arrive, of reaching your side, and when, after the taking of Gyria, the Admiral asked how he could pleasure me, I told him I would sooner carry his despatches to Calcutta than be made captain of the best ship in his fleet. And here, madam, I am, to lay my excuses before you."

"And I'm sure, sir," I said, rising and curtseying, "I am most grateful to you for your entertaining history. Nothing now remains, I think, but for me to bid you a very good morning."

There! could my Amelia herself have bettered that? Oh, my dear, you never saw such a fool as the poor young gentleman looked, standing as though turned into stone. But what a plague are these feeble bodies of ours, that won't second the heroical motions of the soul! My limbs trembled so frightfully that when I turned to reach the window leading to the saloon I had done no more than get my hand upon the *antiporta*, or curtain of reeds, before Mr Fraser was there to block my path.

"Pray, sir, let me pass," said I, very haughtily.

"Not until I have your answer, madam. Was I right or wrong in fearing that you was indifferent to me?"

"Whatever you may once have been, sir, you have lost your right to an answer now."

"Nevertheless, madam, I mean to have it."

"Then you shall have it, sir." This bold front, after such behaviour as Mr Fraser had been guilty of, made me both brave and angry. "I won't deny there was once a time when I indulged a certain partiality for you, but that time is past. It became my duty to uproot from my heart any tenderness that might have found a lodging there for the humble servant of another lady, and if I had not done so, can you believe that your confession that the story was all a trick, designed to save your own punctilio from an imagined slight, is a likely passport to my favour? Sooner than expose yourself to the risk of a rebuff, which you should have known me well enough to be assured I would have made as gentle as possible, you seize upon a childish expedient which don't prove able even to satisfy yourself. You force me unconsciously to deceive my dear good papa, and you expose me to most injurious suspicions from my acquaintances here. And for all this you offer me no amends——"

"Except my poor self." He laughed harshly. "You're right, madam. The compensation en't by no means sufficient. Would it increase its value if it was deferred? If you would be pleased to set me a term of probation, I would do my best to atone for my fault, and to recommend myself to your favour."

"I fear, sir, that my papa would scarcely look favourably on such——"

"Probably not, madam. Have you, by the way, any objection to telling me why you have persisted in refusing, ever since you reached here, to make any of your adorers happy?"

"That, sir, is entirely my own affair."

"Oh, pardon me, madam. From something Mrs Hurstwood let drop, I picked up the notion that it might also be mine."

Have you ever heard anything like the assurance of the man, my dear? "Sir," I said, "I'm not answerable for what any one else may have told you, but I should be false to my sex if I showed any favour to one that has behaved as you have done, and testified so little penitence after it. You'll allow me to say that a more contrite and humble carriage would have become you better this morning, and indeed, Sylvia Freyne's own constitution en't so meek as to offer much prospect of happiness to a gentleman that can come to entreat forgiveness with so stubborn and resolved an air."

"You're like your sex, madam, who wish to see all men their slaves."

He spoke angrily, and turning away, but I fancied not so resolutely as before. I watched to see whether he would turn back. If he had—if by one word or glance he had shown his sorrow—why then, Amelia, your Sylvia would have thrown reserve to the winds, in spite of all her fine words. I'm not naturally exacting, I think, my dear—I don't desire to humiliate the poor man; but what could one hope for from a person that could make an unhappy creature suffer, as he has made me, merely to glorify his own punctilio, and utter no word of regret? I would have given the world to call after him as he went down the steps, but if he's proud—why, so am I.

I was still leaning against the wall (I don't know how long Mr Fraser had been gone) when my papa comes back to tiffing.

"Well, miss," he cried, as he came up the steps, "so all Calcutta is ringing with your doings, hey? Sure two dozen, at least, of my friends have been so obliging as to tell me that you're about to present me Lieutenant Bentinck as a son-in-law. We all hear our own news later than the rest of the world."

"If Mr Bentinck is to be your son-in-law, sir, you must have some other daughter than me, for I en't going to be married to him."

"And quite right too, miss. I would cut you off with an *anna* if you was, for making me father-in-law to a fool. But what's happened to the young 'Squire of the Rueful Countenance that I met just now? Han't he yet made his choice between you and t'other lady?"

"Oh, dear sir, he says there's no one but myself," I sobbed.

"And you'd prefer there should be some one else as well? Come, miss, I can't have you take up with these pagan notions, though you be living among the Moors. Is the gentleman dismissed because he adores no one but you?"

"No, sir, but because he made me believe there was some one else."

"Then, 'tis as well he's gone, for he must be a fool too," says Mr Freyne. "Come, cheer up, my girl, and don't give way to these vapours. What, you want the fool back, do you? Your father's to fetch him, I suppose, and tell him you'll die if you don't have him?"

"No, indeed, sir!" I cried, dashing away my tears. "I—I hate him!"

"Why, then you shan't have him, miss," says my papa.

CHAPTER VII.
WHICH TREATS OF TREASONS, STRATAGEMS, AND SPOILS.

CALCUTTA, *April ye* 15*th*.

Well, Amelia, Mr Fraser is departed, and I have not seen him since he turned his back on me and strode out of the varanda. I don't know whether he desired me to understand his visit as a final and never-to-be-repeated offer of his affections, so that, once refused, the chance of gaining 'em would not present itself again, but his acts seem to give countenance to the notion. So then, my dear, your Sylvia finds herself deserted, but in such a mood, I am thankful to say, that she would not lower herself to call the young gentleman back, even were he descending the steps at this moment. My dear Miss Turnor won't be surprised to hear that her friend has been busy summing up Mr Fraser's defects, in order the more easily to fortify her mind against the reflection that she has lost him. Here's a portion of the list: Item, the gentleman is proud; item, he is over-prudent; item, he resents the discovery of his faults; item, he wickedly risqued his own life and that of another person in a duel over a word; item—but the total would be too long. In short, your Sylvia is occupied, with extreme industry, in proving to herself that the grapes are sour.

I had just wrote this, my dear, when I heard my papa's voice—

"Where are you, miss? What's come to the girl?"

"Here, dear sir; here to serve you," I cried, and ran to meet him.

"Why, miss," says Mr Freyne, "here's the rival prophets both coming up to the house at once. I must have you sit by with your sewing, as meek as if you had never passed a saucy remark on your betters in your life, and take down their doleful prophecies, so as we may laugh at 'em a year hence."

My Amelia knows one of these prophets: 'tis good Captain Colquhoun. The other is a young gentleman of the name of Dash, one of the Company's writers here, the son of an old friend of my papa's, and commended to his favourable notice by his father. Mr Dash is one of those persons who feel themselves competent to direct the whole œconomy of any business in which they are interested, and who, since it han't pleased Providence to place them in authority, bear a grudge against such as occupy the situation they would fain fill.

"So you see, sir," says Captain Colquhoun to my papa, when the gentlemen were seated, "I was right in telling you the Soubah was dead."

(So he is, Amelia. The news was confirmed on Monday, when I wrote you last, but my head was so full of other things that I forgot it.)

"If you'd be so obliging as to say who's to succeed him, it might profit us not a little at this moment, sir," says Mr Freyne.

"Since the Presidency is leaning towards the side of Gosseta Begum, I would lay my money on the Chuta Nabob," says Mr Dash.

"The Presidency," said the Captain, "is doing its best to run with the hare and hunt with the hounds, and that ends in destruction."

"Sure, Captain," said my papa, "you wouldn't have the Council adopt precipitately either one side or t'other?"

"Sir, they have had time enough to make up their minds, and all they have decided is that while they hope the winner will be the Begum, they fear 'twill be Surajah Dowlah. If they had sufficient courage to support their desires, they might turn the scale in the lady's favour, or possessing a little enterprise, they might bind the Nabob securely to their side; but they'll do neither."

"But, Captain," said Mr Dash, "you would not have the Council embark on such enterprises as have brought us so much trouble in the Carnatic?"

"I would have them strong enough to support the right side if they chose, or to defend themselves if they remained neuter," said the Captain. "At present they can't make up their minds what to do in a situation in which it's equally fatal to act too soon and to act too late."

"Like myself, sir, you believe the Presidency will delay to support the young Nabob till too late, and then seek to curry favour with him?"

"Just so, sir; and the ladies and gentlemen here will be eating and drinking, and buying and selling, and marrying and giving in marriage, until the very day that the flood comes, and sweeps us all away."

"Oh, fie, Captain! you're alarming Miss. En't you ashamed to have made the fairest cheek in Calcutta grow pale?"

"Miss is no more alarmed than you are, sir," says Mr Freyne. "She has heard the Captain's prophecies before."

This turned the laugh against the Captain, who sat looking vastly stern and grim, and not a whit shaken in his predictions.

"The flood will sweep us all away," he repeated, "and 'tis well it should. The luxury of our people is grown to an excessive pitch."

"I vow, sir, you're right," said Mr Dash. "The establishments kept up by the President and most of the Council, and their manner of life, not to speak of the entertainments they give, are scandalous."

"I was not pointing at any particular person, sir," says the Captain, with a frown. "The evil is as marked in the case of the youngest writer, since too often he adds to his faults emulation of those above him."

"But what would you have, Captain?" asked Mr Freyne. "Sure the Company can do no more than it does, sending out orders that the writers are to be deprived even of the indulgences most necessary in this climate. Rather than see the youngsters die for the want of these common things, we are forced to wink at their evasion of the orders, as when the writer at Madrass, who was forbid to be attended by a roundel-boy, changed the shape of his umbrella and called it a squaredel, and was waited on by his boy in peace. But the worst of this meddling on the Company's part is that we can't consistently enforce the salutary regulations against drinking, dicing, and debt, and such like, since we have suffered the infraction of the little foolish rules on which they insist so strongly."

"Well," said Mr Dash, "I would have the writers left alone. Some of them will die early, but the strongest will live on, and for them I would have the Company's regulations strictly enforced, when they have reached the higher offices, that is. The election to these offices I would direct by the general vote, which should also have power to remove an office-holder in case of incapacity on his part."

"Come," says my papa, "Bengall will be the paradise of writers, indeed! though I can't but pity the Members of Council when they shall hold their places at Tom Dash's pleasure."

"I'll assure you, sir," says Mr Dash, "the factory would be much better managed, and the Gentoos more friendly to us. At present both they and the Moors are nothing but so many spies on us for our enemies' benefit. And talking of spies, what's your opinion of the French gentleman from Chandernagore?"

"Young le Beaume? A very sprightly and agreeable person."

"I am assured," very mysteriously, "that he's here as a spy on us. Mr Menotti tells me that he left Chandernagore secretly, having been imprisoned for taking a drubbing meekly from another officer, and that he looks to win his pardon by his reports as to our movements and intentions."

"Then Mr Menotti has misinformed you, sir," said Captain Colquhoun, contemptuously. "Mr le Beaume left Chandernagore because, having sent a challenge to a superior officer who he conceived had insulted him, he was accused of threatening his life, and put under arrest. He broke prison to come here, and he won't return unless we deliver him up. I would far sooner believe Menotti to be a spy than him."

"Sir! Mr Menotti is a gentleman of the highest respectability."

"He's nothing but an interloper, sir, and thirty years back would have been harried out of Calcutta. I'm much mistaken if all his wealth is the result of honest trading. He's hand and glove with Omy Chund and the other Gentoos, visiting even at their private houses, which no other gentleman in the factory does, and the President finds him useful as a means of communicating with 'em. If he sells the secrets with which he has been injudiciously entrusted, we have a key to all that betraying of our plans to the Muxadavad Durbar which has gone on for years before poor le Beaume came here."

"Come, Captain, don't talk scandal," says my papa, seeing my eyes fixed eagerly on Captain Colquhoun, for indeed I am perpetually on the watch for any chance of ridding myself of Mr Menotti. "We are as slanderous as any three old tabbies over their dish of tea, and Miss here is listening with all her ears."

"And indeed, sir," put in Mr Dash, "I can't see that we have any reason to regret Mr Menotti's friendliness with the Gentoos. Omy Chund and Govinderam Metre have both been hardly treated, and 'tis well they should be cultivated."

"They are a pair of rascals, sir!" cried Mr Freyne, with a strong word, "and should have been turned out of the bounds when the Company's service was rid of 'em."

"Oh, come, sir, sure you must grant that the Zemindar used 'em with great hardness, worse even than the rest of the Indians he misrules."

"No abuse of Mr Holwell here, sir, if you please."

"But, sir, the place rings with tales of his injustice. There's that affair of Rangeeboom Coberage, Raja Tillokchund of Burraduan's[01] *go-master*—his entire possessions were sold for a debt of seven thousand rupees. That has inflamed the Gentoos, and 'tis not the only case."

"When you have lived a little longer in Bengall, sir, you'll understand that if King Solomon himself were judge in the Cutcherry Court, the losing side would infallibly declare he'd been bribed."

"But 'tis well known, sir, that Mr Holwell increases the Company's revenues by permitting persons of infamous character to settle here on payment of a price."

"That's Mr Holwell's affair, sir, and if it be true, he must settle it with his conscience and the Company, which is for ever pressing him to raise more money. But I entirely disbelieve the report. Why, this very morning there was a dispute in the Council over some vagabond or other, whom Holwell desired to admit, while Drake and the other two were resolved to expel him. I suppose you'll say that the Zemindar had took money from him?"

"Was you present at the Council, sir?" asked Captain Colquhoun.

"No, indeed, Captain. I had some notion of strolling in, but outside the door I heard the angry voices, and the peon told me what was going on, so I stayed away, knowing that poor Holwell and I could do nothing against Manningham and Frankland and the President. They won the day, of course, and as I came back to tiffing I saw a *chubdar* conducting the fellow, whoever he was, out of the place, with the usual rabble at his heels, pelting him with garbage and foul names."

"Sir," broke in the Captain, seemingly much moved, "that's the fault I find in you, that having but one voice in the Council, you don't exercise that one, but leave all things to be controlled by the Committee of Three."

"You're warm, Captain," said my papa, "or you would scarce set to chide me in the presence of these young persons."

"I ask your pardon, sir, but excuse you I can't. Suppose (I say suppose, for I know no more of the matter than yourself) that this vagabond should be a hanger-on of Surajah Dowlah, how will you answer to the Company for your silence?"

"I shall answer with my life, sir, like all here, I suppose," said Mr Freyne, smartly.

"And also with the lives of your wife and daughter, and all the women here, when the Nabob's vengeance comes? Even your sole voice raised on Mr Holwell's side might have brought the Three to reason, but you refused to give it."

"Sure, Captain, you think a mighty great deal of Mr Holwell," says Mr Dash.

"I think, sir, that he's the one man of sense and honour in the Council, beyond a friend of mine that has the sense and honour, but won't employ 'em, and one or two that are like him."

"Well, sir, as I see the gentleman himself approaching, I won't disturb your conversation with him," said Mr Dash, rising and taking his departure in a very marked manner, though laughing.

"How has Holwell managed to disoblige the lad?" says my papa to Captain Colquhoun.

"I don't know, sir, but I would judge he has made some effort to keep him in his place, for which he'll pay dearly, I fear, if the young gentleman's power ever equal his ill-will. Your servant, sir," this to Mr Holwell, who came up looking more serious than ever.

"Good-day to you, gentlemen. Madam, your humble servant. I fear, Captain, that your prophecies are in a fair way to be fulfilled."

"Hey-day!" cries Mr Freyne, "another prophet! Come, sir, what's to do now?"

"You saw a Gentoo fellow drove out of the town this morning?"

"Questionless, sir; as villainous a countenance as I ever beheld."

"Have either of you ever heard of Narransing,[02] gentlemen?"

"Narransing?" said the Captain, musing; "I seem to myself to know the name. Not Rajaram's brother?"

"You're right, sir. The brother of Ramramsing Hircara, the chief of the Chuta Nabob's spies, was expelled from our bounds this morning with all possible ignominy."

"If you're surprised, sir, I'm not," says the Captain.

"Tell us how it happened, sir," said Mr Freyne.

"Last night between eight and nine," says Mr Holwell, "I was surprised by a visit from Omy Chund, bringing with him another Gentoo, whom he presented to me as Narransing, saying that he entered the town in a European dress, and brought a letter from the Nabob. I received the fellow with the civility due to Rajaram's brother, but refused to look at his *perwannah*, which was wrote by Huckembeg, the Nabob's duan, as the President would be in town in the morning. The purport of the piece was to demand the delivery of Kissendasseat, with his women and treasure, on the ground that Radjbullob, his father, when ordered to produce his accounts, said that Kissendass had taken 'em away with him. In the morning I laid the matter before Mr President, with whom were Messieurs Manningham and Frankland, who regarded the affair as an insolent attempt to terrify us, since advices from all quarters report that Gosseta Begum is certain of success. Narransing's coming in disguise, and his sneaking into the place under cover of night, seemed to support the notion, even if they did not show that he wasn't an accredited messenger at all, and the Council would not choose to wait and see how things would turn out. Mr Manningham seemed to be of my way of thinking at first, but he soon agreed with his partner and Mr Drake, and they sent to turn Narransing out of the place. The servants, going beyond their orders, drove him out of the factory, and even off the shore, with menaces and insolence, which seemed somewhat to alarm the Council when they heard it, for they writ at once to Cossimbuzar to bid Mr Watts make things right with the Nabob."

"Make things right!" says the Captain.

"And more," said Mr Holwell, "this morning, when I was about to punish the Jemmautdar[03] of the *chokey*,[04] where the fellow landed, for admitting a person in a European habit unknown to me, he said that the only European he admitted last night was not Narransing at all, but might be any of the gentlemen here. Narransing wore the dress of a common *pycar*,[05] but when they would have opposed his landing, Omy Chund's servants came to say that he was a relation of their master's, and must be let in. What do you make of this?"

"Why, that there's an extraordinary great mystery somewhere, sir," says my papa. "We'll talk of this in the garden, gentlemen, if you please, for there's one or two matters on which the Captain and I would fain have Mr Holwell's opinion. Mind you're not late in dressing for the Masquerade, miss."

Oh, this Masquerade! Was ever any one in a frame of mind less suited to such a gathering, Amelia? I had hoped it might be put off by reason of the old Soubah's death, but it seems that since Mr Drake has heard nothing in an official manner he can't take notice of it; and though I have begged and prayed my papa to permit me to stay at home, he won't hear of it, but insists on my attending him and Mrs Freyne to the Play-house.

April ye 16th.

More troubles and mysteries and perplexities, Amelia! Sure my dear Miss Turnor will begin to think that her Sylvia's presence is as disastrous as that of Helen of Troy to the place she honours with her residence. But to my tale. Yesterday evening I went to my chamber early to dress for the masquerade, and turned sick at heart to look at the dress which Marianna had laid out upon the *cott.* (Did I tell you that a bed here is always called a cott?) It was made after the pattern of that worn by Miss Byron as an Arcadian princess, for Miss Hamlin and I had agreed to wear dresses of a more modern and distinctive sort than the usual nuns and shepherdesses one hears of every day. She chose, therefore, the dress worn by Lady Bella in the 'Female Quixote,' as the Princess Julia, daughter of Augustus Cæsar, and I that of the charming Harriet, although my pleasure in it was sadly damped by the rumour that reached me that Mr Menotti was having a vastly fine suit made for himself as Sir Charles Grandison. Imagine it, my dear! the desecration of so noble a character by this vile wretch's impersonating it. Well, as I stood looking at my gown, I heard a palanqueen arrive, and presently in came Mrs Hurstwood, Miss Hamlin that was, in her ordinary clothes, and frightfully disturbed. The tailor that was making her gown for the evening had run off with the stuff, tempted, as is supposed, by the richness of the blue and silver brocade, and there was no time to make another. Indeed, the poor young lady was in a terrible state, fit to rave. As she sat and bewailed her loss, a thought came to me.

"Oh, dearest miss—Charlotte, I should say—" I cried, "wear my dress, I entreat you, and go in my place."

"And what would Miss Freyne's papa say to that?" said she.

"Questionless, he would be sadly displeased, for I have begged of him in vain to permit me to stay at home. But oh, miss, I have such a terror of masquerades"—"Drawn from Mr Richardson," she put in—"and such a diversion is so ill-suited to my present thoughts and situation, and I am so apprehensive of being spoken to by my persecutor, and perhaps insulted, that if you would persuade Mr Freyne to excuse me, I should be for ever grateful to you. And I know that my papa has a vastly high esteem for Mrs Hurstwood."

"And pray, miss," says she, "will you prefer Calcutta to say you remain at home out of jealousy for my marriage, or grief for Mr Fraser's departure, or sympathy with Lieutenant Bentinck?"

"You terrify me!" I cried. "Sure my papa was only kind in commanding me to appear, if this be the alternative. But," for a sudden thought seized me, "I can't wear this dress. I should feel like a tricked-out skeleton. Pray, miss, oblige me by putting it on. You may be taken for me, but I know you'll hold your own with the boldest wretches in Calcutta"—"I thank you, miss," said she.—"As for me, I'll endeavour to strengthen and calm my mind by wearing the dress of the incomparable Clarissa, who was greater in her humiliation than in her happiest days. My white damask nightgown and satin petticoat, with a morning cap, and my hair in a *dégagé* style, will answer all purposes, and should save me from recognition."

"I vow you're mistaken, if you think an undress and the absence of a hoop will disguise the finest shape in Calcutta," says my Charlotte; "but the notion of deceiving the fellows is agreeable enough. Well, miss, if you're really in earnest, I'll oblige you by wearing your dress."

"I can never be grateful enough to my dear Mrs Hurstwood," I said, and calling in Marianna, we soon had Charlotte dressed in the blue satin waistcoat and petticoat, laced and fringed with silver, the white silk scarf and the fantastical cap, so well known to all Mr Richardson's readers. While I was hurrying into my own gown, my stepmother looked in at the door.

"What, miss! exchanging dresses?" she cried.

"A mishap has come to Mrs Hurstwood's gown, madam," said I, "and she is so good as to wear mine, which I have took a dislike to."

"Oh, very well," said Mrs Freyne. "And you are the divine Clarissa in the Sponging-house, I see. O' my conscience, miss, I wonder at your preference! But your papa and I can't wait for you. You'll follow with Mrs Hurstwood, I suppose?"

"I expect my spouse every moment, madam," says Charlotte, "and I'll assure you we'll both have an eye to Miss's safety."

Mrs Freyne went away, and I finished dressing in much better spirits. But what was my vexation when I arrived at the Play-house with the Hurstwoods to perceive that my naughty, unkind stepmother must have told Mr Menotti of my sudden change of intention, for he came stumping towards me as soon as I alighted from my palanqueen, in a greatcoat with a cape, the collar turned up and buttoned round his chin, a pair of coarse stockens drawn over his own, and an old tie-wig, the very image of the abandoned Lovelace when he forced himself in this disguise upon Clarissa's retirements at Hampstead. I could have wept, Amelia. The sole consolation that offered itself to me (and it did give me a sensible pleasure, I'll promise you) was the thought of the inconvenience the wretch must be suffering from the heat, and the mortification it must have cost him to lay aside his fine Grandison dress. There was no escaping him, for he was the first to observe our arrival, and I was forced to give him my hand, and to endure his talk, which was as free as that of Lovelace, but wanted the wit, until I hated him worse than ever, if that were possible, and seized the chance of our becoming entangled in a crowd of masques to rid myself of his company.

Anxious only to be free from the company of my too importunate Lovelace, I lent a ready ear to a masque who approached me in the habit of a French religious person, and whom I knew, by his air of gallantry, to be Mons. le Beaume. With him was a gentleman most elegantly dressed in a coat of red cloth of silver, buttoned with diamonds, and very richly laced, with waistcoat and breeches of satin. There was large diamond buckles in his shoes, which had monstrous high red heels, and he wore a great forked periwig, all in the mode of fifty years back. I observed this person particularly, because a few minutes ago he had come and tapped Mr Menotti on the shoulder, desiring him, as I think, to present him to me. His address seemed to put my persecutor out of countenance in an extraordinary manner, but he refused very vehemently to grant the request, though the other continued to urge it even with menaces, as I judged by his gestures.

"Fairest Clarissa," says Mr le Beaume, bowing with great ceremony, "here's his Most Christian Majesty the late King Lewis of France, whom the report of your virtues has reached in the other world, and brought him back to earth to show his admiration of 'em."

"Sure his Majesty's admiration of virtue is well known, sir," said I.

"Madam," says the strange gentleman in French, which also Mr le Beaume and I had used, "in his day virtue had not dwelt upon earth in the person of the divine Clarissa. With the good fortune of her example to guide him——"

"If your Majesty desire the divine Clarissa to guide you in the dance," says Mr le Beaume, "there's no time to lose. You can exchange fine phrases out of the romances afterwards."

My cavalier offered his hand immediately, which I accepted, anticipating an agreeable contest of wits in forcing him to discover himself, for, what with his masque and his periwig, I was quite unable to recognise him as any of the gentlemen of the place, while his voice (and he spoke French as I had not thought any of our gentlemen could speak it) was also strange to me. So well did he present his character that he even danced in the French style, which is at once more ceremonious and displays greater vivacity than ours, until my curiosity was piqued in the highest degree. But 'twas not until we were sitting in the inner varanda after the dance, and my partner was fanning me, as is the custom here, that I had any chance to converse with him. His discourse suited less well with his disguise than his dancing had done; for although he made me several genteel compliments in the true romantic style, he turned quickly to speak of the ordinary affairs of the place, and among them of the matter of Kissendasseat. But here I stopped him.

"Pray, sir," I said, "don't mention that person's name to me. For weeks there was nothing talked of in Calcutta but Kissendass and his women, his goods and his sacks of treasure, until I was tired to death of him."

"His refuging here is much talked of, then?" asked the disguised.

"Really, sir, you must know that as well as I."

"Pardon me, madam; how should I know that the ladies condescended to weary themselves with the trifles that interest us poor men? Yet I deserve the rebuke, for en't the lady in this case Miss Clarissa Harlowe?"

"Sure you single me out unduly, sir. The ladies of Calcutta can't be indifferent to events that might prove to be of so much moment to 'em."

"Then has the President's treatment of the Nabob's messenger given rise to apprehension among the fair sex, madam?"

"'Tis but little known as yet, sir, but it's natural there should be some misgivings as to the new Soubah's acceptance of it."

"Poh, poh!" says he. "The President knows what he's about, madam. The Nabob has exposed his weakness by his method of proceeding. Why should he send his emissary to steal into the place in disguise, if it en't that he hoped to gain secretly from the friendship of the Presidency what he knows he can't demand openly and by force?"

"It may be so, sir; but if it be, the insults offered to his servant will give him but an indifferent notion of that friendship."

"You're too apprehensive, madam. You may take my word for it that the Nabob can't afford to resent these insults. He's encompassed with enemies, and he knows the strength of the factory too well to dream of attacking it."

"You're vastly positive, sir; I hope you may be justified. What I find alarming in this affair is the suggestion that there may be some deep conspiracy behind it."

"Conspiracy, ha, ha! Forgive me, madam, but I perceive that even the greatest of her sex en't free from the fault of meeting misfortune half-way. Trust me, in a month or so this alarm will be forgot, and Clarissa will be swallowed up in preparations for making her Lovelace the happiest of men."

"I vow I don't understand you, sir."

"What! don't we all know that in this case the lover possesses the support of his mistress's friends? Happiest of men, indeed! since with the mind and temper of Solmes, he's earned the reward of Lovelace."

"If you're in the confidence of the person at whom you hint, sir, allow me to say that you'll do him no service by these free remarks. Will you be so good as to hand me back to the ballroom?"

"Nay, then," said this strange man, with great warmth, placing himself in my path as he spoke, "is the report true that has reached me, that this pretended Lovelace is but Solmes in disguise? Is it true that his suit, while favoured by her mamma, is distasteful to the amiable Clarissa herself? Speak, madam, and enrol Lewis as your defender until death."

By this time I was heartily frightened, as you may suppose, and anxious only to rid myself of my new tormentor. "Sure you forget yourself, sir, in thus intruding into family matters. I thank Heaven that I have already friends sufficient to protect me, as well as a will that has served me tolerably hitherto."

"Nay, madam," he cried again, seizing my gown as I sought to slip past him, "you're in a trap, believe me. Your mamma is leagued with this Solmes or Lovelace—whichever he be—and resolved on handing you over to him. You'll perceive before long the truth of my words. If you should then be moved to accept of my assistance, a billet addressed to me in character, and sent to the house of a respectable female in the Great Buzar, whom all the Indian servants know by the name of the Mother of Cosmetiques, will find me without loss of time."

I was incensed against the man for his bare-faced proposition, and tore my gown from his hold. "Sure, sir," I said angrily, "you forget the character I have assumed in thus acting up to your own. Be assured there's no help I would not accept sooner than that offered in such a fashion," and I pushed past him, and ran along the varanda towards the door. Here I came upon two gentlemen, who had been watching the dancing, and had stepped out to breathe the air, and to my delight I recognised them as my papa and Captain Colquhoun. I seized Mr Freyne's arm. "Oh, sir——!" I gasped, and burst into tears, and so clung to him, looking like a fool, I make no doubt.

"Can I be of any service to you, madam?" asked my papa.

"Is it possible, sir, that you don't recognise Miss Freyne?" said Captain Colquhoun, with the stiffest air in the world.

"How could a man know any one in that masque?" cried Mr Freyne. "Take the absurd thing off, miss, and tell me what's the matter."

"The—the person with whom I was dancing, sir," I sobbed.

"Well, and what of him, miss? Who is he?"

"I don't know, sir. Oh pray, don't be so sharp with your girl. He—he said——"

"He has offered to insult you, madam?" demanded the Captain, in his sternest voice, which Mr Freyne took as a rebuke.

"I'll manage my own family, sir, if you please, so pray don't favour us with your strait-laced opinion of masquerades at this moment. What did this person say, miss?"

"I—I believe he invited me to run away with him, sir."

"You en't certain? Sure the girl's a fool! She cries out that a person has insulted her, and she don't know who he is, nor can't tell what he said. Where is this gentleman?"

"I—I left him there, sir," pointing to the settee where we had sat.

"And there en't a living creature to be seen! I fear, miss, you are one of those that flee when no man pursueth."

"Sure, sir," says Captain Colquhoun, coming to my help, "you can't doubt but Miss Freyne's delicacy has been wounded by the liberties of speech this person has permitted himself. If he have drunk too freely, he should be removed from the place, both for his own sake and others', and will questionless see the propriety of offering an apology on the morrow. Was it the gentleman habited as King Lewis the Fourteenth, with whom I saw you dance not long ago, madam?"

"It was, sir, but I can't imagine who he may be. He spoke only French."

"You see, sir?" Captain Colquhoun turned to my papa. "I fear Miss has been exposed to the rudeness of one of those rascally fellows that make a practice of insulting ladies at gatherings of this sort, feeling secure of impunity through their disguises. Did he first accost you, madam?"

"No, sir. Mr le Beaume presented him in character."

"Then he'll know him, questionless. Excuse me for a moment, madam," and returning to the ballroom he brought out Mr le Beaume and Ensign Bellamy, the latter wearing rams' horns and an antique habit as Alexander the Great. The two young gentlemen had been dancing together, a thing which is not unfrequent at the Calcutta balls, owing to the small number of our sex that are present.

"Pray, sir," says my papa to Mr le Beaume, "who was the person you presented just now to my daughter?"

"Why, sir, I'm sure I don't know. I named him only by his character, as I heard was the custom at these gatherings, since all present were well acquainted with one another."

"Then you know nothing of the fellow?"

"Nothing, sir, save that I chanced to jostle him in the crowd somewhat roughly, and begged his pardon, which he gave with a very good grace. 'Say no more, Mons. l'Abbé,' he said, speaking in character. 'Do your King the honour of making him known to the divine Clarissa, and all is more than forgiven.' I hope, sir, I han't done any displeasure to the lady in granting his request?"

"Your King, as you call him, sir, has thought fit to use towards Miss a freedom that may be the mode at Chandernagore, but en't so at Calcutta."

"Do I understand you to imply, sir, that this person was an intimate of my own?"

"Come, Mr le Beaume," it was Captain Colquhoun who spoke; "don't be over ready to stand on your punctilio. You see that we must come at the truth of this affair, if only to save the ladies from annoyance in the future. I understand this person spoke nothing but French. To the best of your belief, had you ever met him before?"

"Never, Captain. I know all the officials of our factories at Chandernagore and Sydabad,[06] but he recalled none of 'em to my mind. But, gentlemen, this affair touches my honour. Pray allow me to seek out this person, and bring him here to entreat Miss's pardon on his knees."

"And I'm with you, sir," said Ensign Bellamy. "Sure the matter touches me also, Captain, since I introduced Mr le Beaume as my guest."

"And lent him also your father's best cassock in which to appear?" said Captain Colquhoun. "What will our good Padra say to that, sir?"

"'Tis but his second best, sir," pleaded the Ensign, "and Mr le Beaume passed his word to me to do it no discredit. But now, gentlemen, with your leave, we'll set out to hunt this low fellow."

"Go first to the peon at the door, young gentlemen," said Mr Freyne, "and desire him to let you look at the chitts." (These, Amelia, are the tickets of entrance, as we should say.) "By that means you'll discover who 'twas that represented the French King."

But the two gentlemen returning in a few minutes brought word that there was no such character mentioned on any of the chitts, neither could the peon recollect admitting such an one.

"Poh!" says my papa. "Buxies, that's all! Did you discover whether the fellow be still in the place, gentlemen?"

"He's not, sir," they replied together; "but although several persons had remarked him in the ball-room, no one has seen him leave the Play-house."

"Pray have the goodness to enquire further, gentlemen. There's some mystery here." I thought that he wished to be rid of the young gentlemen, for as soon as they were gone he turned to the Captain.

"What do you make of this, sir?" he asked.

"A spy, I fear. Perhaps from Chandernagore—but no, the lad le Beaume hath an honest countenance, Papist though he be."

"A spy of the Soubah's, then? Watts' letter warned us the place is full of 'em. There's Someroo,[07] that Prussian of Cossim Ally Cawn's, might have got in among us."

"True, but Mr le Beaume would be little likely to mistake a Prussian for one of his own nation. A spy the fellow must be, I believe. Do you recollect the confusion of Holwell's Jemmautdar in speaking of the entry of the Nabob's messenger? Look you there, now. There was two of 'em, after all—this fellow in a European habit, and Narransing in the disguise of a pycar."

"There's more in this than appears, Captain. Do you think this impudent intruder can be Bussy himself, stole hither from the Carnatic?"

"Bussy? My good sir, Bussy is besieging Savanore, and has his hands too full to leave the Decan at present. Besides, why risque discovery by annoying a lady?"

"To avert suspicion from his true object—I don't else know why. Or perhaps his freedoms were only assumed to get rid of Miss while he put on another dress to escape in. He might wear a domino, or obtain some other disguise from one of the servants."

"Perhaps, sir," I ventured to observe, "Mr Menotti may be able to tell you something. He seemed to have some acquaintance with the wretch."

"Pray, miss, why didn't you say that before?" I saw a look pass between my papa and the Captain. "Put on your masque again, and come back to the ballroom with me."

Once inside the Play-house, it was not long before Mr Menotti perceived us, and came to importune me for another dance, which I was charmed to refuse him.

"Miss has danced quite as much as is good for her health," says my papa. "I won't have her try another step this evening. You young fellows should have some mercy on these delicate creatures, for they en't made of iron, and there's none too many of 'em. By the way, sir, who was the gentleman that desired you to present him to Miss, but you refused?"

I was watching Mr Menotti with all my eyes from behind my masque, as you'll guess, Amelia, and it seemed to me that he changed colour a very little. Yet he answered with the greatest unconcern imaginable, "Why, that I don't know, sir, which was my reason for refusing him the honour he asked. He was vastly urgent with me, I'll assure you, but I would not listen to him. I hope he han't tried to force himself upon Miss?"

"Why, sir, he has alarmed her slightly by his importunity, I believe, but that only calls for greater gratitude for your care of her."

Leaving Mr Menotti, we returned to the doorway, where Captain Colquhoun, with infinite kindness, turned the conversation to other matters, until the young gentlemen returned, having done wonders in the way of tracking the Unknown, but accomplished nothing. Learning from a late comer in the ballroom that on entering the place he had seen passing out a tall masque in the veil and robe of a Moor-woman (this was so unusual a habit as to excite his remark, for persons here entertain such a contempt for the Indians that it is the rarest thing in the world to see their dress, which is very handsome among those of quality, copied at these masquerades), they made enquiries among the servants waiting for their masters in the compound, and found that a person so habited had entered a hired palanqueen and departed. The only distinguishing mark that they could discover about this palanqueen was that one of the bearers had a lame leg, but with the aid of this sole clue Mess. Bellamy and le Beaume set out to trace it. After many false starts they were told by a certain Armenian that he had seen such a palanqueen carried into the house of Omy Chund, the Gentoo banker, but on enquiring there they found that it had contained only one of his women, who had gone out to visit her mother. Thus they returned discomfited, but all eagerness to find the stranger. Meanwhile my papa had learnt from me of the direction given by him at the old woman's house in the Great Buzar, and the young gentlemen were very urgent with him to allow them to obtain an order from the Zemindar, and so search the place.

"How would that serve?" says Mr Freyne. "The fellow en't in the house, you may be very sure, and the woman would deny any knowledge of him. Ladies of her trade have many clients whose secrets they are well paid to keep, and she may well have never seen him, and know only that she might possibly receive a letter for him."

"But, sir," ventured Ensign Bellamy, "perhaps Miss would be so good as to address a blank sheet of paper to the woman's care, so that the messenger who came to fetch it might be watched and seized."

"I thank you, sir, no," said my papa. "Miss's name has already been more mixed up in this affair than either she or I care for. I'll speak to Mr Holwell, and get a watch set secretly on the house; but we can't hope the rascal will venture there in person. You'll undertake, young gentlemen, that the matter shan't go beyond yourselves?"

"On my honour, sir," said the two gentlemen, and we were left to muse in silence over this most disquieting affair. I don't know what to think, my Amelia. A sudden sound terrifies me. I am ready to run away from the most harmless stranger. I screamed aloud this morning when I came suddenly upon the *molly* in the garden. Plots and conspiracies seem to be thick on every side of me. I fear, though I don't dare hint this to my papa, that the words of the Unknown regarding Mrs Freyne's compact with Mr Menotti may be true, and what a prospect then opens before me! I know how deeply my dear Miss Turnor will pity her unsuspicious Sylvia, who thus finds herself entangled in a web of mysteriousness.

CHAPTER VIII.
IN WHICH MR FREYNE'S PATIENCE COMES TO AN END.

CALCUTTA, *April ye* 17*th.*

Nothing has as yet been discovered respecting the mysterious affair of which I informed my Amelia in the letter I finished yesterday, and all our minds have been further disturbed by an event that has just occurred. About six o'clock this evening I was taking a dish of chocolate in the varanda before going to change my dress for a water-party to which I was to attend Mrs Freyne, when my papa and Captain Colquhoun joined me. The Captain was in an extraordinary sprightly frame of mind, and all because the Company's ship Delawar, which arrived at Culpee this morning, had brought a warning from the Directors that war with France might be looked for very shortly, and therefore the Fort was to be put in a good state of defence, particularly the cannons on the west front, in case of an attack from the river. My papa rallied his friend on his eagerness, asserting that 'twas the news of a monstrous French fleet a-preparing at Brest, and designed to sail for the Indies under Count Lally to lay waste our factories, that delighted him, since now all his prophecies of evil were in a fair way to be fulfilled. The Captain defended himself with great spirit, saying that he should be thankful if we were not all prisoners to a less polite foe than the French long before Count Lally's fleet arrived, condemning also the slowness of the Presidency in acting on the orders they had received.

"Had I been in command," he said, "the plans for the repair of the defences should all have been put in hand to-day, and the work begun to-morrow, so that all had been done before the Nabob could get wind of our preparations and seek to stop us; but now here's the Three disputing what's to be done first, and whether it be necessary to do anything at all, with as much indifference as if they were considering the siege of Carthage. When the walls are falling to pieces, and the guns lying useless for want of carriages, one would think the Council might be willing to set to work on both the jobs at once."

Mr Freyne made some jesting reply, and seeing that the gentlemen were well embarked on one of their political talks, I slipped away to dress. Marianna was waiting in my chamber, and asked me which necklace I would wear with my yellow gown. Coming to the dressing-table, where she had laid out the ribbons, I remarked something white under the edge of my hand-mirror, and lifting it pulled out a small billet wrote on gilt-edged paper and very finely scented. "*A la très-belle et très-excellente Clarisse*" was on the flap.

"Why, what's this chitt, Marianna?" I said.

"Me not know, missy. Never see it before."

I opened the letter. It was all in French, and signed "Clarissa's slave till death," while at the top stood these words, "Let the amiable goddess of my heart deign to read these lines in secret, and to keep them concealed from all the world." Had the writer been there to watch me, he had questionless been chagrined by the effects of his words, for I did not stop even to read the billet, but ran back to the varanda in a prodigious hurry, and thrust the paper into my papa's hands.

"Why, what's this, miss?" he said, just as I had done.

"A chitt, sir—from the Unknown, I'm sure—he begs me to keep it secret, but I haven't read a word of it. Oh, sir, who can he be?"

"Calm yourself, madam," says Captain Colquhoun. "The billet may only be a jest on the part of one of our young gentlemen."

This notion had not occurred to me, and I waited, something calmer, while Mr Freyne spread out the paper and pored over it, which was not long.

"I'll be hanged if I can make head or tail of the gibberish!" he cried. "Here, miss," throwing it back to me, "make a translate of the Mounseer's love-letter for us, and see you don't miss out none of the hearts and darts, nor abate the poor gentleman's ardours. Read it out, pray; don't wait to write the stuff down."

Now was it not an odd business, my dear, to have to read aloud in the presence of two gentlemen a love-letter of whose contents I had not the slightest knowledge? nevertheless I began boldly enough: "'To the coldest and most charming of ladies, the humblest of her worshippers indites with his heart's blood these lines——'"

"I would the letter had been longer; then he might have bled to death," growled my papa. "Go on, miss."

"'Such, madam, is the admiration I conceived for the incomparable Clarissa on that happy evening when her resplendent charms burst for the first time upon my enraptured gaze, that since she quitted me in anger I have neither ate nor drank nor slept——'"

"Come, if this go on, we shall kill him yet," says Mr Freyne.

"'That the failure of my attempts to conceal the passion with which she inspired me should have alarmed her delicacy were calamity enough, but that she should carry her apprehensions so far as to flee from the expression of my adoration is a punishment that would (I appeal to the charmer herself if this ben't truth) be over severe for the most heinous of crimes. To the worm that was permitted to bask for a few brief moments in the sunshine of her smiles 'tis a veritable sentence of death. But, madam, he who now ventures to address himself to you en't one to welcome death tamely. He'll fight for his life, and such is the love he has for you that he'll gratify it even though he must needs wade through rivers of blood, though Calcutta be razed to the ground in the course of the measures he'll take, and the English swept out of Bengall. But he don't desire to alarm Clarissa a second time by the warmth of the sentiments he entertains, and would therefore only hint that his charmer has it in her power not merely to attach to herself for ever a grateful adorer whom her condescension will have preserved from death, but to oblige her countrymen in the highest degree, and gain for herself a name greater than that of the victorious Mr Clive as the protector of the British settlements in the Indies. Let her but vouchsafe to free herself from the perils of a distasteful alliance that now beset her, and honour her devoted slave by confiding herself to his care. A Christian priest shall be at hand and remove the only scruple that a lady of Clarissa's modesty and prudence might be troubled with in granting such a prayer, and in an hour after the lightest intimation of Clarissa's pleasure has been conveyed to the house named to her two days ago, she shall be safe for ever from the persecutions of tyrannical parents and a tiresome lover.'"

"Well, indeed, miss!" says my papa, "I must make you my best compliments on the style of your adorer's letter. Pray, does he expect love or fear to incite you most to grant his request? And the forethought of the gentleman! 'A priest at hand' in an hour! I vow you're a lucky girl."

"A mighty tasteful piece of writing, indeed!" says the Captain.

But I was in no mind to join in their pleasantry. "Oh, sir," I cried, turning to my papa with the tears in my eyes, "is this a letter that should be sent to your daughter, who has never (if she may humbly venture to say so) given occasion to any to speak lightly of her? En't it enough for me to be pestered with the detestable attentions of this wretch in a public place, that his vile missives must pursue me even into the retirements of my papa's dwelling? Have I deserved this indifference which you, sir, are pleased to show in a matter of such singular moment to me?"

"There, there, Miss Sylvy," says my dear papa, patting my neck in the kindest manner imaginable, while I sobbed like a fool; "don't cry, for you shan't be rallied any more. Don't my girl trust her papa? Sure the Captain and I are both itching to have our swords at the fellow's throat, but we had the same thought of making little of the matter for fear it might alarm Miss and prey upon her spirits. But since she accuses us of indifference, why, she shall know all that we do, and spur us on when our eagerness seems to her to flag. You say your iya knew nothing of this charming billet?"

"So she tells me, sir—oh, pray forgive my undutiful words."

"Tut, tut, miss! I like your spirit. 'Tis well to see a young woman nice about what touches her honour. You're your papa's own girl. And now come, we'll examine the household. Call the servants together, *consummer*."

The butler, who had been summoned by Mr Freyne's clapping his hands, went about his task in no small surprise, and presently had all the servants ranged before us, the upper in the varanda, and the lower remaining modestly in the compound. When they were all assembled, Mr Freyne held up the letter, folded as it had been at first, and asked each in turn whether he or she had laid it upon the Chuta Beebee's dressing-table. Each of them denied it, whereupon my papa offered a reward of ten rupees to any one that could tell how it had got there—an offer that excited the liveliest eagerness, but brought no result. Next Mr Freyne asked what strangers had visited the house to-day, and while the servants were reckoning up beggars and pedlars and messengers bringing chitts, Marianna stepped suddenly to the front.

"Me know, sir!" she cried. "Mother of Cosmetiques here, two—tree hours ago, bring washes and essences for Burra Beebee. She bad old woman, often carry messages for gentlemen; pass Missy's door as she go along varanda, put her hand in, put letter on table, no one see her."

"Upon my word, I han't a doubt but the wench is right!" cried my papa. "The Mother of Cosmetiques here, indeed, and after what we had heard before! Who has ventured to bring her to the house, I should be pleased to know?"

"There's no difficulty about that, sir," says Mrs Freyne, who had come from her dressing-room to see what all this assembly was about. "If you choose to bring out a daughter from home with a pair of red cheeks that make all Calcutta look faded, sure you can't wonder that we poor matrons do what we can to hold our own."

"Here, iya," says my papa to Marianna, "here's five rupees for you, and you shall have the other five if we can convict the hag. You can go now, and all the whole parcel of you. Pray, madam," he turned to Mrs Freyne, "do I understand you to say you're in the habit of employing this female?"

"Why, sir, I heard you talking about her with Miss and the Captain, and when I was at the President's yesterday I asked some of the ladies who she might be. Mrs Mapletoft was so obliging as to favour me with her direction, and I lost no time in engaging her services."

"Why, no indeed, madam, not even when you knew she was embarked on a plot against my daughter's reputation. But you may take my word for it that you've employed her for the first and last time."

"Indeed, Mr Freyne, we shall see about that. The woman's an excellent worthy creature, and I won't have her persecuted. You'll find that she's too useful to all the ladies here for 'em to permit you to drive her out of the place because she has had the misfortune to oblige me."

"We shall see, madam," says Mr Freyne again, and shouts to the servants for his hat.

"Captain, the favour of your hand to the palanqueen, if you please," said Mrs Freyne. "I presume you don't design to go out to-night, miss, as you en't dressed, so I won't wait for you."

And she departed, while Captain Colquhoun and my papa went off together on foot, but not without arming two of the peons with swords and shields, and bidding 'em keep guard in front of the house, to quiet my apprehensions. The time passed without alarm, save in your Sylvia's foolish bosom, as she divided her attention between scribbling a few words to her Amelia and listening fearfully to every chance sound. The gentlemen returned late, and not in the best of humours, though they had gone straight to Mr Holwell, and obtaining an order from him, had entered the old woman's abode and found her at home. She made no difficulty about confessing that she had placed the billet on my table, but professed herself unable to say from whom she had received it. 'Twas a tall European gentleman, speaking the Moors language, she declared, but she should never know him again, for all Europeans are alike. (So the Indians say, Amelia, which is very odd to us, since we find it next to impossible to distinguish one of themselves from another.) Leaving a guard over the woman's house, Mr Freyne and the Captain went to Mr Drake, and were very urgent with him to expel her from the bounds of the settlement at once. But (said my papa) the President, retiring for a moment in the course of the discussion, must have sought and received counsel from Mrs Drake, for he came back to say that he understood the female to be a useful adviser in cases of sickness, and not to be dispensed with by the ladies of the factory, so that he would content himself on this occasion with cautioning her, and promising that in case of repeating her offence she should be drove out of our bounds with ignominy. And this it was that had vexed the two gentlemen, as well it might, to find themselves mocked by a wicked person and his degraded instrument. But your Sylvia, the unhappy cause of all this pother, welcomed their return with delight, her mind having devised a new terror for itself in their absence.

"Do you think it possible, dear sir," I said to my papa, "that this wicked man can be the Nabob himself?"

"What, and speak French like a Frenchman, and pass for a European?" cried Mr Freyne. "No, miss, I don't. By all we hear, Surajah Dowlah is black for a Moor, and speaks no civilised language. But what then?"

"Only this, sir, that—that if this person should unhappily possess the power to carry out the cruel threats he utters in this letter, I thought—it might—might be my duty——"

"To oblige him?" cried Mr Freyne, with a strong word. "Sure the fellow has gauged your constitution monstrous skilfully, miss."

"Oh pray, dear sir, don't wrong your girl so far as to think such a measure would be agreeable to her. But to save the entire factory——"

"The entire factory may go hang before my girl saves it in any such style, and there's an end of the matter!" cried my papa.

"Sure you're no Roman papa, dear sir, or you would instantly sacrifice your daughter for the good of the State."

"No, miss, I en't a Roman papa, nor an Agamemnon neither, to sacrifice my daughter for any cause, whether on account of my own fault (though the Captain do always cast it in my teeth) or of the State's."

"Indeed, sir," says Captain Colquhoun, "I'm in the fullest accordance with you here. Miss don't perceive that this is the wretch's artfullest touch, to endeavour to lure her away by the hope of benefiting the Presidency, knowing that this will be to ruin her through the finest motions of her nature. 'Tis a flattering testimony to you, madam, though it speaks little for the fellow that uses it. As to his power to carry out his menaces, I don't think it need alarm you. He would scarce brag of it if he meant to use it."

"But, sir," I said, "suppose he have the power, and do use it. What will you think of me then?"

"Why, that like another Helen, you've fired another Troy," says my papa, quoting from one of the songs in the cantata sung at the Harmonic Society last night; "and, like the Trojan elders, we shall esteem you the more because we have suffered so much through you."

CALCUTTA, *April ye 21st.*

My troubles en't by no means ended yet, Amelia, although the dreadful Unknown has so far left me in peace since his billet of last Saturday. 'Tis his prophecy uttered at the Masquerade that now threatens to prove true. Passing through the parlour this afternoon, on my way to the varanda, I found my papa and Mrs Freyne there together—a thing unusual at any time, and particularly at that hour of the day, when Mrs Freyne is wont to retire to her chamber in order to fit herself by a second period of rest for the gaieties of the evening. That's a pert remark for me to make, en't it, my dear? I know my Amelia will say so. Questionless 'tis made because I can't find it possible to sleep for two entire hours both before and after dinner, and therefore am jealous of one that can. But oh, my dear Miss Turnor, I wish I knew why my stepmother dislikes me so terribly. Perhaps you'll tell me that 'tis because I am not so complaisant towards her as I ought to be. But indeed I do all I can to oblige her, though I must confess I don't feel towards her as I should wish to be able to do. "See there!" you'll say, "you wonder that Mrs Freyne should dislike you when she sees you dislike her." True, my dear, but I was prepared when I came here to exhibit the greatest complaisance imaginable, while she (I must say it) did not even feign the slightest sentiment of kindness towards me. There, Amelia! your Sylvia is a saucy ill-mannered creature, passing judgments that don't become her on her elders and betters, and accusing them of misusing her instead of bewailing her own failures in duty towards them. But indeed my mamma has done me an ill-turn this afternoon, as you shall hear.

"You'll oblige me by telling me what you have against him, sir," she was saying, when I came into the room. "I understand he's a nobleman in his own country."

"That's very likely, madam. I have known several noblemen of that sort."

"I'm sure he has money enough," says Mrs Freyne, angrily.

"True, madam; too much. I should be glad to know how he gets it."

"By honest trading, sir, of course. I wonder at your remark."

"No interloper could make by honest trading in these days the fortune Mr Menotti boasts of," says my papa. I jumped when I heard the name.

"I see it en't no good my taking the poor man's part, sir. You have conceived a spite against him."

"You do me too much honour, madam. I'll refer the question to the party it concerns most deeply. Here, miss, your mamma is pressing me to marry you to Mr Menotti. Will you have him?"

"No, sir, I thank you," said I, with a curtsey.

"Then that settles the matter. My girl will never find me forcing her inclination when it jumps with my own," and Mr Freyne laughed as he patted my neck. The laugh seemed to displease my stepmother.

"Perhaps you en't aware of it, sir," she said, "but you'll be charmed to know you are the laughing-stock of Calcutta for your usage of Miss there. They say she turns you round her little finger."

"She could not turn me round a prettier nor a smaller one, madam."

"Oh, pray spare me these endearments, sir, which befit your age as little as they do your relation to Miss. You won't listen to me now, but perhaps some day you'll think of what I have said. Why don't the girl get married all this time? The gentlemen come crowding to you, and you give 'em their *congé* one by one, and Miss Saucy-face sits in the corner and simpers. She'll disgrace you one of these days running off with some blackfellow or other."

"Pray, madam, remember you're speaking of my daughter."

"Am I likely to forget it, sir? Mr Freyne is so nice about his daughter that no one may use a free word in speaking of her, but his wedded wife might look far enough for his assistance if she desired it."

"My sword is at your service, madam—whether to vindicate your honour or my own." I had never heard my papa speak with so terrible a voice, and he stood before Mrs Freyne's couch and looked down at her. She laughed lightly—but was it my fancy that it was also consciously?—as she rose and swept away.

"I won't forget your obliging offer, sir, I'll assure you; but I have a notion your sword may be needed first in a quarter more interesting to yourself. Do you know what all Calcutta is saying about your dear Miss, and the reason why she don't marry? Because she don't dare. She's married secretly already, to some fellow she met on her voyage, by a Popish priest somewhere or other, and she has persuaded you that it's owing to her extraordinary delicacy she can't find any one in Bengall good enough for her."

"Indeed, madam, your liberality is too great. Not content with robbing my daughter of her reputation—for your own benefit, I suppose—you make me a present of a son in law, all in one day."

Mrs Freyne laughed again as she stepped out on the varanda. My papa watched her out of sight, then turned to me with a frowning brow—

"Is this true, miss?"

"Oh, dear sir, can you believe such a thing of your girl?"

"No prevarication, miss. Give me an honest yes or no."

"Why, no, sir. There's no truth in it."

"Will you swear it, miss?"

"On my honour, sir."

"No, miss, that won't do. Sure I can't accept an oath by the very thing that's in dispute."

"By your honour, then, sir, which is as dear to me as to yourself, and which will be stainless indeed if it receive no more disgrace than I have done it in the past." I sobbed out this upon my knees, for my papa's words cut me to the heart. At any other moment he would have sought industriously to comfort me, but now he was walking up and down the chamber with his brows knit and muttering to himself. Presently I could bear it no longer, and throwing myself in his way, catched his feet. "Oh, sir," I cried, "don't condemn your girl unheard. What have you ever found in her to justify you in believing she would deceive you? Ask me any question you choose, dear sir, and I'll answer it on my knees. I have had many things to trouble me of late, but my papa's countenance has helped me to endure them. If he forsakes me, what refuge have I but death?"

"Don't talk of things you know nothing about, miss. I do accept your word, and it's well for you I have no cause to do otherwise. But all Calcutta don't know you as I do, and what's to be done to convince 'em? The tale fits only too well with your constant refusal to marry. Why han't you married, miss? You have had chances enough. I believe there en't a man of suitable degree in the place but has laid himself at your feet. Pray, what are you waiting for—the Grand Turk or the Great Mogul? I can tell you this, you'll marry the first honest man that asks you after to-day, and no more pother about it, by——"

"Oh, dear sir, don't swear it!" I cried, and ventured to cling to his upraised arm. "Pray think that the wicked person who spread this slander may have anticipated this very resolve of yours, and counted on benefiting by it, and so you may hand me over to the most dreadful tyranny. Won't my papa pity his girl at all?"

"If I was a person of sense," says my papa, angrily, "I should refuse to be moved by that pert tongue of yours, miss, but I can't hear my Sally's girl pleading and remain unmoved. But Miss Sylvia Freyne may be sure of this, that I'll find her a husband before another week is out."

CALCUTTA, *April ye 27th.*

Oh, my dear, the husband has been found, and who do you think he is? But I'll tell you the tale as it happened.

"What do you think of Captain Colquhoun, miss?" says my papa to me, as we were taking the air in the garden before breakfast this morning.

"Think of him, sir? Why, what could I think but that he's a vastly agreeable and respectable person, and my papa's most esteemed friend?"

"I'm charmed that your opinion's so favourable, miss. The Captain is coming to see you this morning."

"Coming—to—see—me—sir?"

"Why, yes, miss. He has done you the honour to ask you of me in marriage, and I desire you'll entertain him as your future spouse."

Was I very saucy, Amelia? I did not design to be so, but the words escaped my lips. "But, dear sir, I can't!" I cried.

"And why not, miss, pray?"

Now here, Amelia, was your poor Sylvia in a pretty confusion. Why not, indeed? Even to myself I could not produce any reasons; I could only feel them.

"Sure it's impossible, sir. I never dreamt—— The gentleman is surely a sworn bachelor. I esteem him most highly, I'll assure you, but any closer tie—— Dear sir, the Captain's age, his—his wisdom—he could never put up with an ignorant girl like me. Pray, sir——"

I could say no more, and my papa regarded me sternly.

"This charming prudishness won't weigh with me, miss. I believe I have indulged you excessively, allowing you the whole of the cold weather to make your choice. I vow I never looked to keep you longer than a month, and I wish heartily I hadn't done it. No, miss; this season of reigning as a queen, and holding all Calcutta in suspense, and setting all the young gentlemen at enmity, has lasted too long, and you may thank me for ending it before you find yourself excelled by the young ladies arriving this year from home. Not that you shall have the chance of calling me unreasonable. If there's any gentleman in Calcutta that you would honestly prefer to the Captain as a spouse, name him, and I'll set on foot a treaty with him at once."

"Dear sir, there en't one. But won't you permit your girl——"

"No, miss, I won't." I could see by my papa's face that he was hardening his heart against me. "I won't have it said that my foolish desire to have your company at home has led me to spoil your chances of marrying. And what's more, the injurious things that are being said about you demand that you should be married as soon as possible as their best contradiction. Why, it fell to me to-day to reprove a young fool of a writer, who had bribed a Popish priest to marry him to a country-born wench in the Portuguese quarter; and pointing out to him that his proceedings showed he was ashamed of what he was doing, or he would have sought to get married in the church by the Padra like an honest man, he told me that he was not alone in preferring a private wedding, for there was one of my own family that was commonly reported to have done the same. What do you make of that, miss?"

"Oh, sir——" I sobbed, and stopped. "Will he say this everywhere?"

"I think not," said my papa, very grim. "I promised to cane him round the town if he did not instantly unsay his words, or if he ever repeated 'em, and he saw his error, and begged my pardon. But what he says, others are saying, and I don't choose they should say it of my daughter. You may be as whimsical and as humoursome as you like, miss, and play off all your pretty airs and graces on me, but it won't do you no good, nor advantage you one whit. I am acting for your good, and you know it; and I don't despair that one day you'll have the grace to thank me for it, when you judge that your punctilio has been satisfied by the proper amount of sulking."

He made as though to leave me; but 'twas my last chance, and I could not see it slip away. Springing after him, I was bold enough to seize his arm. "Dear sir," I said, "you have forbid me to plead for your girl, and she perceives she need expect no softness from her papa. But think at least of your friend. Is it acting a friendly part by him to seek to force into his arms an unwilling bride? That's all I ask you."

"But why should the bride be unwilling?" cried Mr Freyne, turning upon me angrily. "I offer her the whole of Calcutta from which to choose, and she's still unwilling. There must be some limit even to a lady's reluctance. Perhaps the cause lies outside Calcutta—hey, miss? Perhaps you'll be so obliging as to tell me exactly what there is between you and the sea-officer, the Captain's cousin, or perhaps you're held back by an oath?"

"Why, no, sir, for there's nothing to swear about. There's nothing whatever between your daughter and Lieutenant Fraser."

"Not so much as a promise? I had your word for it that there was no marriage."

"Not even a promise, sir. I don't deny that the gentleman came desiring to obtain one from me, but we parted in anger."

My papa looked at me with a suspicion that convinced me I owed this strange harshness of his to some fresh tale of Mrs Freyne's. (Don't scold me, Amelia. Can you say that she don't seek to separate my father and me by means of tales?) "And you wish the young gentleman fetched back, miss?"

"Why, no, sir, certainly not," my cheeks aflame at the very thought.

"Then you would prefer to wait in case it might please him to come back, and so find you meekly ready for his arrival?"

"I don't think your girl has merited these sarcasms, sir."

"Then show it by marrying the Captain, miss."

"If you command me to marry the Captain, sir, I will obey you."

"No, miss, I don't command you. I won't give you that excuse for saying you was forced into a marriage by your father's tyranny. You know that it's my strong desire that you should marry the Captain, and as you have always shown yourself a dutiful daughter until now, I expect that desire to prevail with you in the absence of any weighty reason that might make your compliance wrong. If there be any such reason, I'll hear it with patience. If not, I look to you to justify the consideration I have extended to you in the past by your behaviour now."

"I'll do my best to satisfy you, sir," I said, sighing. For oh, my dear girl, who could continue to resist when urged in such a manner by such a father? Had the parents of the noble Clarissa treated her with so reasonable a kindness (for I know my papa is only cruel to be kind), sure she must have succumbed to their softness where she was firm against their invective. But perhaps you won't agree with me. Then, Amelia, be very sure your Sylvia en't a Clarissa. But then, neither is Captain Colquhoun a Solmes. He's all that is excellent—his only fault that he is not Fraser. And indeed, my dear, that's as well, for I should be sorry to think there was two men like the lieutenant in the world. There's a double meaning here, you'll say? Why, so there is. I will stop.

I take up my pen again at night. During breakfast my papa preserved the same unbending sternness towards me, so that I could scarcely eat, and was like to choke more than once. The only person at their ease was Mrs

Freyne, who talked and laughed with the most charming sprightliness. When the meal was over, and your unhappy Sylvia was creeping away to her own chamber, Mrs Freyne called to me as I passed her door.

"So I hear you've added another to the list of your conquests, miss. 'Tis a little hard on the poor gentleman to have to pay so dear for merely taking up your defence in public, en't it?"

"Sure, madam, you're better informed than I."

"Why," says she, "it seems that after mess yesterday, when the gentlemen had perhaps drunk somewhat freely, your name was mentioned among 'em, and the story which is in the mouths of all Calcutta not obscurely hinted at. Up darts Captain Colquhoun, and calls on the speaker ('twas young Waring, I fancy they told me) to withdraw his words, which he had the best authority for knowing were altogether false. The young gentleman demands with great spirit what right the Captain had to interfere in the matter, to which he replied, quick as lightning, that his right was that of a suitor for the lady's hand. On this Waring offers his apologies, and the matter drops; but coming to your papa's ears, he jumps at the notion, and forces the Captain to turn his expedient into a reality."

"I'm sure, madam, I am prodigious grateful to you for telling me this," I said, as I went on my way. And indeed, Amelia, the history comforted me not a little, for if not the Captain's heart, but only his politeness, was engaged, it should not, surely, be impossible to turn him aside from his object. Hence, when Marianna came to tell me that Captain Colquhoun was waiting for me in the saloon, I put a bold face on the matter, and having dried my eyes and settled my cap, walked into the apartment with as easy an air as I could assume, though my heart was thumping as if it would burst.

"Madam, your most obedient!" said he, with his stiff bow.

"Sir, you're very welcome," said I, as well as my trembling lips would allow me.

"Dearest madam, why this agitation?" said the kind gentleman, as he took my hand to lead me to a seat, and found it cold and shaking. "I hope I han't incommoded Miss Freyne by so early a visit?"

"Indeed, sir, I had rather you came early," I said, for I don't know how I had lived the day through in anticipation of his coming.

"Questionless, madam, my good friend Mr Freyne has informed you of my object in waiting upon you this morning?"

"He has told me of the honour, sir—" I could not get out another word.

"And may I venture to hope that Miss Freyne shares in the kind opinion expressed by her papa?"

I saw my chance, Amelia, and rushed at it. "Dear sir," I burst out, all in a flurry, "it's been told me that you're paying me these addresses out of a notion of honour, feeling yourself bound by a declaration you made in public yesterday. I can't be too grateful for your defence of me, but it would give me infinite pain to think that you held it necessary to carry the matter any further."

"Even though it gave me infinite pleasure, madam? Has my dear Miss Freyne never guessed that she had another humble servant besides the young sparks that flutter about her so gaily? Ah, madam, they see you only in company, outshining, it's true, every other lady present, yet still one amongst many; but you have permitted me to behold you continually in the softer and more endearing character of a daughter in her father's house, and the repeated sight has graven upon my heart an impression too deep to be effaced. Does Miss Freyne grudge having lost the triumph of enrolling a new admirer? I know her tender spirit would not seek to gratify itself with the spectacle of the distress of another hopeless lover, and that I have been since first I perceived my case. But the event of yesterday gave me fresh food for thought. When I had silenced the slanderer by the revelation of a passion of which no one had dreamt, the notion came to me, 'What if this amiable lady would be willing to accept the devotion her Colquhoun would so gladly offer her? A genteel abode, a respectable competence, the protection of a husband, and all else that could be done or given by a man who would lay down his life to oblige her, would be at her service.' Pray, madam," for I had strove to speak, "hear me out. You don't need to remind me that I am old, and scarred with long years of war both in Europe and the Carnatic—I know it too well. But, on my honour, I don't think you would find me an unkind spouse. I would never seek to deprive you of the diversions natural to your sex and age; on the contrary, I would feel honoured in attending you to 'em. The desire for knowledge, which displays the ingenious bent of your mind, I would do my best to gratify. Your heart, as I know well, I can't aspire to possess, but if respect and complaisance could win it, even that treasure would be mine—in short, if Miss Freyne could tolerate me as a spouse, it should go hard with me if she were not happy, or at least contented in her lot."

"Oh, dear sir," I cried out, "cease these too kind remarks before I am crushed to the dust under such a load of obligation. Every word you have spoken has planted a dagger in my heart. I entered this room almost resolved, as I had promised my papa, to accept your proposals, but now I can't do it, when I see that your heart's engaged in the matter, without telling you the truth. My heart is given to another. If I could have recalled it, the thing had long been done, but I can't, and there the matter lies."

"Is the gentleman alive, madam?"

"Oh yes, sir; but we have quarrelled."

"I need not ask, madam, on whose side the fault lay."

"Indeed, sir, he has used me cruelly, though I would tell this to no one but you."

"Could you oblige me with this person's name, madam?"

"Oh no, sir!" I went cold all in a moment at the thought that the Captain might seek out Mr Fraser and fight him, perhaps kill him. "I was over hasty. The blame was certainly in great part mine. The gentleman sought to test my sentiments for him by means of a fantastic device out of a novel, and I, not knowing his expedient, believed him false to me. Then, when next we met, he failed to express the contrition I fancied was called for, and I stood upon my punctilio, and refused to forgive him without it, whereupon he went away in a rage. You see that I am at least as much to blame as he."

"No, madam; I see that the puppy has a stouter defender than he deserves, that's all. But pardon my speaking so of one dear to Miss Freyne. You anticipate that this person will return to you?"

"No, sir, I have not the slightest cause for thinking so. My reason for mentioning the matter at all was a desire to deal fairly by you. I esteem you as the best person in the world, next to my papa, and with Heaven's help I'll do my best to make you a dutiful and, I hope, an obliging wife, but I can't delude you into believing that Sylvia Freyne has still a heart to be won."

"Do you know, madam, that you are placing me in a most cruel situation?"

"Dear sir, forgive me. I am a sad selfish creature, I fear."

"My own heart, madam, would prompt me at once to leave you free, but such a course would only expose you the more to the tongues of the injurious busy-bodies of this place, as would your rejection of my proposals."

"But I han't rejected 'em, sir."

"To accept them, madam, would be even more dreadful. Suppose this person, of whom you have told me, should in time repent of his behaviour, and return to find you married? I am not, I hope, a jealous man, I believe in your virtue beyond all possibility of doubt, but how should I feel to see two young persons, well qualified to make each other happy, condemned to an eternal separation, and all through me? The higher the virtue they displayed the more poignant would be my sufferings. What man of honour could endure such a situation with contentment, even with complacence?"

"Dear sir, you torture me. Tell me what to do, and I'll obey you."

"Why, madam, I don't know myself. I will go back to my quarters and think the matter over, not forgetting to seek guidance where alone it is to be found, as I trust Miss Freyne will do also, and if I see a way out of the trouble I will wait upon you again this evening. Trust me, madam, you shan't be forced into so repugnant an alliance if I can save you."

I cried out against his words, but he was gone.

CHAPTER IX.
TREATING OF LOVERS AND FRIENDS.

CALCUTTA, *April ye* 28*th*.

To continue the history, in which I know my dearest Amelia is most painfully interested, I returned to my own chamber after the Captain's departure, and did my best to comply with his desire, though with little faith, I fear, in the possibility of obtaining an answer to my prayers. For indeed, Amelia, what plan could be devised whereby might be satisfied not only my papa's punctilio and Captain Colquhoun's honour, but also the prying eagerness of the scandal-mongers of this place? I told myself that there could be none, and endeavoured to bring my mind into a state of resignation—a task that was rendered far harder by the recollections of Mr Fraser that had persisted in forcing themselves upon me all morning. For this is the worst of my misfortunes, that I can't fail to perceive in the Captain a nobler spirit and a more obliging disposition than in Fraser, and yet (a plague on Sylvia Freyne's perversity!) I love the meaner man and not the greater. I scolded myself for this preference. I sought to reason myself out of it, but all in vain, for the whole time I knew that if by some miracle Fraser should return at that very hour, and declare his repentance by the smallest word, or even with a look—aye, perhaps without even that—I should forgive him and love him, not better, that were impossible, but with a far more respectful affection than before. I am fully sensible that many writers, and in especial the ingenious Mr Richardson, would counsel me that 'twas my duty to resist a wilful passion of this sort, and endeavour to uproot it, and I should have hoped to do so, had time been allowed me. 'Tis the entering on new and all-important duties with a mind thus preoccupied that I dread, for fear lest, after all, my efforts should fail. "You can but try," says everybody; but, my dear, it seems to me an extraordinary grave thing to make this sort of experiment, as I may say, in our lives, whereof we have but one apiece, whether to be gained or lost. For if we lose, what then, Amelia?

Spending my morning in reflections of this sort, my dearest girl will readily guess that when the hour for tiffing arrived I was in no state to make a public appearance. Sending Marianna to beg Mrs Freyne to excuse me from attending her at the meal, I turned over on my couch, and sought to cool my hot face with Hungary water. While thus occupied, in comes my papa.

"What, miss, sullen?" he said angrily, seeing me all in a heap on the couch, with my hair about my face and my cap awry.

"Indeed, indeed, sir," I cried, rising from the couch and falling on my knees before him, "I am trying to mould my mind to your will, believe me. Only remember how your goodness has always indulged your girl in the past, and you'll perceive how difficult she finds it to accommodate her behaviour to your present awful severity. Pray, sir, don't think I regard it as ill deserved—I believe I know my faults—but bear with me for to-day, I beg of you."

"You're a strange unaccountable hussy," says my papa, but not so harshly. "What do you want, miss, I should like to know? Well, cry your eyes out to-day, if you will have it so, but mind, no sulking to-morrow, on pain of my gravest displeasure."

I heard him sigh impatiently as he went away, and (undutiful wretch! you'll say) the sound rejoiced me, for I knew that whatever my stepmother's arts had been, they had not availed to estrange my papa's heart from his girl. My next visitor was Mrs Freyne herself, who came creeping in, with her finger to her lip, after my papa was gone back to his *dufter-conna.*

"So you're to marry the Captain, miss?" she said in a half-whisper; "I hope you're pleased with the prospect?"

I could not think of any answer to make, and she went on, "Now, miss, I know you've often taken it vastly unkind in me that I've chanced to disoblige you now and then, but I'll assure you I en't really ill-natured. I won't see you drove into a distasteful marriage without offering you a hope of escape. What do you say to marrying a rich and handsome young gentleman that's dying for you, instead of your solemn-faced, miserly old Scotchman?"

"Who's the gentleman, if you please, madam?"

"As though you needed to ask! 'Tis Menotti, of course, with the most elegant residence and keeping the best company in Calcutta. Come, miss, a chitt from me will bring him here in ten minutes, and Padra Mapletoft with him, and you shall be married quietly in your chamber, with no fuss or confusion. Then you can go home with him at once if you please, or if you choose still to play the prude and torment the poor man, he'll be content not to claim you until you're reconciled to the notion. Here's pen and ink, I see—shall I write?"

Now it may appear strange to my Amelia, but this proposition of Mrs Freyne's went far to reconcile me to quite another notion than hers. 'Twas possible, then, to meet a worse fate than to be compelled to marry an excellent good man that one did not love—even to lay oneself under an eternal obligation of the same nature to a wicked person that one hated.

"I thank you, madam," I said, "but if I must marry one or other of the gentlemen, I'll choose the Captain."

"Then you're a fool," says she, "to choose a poor beggarly captain of Company's troops, with whom you may be grateful if you get a silk gown once in ten years, in preference to one that will load you with the finest jewels and richest stuffs that can be had. I wonder, miss, where the obliging disposition is, with which the gentlemen all credit you, when you can doom to despair an adorer that has worshipped you so long with the utmost devotion, and for no reason at all?"

"Indeed, madam, I have my reasons. Mr Menotti's manner of life, his free language even in the company of ladies, and the indifferent esteem in which he is held by persons of honour, are sufficient reason for me."

"Well," says Mrs Freyne, as she left the room, "if you'll do me the favour to look at yourself in the glass, miss, I think you'll say that if Mr Menotti saw you now, your looks would be a sufficient reason for his not marrying you."

"Ah," I thought, "I see now why Mr Freyne has been urged on to force me into marrying the Captain, and why I have been sought to be privately dissuaded from the match. The Unknown was a true prophet."

Now this slight encounter with Mrs Freyne proved a huge refreshment to me, so that I rose and summoned Marianna to dress my hair and help me change my gown. And, indeed, it was well that I did so, for before dinner, while it was still the heat of the day, I was told that Captain Colquhoun was again awaiting me in the saloon. I sought in vain to read his face when I entered the room, but as he led me to a seat I observed that he had a letter in his hand, which he presently opened, showing me that it had another enclosed in it.

"This pacquet," madam, he said, "I found lying at my quarters when I returned from attending you this morning. I have brought it here because I fancied Miss Freyne might be able to help me respecting its contents."

"Indeed, sir, I hope you'll command me," I said, out of measure astonished at such a sudden change of address.

"It comes," he said, "from my cousin, the young gentleman that was staying with me a fortnight or so back. He begs me to deliver the enclosure to a lady of whom he is enamoured, and whom—so far as I can make out—he offended grievously before his departure, but he don't mention the lady's name. 'Tis a wild fantastical piece of writing, but he appears to consider I would know his mistress. Yesterday I would have returned him the paper, having no notion who the divinity might be, but this day has taught me more things than one. Have you any knowledge of the lady, madam?"

"Oh, sir," all impatience, "pray, pray give it me." The Captain laid the letter in my hand, but I delayed to open it, partly through a real misgiving, partly through a foolish readiness to tease myself by postponing my happiness. "It en't directed to me, sir."

"If you think it en't designed for you, madam, pray hand it back to me with the seal unbroken," says the Captain, in a severe voice of rebuke; but that I could not do. The horrid doubt that I might find the letter wrote after all to some other lady made my hands shake as I tore it open, but then I cried out with joy. Oh, the dear, blessed words, Amelia! fantastical, if you will (sure poor Fraser must have gathered 'em from a novel, as he did that unlucky expedient of his), but for all that the sweetest, the most charming that ever assured the fearful heart of a poor creature that had sad cause to mistrust her lover. I copy them for my dear friend:—

"To the incomparable Mrs SYLVIA FREYNE.

"If, madam, you deign to permit your eyes to rest upon the lines which the wretch who now addresses himself to you has dared to trace, it may perhaps serve to mitigate your just resentments when you learn that ever since he parted from you he has been a prey to the pangs of that remorse and contrition which is properly his lot. 'Tis true, he quitted your presence with an air of hardihood and bravado, as tho' he had the effrontery to believe that he might remain unscathed by those arrows which had been planted in his guilty heart by your reproof of him, and this tho' the wounds they caused (which have never ceased to throb and smart) were even then beginning to fester. The suffering wretch has no art to alleviate his pains, and in his despair he throws himself at the feet of the righteously offended charmer, to ask whether she who inflicted the hurts will be so divinely obliging as to chase 'em away. That the punishment is merited he dares not deny (yet not with such an affectation of humility as might seem to seek to disarm the just wrath of the lady to whom he applies himself), but will Miss Freyne's tender heart permit her to use her suppliant as the savages of the Virginias their enemies—viz., to set 'em up and shoot arrows into them, and leave them to expire in their agony? Since quitting Calcutta, the miserable object of her displeasure has failed to enjoy a moment of ease from the torment of these cruel barbs in his vitals, and now, his vessel being forced by the stress of a storm to seek shelter in the port of Vizagapatnam, he gazes across the raging billows in the direction of the city that holds his mistress, and longs for the power of throwing himself in reality at her feet, where he might demand pardon too urgently to be withstood, and receive the assurance of his felicity from the kindest lips in the world. But honour draws him back to Madrass, for his orders were strict against lingering on the road, and the lady he ventures to adore would be the last to desire to lure him away from his duty. Won't the amiable Sylvia grant her Fraser a word of kindness, whether traced by her own fair hand, or confided to the mediation of his kinsman, that may salve his wounds and send him victorious to fight his nation's battles?

"*P.S.*—Dearest madam, I love you with all my heart and better than my life. Forgive my unlucky trickery, and also my cursed rudeness, and rejoice your most humble and devoted servant,

C. FRASER."

My happy tears fell fast (indeed I could not restrain 'em), on this charming, charming post-scriptum. "Oh, sir," I cried to the Captain, "how shall I ever thank you for handing me this dear, this affecting letter?" But no sooner were the words out of my mouth (as they say) than I remembered, what my foolish ecstasy had made me forget, the present posture of my affairs. "Dear sir," I said, "pray forgive me. What must you think of me?"

"Nay, madam," was the Captain's reply, "'tis of my cousin Fraser I am thinking. Sure the lad should have been named Jacob, and not Colvin, for he and his have supplanted me these two times."

"Oh, sir," I said, "you do me wrong, and your cousin also. See," and I made as though to tear up Mr Fraser's letter, but could not bring myself to do it, and only crushed it in my hand, "this late though happy repentance on his part can make no difference to the engagement into which I entered with you this morning. My dear Captain Colquhoun won't grudge me, I'm sure, the happiness of knowing that I had misjudged one so nearly related to him, but that pleasure is in itself sufficient. I am yours, sir, and it shall be my constant effort, I'll assure you, that what you have just witnessed shall never be recalled to your mind."

"Nay, madam," said he again, with what Charlotte and I have been used to call his wooden smile (oh, my dear, how the memory of our pert jests concerning the noblest of men shames me now!) "when Jacob hath gained both the birthright and the promise, what remains for poor Esau but to flee into the wilderness from the face of his brother?"

"Dear sir, what do you purpose doing?" I cried in great alarm.

"Nothing that need terrify you, madam; merely to withdraw my pretensions in favour of him who has the best right to your hand, since for him your heart goes with it, and to endeavour to find my happiness in that of the lady I most admire and of the man who must needs be worthy since Miss Freyne prefers him to so high a place in her esteem."

"Sure, dear sir, you must be a philosopher?"

"I am more concerned to be a Christian, madam. But," seeing that I was much abashed, "don't let my sour humour put Miss Freyne out of countenance. Be assured, madam, that when I leave you 'twill be to set my wits at work to devise a means of escape from this situation that shall satisfy both Mr Freyne's punctilio and yours, and if I find a chance to throw in a good word for your Fraser, it shan't be lost."

"Oh, sir, dear sir, if there was anything I could do!"

"There's nothing, madam. Miss Freyne's kind heart must not concern itself with the old man's misfortunes. 'Serves the old fool right for falling in love at his age!' the world will say, but Alexander Colquhoun himself thinks no shame of it, and he is tough enough to bear the consequences without whimpering. Nay, madam, I protest you honour me too much——"

For when he stooped to kiss my hand, I had seized his and kissed it instead. And, indeed, Amelia, even now that I am cool, I will defend my hasty action to you or any other person. Would not you have been proud to kiss the hand of Sir Charles Grandison? and though you may smile to think that I should have discovered the features of that great and good man in a poor captain of Company's troops, yet I defy you to produce any person of this age whose disposition will more nearly approach that of Mr Richardson's noblest and most elevated character.

As I returned to my own chamber a little later, I met my papa.

"Well, miss, and where's the Captain?" he asked me.

"I believe he's gone back to his quarters, sir."

"And what's settled, hey?"

"I think the Captain will wait upon you to-morrow morning, sir."

"Pray, miss, why don't you answer my question? Is all right between you and the Captain?"

"I—I don't know, sir," and I burst into tears, which displeased my papa so much that he ordered me to go to my chamber, and not to show myself in his sight for the rest of the day.

The remainder of the afternoon I spent in scribbling these pages to my Amelia, until my eyes ached so badly I could write no more, and also (I'll confess it) in reading again and again the dear delightful letter that assured me of Fraser's penitence and faithfulness. My beloved girl will wonder that I could take so much pleasure in that which had so sadly disobliged the dear kind gentleman I had seen so lately, and indeed I was ashamed of my own delight, and astonished at it. I put the letter in my bosom at last, and crept like a mouse into the saloon, which was not lighted, since Mrs Freyne was spending the evening abroad. But outside in the varanda sat my papa, meditating, I fear, on the humours of his troublesome girl, and though he had forbid me his presence I could not endure not to be near him. Seated, therefore, on the straw matting (this is used instead of a carpet), close to the open door that leads on the varanda, and sheltered by the *antiporta*, I ventured to watch him, with all the love and reverence in my gaze that ought to, and does, fill my grateful heart on the slightest thought of him. He appeared troubled, and I knew that he felt the want of the Captain's company, who is so often with him of an evening, but before very long Mr Dash was announced, and the two gentlemen sent for their *hookers*[01] (have I said that these are a strange sort of tobacco-pipe, with a vessel of water and a long tube like a serpent and all manner of outlandish additions belonging to 'em?) and began to smoke.

"I looked in at the Captain's quarters as I passed," says Mr Dash after a while, "thinking he would be coming to pass the evening with you, sir."

"And you found him abroad?"

"No, sir, but he was too busy to stir a foot. Questionless that sergeant of his has been in trouble again, and is condemned to pass the night in the black hole for brawling, after smuggling a jar or two of arrack into the guard-room, and the Captain's preparing a new scheme for his reformation."

I knew well what Mr Dash meant, for Captain Colquhoun had often told me of this man, who is an extraordinary good soldier so long as he can resist the influence of strong liquors, and had even requested my opinion on the possibility of depriving him altogether of the indulgence, which in this climate is so often abused; but I did not believe that 'twas this matter which was exercising the Captain's mind this evening. I sat listening while my papa and Mr Dash spoke of the overbearing and threatening carriage of the new Soubah towards us, and wondered whether he would permit himself to be appeased by the genteel congratulatory letter sent him by the President as soon as he was formally proclaimed in Calcutta. My papa made sure that all would be well, since the Nabob had received the letter favourably, and shown no resentment for the injurious treatment of his messenger in the matter of Kissendasseat, but Mr Dash pointed out that Surajah Dowlah had already seized and imprisoned one of his rivals, namely, Gosseta Begum, his uncle's widow, and was commonly reported to be about to march against t'other, his cousin the Purranea Nabob, so that he was destroying his enemies one by one, "and after Sucajunk," says the young gentleman, "our turn will come."

My papa made some jesting answer to the effect that Mr Dash had taken the infection of Captain Colquhoun's apprehensions, and after that I believe I must have fallen asleep where I was crouched, for I woke up with a great start and my heart thumping, to find Mr Dash gone and Mr Menotti shouting on the varanda, while my papa sought to quiet him.

"I tell you, sir," he cried, "I found one of Omy Chund's peons (and I believe 'twas Juggermunt Sing, their Jemmautdar and the biggest rascal of 'em all, but I could not make sure in the darkness) lurking in your grounds, with a billet upon him addressed to Miss."

"Sure the fellow must be the biggest fool of 'em all if he handed the chitt to you, sir, in mistake for Miss," says my papa.

"Sir," says Mr Menotti, with a very haughty air, "I addressed myself to the rogue with authority, demanding what he was doing in such a place."

"Ah, and what did you say the place was, sir, by the bye?"

"Why, sir, the great thicket opposite Miss's window."

"Indeed, sir! and may I ask what you was doing in such a place?"

I thought Mr Menotti seemed confounded for a moment, but he answered quickly, with a monstrous effrontery, "Why, sir, I saw the fellow sneaking into the shadow of the thicket, and thinking I knew his villainous countenance, my concern for your interests induced me to follow him. Recognising me as an acquaintance of his master's, he was so imprudent as to declare his errand, when my regard for Miss's honour at once put me upon getting hold of the letter he carried, which I did by promising to deliver it to the proper person. The wicked wretch had been haunting the spot for hours without being able to have speech of Miss, and being a simple sort of fellow, one of those Sykes[02] from the Mogul's dominions, and not a Gentoo, he was easily persuaded to deliver it up."

"Sir, your concern for my honour and my family's does prodigious credit to the goodness of your heart. Did you dismiss the fellow in peace?"

"Why, no, sir; the billet once in my hands, it was no longer needful to dissemble the fury that possessed me, passing all bounds when I perceived the nature of the vile piece. For seeing that the letter was from the hand of the abandoned deceiver, whose shameless attempts have twice been frustrated by your vigilance, and that it contained a condolence with Miss on the tyranny by which you, sir, was endeavouring to force her into marriage with an elderly suitor, and an invitation to her to meet the writer on that spot at a certain hour this very night, with a view to eloping with him, I fell upon the messenger in my rage, and kicked and cuffed him so soundly that he may be thankful to have escaped with his life."

"Sir, you lay me under an ever-increasing debt of obligation. The Unknown must be but new at his work to send his letter open and unfolded."

"Indeed, sir, it was folded and sealed, but my transports of indignation would not permit me to hand the vile scrawl to Miss."

"Nor to me neither, I suppose, sir? Perhaps, having perused it at your leisure, you'll now pass it on to me."

"Why, sir, I tore it into a thousand pieces and scattered 'em abroad. Would you have it pollute the sight of any but myself?"

"Sir," says my papa, with his most awful air of severity, "I would have you act as a person of honour, if it be in your power. I have such confidence in my daughter that I'm persuaded, had the billet reached her, it would be in my hands at this moment. You have thought fit, not only to open and read, but to destroy, a letter addressed to a lady with whose actions you have not the smallest concern, and by alarming the messenger, to prevent our having any hope of catching his villainous principal in his own trap. You'll oblige me excessively if you'll inform your friend Omy Chund that my gardens en't designed as lurking places for his peons, and you'll double the obligation by taking the same information to heart for the future with regard to yourself. I will wish you a very good evening, sir."

Never, Amelia, have I seen a person look so foolishly confounded as Mr Menotti when my papa bowed him off the varanda, and called to the servants to conduct him to the gate. But oh, my dear, how fearful is this proof that the Unknown has not yet ceased his wicked attempts upon the reputation of your poor friend! Observe how quickly the news of my papa's pressing on me the Captain's suit has reached him (though I might give a guess as to the means, since Marianna tells me that Mrs Freyne's iya Bowanny was despatched to the Mother of Cosmetiques this morning on an errand for some lipsalve), and how promptly the vile wretch acts. My mind is filled with terror by these continual plots against my peace (for what, pray, was Mr Menotti doing in the garden?). The only ray of hope that I can see is the chance that the second vile wretch, desiring to better his position with my papa, may have invented the whole affair. But this hope is destroyed by what I hear this morning (for I have not added a new date, since I desired to keep all the events of yesterday together), that Mr Menotti has quarrelled with his friend Omy Chund, and that the two, each threatening to betray some damaging fact that was come to his knowledge about the other, were with difficulty separated without bloodshed by the bystanders.

April ye 29th.

Rising at my usual hour this morning, I dressed myself very carefully, putting on the carnation-coloured ribbons that are always my papa's favourites, and a gown of printed muslin that he had brought me himself from Dacca. So fearful was I of meeting Mr Freyne, or at least of displeasing him by anything in my carriage or appearance, that I loitered before the mirror, altering a bow here and a knot there, until the bearer (who is as we should say Mr Freyne's gentleman, but black, of course) came to tell Marianna that his master was waiting. Then you will guess, Amelia, how I hurried out, but slackened my haste as I approached my papa, my feet almost refusing to carry me, such was my state of apprehension. What was my relief when Mr Freyne saluted me most kindly and pleasantly, and bade me pour him a dish of tea before it all became cold. My fears were almost vanished under the influence of my dear papa's agreeable conversation, when (the meal being ended and the servants retired) he sent me cold all over with—

"I must make you a compliment on the state of your affairs, miss. What with your modesty and your reserves, you've brought 'em to a pretty pass!"

"Indeed, dear sir, pardon me—I can't help it," I stammered.

"I had the Captain here last night," says my papa.

"Last night, sir? the Captain? and what—what—?"

"What was you thinking about, miss, to tell him you loved another?"

"I durst not deceive him, sir."

"Do you know you're a troublesome, humoursome baggage, miss? What do you think your whimsies have cost the poor Captain?" He threw a great parcel of papers into my lap. "There, take 'em, and see what they come to. On my life, I'm ashamed to touch 'em."

I unrolled the papers. They were Indian bonds of great sums, three hundred and five hundred pounds, and the like. I sought to reckon up their value, as my papa bade me, but could not come at it in my confusion.

"Pray, sir, what's all this money?" I said, trying to speak calmly.

"Why, that's your ransom, miss, to deliver you from the Captain's clutches, though why he should have to pay it puzzles me."

"Sure, sir, you must be jesting, and yet it en't like my papa to rally me on so sorrowful a subject."

"Sorrowful indeed, miss. I would pay down myself that sum you hold if it would free me from the reproach of having brought so much misfortune upon a man that I esteem the very chiefest of my friends, when I thought only to do him good."

"But, dear sir, is it I that have done him harm?"

"Yes, miss, you, and that long Scotch lad of yours, and the tattlers and scandal-mongers of this place, and I myself, as I said."

"You terrify me, sir. What's happened to the Captain?"

"Oh, nothing, miss," says my papa; "only that he has been robbed of his mistress and a matter of five thousand pounds besides."

"This money that's here, sir?"

"Yes, miss; the sum he makes over to you to compensate you for breaking off his addresses."

I was filled with horror. "But you would not dream of accepting it, sir?"

"Why, miss, I must; that's the cursed part of the business. Say that the Captain breaks off his courtship, which is become the common talk of all Calcutta. Did you refuse him? Then the gossip was true, and you was bound by some earlier engagement, so as you durst not marry him. Did he withdraw from his suit? Then you may be assured that he had discovered some spot on the lady's reputation. Did I put an end to the affair? Why then, I was aware of something improper, and as a person of honour, refused to permit my friend to sacrifice himself. The lady's in the wrong, you see, however you take it."

"But, sir, how can this horrid, this dreadful money make things better?"

"Why, just in this way, miss. The Captain came to me last night, and told me you had received his addresses with the dutiful acceptance I had prepared him to expect in you. 'But presently,' says he, 'talking with Miss, I discovered that if she honoured me with her hand, I could not hope to make her as happy as a lady of her beauty and merits has a right to expect. To force myself upon so charming a creature without that assurance which I failed to obtain would be to inflict undeserved misery on her, and a richly merited remorse on myself, but I am sensible that I would do her only a less harm by withdrawing from my suit. As a testimony, then, of my regard for the lady's worth, and a compensation to her for the breaking-off of the match, I desire to make over to you for her use the sum of five thousand pounds, to be settled strictly upon herself,[03] whomsoever she may marry, and I will take it kindly in you, sir, to allow her to exercise her own choice in that particular.' That I promised him at once, for 'twas all I could do for him, and indeed he has found the only way out of the difficulty."

"Oh, sir," my voice was choked, "forgive me, but mayn't it be said that the dear gentleman paid down the money sooner than marry me?"

"No, miss, it mayn't; for what man in his senses would allow himself to be forced into paying down such a sum without a fight at the law? And having paid it, would he be likely to remain friendly with the lady and her family? or more, would he use his best efforts to marry her to a relation of his own?"

"Oh, sir!" This took me quite aback, as the sailors say.

"Yes, indeed, miss. There was an understood condition attached to the gift that if Mr Fraser should pay you his addresses, and they were agreeable to you, I should offer no objection to your marrying. I hadn't been aware hitherto that I was such a tyrannical parent that 'twas necessary to buy my consent to my daughter's marrying the man she had a fancy for, but I suppose I can bear the blame if it's to pleasure the Captain. And now, miss, let me know your thoughts on the subject. Do you desire to marry the fellow?"

"Oh, sir!" again covering my burning face with my hands.

"Come, miss, there's no need to play the prude with me, is there? You told me once you hated the gentleman; am I to understand that you love him now?"

"Sure, sir, that's a question should be asked by Mr Fraser himself if your girl is to answer it," I began, pertly enough, but burst into tears, and cried bitterly, only finding words to entreat my papa to return the money to the Captain, for I could not endure to lie under such an obligation to him. But this Mr Freyne refused, very gently and patiently, pointing out that to return the money would not only disoblige Captain Colquhoun, but also set about again all those injurious rumours which he had been at such pains to silence, and adding that if the Captain could sacrifice the best part of his savings to endow me with the money, I might at least mortify my pride so far as to accept the sacrifice gracefully.

"Though I shall be forced to raise an army to protect this girl of mine," says my papa, "for after all her adventures (no, miss, I don't intend it unkindly) hitherto, what will it be now that she's a fortune as well as a beauty? 'Twill be necessary to fortify the house, questionless, and hire a garrison of *buxerries*."[04] (These are the Indian mercenary soldiers that fight for pay.)

This was said while my papa was comforting me with great kindness, and in his rallying style bidding me never again show myself so strange and obstinate as I had during the last two days, for it had cost him so much to be stern with his girl that he could not hope to achieve it a second time. "And indeed," he said, "we can't look to find every day a gentleman that's willing to pay five thousand pounds for the privilege of being refused by Miss Sylvia Freyne, so pray, miss, make sure of your own mind before the next suitor comes."

"Why, sir," I said, "'tis my misfortune that I did know my own mind, for sure I must otherwise have been captivated by the justice and nobility of the Captain's sentiments. But, sir, the dear gentleman has certainly failed in generosity in this one particular of the money, for how can a poor creature that's crushed under such a weight of obligation ever make proper acknowledgments to him?"

"Nay, there you're wrong, miss," says Mr Freyne. "The Captain gave it as his particular request that I should entreat you never to mention the matter in his presence, nor even to hint at it, since otherwise you'll force him to cease those visits here which are the great happiness of his life."

Was there ever such a man, Amelia? The kindness, the delicacy of this behaviour—but no, I shall weep again if I write more on this topic, and I have wept so much of late. But there the Captain sits in the varanda with my papa at this moment, and makes his stiff bow and smiles his wooden smile if I interrupt them, as though nothing had happened between now and a week ago.

May ye 11*th.*

This morning I went to pay a visit to my dear Mrs Hurstwood, whom I have hardly seen for a month. In the very week after her wedding, the dear creature was seized with fever (owing to a chill taken at the Masquerade, said Dr Knox), and as soon as she was a little recovered, her attentive spouse carried her by boat to Ballisore, so that I have lacked her sprightly counsel for some time. I was all eagerness to visit her as soon as I heard she was returned, and my papa having occasion to drive as far as Surman's, offered to take me with him in the chaise, and fetch me again when he passed in the evening. It so happened that when we reached Mr Hurstwood's house the good man himself was standing on the steps, about to depart to his business at the Fort, and welcomed us with great warmth, complimenting Mr Freyne on his horses, and declaring that he should no longer be apprehensive for his Charlotte's cheerfulness since he could leave me to spend the day with her. My papa continued his ride, and Mr Hurstwood carried me to Charlotte's closet, where she was lying upon a couch. She jumped up on seeing me, and we embraced one another very tenderly, while her worthy spouse rubbed his hands with delight and made us both as many foolish compliments as if he had been Miss Grandison's Lord G. himself. He displayed a monstrous anxiety lest I should imagine he had neglected or ill-used his Charlotte, which made us both laugh, for indeed I believe if the dear girl had a fancy for the Peacock Throne of Delly he would beggar himself to obtain it for her.

"Ah," says Mrs Hurstwood, with the longest face imaginable, as the good man still lingered, "you don't know all my trials, miss. Mr Hurstwood is trying to get rid of me."

"My dearest life!" cries the poor gentleman, quite confounded.

"Why, yes, sir. Did you never hear of the woman who was killed with kindness?"

"Ah, madam," says Mr Hurstwood, with a broad smile that he sought in vain to restrain spreading over his visage, "our dear Charlotte's sprightly wit is like our mangoes here, which are only disagreeable before you are arrived at their full flavour."

"I vow, sir, you're a sad flatterer," cried she. "Pray get you gone to your business, or my talk with Miss Freyne will never be done. Oh, we have extraordinary weighty matters to discuss, I'll assure you."

"And how does my Charlotte find herself?" I asked her, when her spouse had at last withdrawn, with many bows and scrapes and farewells, and she had sent away the iya that we might talk with the more freedom.

"Why, I'm as well as my Sylvia," she said; "but it pleases Mr Hurstwood to sit and look at me reclining here, instead of spending the evenings abroad, and I'm lazy enough to pleasure him. But I won't give way no longer, or I doubt I shall grow like some of our ladies here that rarely stir from their couches. I shall be taking to a *hooker* next to soothe the mind, as they say. Has my Sylvia ever catched Polly Dorman enjoying hers? I don't know when I have laughed more, to see her so excessively happy. But no, my dear, I shall go into company and take you about, for from all I hear you want a duenna sadly. So your adventures han't ceased in consideration of my absence? I understand that things are come to such a pass with you that Mr Freyne would feel no surprise if a *coffle*[05] of Moguls came demanding you for the Emperor's seraglio, or an embassy of Russes to invite you to become the bride of their mad Czar. Now tell me all about your lovers and their vows."

I had a prodigious deal to tell her, as you will guess, even allowing her to hear a portion of Fraser's letter (not the post-scriptum, oh no! none but my Amelia shall be obliged with the knowledge of that), and moving her to tears with the history of Captain Colquhoun's singular generosity. When all was done—

"And so," said she, "the poor Captain is to intimate to your Fraser that if he choose to honour Calcutta with a second visit he'll be welcome?"

"Why, no, my dear, not exactly. Mr Fraser was to join his ship at Madrass, if the fleet was arrived there, and after that he may go anywhere, and I never know whether he's even in these seas at all. But if his duty should bring him anywhere near Calcutta, or the Admiral should choose to employ him again with despatches——"

"Why, then, he'll find Mr Freyne ready to meet him with open arms, and Miss in the background, all smiles and tears and blushes——"

"I protest, madam, you're too bad!" I cried. "One might fancy I was——"

"A boarding-school Miss? and so you are, my dear, or was, not so very long ago. But she shan't be rallied if she don't like it. And what of all the other lovers who en't able to pay down five thousand pounds to win their freedom?"

"Why, Mr Menotti's forbidden the house by my papa."

"And he has quarrelled with your mamma as well? Oh, I know it; Mrs Mapletoft told me about it yesterday. 'Twas at her house, under colour of a dispute at cards. The gentleman accused the lady of having played him false, and she retorted by threatening to betray what she knew of him, to which he replied that he also had tales to tell if necessary. What do you think of that?"

"Sure their falling-out is the best thing that could be for me."

"Why, yes, if they remain unreconciled. But they won't, my dear. With the hold he has over her, she don't dare disobey him, and the easiest way of gaining his favour is to sacrifice you. So my dear Miss must look to herself. Be careful about your palanqueen-bearers at night, for remember your beloved Miss Byron was carried off by treacherous chairmen, and don't suffer yourself to be persuaded into entering any chaise or budgero but your papa's. You don't want me to warn you not to wander away with Menotti at any party of pleasure."

"Come, my dearest life," it was Mr Hurstwood who entered, as gallant as ever, "tiffing is served, and sure you and our dear Miss Freyne must be prodigiously hungry after so long and serious a conversation. I have a piece of news, also, that Miss Freyne's good papa will be glad to hear. Can you credit it, madam, that our Council have at last plucked up courage to defy the Nabob? It seems that seven or eight days since he sent by the hand of one Facquier[06] Tongar" (these *facquiers*, Amelia, are accounted holy men among the Moors, as the *gioghis* among the Gentoos) "to demand with threats the destruction of the new fortifications that he heard we were making; but the Presidency, seeing in the demand only an attempt to extort money from us, made bold to refuse it. To-day is come a second messenger, with a *perwannah* wrote on the day of the Soubah's starting at the head of his army against the Purranea Nabob, with very stringent orders that the ditch and wall which, as he hears, we are making round our territory, should be instantly stopped. This wall and ditch, of course, are nothing but an invention of the French who have his ear; but Mr Drake has returned by the messenger a letter saying that the slight repairs in hand on our defences are needed in case of war with the French, and he won't stop 'em, but that no new works have been devised. I did hear a rumour of the several messengers having been dismissed with contempt, too, but at least you see that we shall venture to hold up our heads to Surajah Dowlah yet."

CHAPTER X.
IN WHICH THE FLOOD BEGINS TO RISE.

CALCUTTA, *May ye 26th.*

Yet another attempt, my dear! and devised with such singular effrontery that but for the signal goodness of Heaven in frustrating the design, your Sylvia must by this time have found herself the unwilling bride of the daring wretch who pursues her with so much persistence. But here I am running on, as usual, instead of proceeding orderly. Well, my Amelia must know that last night was a party of pleasure given by Mr Kelsall, one of the elder gentlemen here, in his garden at Chitpore, which is about a league from the town, but within the circuit of the Morattoe-ditch. Coming ready dressed into the varanda, I found my papa still smoking his *hooker* in his ordinary clothes and without his wig.

"Why, sir, en't you coming with us?" I cried.

"No, miss; and I han't never designed to."

"Oh, pardon me, sir. When I heard we were going by water, I thought you must be about to honour us with your company."

"Why, no, miss, that's nothing but Madam's old pique against her palanqueen." (For you mayn't be aware, Amelia, that Mrs Freyne uses this equipage as little as she can, and all because she en't permitted to adorn the poles of the machine with a tyger's head in silver, this ornament being reserved for the ladies of the President and the second in Council, and much coveted by those of lower rank.) "I purpose passing a quiet evening here with the Captain."

Leaving my papa, I attended Mrs Freyne to the river-side, where our budgero, the rowers wearing Mr Freyne's livery of white dresses and orange-coloured ribbons, was awaiting us, and carried us quickly to Chitpore. Mr Kelsall's garden is situated on the bank of a rivulet that serves to continue the Morattoe-ditch as far as the river, and before reaching it one passes another garden called Baugbuzar or Perrins, where stands a redoubt or fortification on a projecting piece of land, which was planned by Colonel Scott, when he was sent here to improve the defences of the place, to command both the river and the rivulet, and also the high road which crosses this last by a bridge. I am thus particular in my description that my Amelia may understand the later events. On arriving, we found all Calcutta gathered in the gardens. The rivulet was full of budgeroes three deep, moored to the bank and to each other, while not a few ladies and gentlemen had travelled by land in chaises or palanqueens. The garden, which has only been lately laid out, was prodigiously admired, and in particular a pavilion or summer-house, just finished to Mr Kelsall's own design—an elegant building of stone in a neat octagon shape. Mr Kelsall offered us a very genteel entertainment, for there was not only a *notch* for those to watch that chose to sit still, but also a band of music for dancing, and again pleasant alleys, lighted up by huge numbers of little earthen lamps, in the Indian style, in which to roam, while the dessert was one of the richest I have ever seen, including even ices (my Amelia will guess how grateful, and at the same time how costly, is this sweetmeat in such a climate), which are manufactured by the Indians in some artificial and ingenious manner that I don't pretend to understand. I felt quite at my ease, for although Mr Menotti was present, he made no attempt to force himself either on me or on Mrs Freyne, which gave me confidence that they were as yet unreconciled, but I experienced a good deal of annoyance from a trick played by certain of the young gentlemen, among whom were Ensign Bellamy and his friend Mr le Beaume.

To understand my mortification, you must be told that Ensign Bellamy had entreated me a week ago to tell him what gown I purposed wearing to this entertainment, and on learning 'twas my blush-coloured paduasoy and white satin petticoat, had entreated me very earnestly not to change my mind, which I promised, fancying that he designed to present me with a nosegay or some such trifle, but little guessing to what I was committing myself. Judge, Amelia, of my disgust when on entering the ground there came forward to meet me no fewer than eight gentlemen, ranging themselves on either side of me like a guard, and every man in my livery, as the wild fellows called it, viz., a pink silk coat laced with silver, and white satin waistcoat and breeches, all to match my gown! I'll assure you there was plenty of mirth for the general company in this odd sight, but very little for me, and when I could draw Ensign Bellamy aside, I reproved him very seriously for the extravagance of his conduct, and especially for putting off the Company's uniform that he might wear mine. To this he replied that he had allowance not to wear his uniform for this one night, and that he and the other young gentlemen had designed the spectacle by way of protest against the arrogant assumptions of Mr Fraser (whose pretensions, by the way, my dear, are now pretty well known, at least to the unlucky remainder of my suitors, since Mrs Hamlin became acquainted with Captain Colquhoun's generous conduct). When that presumptuous person should venture to show himself in Calcutta, says Mr Bellamy, he and the rest would make a point of wearing these same suits of clothes, to assure him that there was, at any rate, eight gentlemen of Bengall who were ready to resent his robbing them of their goddess, and would call upon him to prove his right by the sword.

I was more amused by this rodomontade than my Amelia will anticipate, for I knew these young fellows to be persons of sense and honour, and not traitors and ruffians like certain I could name, so all I said was to engage Ensign Bellamy and his companions to be bride-men at my wedding, warning 'em that any one picking a quarrel with Mr Fraser would instantly forfeit the privilege. This condition was received by the gentlemen with a prodigious amount of laughter, for ladies are so few here that a certain modest assurance is gained in speaking by our sex, which the other are all too ready to applaud and obey, and they all vowed they would run no risque of incurring so dreadful a penalty. Thus then to supper, which was served in the summer-house, while the music played without, making a very agreeable effect, and all the company were complimenting Mr Kelsall on the elegance of his entertainment and the taste displayed in the laying-out of the garden, when in a pause of the music there came the sounds of a horse's feet on the high road leading from Calcutta.

"Sure one of your guests is arriving late, sir," says one of the ladies to Mr Kelsall.

"Why, he'll find a few pickings yet, madam," said he.

Presently Mr Kelsall's banyan brought in Mr Dash in a riding-dress, his whole appearance much disordered.

"I hope there's no bad news, sir?" says our host.

"I doubt but I'm a sort of skeleton at your feast, sir, but I thought all the company would be concerned in what I have just learnt, which must be my excuse for breaking in upon the ladies in this attire. The letter wrote by the Governor and Council in reply to the Soubah's last *perwannah* reached him eight days back at Rajamaul[01] on his way to Purranea, and on receiving it, he gave instant orders to cease the advance against his cousin, and returned to invest our factory at Cossimbuzar."

"Why, the fellow has some mettle in him after all!" cries Ensign Bellamy. "Sure we shall have some fighting now, gentlemen."

"I would not have you too sure of that, sir," says Mr Dash. "The President and the Select Committee, who are considering the news, may prefer to disarm the Nabob's enmity by destroying such of our defences as en't ready to fall down of themselves."

"That's our newly-repaired row of guns on the west face of the Fort," says Ensign Piccard, with a groan.

"And the redoubt here on Perrins Point," says Mr Kelsall.

"Nay, sir," says Mr Dash, "'twill be even this pavilion of yours, perhaps. The Indians all take it for a work of defence."

"I'll be hanged," says Mr Kelsall, very red in the face, "if I'll pull down my new summerhouse for any Soubah that ever sat on the *musnet*!"

"Sure, sir, you underrate the meekness of our Government. The Council will do it for you, sooner than affront the Nabob."

"Oh, sir," says Mr le Beaume, "pray don't slander your countrymen. I could not credit such a thing of the great British nation."

"Come, gentlemen," says Ensign Bellamy, "fill up your glasses. Here's to a speedy campaign and a brisk one! When we have sacked Muxadavad, we'll set Miss Freyne on the *musnet*, and she shall rule Bengall as now she rules Calcutta!"

The party now began to break up, Mr President and the members of Council having left before the general supper, in expectation of receiving letters from Cossimbuzar, and no one feeling inclined for further merry-making in view of the news that was arrived. At the small *gott* by the side of the rivulet there was a prodigious confusion, every one desiring to get on board of his own budgero at once, so that some whose boats were on the outside even clambered across those which intervened, and thus were able to depart first after all. In the crowd I was separated from Mrs Freyne, and with Ensign Bellamy, who was conducting me, went looking about in vain for our budgero, which was not where we had left it on arriving.

"Pray, madam," said the young gentleman, "suffer me to leave you here a moment, while I run to the end of the press of boats and see whether your servants have moored yours there. I'm ashamed of dragging you about in this style."

But no sooner was Mr Bellamy gone than I heard Mrs Freyne calling me from behind (have I mentioned, my dear, that my stepmother's voice is a little shrill?), and looking round, saw her standing on the deck of a budgero in the line nearest the *gott*, and beckoning to me with her fan. 'Twas a marvel to me how I had missed her, for I could discern the white and orange liveries even where I was. I turned to call Mr Bellamy back, but he was gone too far to hear, and I returned alone to the budgero. Mrs Freyne was no longer on the deck, but there was two or three of the young gentlemen there that attend upon her continually.

"Mrs Freyne fears she has took a chill, madam," says one of them as I came up, "and won't therefore stay on deck, but she desired you would attend her in the cabin."

He offered his hand (I think the fellow was Lieutenant Bentinck, but he was so muffled in his cloak that I could not be certain), and I accepted of his help to step on board. Before I could do more than turn in the direction of the cabin, however, I heard Ensign Bellamy's voice on the bank behind me.

"Madam, madam! you are in error. I have found your budgero at the end of the line, with Mrs Freyne on board. Pray let me conduct you——" He needed to say no more, for I wrenched my hand from the fellow that held it (though indeed the wretch tightened his grip until it was like iron), and seeing that the boat was already moving from the *gott*, sprang with all my strength to the shore, the Ensign's outstretched hands catching mine in time to prevent my landing on my knees on the steps.

"Thank heaven, madam, that you're safe!" he cried. "I feared you was certain to fall into the water, or at least to receive some hurt in jumping, but I durst not delay." His countenance was very pale. "That was Menotti's budgero."

"But the liveries—Mr Freyne's colours?" I stammered.

"Mr Menotti's ribbons are pink, madam, you'll remember, and by this torch-light——"

"But I saw Mrs Freyne calling to me from the deck!" I cried, foolishly enough, clinging tight to his arm as he guided me along the *gott*.

"Impossible, madam," says Mr Bellamy, looking me straight in the face. "Mrs Freyne arrived at your budgero at the same moment as I myself—although she crossed from another boat."

"Questionless I made a mistake," I said, but my heart would not cease thumping. Was it possible that my papa's wife could lay such a plot against the honour and happiness of his daughter? "Pray, sir," I said to the Ensign, "be so good as to attend us home to-night."

"With pleasure, madam," said he, "if I may bring Mr le Beaume."

I had no chance to answer, for we had reached the budgero, where Mrs Freyne was standing outside the cabin speaking to the chief of the boatmen. "You had better push off," she was saying. "The Chuta Beebee must be returning in some other budgero with her friends. I can't wait here all night."

"Oh, pardon me, madam; I have found the vanished fair," says Ensign Bellamy, handing me on board. "May I venture to entreat a passage on your vessel for myself and my friend le Beaume? My father always warns me that he won't stay for me at these entertainments, and to-night he departed early with the other great folks, leaving us two poor babes in the wood to get home as best we might."

"Oh, pray summon your friend, sir," says Mrs Freyne, to whom this speech had given time to recover her countenance, for she had changed colour at the sight of me. "Me and Miss will be enchanted to have your company."

I dare to say that my stepmother blessed the young gentlemen as heartily in her mind as I did, for I can't conceive how she and I should have faced one another, or how we should have conversed, had we been left to ourselves. As it was, we were attended gallantly home by Mess. le Beaume and Bellamy, and I fancy the latter gentleman must have got a word with my papa, for as I bade him good-night Mr Freyne said to me, so as only I could hear—

"So I understand that my girl en't safe in company without her papa? After this evening, miss, I'll take care to go out with you, unless your friend Mrs Hurstwood will take charge of you. But indeed I shall be forced to send your Fraser a despatch to come here post-haste and take you off my hands, for you're a sad tiresome piece of goods, dragging me away from my quiet *hooker* on my own varanda."

"Oh, dear sir, let me stay at home with you, and I shall be quite content," I cried, and went to my chamber, to wake up again and again in the night thinking that I was sailing on one of the slimy, feverish channels of this horrid river, in the power of the vile Menotti, and bound for the nearest European factory where a Popish priest was to be found. My Amelia won't be surprised, seeing how nearly successful the wicked attempt proved, that my only comfort lay in my papa's promise for the future, although I won't deny that I was thankful to have been saved without another of those public discoveries in which your poor Sylvia's name (I think I may say without her fault) has been too much mixed up.

May ye 27th.

To-day Captain Colquhoun visited my papa for tiffing, and told us, with the most vehement disgust, that the Council had stopped all the work that was being done to repair the fortifications, and were sending very humble letters through Mr Watts to the Nabob, representing that since they were building no new defences it was impossible they should cease working on 'em, as his Highness ordered, but that what little they could do to pleasure him was already done, and in consideration of this would he be graciously pleased to withdraw his army from before Cossimbuzar, and leave our factory in safety?

"For Britons to cringe before Surajah Dowlah is an unpardonable sin!" cried the Captain.

"Why," says my papa, "they argue that he that is down needs fear no fall. If they wallow in the dust before the Soubah, 'tis quite clear that he can't kick 'em any lower. So that they save their private property and get off with a whole skin, what's Britain's honour to them?"

"In that," cried the Captain, "I'm convinced—and I might almost say I rejoice to think so—they're wrong. If the Soubah is set on the capture of Calcutta, all their humility won't turn him aside, and I believe he is."

"But sure he won't be such a fool as kill the goose that lays the golden eggs?" says my papa.

"Why, sir, he hopes to make the goose his own. The French have assured him that all the Rajas of the province have laid up their revenues in our Fort for safety, and he looks to lay hands not only on them, but on all our customs and dues for the future. Whatever good advice his grandfather Ally Verdy may have given him to leave us alone, as Mr Holwell insists he did, I can't doubt but he designs to strip first us, and then the other European factories, of all our privileges."

"But we shall have a word to say to the gentleman first, Captain."

"I doubt it, sir; for if so, why are we neglecting our defences, which if they were in good order might enable us to hold out against the Nabob until the rains begin, or even until this year's fleet arrives from home? Under the guidance of Mr President and his two friends we are dancing smiling to destruction."

June ye 1st.

Oh, my dearest friend, Mr Dash and the Captain were right in their prophecies of the behaviour of the Presidency. Sure the wretch Surajah Dowlah must be rejoicing beyond measure over the terror his name inspires in European breasts! But why should the Council have begun by taking part with his rivals, insulting his messengers, and withholding the customary presents made to a new Soubah, if all they designed was to fall on their knees in the most pitiful submission as soon as he moves his army a step in their direction? I can't write coldly, my dear. I feel the humiliation of the factory so keenly that my pen digs holes in the paper, and I wish it were a sword, and I a man to fight Surajah Dowlah with it. This day there came letters from Cossimbuzar to the Council, Mr Watts writing that yesterday week one of the Nabob's captains, a Jemindar named Aume-beg,[02] encamped against the Cossimbuzar factory with a considerable force, which was strengthened later by more troops and two elephants. Prevented from forcing the gate by the coolness of the sergeant on guard, who fetched out his men and bade 'em fix their bayonets, the Moors called a parley, of which Mr Watts took advantage to get in provisions and water and load the great guns of the place. Nothing coming of the first parley, the factory continued to be besieged, and on the 28th of May Dr Forth was sent out, who had attended Ally Verdy Cawn in his last illness, accompanied with a *mounsee*,[03] or Persian secretary, to endeavour to arrive at an accommodation, and 'tis the demands then made upon him that Mr Watts has forwarded by special messenger. The chief of these is for the demolition of our new works at Baugbuzar, and of Mr Kelsall's summer-house, which last they take for a fortress because, while the land lay waste, a parcel of shells was proved there from time to time. Mr Watts advises the granting of these demands and the appeasing of the Nabob by means of a genteel present, considering that, like his grandfather, who extorted from us in the course of his reign near 100,000*l.* in all, Surajah Dowlah designs to stop all our business until his rapacity be satisfied.

My Amelia will have learnt from my letters so much of the character of the wise and valiant persons who are our governors that she won't need to be told what was the immediate impulse of their hearts on reading this alarming news. But for the sake, I suppose, of setting themselves right in their own eyes, what do Mr President and his friends, Mess. Manningham and Frankland, do? They call together the five captains of the Company's forces here (Captain Colquhoun, of course, being one) and ask them very seriously whether they believe it possible, with a hundred men from the Calcutta garrison, to attempt the relief of Cossimbuzar against the Nabob's army of 12,000 trained soldiers, supported by a train of artillery! You won't wonder that the poor men declared the notion to be an extravagant one, but they added that the force at Cossimbuzar was sufficient, and the factory strong enough, to beat off the enemy if wisely handled. But the humane gentlemen to whom our destinies in this country are committed did not offer to repeat this hard saying to Mr Watts. In their care for the lives of our people at Cossimbuzar, they sent for presentation to the Nabob an *arasdass*,[04] or humble petition, couched in the most submissive terms imaginable, and yielding all he might choose to ask, while they promised prodigious rewards to the *cossids*[05] or messengers if it should reach Muxadavad in thirty-six hours. At the same time they gave orders for the destruction of poor Mr Kelsall's pavilion and of the draw-bridge and outworks at Perrins Redoubt, and this is going on as I write. O' my conscience, Amelia, if my pen were the sword I spoke of just now, and in a manly hand, it would not be against the Nabob I would turn it, but upon his honour the President and his two like-minded advisers.

And how, think you, my dear, are all our minds occupied in this moment of humiliation and disgrace? (Though indeed the three gentlemen at the head of affairs are in high spirits, regarding themselves, so it seems, as the saviours of their countrymen, and looking askance only upon the dejection and uneasiness of such persons as Mr Holwell and Captain Colquhoun.) Why, Amelia, with a play, which the young gentlemen are so good as to promise us a fortnight or so hence! The Play-house en't generally in use but in the cold weather; but now the work on the defences is stopped (and indeed it's well the Nabob is so merciful as not to demand the levelling of the walls of the Fort itself, for I think the Council would have pleasured him), and there's nothing for the officers to do (for there's but little drill at any time, and to begin it now might anger the Soubah), while the writers are idle for the general stoppage of business, even Captain Colquhoun says 'tis a good thing for the lads to have something to do that may keep 'em out of mischief. They had designed to present to us "Venice Preserved," since Ensign Bellamy owns to a particular ambition to essay the part of Belvidera; but on its being pointed out that the season was too hot and the times too grave for tragedy, they were obliging enough to substitute a comedy, "The Conscious Lovers," which I am very curious to see, as the work of one of the writers of my dear 'Spectators.' The first performance is promised before the rains, which are expected to begin somewhere about the 15th (fancy, my dear, a rainy season, such as Robinson Crusoe experienced!), and I suppose 'twill give us something to talk about when we are all forced to stay indoors.

June ye 7th.

I am writing in the morning, between breakfast and tiffing, to tell my Amelia of the extraordinary events that have, I trust, served to rid me of one at least of my persistent persecutors, though at a grievous cost, I fear, to my papa and to this place. Throughout the whole of Saturday, the day before yesterday, Mrs Freyne was vapourish and difficult to please—not spending the better part of her time in her own closet as usual, but wandering from room to room, taking up and casting down again now this piece of employment and now t'other, and crowning her uncertain behaviour by despatching a messenger to say she would not be present at Mrs Mackett's rout, just when it was time to start. My papa and I were playing chess on the varanda when she joined us, still in her undress.

"You'll be late, madam," says Mr Freyne.

"Oh, I sent a chitt to say I'm not coming," said she, approaching us to look at the board. "There's a move I want you to show me, sir—that which you was discussing t'other night with the Captain."

"When I've had my revenge on Miss, you'll find me at your service, madam."

"But sure you're finished with your game already, Mr Freyne."

"Yes, madam, but Miss has beat me, and in doing so she has let me see a means of defeating a plan of attack that she employs vastly too often for her own safety. I have made up my mind to conquer her this time."

"But pray, sir, show me this first," and Mrs Freyne began to move the pieces on the board; "and perhaps Miss will oblige me by fetching the book of plays which I was reading this afternoon and left in the arbour at the end of the garden. Then there'll be no time wasted."

"The servants are at your disposal, madam, to run your errands."

"Indeed, sir, how you can call these two steps an errand I don't know. Miss can take her iya with her if she's frightened."

"Frightened, madam? The girl don't wander down to the end of the garden at this hour without me and half-a-dozen peons besides, all well armed, I can tell you that."

"I'll assure you, sir, you are become a laughing-stock in Calcutta, with these absurd precautions. Do you forbid your daughter to oblige me?"

"Unless she desire to disoblige me, madam."

Upon this Mrs Freyne burst into tears, lamenting that she was the most miserable woman in Bengall, and that Mr Freyne had not the slightest consideration for her, and encouraged his daughter to insult over her, and so went sobbing to her own chamber, while my papa continued his game.

"Perhaps, sir, Mrs Freyne is sick?" I ventured to say.

"No, miss, I fancy she's sorry, and I'm glad of it." Mr Freyne would say no more, and I durst not ask him his meaning.

It must have been about midnight—perhaps somewhat later, for I had been asleep some time, after the customary struggle with the heat—that I was woke up by a tremendous clatter. Voices, the clash of swords, and pistol-shots were all resounding close at hand, and Marianna, who sleeps across my door, came screaming to tell me that the house was attacked, and we should all be murdered. As I sat up in bed, all trembling, to listen, my papa, in his night-cap, suddenly looked in at the door. He was buckling on his sword over his morning-gown, and there was a pair of great pistols sticking out of his pocket.

"Get into your *tuszaconna*[06] with your iya, miss," he cried, "and lock yourself in, and don't unfasten the door for any one until I bid you."

I lingered only to throw on a wrapper and a pair of shoes, and obeyed him. The *tuszaconna*, or as we should say wardrobe, is the closet in which my gowns and jewels are kept, lighted only by one small window high in the wall. Here Marianna and I locked ourselves in, and not satisfied with that, dragged one of my trunks against the door, and sat upon it (and upon my honour, I don't know which of us trembled the most. The poor wench had lost all her English in her fright, and bewailed herself in some Indian tongue, calling at times upon her Popish saints in scraps of Latin, while your cowardly Sylvia shook so much that the door trembled against which she leant).

The confused noise of fighting now ceased suddenly from the front of the house, and there was a rushing along the varanda outside our place of refuge. My heart was in my mouth, for I knew that the robbers must be making for my chamber, "and in a minute (I thought) they'll guess our hiding-place and break open the door, and then——" But almost at the same moment I heard the door of the chamber burst open again, and my papa's voice cheering on the servants; and so well did they second him that the invaders never penetrated inside the room, but were turned back on the varanda. The noise of the fighting was so dreadful that I could not remain without seeing what went on, and, climbing on a great wooden chest, I peeped out of the window, in time to see the robbers driven off by my papa and the servants, leaving two of their number prostrate on the ground. One of these was a European wearing a masque, who had been knocked down with a blow from a club by our head-peon.

"Throw some water over him and revive him, Jemmautdar," says Mr Freyne. "He has to answer to me for the night's work."

But when the Jemmautdar obeyed, and plucking off the fellow's masque showed his face as he began to recover his intellects, I could have screamed, for it was Mr Menotti. He looked about him like one dazed.

"Your servant, sir," says my papa, standing before him with his sword out. "When you're ready, I'll trouble you to draw."

"At your service, sir," said the villain, fumbling for his sword, which one of the servants, at a glance from Mr Freyne, picked up and gave to him, whispering something at the same time to my papa.

"What, the Cotwal[07] coming round with his peons?" cried Mr Freyne. "Why don't he come when he might be some use? However" (looking scornfully upon Mr Menotti, who was risen from the ground, but stood swaying uneasily about), "you look none too steady upon your legs, sir, and I've no desire to murder you, though I could wish my Jemmautdar had done his work more thoroughly. You shall hear from me very shortly. Two of you take him and set him in the road outside."

"I shall anticipate with pleasure the arrival of any friend of yours, sir," the hardy wretch succeeded in saying before he was seized by two of the servants and run across the compound and through the gates. By this time I was descended from my perch and had opened the door of the hiding-place.

"Oh, dear sir," I cried, catching my papa's arm, "you en't going to fight that barbarous man?"

"Why, miss, would you have me let him go free? I would shoot him as I would a mad dog."

"But, sir, a mad dog could not shoot my papa. Why give this miscreant the chance of doing further harm?"

"Would you have me shoot him from behind a wall, miss? Or do you wish all our family affairs spread out for the gossips of Calcutta to feast upon by a trial at the law? No, leave these matters to me, and go to bed again. You may be thankful I took it into my head to sit up to-night, for the *pyke* was bribed."

"I am, dear sir, I am indeed!" I cried out, but my papa bade me curb my gratitude and go to bed. And this I did, but my Amelia will guess that there was vastly little sleep for me in the rest of the night, what with thinking of my narrow escape and of Mr Freyne's projected duel, and endeavouring to frame such affecting arguments as might induce my papa to leave the wretched Menotti to the torments of his own conscience. But I had not the chance I anticipated to display my logical acuteness, for as soon as I had joined Mr Freyne for early breakfast, there came out on the varanda my stepmother's iya, Bowanny, and said that her mistress had been sobbing and crying all night, and now begged that we would both attend her to hear what she had to tell us. I was prodigiously astonished by such a request, but Mr Freyne seemed in no way surprised, and strode off to his lady's bedchamber without a word. We found Mrs Freyne, still in the undress she had worn the night before, reclined on a couch, with her hair all tumbled about, and no cap on.

"You see before you, sir," she said, "the most miserable woman in India."

Mr Freyne. I fancy, madam, I heard you say something of the same sort last night.

Mrs F. Cruel and hard-hearted man! Would you make the way of penitence as hard to your unhappy wife by your coldness and harshness as you have made the way of concealment easy? But, no; I won't be led into unbecoming recrimination even by your ill-timed derision, sir. I have sent for you that I may confess the steps by which, as a young and ingenuous creature slighted by her spouse, I was led into inexpedient acts through the arts of an accomplished villain.

Mr F. (*excessively angry*). Pray, proceed, madam, but if you are confessing your own sins you may as well leave mine alone. 'Tis scarce your part to complain of neglect.

Mrs F. In spite of your unmanly taunts, sir, I'll strive to preserve both my purpose and my calmness, remembering that I asked your daughter to attend you merely to show that I had nothing in my confession of which to be ashamed. You thought fit, sir, some short time after our marriage, to place a restriction on my diversions, desiring me never to play games of chance for any but beggarly sums. You had reasons for thus limiting me, you said. I didn't ask 'em then, and I don't now, but I suppose you feared I might dissipate the money I brought you. Well, sir, you must have known that if you would not oblige me with the means of play, others would, and I felt little difficulty in accepting their kindness. The chief of these obliging persons was Mr Menotti.

Mr F. Woman! is this true that you tell me?

Mrs F. (*with her handkerchief to her eyes*). No unkind rudeness shall hinder me from confessing the truth. The gentleman whose name so disturbs you, sir, obliged me at various times with sums of money, professing himself amply repaid by my countenance and conversation, possibly also by his persistent good fortune at the cards. But when your daughter arrived from home, I perceived a change in him. He began to hint at a certain means of discharging the debt of gratitude I owed him, and I demanded of him eagerly what it might be. You know it now as well as I. The fool was fallen in love with Miss—but why, I know no more than why she persists in refusing him. The match was an extraordinary good one for her, far better than any she could have looked for in England, and I experienced a glow of satisfaction in thus discharging in the most exemplary style my duties to you, sir, to your girl, and to the gentleman to whom I was so much indebted. Your conscience, sir, will tell you, and so will your daughter's tell her, that I did all in my power to bring about the happy consummation which has all along been frustrated by your fatal easiness and softness of temper, and the pert wilfulness of Miss—

Mr F. Aye, madam, all in your power—I'll grant you that.

Mrs F. I thank you, sir. At least, then, I need not reproach myself with my unhappy failure here. It happened, alas! that Mr Menotti was disturbed by the appearance of two other suitors for his charmer's favour—the Fraser fellow upon whom Miss's inconstant fancy is fixed for the moment, and him whom you call the Unknown—and the balance of the poor gentleman's judgment was unsettled. Not knowing his true friend, he went so far as to turn his resentment against me. Had he but confided in the purity of my motives, all had been well, but he saw fit to attempt to increase his influence over me by means of threats. He had learned, he said, from my conversation, certain important matters of the Company's, which I must have heard from you, sir, and these facts, dropped innocently by me, he had made use of to ingratiate himself with the Chuta Nabob, with whom he had had friendly relations for some time.

Mr F. (*bitterly*). In other words, the fellow is and always has been one of Surajah Dowlah's spies, and my wife's another of 'em.

Mrs F. I am resolved, Mr Freyne, to bear with patience all your injurious remarks until you have heard me out. If I had not felt it possible to confide to you the difficulties I was in about money, you'll guess that I could not endure the thought of your becoming sensible of the new and shocking trouble into which my easiness of temper had led me, and 'twas this Menotti threatened me with when he saw his hopes in danger. But when he discovered the renewed assiduities of the Unknown by that letter he intercepted in the hands of Omy Chund's peon, the current of his thoughts was changed again, and he proposed a settlement at once so charming and so honourable that I could not but accept it. The poor man was much upset to find the Unknown plotting against him in a matter in which his heart was so deeply engaged——

Mr F. And who, pray, is the Unknown, madam? for he en't unknown to you.

Mrs F. Why, sir, he's no other than the Nabob's Frenchman, Sinzaun.

Mr F. And my wife knew our subtlest enemy to be in the place, meditating dishonour to my daughter, and destruction to the factory, and never——

Mrs F. And never warned you, you would say, sir? No, indeed; where was the need of making a fuss and pother when things could be managed in a way vastly more agreeable to all parties? Finding, I say, that Sinzaun was working against him in the matter of Miss, and knowing that he had the ear of the Nabob, Menotti conceived the plan of atoning nobly for his former errors. He promised me that if my efforts to marry him to Miss should be successful, he would not only keep silence on the matter of the money and of my incautious admissions to him, but he would reveal to the Presidency all his dealings with the Nabob, and assist 'em to lay their hands upon

Sinzaun, thus frustrating all Surajah Dowlah's monstrous schemes against the town. Could I hesitate in such a case? Would Mr Freyne have me weigh a young creature's silly likes and dislikes against the safety of the whole factory, and the lives of all the Britons in Bengall? Your wife en't such a sentimental fool, sir. I did my best to pleasure Menotti, and I en't ashamed of it.

Mr F. And your design in telling me this, madam?

Mrs F. Why, sir, now that Menotti is defeated, I know he won't scruple to tell you a parcel of lies about me, and I desire to be beforehand with him.

Mr F. You desire me to proclaim to the Council, and so to all Calcutta, the iniquitous behaviour of my wife, madam?

Mrs F. (*weeping*). Indeed, Mr Freyne, you're cruelly hard. I would have you catch Menotti red-handed, so as no one will give any credit to his tales. I know (for I've made it my business to find out, that I might have some hold over him) that when he pleads indisposition as an excuse for absence from church on a Sunday morning, he goes disguised into the wood beyond Baugbuzar, and there receives messages from the Nabob through Monickchund the Governor of Hoogly. If you catch him to-day in the act, we're safe. Had he succeeded in his last night's design on Miss, he would have delivered up the *hircara*[08] that brings the messages to the President, as a proof of his good faith, but now that he has made an open enemy in you he'll think his only hope of her lies in the Nabob.

Mr F. I'll send a chitt to Mr Holwell. And now, madam, and you, miss, no more of this shameful matter. I think I have sufficient credit in the place for the Council to help me in preserving the honour of my family if it's possible to do so, but if not, then the shame is hers that first tells a word of the tale. Your debt to Mr Menotti, madam, shall be discharged, if you'll oblige me with the particulars.

Mrs F. I'm sure, sir, my maiden-money will far more than suffice——

Mr F. That, madam, you were careful to dissipate in your first year of married life. You had play-debts to be paid then also, if you'll remember.

Mrs F. I vow, sir, you're monstrous unkind!

My papa stayed to hear no more, and I followed him from the chamber, only to discover that he felt the strongest repugnance to denouncing Mr Menotti to the Presidency. "I had the fellow in my power last night, and let him go," he said, "but now, instead of avenging my own quarrel on him, I set the law on his track, for all the world as though I feared to meet him." In this style he continued to combat all my arguments, until I was frightened to death that he would propose to fight the wretch before laying an information against him, but at last he yielded to my representation of the inexpediency of exposing the entire factory to destruction for the sake of a piece of punctilio, and went to write his letter.

Oh, my Amelia, what a dreadful burden must Mrs Freyne have been bearing during all these months, while all the time your naughty Sylvia was judging her with an unkindness that I can't doubt has often aroused your disapproval! Is it any wonder that she has appeared peevish and difficult? How all the reports concerning the Soubah's designs must have startled her, knowing that his excesses might be encouraged by the repeating her unguarded words! Could any assembly of motives have been so strong as the desire to save her own reputation, not only in the eyes of Calcutta, but in those of her spouse, and to deliver the whole factory from destruction? One can't feel surprised that your poor Sylvia's preferences weighed but lightly in the opposite balance. But what a Sabbath was this, my dear, beginning in so awful a manner, for Mrs Freyne, for your unhappy girl and her honoured papa, and for the wretched Menotti! There was rumours when we came out of church that Cossimbuzar was fallen, in spite of the submission of our rulers, but this is not confirmed. Still, the President ordered on the spot a report of the defences of Fort William to be made and laid before him to-morrow.

CHAPTER XI.
SHOWING HOW THE FLOOD CAME.

June ye 8th.

Oh, my dear, Cossimbuzar is fallen without striking a blow, and if all be true that we hear, Surajah Dowlah is already marching on Calcutta! Mr Dash came in just after I had finished writing to you this morning, and related the dreadful history to my papa, as he had heard it from being in the vicinity of the council-chamber when the letters arrived. On the 1st of this month, the very day that our rulers despatched their humiliating *arasdass* from Calcutta, the Nabob sent three Jemindars and Radjbullobdass, the father of Kissendasseat, to hold a parley with Mr Watts, who told them, in spite of the objections of his own officers, that he would trust himself with them if the Nabob would send him a beetle. This is with the Indians a sign of ceremony and friendship, for they wrap this beetle, which is called *pawn*,[01] in some sort of leaves, and chew it. I don't doubt but my Amelia, on hearing of this disgusting custom, will unite with me in thinking that to polite minds it would be more agreeable to dispense with both the sign and the friendship. However, the beetle was sent on a silver plate, and Mr Watts, following the meek example of our Council here, humbled himself so far as to enter the Soubah's presence with his hands across and tied round with a *puckery*,[02] which is the strip of stuff that the Moors twist into their turbants. That Surajah Dowlah was not to be disarmed by this show of humility the poor gentleman quickly discovered, for he was at once threatened with death for his offering such a hardy resistance, and was only saved by the mediation of the son of the *duan* Huckembeg, who told the Nabob that Mr Watts was a good sort of a man, that was come at great peril to embrace his footsteps. Whether 'twas the threats or the mediation I don't know, but Mr Watts was so strangely affected that he forthwith signed a *mulchilca*,[03] which is an instrument enforced by a penalty, by which he not only surrendered his own factory of Cossimbuzar, but also pledged the Council here to demolish their fortifications, as well the old as the new, within a fortnight, to give up those of the Nabob's subjects they were protecting against him, and to resign the privileges anciently granted to the Company with respect to *dussticks* by making good the losses the Soubah had sustained through them. Seeing their chief in the enemy's power, the garrison of Cossimbuzar felt constrained to fulfil his covenant, and admitted the Moorish army, who treated the unhappy gentlemen with such detestable cruelty that Ensign Elliott, who commanded the military, shot himself in a frenzy of shame. May Heaven pardon the poor man this rash act! Alas, there may be others that will need the same pardon before very long.

Momentous though this news be, 'twas not all that Mr Dash had to tell. Lowering his voice, he asked Mr Freyne with an air of becoming reserve whether it was true that a gentleman of this place had been detected in supplying information to the Nabob. To this my papa replied that he had often heard hints to the effect that some such treachery must be at work, but he had received no word of its having been brought home to any one in particular; and the young gentleman went away disappointed. Shortly after his departure we heard a great beating of drums from the direction of the Fort, which threw me into a prodigious fright lest the Soubah's army should be already approaching the town. But Mr Freyne sending out one of the servants to ask what might be the cause of the noise, we learned that the President, who, it appears, has at length mustered courage to offer a resistance to the demands of the Nabob, was summoning all the inhabitants to the Esplanade[04] before the Fort, in order to concert measures for defence. Upon this Mr Freyne ordered his chaise, and while arming himself with sword and pistols, was so good as to offer to carry me with him to see the muster, if I chose. My Amelia will guess that I flew to change my gown at once, for I felt an extraordinary anxiety to see how the Council would bear themselves in this alarming situation; but fastened to my pincushion I discovered something that diverted the course of my thoughts altogether. It was a billet like that I had found on my table before, but folded smaller, and superscribed "Lewis to Clarissa" in French. Inside it was wrote, also in French:—

"It is with the most poignant anguish that the unhappy lover quits the vicinity of the coldest and most charming of women, to whom he has ventured to offer the incense of his unavailing adoration. When a more propitious fate shall place him next at the feet of his goddess, it may be that apprehension for her own safety may serve better to melt Clarissa's icy heart than pity for her slave has succeeded in doing, and that she'll see fit to grant him those tokens of her favour which his humble passion has never ceased to entreat."

The menacing style of this message filled me with alarm, but remembering that the writer announced his departure, and that 'twas possible he might never return, I took courage after a moment. Otherwise, I could not but feel apprehensive in the extreme to discover that the person whom Mrs Freyne had revealed as the apostate Sinzaun should still be seeking to enter into communications with me. This Sinzaun, I must inform my dear girl, is a most notorious renegade Frenchman, who is not only a trusted leader of the Nabob's army, having the management of his train of artillery, but also the vilest of his boon companions in time of peace. His skill had not been needed in the Cossimbuzar matter, but now he was questionless returned to lead his master's forces against Calcutta. I carried the wretch's billet to my papa, who read it with great anger; and I ventured to put a question that had troubled me more than once since the day before.

"Had you been sensible, dear sir, who the bold enquirer was that demanded your daughter, and known that he had, as he claimed, the power to save the factory from the Soubah's vengeance, would you have chose to oblige him?"

"I'm afraid," says my dear papa, "that my Sylvia Freyne believes me either a coward or a fool. Even had I been base enough to deliver up my daughter to the ruffian's demands, what security have I that the rogue would keep his word, and not take the girl first and the place afterwards?"

This view of the matter had not occurred to me, and I'll own that it relieved me from the apprehension I had felt that it might be my duty to sacrifice myself for the safety of Calcutta. Not, my dear, that I had clearly faced the possible necessity of such a shocking act, for I would not have you think me more heroical than I am, but that the dreadful notion had crossed my mind and reduced me almost to despair. Well, my papa and I rode to the Fort, and heard what Mr President had to say of the unexampled ingratitude and perfidy of the Nabob, and of the certainty that he and his army would be speedily crushed by the valour and readiness of the inhabitants of Calcutta. The five captains of the troops had given it as their opinion in writing that there was in the place an abundance both of arms, ammunition, and provisions, and a plan had been drawn out for constructing such additional defences as might reasonably be completed in a few days. But it was necessary that there should be men behind the defences, and therefore his honour trusted that every inhabitant of the place that was fit to bear arms would enrol himself immediately in the militia, and give unremitting attention to his drill until he was called upon to practise in war what he had been taught. This discourse of the President's was very well received, though with less of excitement, I fancy, than he had anticipated; and all of the male sex present, gentlemen and common persons and Armenians and To-passes alike, made haste to give their names to those who were about to enrol 'em. It was now too late to do any more that evening, and after appointing a meeting of the new-raised militia for this morning, on the green to the south of the Fort, that they might begin to be instructed in their weapons, every one returned home.

The ordinary business of the place being quite at a standstill, Mr Freyne betook himself to-day after the early meal to the Park instead of his *dufterconna*, and brought home with him to breakfast Captain Colquhoun and Mr Holwell, who were deputed to ride to Perrins Gardens and see what might be done to restore the redoubt there, which was so foolishly dismantled in the panic of last week. Mrs Freyne pleading indisposition as an excuse for her absence, I was set in her place at the head of the table, and found that the gentlemen were not in the highest of spirits.

"I could scarce believe my ears, Captain," says my papa, "when I heard that you had signed the assurance given by your comrades of our sufficiency of munitions."

"You can't blame me more than I blame myself, sir," said the Captain. "'Twas an unpardonable piece of confidence in me to take Captain Minchin's word for the amount of the stores, without regarding their quality and condition."

"Then you are satisfied as to the quantities mentioned, Captain?"

"By no means, sir. When my suspicions were first roused after signing the assurance, and I asked of Captain Minchin how he had prevailed upon Captain Witherington to make his returns so promptly, he told me with the greatest coolness in the world that Witherington had failed to send in any accounts at all, so that he himself had done his best to estimate what we ought to have in hand, and had assured us of possessing it."

"Witherington ought to be hanged!" says Mr Freyne.

"Indeed, sir," says Mr Holwell, "the poor gentleman is a most laborious, active creature. It en't his fault that his intellects are confused by all these sudden events. With a commander that would keep an eye on him, and see that he did his duty, we should have in him an excellent good officer."

"We don't possess such a commander in Mr Drake," said the Captain, "for Witherington finds all his complaints allowed, and en't forced to do anything. Captain Minchin assured me that when he represented to the President the danger of leaving the whole charge of the Train in the care of such a man, all the answer he received was that Witherington was such a strange unaccountable creature that his honour could do nothing with him."

"Yet the fellow makes more noise and bustle about doing nothing than the Council themselves," said my papa. "So you have examined the stores, Captain?"

"I have, sir, if indeed they're worthy to be called stores. There's but three hundred and fifty barrels of powder, and the most of that bad, no bombs nor grenadoes, except a few spoiled shells that will do more damage to us than the enemy; the grape is all eaten up with worms, and there's no cartridges ready."

"And the guns," says Mr Holwell, "are still without carriages, and the embrasures broken down, while any gunner that's fool enough to try to work his piece on the Fort walls will go through the roof into the chambers below."

"And our army of defence," says the Captain, "with no disrespect to either of you, gentlemen, is a fit match for its weapons. With a garrison of less than two hundred, counting the officers, and of which not ten of the rank and file have seen any war service, we may be thankful if we can hold out for a single day."

"Come," says my papa, "think of Colonel Clive's achievements with a force near as bad, and of your own experience in the Carnatic, sir."

"Ah, sir, here we lack Colonel Clive. And I am not (though it shame me to say it) the man to take his place. If the President had broke Captain Minchin as he had designed doing, and placed Captains Clayton and Witherington in some such subordinate situation as befits their lack of military experience and judgment, maybe Captain Grant and your humble servant might have made shift to show a good front to the enemy, but with five persons in equal military authority, and his honour and the Council interfering perpetually in matters which are none of their province, the thing is hopeless."

"But sure, sir," said Mr Holwell, "you have Captain Grant as adjutant-general, and Captain Minchin made merely commandant of the Fort, where his lack of military qualities can't do much harm."

"Not if we were about to defend the town, sir, but when we are driven back upon the Fort, as we must very quickly be, he has all the chance for mischief that he needs. And were Captain Grant twenty adjutants-general in one, he would still have Mr President for his commander."

"Aye," says my papa, "the Quaker is quaking now in good earnest. But you seem at present to wish to defend the town, Captain, and I thought that you scouted the bare notion hitherto."

"Why, sir, had I been in command, I would have called in the gentlemen from the other factories, and their garrisons with 'em, a month ago, and added them to our force here, whereas now they are refuging with the French and Dutch, or must be snapped up by the Nabob as he advances, since the summons to 'em only went out yesterday. In the former case, with the aid of the forced labour of the black inhabitants, we might have extended the Morattoe-ditch round the town with some hope of defending the space enclosed in it, but as things are, I confess indeed that the Fort is our only hope. The plan adopted by the Council on the advice of the engineer officers, which neither carries out Colonel Scott's scheme of defending the whole space of the town nor contents itself with maintaining the Fort, as should be the case in our present untoward circumstances, is doomed, I am convinced, to failure."

"Sure, sir," said Mr Freyne, "you would not have took the responsibility of destroying the church and all the houses near the Fort, as you pressed upon the gentlemen at the council of war?"

"Aye, sir, that I would, instead of leaving 'em as so many fortresses for the enemy. But when every gentleman that has a brick or *pucca* house wants it included in the defences, and none must be destroyed lest the Company should refuse to pay compensation, how, I ask you, is this to be managed without frittering away in continual stands and retreats the best strength of our small garrison?"

"Ah, Captain," says Mr Holwell, "you should have supported me in the matter of Tanners. Why, sir, I looked to you as my certain upholder, and yet there was none but Captain Grant and that gallant lad le Beaume besides myself to perceive the advantages we should gain in possessing an abundant store of provisions and a retreat both for the ships and ourselves, unless the Nabob should divide his forces to attack us."

"And what of dividing our own forces, sir?" asked the Captain. "They are far too small as it is for the extent of our defences, and to send half of 'em five miles off on t'other side of the river would be madness. And as for the Nabob, why, Monickchund and the Hoogly garrison alone could deal with any force we could send to hold Tanners without our being able even to offer to relieve it."

"But help may yet reach us, sir, from Madrass or Bombay."

"Scarcely, sir, unless they have been warned of our plight in a vision, for now that the sea is shut by the *munsoon*, our letters despatched yesterday by the country messengers can't reach even Madrass in less than a month."

"But the French and Dutch may yet determine to assist us, Captain."

"They may, sir; and if they should, I'll freely allow that the humble and imploring letters of the President and Council to 'em were justified. But I fancy they won't."

Here I saw Mr Dash come into the compound in haste, as though brimfull of news, but looking askance at Mr Holwell, against whom, as my Amelia will recollect, he cherishes some pique. Observing, however, that

Mr Holwell did not remark his presence (for indeed, I doubt if the good gentleman know more of him than his name), Mr Dash joined himself to the company, and slipped quietly into a seat close to me.

"The rumour of which I asked Mr Freyne last night is true, madam," he said.

"That concerning a treachery on the part of some European, sir?"

"Even so, madam. The thing is fairly proved, and Miss Freyne should be doubly rejoiced at the discovery, since the traitor is a person that has often, I believe, disobliged her. 'Tis Mr Menotti."

"I protest, sir, I don't see why I should rejoice to find that a person who had professed esteem for me is a traitor."

"Why, madam, see how your cold treatment of the fellow is justified! And there's another reason for you to triumph. I understand that the information on which Mr Menotti was captured came from a lady who was petted[05] by his neglect of her for a more youthful rival—yourself, madam."

"Indeed, sir," I said, flirting my fan and looking at him very complacently, "I don't see what time the gentleman you mention had to spare for any other lady, for I should have said that he spent it all in forcing himself upon me."

I knew that the young gentleman would set Sylvia Freyne down for a jealous coquette, but that was better for him than to spread about his first tale, for what would be said of my stepmother if it became known that she was the lady who accused him? "Pray, sir," I went on, "tell me how the discovery was made."

"The information was received, madam, on Sunday morning, and spies were set on Mr Menotti's house in consequence. During the time of divine service (he alleging wounds received in an attack made upon him by footpads in the street the night before as an excuse for remaining at home), he was observed to steal out in the disguise of a *deloll*'[06] (this is an Indian broker, of a grade higher than a *pycar*, Amelia), "and was followed as far as Chitpore, where he passed the rivulet by the bridge, and entered the *top*[07] of trees on t'other side. The *hircaras* following him discovered a second person habited as a facquier, who presented certain papers to Mr Menotti, upon which the two were taken prisoners before they could separate, the stranger proving to be an emissary of Monickchund, the Phousdar of Hoogly. Mr Menotti was very earnest with his captors to believe that he had devised a plot to entrap the Nabob's agents and deliver them up to the Council, and offered, in proof of his sincerity, to guide the party to the lodging of the abandoned renegade Sinzaun, who, he said, had lain for more than a month in the place. But the wretch must have received warning in some way, for the lodging was empty, though the inmate had not long quitted it. This attempt falling out so badly, the President was not inclined to leniency by the perusal of Monickchund's letters, which included a pretty broad hint to the effect that Mr Drake was an object of the Nabob's particular aversion, and had better be removed. Mr Menotti was ordered to prison, and the President was stirred up to make the affecting and patriotic speech in which he recanted yesterday from his faith in the Nabob."

"And did the wretched Menotti offer no further defence, sir?"

"Why, madam, he declared himself the victim of a conspiracy to ruin him between the lady I mentioned and her spouse, and hinted also that old Omy Chund would be found to be concerned in plotting with the Nabob; but the President, while promising to keep Omy Chund under his eye, refused to arrest him on such suspicious testimony, and committed Mr Menotti to the prison in the Fort, where he might remain secure until the present alarm be past, and prepare to confound his persecutors when an enquiry is made afterwards."

"You observe, gentlemen," said Captain Colquhoun, catching Mr Dash's last words as he rose from the table, "that even his honour don't yet believe in the reality of the danger that threatens us. I doubt but the Council won't perceive until the Fort is in the Nabob's hands that they have been sporting on the edge of a volcano."

June ye 15*th*.

Oh, my dear, sure Heaven must have devoted this unhappy place to destruction, for all that is said and done by way of defence is either wrong in itself or performed at the wrong time! True, the militia has been drilled morning and evening since I writ last, and makes a brave show, divided into two companies under Mr Holwell and Mr Mackett. Nor is this all, for Mr Manningham is their colonel, and Mr Frankland lieutenant-colonel, while the Rev. Mr Mapletoft and several gentlemen are captains. They were so obliging as to offer my papa a commission, but he refused it, saying that he counted it a greater piece of distinction to be a private man in this force than an officer, for it numbers only two hundred and fifty all told, and of these twenty-three of the Europeans are captains and mates of the shipping in the river, and must return to their vessels in the event of fighting, while a considerable number are Armenians, in whose valour so little confidence is reposed that they are detailed to guard the Fort itself, under command of Ensign Bellamy, who has just received his commission as Lieutenant. I'll assure you, Amelia, the poor young gentleman's disgust at his troops and his post is beyond words.

The defences also are well advanced, three principal batteries having been constructed, one to the north, close to the Saltpetre Godowns, on the cross-road that passes behind the Fort and leads by way of the strand to Chitpore; one across the avenue leading to the eastward which is called the Loll Buzar, in advance of the great gateway of the Fort, and having the Mayor's Court on its left and the Park on its right; and one some three hundred yards to the south of the Fort, at the corner of the burying-ground, and commanding one of the principal roads. Behind this last is a second battery, situated close to the front gate of the Park, and the eastern battery has a slighter one some distance in advance of it, while the Fort gateway itself is to have the additional defence of a work called a ravelin, which is not yet completed. All the smaller lanes and by-ways are blocked with breastworks made with pallisadoes, and where the ground is open, as in the Park, it has been cut up into trenches, to prevent the approach of elephants or cannon. To defend all these works, our small garrison has been augmented to the number of fifteen hundred by the hiring of a thousand *buxerries*, which are mercenary Indians armed with matchlocks. On the other hand, our governors are disappointed of the help they hoped for from the Dutch and French, for while the first refuse either to make or meddle in our dispute with the Nabob, the French are good enough to offer our whole factory to refuge at Chandernagore, where (say they) there's more hope of a successful defence. 'Tis some slight consolation to my papa and me that the Council have replied to this piece of gasconading only by a request to the French to assist us with a present of ammunition, that we may defend ourselves here.

Six days ago, as we hear, the Nabob quitted Cossimbuzar with his army, and began his march towards us, in spite of the intercessions of three of his own subjects, Roopchund and Mootabray, the sons of Jugget Seat, his own *shroff* and money-lender, and Coja Wazeed, a respectable merchant of Hoogly. That these disinterested persons failed in their benevolent designs is in great part due to the submissive and terrified letters sent by our Presidency to Mr Watts, which have continued to arrive long after Cossimbuzar was taken, and, falling into the hands of the Nabob, have confirmed him in his contempt and hostility for us, and he is marching forward with an incredible rapidity, so that many of his soldiers fall dead each day from the fierce rays of the sun. The news of the Soubah's approach reached us on Saturday, and the next day was such a Sabbath as I should think Calcutta never saw before, nor is likely, should it escape the ruin that seems to be impending, to see again. For first of all, there was a letter intercepted from Rajaram Hircara, the chief of the Nabob's spies and the person that sent his brother Narransing to demand that Kissendasseat should be given up, addressed to Omy Chund, advising him to escape from Calcutta to join with the Soubah while there was time. This coming so soon after Mr Menotti's accusation against Omy Chund moved the President and Council to alarm, and they had the old man arrested at once and lodged in the Fort, setting a guard over his effects. Orders were also issued out to stop all the Moors' boats passing up or down the river, and to seize two Moorish ships that were lying at anchor, which was done. Then, as though this were not turmoil enough for one day, some busy-body, finding the defences pretty well advanced and no feats of arms doing, revived Mr Holwell's discarded notion of an attempt on the fort named Tanners, which the Moors call Mucka Tanna, situated some five miles down the river on the opposite bank. So confident were our rulers in the strength of our mighty army, that all Captain Colquhoun's prudent representations were thrown to the winds, and all morning were preparations going forward for sailing against Tanners at noon, though the Captain warned them additionally that no success could be looked for in an enterprise that was commenced by profaning the Sabbath.

It appeared for a time, however, as though these prophecies of evil were to be falsified, for on our troops approaching Tanners in the evening in two ships and two brigantines, and landing in company with the Europeans and Lascars from the vessels' crews, the Moorish garrison fled, without scarcely any resistance at all, so that our people entered the place in triumph and disabled or threw into the river all the great guns of the fort. But this piece of bravado has proved the destruction of the enterprise, for yesterday morning came Monickchund, the Moorish Governor of Hoogly, with two field-pieces and two thousand men, who fired very smartly with their small arms, and to oppose whom our people had no cannon, and were drove out with little difficulty. Last evening and throughout to-day our vessels have been employed in vain trying to dislodge the enemy a second time, in a genteel sort of style without any fighting, and even a reinforcement of thirty men from our small garrison had no effect, so that the ships are dropped down with the ebb of the tide to lie quiet for the night.

Dreadful though this reverse is in a country where such extravagant value is placed upon the slightest piece of success, an event of far greater horror occurred yesterday in Calcutta itself. It was resolved by the Council, who feared further treachery, to arrest Omy Chund's relations and his friend Kissendasseat as well as himself, and a parcel of peons was sent to their houses with this object. Resistance was offered at both places, and Kissendass, who had raised and armed a force of men in the evident intention of joining with the Nabob when he arrives, succeeded in driving off his assailants and taking some of them prisoners, whom he used in the most shameful manner imaginable, until his house was fairly taken by storm by Lieutenant Blagg and a force of thirty Europeans, who discovered an incredible quantity of arms, as well as much treasure, concealed in it. At Omy Chund's house, and this is the horrid part of the affair, his brother-in-law Huzzaromull, who was the person most sought for, hid himself in the Ginanah among the women, while the place was defended by Omy Chund's peons and armed domestics, to the number of three hundred. The fight going against them, the head Jemmautdar, Juggermunt Sing (the same man that Mr Menotti catched in my papa's garden with Sinzaun's letter), stabbed all his master's women, to the number of thirteen, to preserve them, as he believed, from disgrace, and fastening up the doors, set light to the place. Huzzaromull, having no mind to be burnt alive, surrendered himself, having lost his hand in the fight, and there's a rumour that the perpetrator of the fearful deed, Juggermunt Sing himself, was conveyed away by his fellows covered with wounds. But oh, my dear, think of all these poor Gentoo women and their children, murdered in this barbarous fashion! Pray heaven the guilt of their innocent blood may not come on us, who are indeed remotely, though not directly, responsible for its being shed.

FORT WILLIAM, *June ye* 17*th*.

We are besieged, Amelia. Yesterday morning, some time before noon, when the ships, which had come up with the flood-tide, were preparing to drop down to Tanners again, all thought of the continuance of that enterprise was forbidden by a brisk sound of firing from the direction of Chitpore. The vanguard of the Nabob's army was arrived at Mr Kelsall's garden, under the command of Meer Jaffier, his *buckshy*[08] or chief general officer, and firing on the Prince George sloop of eighteen guns that lay off Perrins Redoubt. As you will guess, my dear girl, we had all received our orders in the event of this crisis, and had our effects packed in readiness for transport, so that as soon as the firing was heard, and the military and militia were repaired to their posts, we European women quitted our houses, and ourselves in palanqueens, and with our trunks carried on bullock-waggons, took refuge in the Fort without much confusion. Everything, of course, must necessarily be abandoned, with the exception of our clothes and jewels and our bedding, which is always carried about with them by travellers in the East, and which we should need in the Fort. Here the state apartments belonging to the Company were prepared for the fugitives' reception, and the gentlemen who lodge within the walls were also most obliging in leaving their rooms free, and huddling into the varandas themselves. Mrs Freyne, who is still indisposed, was disturbed to discover that the state apartments were already seized upon when we arrived by the ladies who live nearer at hand, or whose spouses are of higher rank in the service than my papa, but we were made welcome to have our choice of all the young gentlemen's chambers, and found ourselves at last settled in two tolerable rooms, in as cool a situation as we could hope for. Next to us, to my great delight, is my dear Mrs Hurstwood, whose fever has attacked her again to such a degree that she had to be brought into the Fort in a palanqueen of the French shape, which is like a couch covered in with a waggon-top, but her disposition is the cheerfullest in the world, and she declares that the having her Sylvia so close at hand will alone suffice to cure her. My Amelia will guess that I had plenty to do, even with the help of our three iyas (who were more minded indeed to sit down and bewail themselves), to make my two sufferers comfortable, while disposing our trunks and other effects to serve for chairs and tables with some air of neatness and order. When I had time to give my attention to public affairs, I learned from one of the young gentlemen, who came good-naturedly to see whether he could offer me any assistance, that the greater part of the black inhabitants of the town was fled, as were also most of the servants of the Europeans, and among them all the cooks, so that though the place was well supplied with provisions we bade fair to starve in the midst of plenty. But if the Indians are gone, the half-blood Portuguese and other black Christians are all crowded into the Fort, to the amount of two thousand—men, women, and children—so that 'tis scarce possible to move about the courtyard without tumbling over some of the refugees; and, with their chests and bundles, the place is like a fair, though lacking the ease and cheerfulness. However, a certain number of 'em are chose out to act as cooks, so that they are not without some use to the garrison and ourselves.

'Tis some slight consolation, in all this alarm and confusion, that throughout yesterday the honours of the fight remained with us. In command at Perrins Redoubt is Mr Ensign Piccard,[09] a young gentleman that has seen war service on the coast of Choromandel, and has profited by it. With him were only twenty Europeans, though these have since been reinforced by fifty more under Lieutenant Blagg, and this small party, with two field-pieces, maintained themselves with complete success against four thousand matchlockmen of the Soubah's, with whom was a battery of four cannon and other pieces carried on the backs of elephants. Shortly after sunset, seeing the piquet under Captain Clayton advancing against them, the enemy retired, leaving seventy-nine dead on the field, and encamped in the *top* or grove on the further side of the rivulet. Here, after consuming their evening meal, they betook themselves to sleep, as is the custom of the Indians, and this being suspected by Mr Piccard, he crossed the rivulet with a party of his men, seized and spiked up the enemy's guns, and beating up the thickets in which the Moors lay, drove 'em all out, and this without losing one of his people; the spirits of those in the Redoubt being further cheered by observing the enemy, as soon as they were recovered from the confusion into which they had been thrown, filing in very large columns towards Dumdumma, as though they designed to abandon the siege.

But this, alas! was not to be. Oh, my dear, how do our sins return upon us! Who does my Amelia think had entered the Nabob's camp in the interval between Ensign Piccard's attack and the departure of the enemy? None, my dear girl, but Juggermunt Sing, that Jemmautdar of Omy Chund's of whose terrible and resolved behaviour I wrote you two days back. With invincible spirit this man, although covered with wounds and concealed timidly by his countrymen in some of the black houses, caused himself to be set on a horse, and being carried to Meer Jaffier the Buckshy, told him there was no need to sacrifice his men's lives in attacking the bridge which was defended so stoutly by our people at Perrins, for that the Morattoe-ditch did not near extend round the town, and he himself could show him certain undefended passages by which he might enter our bounds on the eastward. This, then, was the secret of the enemy's movement, which brought 'em as far as the old entrenchments at Cow Cross, where they encamped behind the Brick-kilns, their tents extending from the Bungulo[10] as far as Govinderam Metre's garden on the Dumdumma road. Nor was this all our misfortune, for at Cow Cross bridge were posted by far the greater part of our *buxerries*, to the number of near a thousand, and these seeing the enemy approaching, at once joined with them, thus leaving the way into the settlement open.

Such, then, was our situation this morning, Amelia, the enemy entering the skirts of the town and plundering and burning wherever they went, especially the houses of the black merchants lying near Chitpore. They have set fire to the Great Buzar and many parts of the Black Town, and we, for our part, have fired the Buzars and poor mean huts to the east and south almost as far as Govindpoor's, so that there's a vast expanse of fire and smoke all around us, producing a scene too horrible to describe. This evening a party was sent to drive out the Moors from the merchants' quarter by the river, and brought back a few prisoners, from whom it was discovered that a general attack upon our outposts is intended to-morrow. This has led to the recall of Lieutenant Blagg and his reinforcement from Perrins, and the troops are ordered to remain all night under arms. One more piece of news has reached us. The reply from Chandernagore to our genteel letter asking the French to assist us with ammunition is a cold refusal. They have only sufficient, they say, for their own needs. Yet we learn that they were obliging enough to supply the Nabob with two hundred chests of powder when he lay across the river from them at Banka Buzar. Questionless we are intended to be grateful that they don't actively join with Surajah Dowlah against us, though we hear that in his army is a body of fifty deserters from Chandernagore, whose escape has been connived at by their superiors.

FORT WILLIAM, *June ye* 18*th*.

I am writing these lines tormented by the most cruel anxiety. All is lost, Amelia, or very nearly so. The women and wounded are to be put on board the ships this evening, while the small remnant of our defenders endeavour to maintain themselves in the Fort, which alone is left to us, against a triumphant and exulting enemy. The Company's ship Doddalay[11] and seven smaller vessels lie at a convenient distance from the Fort, and Mess. Manningham and Frankland are gone on board to provide for the reception of us unfortunates, while here every one is occupied in making sure that she shan't be saved and her possessions left behind. Mrs Freyne is more sprightly than I have seen her for a fortnight. In an agreeable undress, she sits enthroned on piles of bedding, directing the trembling iyas as they cord the trunks, while my poor Charlotte lies almost speechless, exhausted by the heat and the violence of the fever that has held her all day. You'll wonder that I can write at such a moment; and, indeed, I wonder at it myself. But, Amelia, my papa, my dear and honoured father, the kindest of men, is missing. I have been hurrying hither and thither, demanding of every European I met whether they could tell me anything of him, but all they can assure me of is that no one has seen him either slain or seriously wounded. Captain Colquhoun came upon me while I was seeking to obtain some news from a parcel of frightened To-passes, and fairly led me back by the hand to our lodging.

"You would oblige your good papa much more by remaining calm, madam," he said; "for indeed I can imagine few things that would displease him more than to see you wandering about the Fort unattended at such a moment. Do me the favour to sit down quietly and occupy your mind in some suitable manner, and you shall have the earliest news I can procure you."

Thus it is, then, that I am writing to my Amelia, and as the embarkation is not yet begun, I will endeavour to fulfil the Captain's request by setting down something of the history of this day of disaster, for there en't likely to be much chance for writing on board of a crowded ship, and, indeed, who knows what may be the fate of all of us in another few hours?

The day began with an attack made on the South Battery, where Captain Colquhoun was in command, with my papa among his troops. The enemy, taking possession of the houses on either side of the road in front of the battery, kept up a brisk fire upon the defenders with musquetry and wall-pieces; but the Captain held his ground, and placed garrisons in the different buildings flanking him on the left as far as the Rope-walk, to guard against any attack from that side. He was assailed with the same smartness until noon, when the enemy drew off for a while. The next battery to be attacked was that on the north, which was held by Lieutenant Smyth, who was so happy as to be able to beat off with little loss the assaults made upon him, thanks to the advantages of his situation and his skilful disposition of his men, although the Moors whom he repulsed did but join with those ranged against the Eastern Battery, which was attacked with the greatest resolution of all. Captain Clayton was in command here, supported by Mr Holwell and a party of militia, and having as an advanced post on the right the Gaol, whither Mr le Beaume had entreated to be allowed to betake himself with forty of our remaining *buxerries.* In advance of this again was the slight work I have mentioned before, defended by a platoon of Europeans with two field-pieces, which bore the first brunt of the assault. Seeing themselves threatened by some thousands of the enemy, who found shelter from their shot in the thickets, this small party at length retired upon the Gaol with their guns, when the Moors, taking advantage of an undefended passage, seized the three European houses in the Rope-walk to the rear of the Gaol, and fired from them so furiously that Mr le Beaume was forced to spike up his guns and retreat to the battery. This was now attacked so hotly from the three houses on the right, and also from two on the left, that only the men working the guns could remain in it, and by the loss of the pallisado on the right it became almost untenable, Captain Clayton having rejected with displeasure Mr Holwell's suggestion to occupy the buildings on either side with musquetry. In this unhappy state of affairs Mr Holwell rode back to the Fort to demand reinforcements from the President, for the importance of retaining this commanding post was universally admitted, nor was there any thought of retreat among the defenders themselves; but on his return he was met by the disorderly array of the troops from the battery, whom Captain Clayton had withdrawn in such haste that he left his ammunition behind him, disabling his guns also so slightly that the enemy, who now flocked into our abandoned work, manifesting their joy by excessive shouts, were able to drill them and turn them on the Fort. Oh, Amelia, figure to yourself the anguish of this moment to us who had been enquiring eagerly all day for every the least piece of news, and now saw our brave men disgracefully led back into the place by their incompetent commander! But there was worse still to come.

The capture of the Eastern Battery left the Soubah's whole force at liberty to hurl itself upon that to the south, where Captain Colquhoun found himself in danger of being surrounded. The enemy, who now filled the Rope-walk, broke through the breastwork between Mrs Putham's house and Captain Minchin's, and crowded into the lane at the back, hoping to take him in the rear. Finding himself pressed also in front, from the great road leading to Surmans, he was forced to call in the flanking parties that he had posted in the houses near, and retreat upon the inner battery close to the Park gate, leaving one of his field-pieces at the corner of the Park wall to cover his retirement. This necessary movement left Lieutenant Blagg and a party of volunteers, who had not been able to obey in time the order to retire, surrounded by the enemy on the top of Captain Minchin's house; but although the Moors held all the houses around, and the very rooms below the roof on which they were, these brave men fought their way down the stairs and broke through the hostile crowds that thronged the whole square with their bayonets, until they reached the cannon at the corner of the Park, which covered their retreat also to the inner battery before it was spiked up and abandoned. The incredible slaughter of the enemy made by this brave band, and the skill and deliberation with which Captain Colquhoun had conducted his retirement, bringing with him all his ammunition and all the guns but that one which was spiked up, made the affair rather a triumph than a reverse; but what was his mortification and that of all with him to receive orders from the Fort to retire from the second battery also, although it was within pistol-shot of the walls, and commanded two out of the three roads of the place! I could almost wonder that the gallant gentleman did not refuse to obey (or rather I should do so did I not know his strict notions of discipline), but leaving an officer with thirty men, my papa among them, to hold the Company's house outside the walls, he returned reluctantly with his troops, to find that those in command had lost, during the trials of the day, the little spirit and wisdom they had possessed. Not content with having compelled the abandonment of the South Battery after the loss of that on the east, the Council now ordered a retreat from the post which Lieutenant Smyth had defended with so much success on the north, sending also boats to recall Ensign Piccard and his party from Perrins to garrison the Company's house, and ordering the Prince George to fall down from Baugbuzar to her usual station opposite the Fort.

No words of mine can describe, Amelia, the state of affairs when this disgraceful resolution was made known—the consternation of the English at so unnecessary and damaging a retreat, of which the remaining *buxerries* and all the Lascars but a few quickly showed their opinion by going over to the enemy, the stupefaction of the To-passes and Armenians among the militia, and the frightful uproar among the three thousand servants and black Christians that crowd up the Fort. All this needs to be seen and heard to be appreciated, but her Sylvia's misery my dearest girl's sensibility will enable her to picture, since the party left by Captain Colquhoun at the Company's house came in, on being relieved by Mr Piccard, without Mr Freyne.

(*In the original letter the following is written hurriedly in pencil.*)

I am scribbling these few lines on the last sheet of my unfinished letter, in case I should never despatch another to my Amelia. I shall entrust it to Mr Hurstwood, who is going on board the Doddalay to see how his Charlotte finds herself, but only for a moment, since a fresh assault of the enemy upon the Fort is momentarily expected. But why am I not on board? you'll say. Because my duty holds me here, Amelia. I was actually in the boat with Mrs Freyne and other ladies, and on the point of putting off from the Gott, when there comes running a servant of Omy Chund's who is permitted to go freely about the Fort to wait upon his master, and cries out to me that he had found Fahrein Saeb (so the Indians call my papa), grievously wounded, but still living. Was it possible for me to persist in going on board the ship after hearing this, my dear? Sure my sweet girl would tear me from her heart had I given the notion a moment's thought. Mrs Freyne is herself ill, and was so prodigiously alarmed at the idea of delaying any longer, that I feared a screaming-fit, and begged the boatmen to put off at once without me, which they did, while I returned with the Indian to one of the ground-floor chambers of the Fort, where they had carried the dear gentleman and laid him on a bedstead. It seemed that he had been struck down by a blow from the butt-end of a musquet or other heavy weapon, and then stabbed and hacked in the most cruel and fiendish manner, so that he was as near as possible dead from want of blood. The good Padra Bellamy and Mr Holwell did all in their power to stanch the wounds, for Dr Knox was nowhere to be found, but all was in vain until the poor servant (who had heard, he says, that Fahrein Saeb was missing, and since he had always used him civilly and been friendly with his master, went to search for him in the grounds of the Company's house and found him) proved himself indeed a good Samaritan, bringing some odd sort of salve that was extraordinary effectual, and bidding us on no account move the sufferer before morning, lest the blood should burst forth again. Here, then, I am, my dear, watching over my papa, in company with a Portuguese woman that Mr Holwell has fetched to be with me, not knowing whether I shall see the light of another day, for the enemy, grown bold, as they may well be, with their continued and undeserved successes, are gathering themselves for a general attack. Farewell then, my dearest, my best beloved friend. If this is the last you hear from me, preserve a little kindness in your heart for

your SYLVIA FREYNE.

CHAPTER XII.
PRESENTING ONE OF THE WORLD'S TRAGEDIES.

(The account contained in this chapter belongs to a letter written some months later, but it is introduced here in order that the current of the narrative may not be interrupted.)

However long I may live, Amelia, I am assured I shall never find weaken the remembrance of the period of three nights and two days which began with the departure of the European women from the Fort. All the events of my life before it seem pale and distant, and as for those that have occurred since—why, my dear, they are so little real in comparison that if I so much as close my eyes, without any design of recalling the awful past, I find myself in it again. After this, you need only to be told that I am sometimes thankful for even this frightful relief from the realising the cruel situation in which I am at present, to perceive your poor Sylvia's sorrowful case. 'Tis in part for this reason that I am forcing myself to set down in writing the whole shocking history.

After the council of war held on the Friday evening, at which it was determined to send the European women at once on board ship, there was a continual diminishing of the garrison of the Fort. Outside the walls our people were still holding Mr Eyre's house on the north, Mr Cruttenden's and the church on the north-east, and the Company's house on the south, but this last post was evacuated before eight o'clock, the defenders being too severely galled by the fire from the next house, which was occupied by the enemy. The south side of the Fort was thus left exposed to attack, for our guns (mounted on the roof of the godowns which rendered the two bastions on this side useless) failed altogether to do any damage to these *pucca* houses, which we could neither hold nor destroy. Since affairs began to look so black, such of the garrison as held their lives more precious than their reputation took advantage of the passing to and fro of the boats conveying the ladies to slip off to the ships themselves. A monstrous example was set by Mess. Manningham and Frankland, the third and fourth in rank in the Council, and Mr Drake's constant allies in the work of governing, who, offering their services to attend the ladies and see them safely on board, chose to remain in the Doddalay, of which vessel they, with the President, were part owners, in spite of all the urgent messages sent to bring 'em back. There followed them, among other private persons, three lieutenants of the militia, and worse still, one belonging to the army. It was Mr Bentinck, Amelia. All this time the enemy were gathering their forces for an assault, and approached the walls about midnight, intending to escalade 'em. Inside the Fort a general alarm was beaten three times, but only such of the garrison as were on duty responded to the call, the rest having thrown themselves down in any corner, worn out with fatigue, or being disgusted with the behaviour of their leaders and the want of food,—for though there was plenty to be had, no one had chanced to keep an eye on the Portuguese cooks, and they were run off. This great beating of drums, however, alarmed the enemy so terribly that, fancying the whole garrison, rendered fierce by despair, was gathered in arms to oppose 'em, they withdrew from their attempt, contenting themselves with shooting a few fire-arrows into the Fort, and now and then sending off a cannon-shot.

While all this was passing, I sat watching beside the senseless form of my dear papa, who never moved nor opened his eyes while the effect of the salve with which the Indian had dressed his wounds lasted, which was the whole night. I was not left altogether solitary, for one gentleman after another was perpetually coming in to ask whether he might be permitted to do anything for me, and this proof of the esteem felt by all for Mr Freyne and their obliging kindness to myself affected me very sensibly. Soon after eleven o'clock in came Captain Colquhoun, whom I had not seen for some hours, and eyed me with great sternness.

"You have no business here, madam," says he.

"Indeed, sir, I think I have," said I.

"I would I had known ten minutes ago where you was, madam. I promise you I would have packed you off on board the Diligence, with Mrs Drake and Mrs Mapletoft and the two other ladies that were left. Mr le Beaume was there too, badly wounded, and you could have acted nurse-keeper to him, if you're so fond of the part."

"There's no question of fondness, sir. I'm but doing my duty."

"What can you do for your papa that any of us can't do, madam? If he were in his senses, 'twould please him best to know that you was safe on board the shipping, not thrusting yourself into danger here," and the good gentleman went away in a rage, to seek, I fancy, for some means of getting me out of the factory, but there was no more boats plied that night.

Mr Secretary Cooke was the next person that looked in, I think, to tell me that a second council of war was about to be held (this was after the enemy had desisted from their design of attacking us), and some time later Mr Dash came to tell me that the council was broke up.

"But what was the decision arrived at, sir?" I asked him.

"None at all, madam. A cannon-shot passed through the consultation-room, and no one waited for another."

"But, sure, sir, something must have been resolved upon?"

"Indeed, madam, there never was so good-natured an assembly, for it left every member to believe that his own proposals would be followed."

"But were there many different plans proposed, sir?"

"As many as there were members, madam, and that was any one that cared to take part. Mr Holwell was all for an orderly retirement after holding the place for one day more, in order that the Company's papers and treasure might be put safely on board the shipping, but Mr Baillie opposed him. Others were for evacuating the Fort at once, and Captain Colquhoun was for holding it as long as the walls stood, in the expectation that the rains, which are now some days overdue, must compel the Nabob to raise the siege before long."

"That's the Captain, indeed! And was he well seconded, sir?"

"But poorly, madam, since Captain Witherington, who has succeeded in counting up his munitions now that there's so little to count, declares that our powder is only sufficient for two days more, or three if it's well husbanded. But as I said, what with every one talking at once, and the absence of any sort of control, no one knows what plan was decided upon or what rejected."

I heard nothing more certain than this until the morning, when Mr Hurstwood, who had returned punctually from the Doddalay the night before, with his Charlotte's full consent and approbation, came in and told me that all the Portuguese women and children were to be embarked at once, but whether this portended a general retirement or not, he could not say. The duty of seeing these unfortunate persons put into boats and despatched to the ships fell to Mr Baillie, who set to work very early, with all the disinterested kindness and generous activity imaginable. Our short season of peace was now over, for with the light the firing upon us began more fiercely than ever. So wickedly ingenious were the enemy that they had employed the hours of darkness not only in filling up the ditches which we had dug across the Park and other open grounds (and which had served them for ready-made breastworks behind which to fire at us the day before), and bringing their artillery over 'em, but in turning against us the abandoned guns of our own Eastern Battery, which did us more damage than all their own weapons. Not content with this, they had mounted cannons at the gates of Mr Bellamy's compound and the Play-house compound, which commanded the church, as well as three at the corner of the Park, two in the Loll Buzar beyond the Gaol, and two at a spot near the

Horse-stables, from all of which they rained their missiles upon us, while *shamsingees*[01] and wall-pieces were fixed at every corner, and *bercundauzes*[02] or matchlockmen were in readiness to shoot at any person that appeared on our walls. Finding that the enemy had not seized upon the Company's house, which he had been forced to abandon the night before, Ensign Piccard led out a party to occupy it again, in the hope of at least diverting a portion of the firing from the Fort; and the President, adventuring his person boldly enough, made the tour of the ramparts, and finding it almost impossible to hold them in their ruinous state, which every moment became worse, ordered them to be strengthened with bags of cotton, affording a very sufficient protection against bullets. Seeing his honour and Mr Holwell, with Mr Hurstwood and Padra Mapletoft, busy in front of the chamber where I sat in cutting open the bales and filling the cotton into bags to carry it to the ramparts, I made bold to offer them such help as I could in closing the bags, and we all worked hard for some minutes, until a messenger came to call away Mr Drake, to whom, just as he was departing, Mr Hurstwood cried out that he would go on board the Doddalay again for five minutes to see his lady, and return at once. Mr Holwell also going off, there was only the Rev. Mr Mapletoft left, who came and looked in upon my papa, and said in a dolorous voice that he had understood a retirement was decided upon, and he wished some gentleman would be so wise as to begin it, which on Captain Colquhoun hearing, who came up at the moment, he rebuked the Padra very sharply for his dejected air, and bade him take pattern by the excellent Mr Bellamy. I don't know how the poor divine covered his confusion, for on entering the chamber I found to my delight that my papa's eyes were open, though he was not looking at me, but at Captain Colquhoun.

"Captain," he said, very feebly, "we en't going to leave the place to those Moorish swine, as the parson said, are we?"

"Not while we have a charge of powder left with which to fight 'em, sir."

"I'm with you, Captain. But what's my girl doing here? Where's the other women?"

"On board the shipping, sir, where Miss ought to be."

"So she ought. Get her on board, sir, pray."

"The first chance I have, sir; trust me."

"Sir," I said, following the Captain out of the chamber, "I would not withstand you in my papa's presence, for fear of disturbing him, but I won't go."

"By Heaven, madam, but you shall, if I have to carry you down to the Gott. There's no women's work before us here."

And he hurried away, but could not immediately carry out his intention, for there happened all at once a whole quantity of disasters. Ensign Piccard's party in the Company's house, having been attacked by the Moguls in overwhelming numbers, were forced to retreat back to the Fort, every man of them being wounded, and their leader very seriously so. As though this were not enough, almost at the same moment the piquets that held the church and Mr Eyre's and Mr Cruttenden's houses, whether on receipt of an order or on their own motion I don't know, also left their posts and came in, so that we were now reduced to the Fort itself and the Gott which it commanded, and which was defended on either side by a weak wall with a gate of pallisadoes. The enemy, scattering themselves along the bank of the river, began now to shoot fire-arrows into the shipping, and this so terrified those on board the vessels that they were seen to be weighing their anchors in preparation for dropping down the river. At this dreadful sight the terror and confusion in the Fort became extreme. Many of the boatmen detained at the wharf had made their escape in the night with their craft, and Mr Baillie was met with the utmost turmoil and difficulty in his humane task of embarking the Portuguese Christians, a good number of whom were drowned in their haste and terror, but the consternation was now spread to the Europeans. The President was going hither and thither in an odd hurried sort of style, giving orders for the defence of the wall that connected the south-west bastion with the line of guns over the wharf, but no one offered to obey him, for there was no one at hand to manage the two field-pieces that were there. Presently a person came to acquaint him that all the gunpowder left was so damp and spoiled as to be useless, a piece of news that appeared to give him great concern, as well it might, although it was afterwards proved not to be true. Mr Drake went away to consult with his officers, and for some time we heard nothing but the firing, until Captain Colquhoun came running, and seizing my wrist, cried out to me to follow him at once.

"I won't leave my papa here, sir," I cried.

"If he's moved he'll die, madam."

"Then I'll stay and die with him, sir."

"No, you won't, miss," cried my papa, in a voice of extraordinary strength. "See," and he plucked at his bandages, "if you don't go I'll loosen these and bleed to death, and you'll have the recollection that you're your father's murderer."

"If my papa will drive away his girl by such a cruel means—" I cried, but Captain Colquhoun dragged me from the place, choking with sobs, and hurried me towards the back gate of the Fort. The Gott and the steps were crowded with people, all crying out that the enemy were forcing the pallisadoes from the side of the Company's house, but there was only two boats in sight. One was already putting off, with Captain Minchin and Mr Mackett in it, t'other was still at the steps, and Mr Drake was in the act of stepping on board, Captain Grant and one of the engineer officers following him. By the time we were arrived at the head of the steps, this boat also had put off, the President's black footman, who had stood with his sword drawn guarding it in readiness for his master's escape, clambering in from the shore. Captain Colquhoun pulled me down the steps.

"Gentlemen," he cried, rushing into the water up to his knees, "wait a moment! Put back and take the lady on board. Mr President! Captain Grant! do you call yourselves men, sirs, and leave a woman to perish? Think of your own wives and daughters, and of the fate to which you are condemning Miss Freyne! May Heaven's curse light upon you," and he went on to call down the most fearful imprecations, such as it made me shudder to hear, for the rowers were rowing with all their might, and none of the persons in the boat had made so much as a motion to put back, nor even appeared to listen.

"We can do better than curse, Captain," said one of the gentlemen standing on the steps, who had his piece in his hand, and he levelled it and fired. Several others followed his example, and the bullets went skipping into the water round the boat, but none of 'em took place, and these last and worst of our deserters arrived safely on board of the Doddalay, which had by now dropped down as far as Surmans. Many others, so we learned, were escaped before them, and among these were Padra Mapletoft and Mr Dash. Mr Hurstwood, who had not returned from the Doddalay, was carried off along with it, against the good gentleman's will, I can't doubt.

Captain Colquhoun led the way back into the Fort, walking with hanging head and his eyes cast down, and when all were inside, locked the west gate, to prevent any further desertions. Another council of war was hastily summoned, at which Mr Pearkes, the senior member of Council remaining in the factory, yielded his right in favour of Mr Holwell, who was welcomed without a dissenting voice as governor of the Fort and commander-in-chief. This having been determined, Captain Colquhoun remembered that he had been holding me fast by the wrist the entire time, and led me back to my papa without a word.

"We were too late, sir," he said, in a broken voice, when we entered the chamber, and my poor father uttered a heart-rending groan.

"Unhappy girl!" he cried, looking sternly at me; "it had been better you had died with your mother than lived to see this day."

I could only sob, and my distress melted the Captain.

"Come, sir," he said; "we'll hope things en't so bad. From all quarters of the Fort they are hanging out signals to the ships to come back to their stations and take us off, and 'tis unpossible that those on board should be so flinty-hearted as to disregard us. Please Heaven, we shall all be took off orderly to-night, as Mr Holwell proposed at the council."

"And if the Moors break in first," says my papa, "why, you must do the last kindness to my girl if my hand fail me. See that my pistols are charged, and lay them here beside me, old friend. The dogs will give warning enough of their approach when it's time to use 'em. Stop crying, miss, and come near and give me a kiss. You meant well, and it en't your fault that you're a fool, staying here to make your father's end a miserable instead of a happy one."

I entreated the dear gentleman's forgiveness with tears, as I knelt on the floor beside him, and my grief so wrought upon his tenderness that he was moved to take a more cheerful view of our situation, encouraging me with hopes that the ships would return with the flood-tide, and take off the whole garrison. Presently there came in the Gentoo, Omy Chund's servant, whom we now knew to be the person that had raised the alarm of the enemy's breaking through the south-west pallisado, which was proved to be false, though not before it had frightened away Mr Drake and his friends; but asking the fellow why he spread such a report, he answered that he had believed it to be true. He brought with him a second small quantity of the salve, which he said was all he had, and, having promised that by his master's order all his interest should be exerted in favour of our safety and honourable treatment should the Moors break into the Fort, departed again. About this time there fell on us the most cruel disappointment of all. The sloop Prince George, which had been ordered down from Perrins the night before, and was still lying opposite our south-west bastion, was signalled to approach closer, in the hope that she might be able to take us off. Mess. Pearkes and Lewis, going off to her in one of her boats that she sent on shore, carried instructions to her commander to bring his ship as near the Fort as possible, and this gentleman had sufficient courage and humanity to obey. But as the vessel approached us, and all watched her with tears in their eyes, thinking that safety was at last within reach, what was the general consternation when, owing either to the timid incompetency, or, as some said, the treachery, of her pilot, she run aground on one of those sand-banks that are everywhere lying in wait for unwary wretches in the course of the deceitful Hoogly! This destroyed our last hope of escape by water, for she could not be got off (those on board of the other ships making not the slightest offer of assistance), and her crew saved themselves at last in their boats, which durst not approach the shore.

But what shall I say of the conduct of the President and those with him on board the shipping, who took no step to save the wretches they had so basely abandoned? Either on Saturday or on Sunday they might have stood up the river with the flood, and with the aid of their crews and of the stores of munitions aboard of them, have turned the entire course of affairs, or at least have taken off the garrison and the Company's papers and treasure without the loss of a single man; but in spite of all the urgent and affecting signals made to them, they did nothing. Nay, had they dropped down the river out of sight, for safety's sake, one might forgive them better, but they lay off Surmans, in full view of us, for over four-and-twenty hours, as though to feast their eyes upon our dying agonies, and stood away only when they perceived that the worst had happened (though how fearful that worst was to be they could not have guessed).

As for those who were thus deserted, in spite of their natural resentment and despondency, they prepared to fight to the last under the new commanderie, and die as becomes Britons. Bales of broadcloth were got up from the warehouses, and built up into traverses along the eastern wall and its two bastions, which were swept by the enemy's fire from the church, and with these, and the bags of cotton placed along the other ramparts, some shelter was obtained for our wearied garrison. Towards noon the enemy, being questionless disappointed that we had not offered to surrender the Fort to them in the panic at the President's departure, drew off a little, and made no more attempts at storming our defences either that day or night, contenting themselves with keeping up their constant fire of cannon and musquetry, to which we were by now well accustomed. Will it surprise you, Amelia, to learn that your Sylvia passed that afternoon in sleep? I'll assure you that I can hardly believe it of myself, and yet I had not slept all the night before, and even our dangerous situation, and the cruel anxiety I was in, could not keep me from drowsiness. Mr Bellamy coming in, fresh from the walls (where, good gentleman, he had fought as well as any lay person of them all), to see my papa, found me fallen asleep with my head on the sufferer's pillow, and bade me go into the next room and rest, while he watched beside the dear gentleman. I was very reluctant to go, for my papa's least movement made his wounds begin to burst out bleeding afresh; but on the Padra promising to call me the moment that there was any change, I obeyed him, and slept until it was dark, when I waked up to find the enemy still cannonading us, and fire-signals burning instead of flags to summon the ships. That night passed much as the last had done, the gentlemen coming in every now and then with the most agreeable punctuality to exhort me to keep up heart, for if we could only maintain ourselves until the following night, Mr Holwell was devising a scheme with Captain Colquhoun for cutting our way through the enemy, and retiring to Surmans, where we might get on board the ships. The enemy had fired all the European houses in the town, except those which gave them a footing from which to annoy us, and the dreadful glare and heat was most distressing, although the Moors remained tolerable quiet.

The morning of Sunday the 20th of June found our garrison divided between resolution and a desire to capitulate. The gentlemen of the Service and the officers, both those of the army and the ships, were resolved to preserve their honour by dying where they stood rather than yield, but there was a discontented spirit abroad in the lower ranks, which were full of Dutchmen, To-passes, and Armenians, few English being left. Among these men Mr Holwell divided three chests of treasure in the hope of pacifying them, and even went so far in yielding to their demands as to send to Omy Chund in his prison, requesting him to accept of his release and go to treat with the Nabob for us. This the vindictive Gentoo refused to do, but consented to write a letter from his cell to Raja Monickchund, the Phousdar of Hoogly, entreating him to intercede with the Soubah on our behalf, and this letter Mr Holwell threw over the wall when the enemy had opened their attack upon us again with the daylight, but the humiliating expedient had no effect, for there was a very determined attack made at noon on the north side of the Fort, which the enemy sought to escalade under cover of a prodigious fire from the ruins of Mr Cruttenden's house. They were again beat off, but not without a dreadful struggle, in which five-and-twenty of our bravest remaining defenders were killed, and over seventy received wounds. So stubborn was the fighting that it seemed to me more than once that all must be lost, and I was like to cry out with joy when the news of the enemy's repulse was brought me by that sergeant of Captain Colquhoun's of whom I have told you before. This worthy fellow, who is named Jones, came to me running with all his might, and with one hand clapped to his face.

"So please you, madam, the Moors is drove off again," says he, and would have hasted away at once, but thinking he must have received some wound, I asked him why he ran in so odd a style.

"Why, madam," says he, "you've heard as how I've promised the Captain to touch no spirits until he gives me leave, and I've kept it, too. But when the other men broke into the arrack storehouse just now, where they're making themselves as drunk as fiddlers, I knew as how the devil was setting a trap for me, and I says to myself as I'd not linger a moment before getting back to the Captain, nor give myself the chance of so much as smelling the stuff."

And away he went, holding his nose as before. It pleased me that he should be so anxious to keep his promise to his Captain, and I told my papa of it, but to my grief the tale threw him into a great melancholy, for he began to lament that in all his life he had never done so much kindness to any fellow-creature as to help him to withstand his temptations. I sought to comfort him with the recollection that at least he had never led any astray, but he refused to listen to me.

"All my life," he said, "I have been satisfied to be of the breed of Democritus, smiling at what was evil, and admiring what was good—and staying there. My natural easiness of temper has made me believe that I was right so long as I did no wrong, nor interfered with others' doing it if they pleased. I thought that if I did no good, at least I did no harm, and now I am reaping the fruits of my foolishness. My wife has taken advantage of my slackness—nay, let me rather say that I in my slackness have suffered her to bring disgrace on herself and destruction on the factory. My daughter is here exposed to the worst of perils instead of finding herself safe under the protection of a husband, and my business here—how shall I answer for it to the Company, to the women that are left homeless, or to the brave men that are foredoomed to perish within these walls? 'Twas in my power to have spoke and voted in the Council for wise and prudent measures, perhaps to have restrained the extravagancies of the President and his two friends, but I did it not, I loved my ease too well. And this is the end of it all. Truly I have left undone those things which I ought to have done."

I was beyond measure affected to hear such words from my papa's lips, and seeing Mr Bellamy crossing the court, all blackened with powder and stained with blood, I ran out in the sun to him, and prayed him to come to the dear sufferer. Such was the kindness of this good man that he robbed himself of the rest which he so much needed, and gave up the time for it to Mr Freyne, sitting beside him and reading passages from the Scriptures, bidding him also look away from the life of which he was now ashamed to that of Christ who had died for him, and not add to the sins which he deplored that of unbelief and of the rejection of God's mercy. Nay, he was even so thoughtful as to comfort him concerning the poor girl that he was leaving, as he feared, to the most extreme peril, saying that when man's power was utterly at an end, then was the time for the manifestation of the power of God. And how often the good Padra's words have served to comfort me since that day, I could not tell you, Amelia.

About two o'clock, the attack being renewed, Mr Bellamy was compelled to leave us to take his place on the walls, and my papa fell into a kind of slumber, with his hand clasped in mine. After a while Lieutenant Bellamy came to tell me that the enemy had desisted from their efforts and betaken themselves to places of shelter out of the reach of our fire, where, said he, 'twas to be hoped they would stay, for nearly all our common soldiers were so drunk with the arrack they had stole as to be lost to all sense of duty. After this all was quiet until a little after four, when the Gentoo, Omy Chund's servant, came running, and with a naked scymitar in his hand took up his post before our doorway. On my asking him what was the matter (for I had learnt to speak Moors well enough to understand the servants and they me, though but in a broken manner), he told me that the enemy having shown a flag of truce, Mr Holwell had replied with another, throwing over the wall also a letter addressed to Raja Doolubram, the Nabob's *duan*, asking for terms. While our people's attention was engaged by this parley, the enemy all flocked out of their hiding-places, and made fierce attacks both on the eastern gate of the Fort and the pallisadoes on the south-west, wounding Mr Baillie with a musquet-ball as he stood by Mr Holwell's side. On Mr Holwell running down to the parade to summon our common men, he found the few that were not drunk asleep, and those that were drunk, hearing of the danger, broke open the western gate, headed by a Dutchman of the Train, seeking to escape along the slime of the river, and so admitted the enemy. Hurrying to the south-east bastion Mr Holwell met with Captain Colquhoun, and the two gentlemen agreed that no further resistance was possible, since the Moors had also, by using bamboos for scaling-ladders, succeeded in great numbers in escalading the south wall, by means of the roofs of the godowns built against it, and were pouring into the Fort. The Gentoo added that he had seen the two gentlemen give up their swords to a Jemmautdar of the Nabob's, and that he had hastened hither to defend us with his life, as his master's orders were.

Resolved to second to the best of my power the efforts of this human pagan, I catched up Mr Freyne's pistols, and stood with one of them in each hand, while the shouts and cries of the victorious Moguls approached nearer, although none had as yet penetrated to our neighbourhood. I thought I had passed through the bitterness of death, Amelia, and 'twas like a new life when I saw Captain Colquhoun and his sergeant come hurrying across the courtyard, in company with one of the Moorish Jemmautdars and ten or twelve of his men, while the poor Gentoo that guarded us was so confused by their sudden appearance that he fetched a great blow at the Captain with his scymitar, but the sergeant warded it off, and no harm was done, though I cried out aloud in my fright.

"Madam," says the Captain, brushing the Gentoo aside, and coming into the chamber, "this Jemmautdar here en't so vile as the most of them, and has promised, in return for receiving all our valuables, to save us from the ill-treatment of his fellows. Pray give him any jewellery you may happen to have about you, and he'll conduct us to our friends, the rest of the prisoners."

My dear girl will guess that I did not delay to give the Captain my brooch and rings, my silver-framed tablets, and even the coral pins that fastened my handkerchief, to present to the Moor, observing that the poor gentleman himself had been robbed not only of his watch and shoe-buckles, but of the very buttons from his coat. My papa's pistols, which were mounted in silver, next excited the covetousness of the Jemmautdar, and Captain Colquhoun bade me give them up to him, making a sign to me that he himself had still a weapon concealed on his person. Since we were now robbed of everything, the Captain bade me pull the frills of my cap over my face as far as I could, and he and Sergeant Jones took up the two ends of the bedstead on which Mr Freyne lay, to carry it out. But to this the most strenuous objection was offered by Omy Chund's servant, who declared himself fully equal to protecting us if we remained where we were, and brought the Jemmautdar over to his side by means of signs which we could not comprehend. I was in terror lest the Captain and his man should be dragged away, and my papa and I left to the poor protection of this one Gentoo with his scymitar, but Mr Freyne settled the matter for himself.

"I don't desire to be separated from my friends," he said, awaking, as it seemed, from sleep. "My daughter and I will share the lot of the other prisoners."

The servant offering no further opposition, we quitted the chamber, I keeping close to Captain Colquhoun, and the Jemmautdar and his men acting as our guard. Not knowing what sights of horror might meet my eyes, I durst not look around me, but we passed unmolested—the Moors, as I learnt, being so busy with the spoil they had found, such as bales of broadcloth, chests of coral, plate, and treasure, in the private rooms of the gentlemen in the factory, that they had no time to observe us, and we arrived safely in the arched varanda in front of the barracks that extended from the great gate of the Fort to the south-east bastion, inside our eastern wall. Here were gradually gathered all that had escaped the perils of the day, including, besides ourselves, Mr Holwell, Mr Secretary Cooke, Mr Bellamy and his son the Lieutenant, Mr Eyre, Mr Baillie and several other members of Council, Captains Clayton and Witherington, a number of young gentlemen of the Service and the army (among them that gallant officer Mr Ensign Piccard, who was almost disabled by his wounds), several masters and mates of ships who had chose to remain with us when their fellows abandoned their duty, and some common soldiers and militia, both white and black. Oh, my dear, all these brave gentlemen! Sure I could weep tears of blood, to think of the awful fate of the best and noblest of our people in this factory, while the cowards and deserters stood aloof in safety.

About five o'clock the Nabob and his brother entered the Fort in state, being borne in ornamented litters, and Surajah Dowlah, having ordered a guard to be placed over the treasury, proceeded to the principal apartments of the factory, where he set up his throne and held his Court, receiving the compliments of Meer Jaffier the Buckshy, and the rest of his attendants. Having indulged himself in this fanfaronade, the victor sent for Mr Holwell to attend him, whom we saw depart with great grief and apprehension, but had presently the delight of welcoming him back unhurt, though with a countenance expressive of the utmost concern. After telling us that the Nabob had declared himself exceeding dissatisfied with the small quantity of money in the treasury, and had loudly expressed his resentment at our presumption in defending the place so stubbornly with such a small garrison, demanding also why Mr Holwell had not had the prudence to make his escape with the President, but ending with a promise that no harm should befall the prisoners, the good gentleman admitted us into the secret of his dejection.

"One of the first acts of the Soubah on entering," he said, "was to have Omy Chund and Kissendass fetched out of prison, whom he received with the greatest imaginable civility, and presented 'em both with *seerpaws*."[03] (These, Amelia, are vests of honour, given by a ruler to those he most affects.) "You may well look astonished, gentlemen, knowing that the shelter given to Kissendass was our chief alleged crime in the Nabob's eyes, but there's worse yet. Have you forgot that in the same prison with the two Gentoos was a European, suspected, like them, of trafficking with the enemy? I understand that when the prison was broke open the unhappy man had almost secured his freedom by promising to show the Moors that discovered him where he had buried a prodigious treasure, but, as you are sensible, Omy Chund never forgives, and sure Mr Menotti made him his deadly enemy when he sought to save himself by casting suspicion on him. Not that Omy Chund appeared in the matter, save by preventing Menotti's escape, for there was another ready to do the business. When the wretched man was brought before the Soubah, there stood out to accuse him a person somewhat of a European aspect, but dressed like the Moors, and this I discovered to be the renegade Frenchman, Sinzaun, the master of the Nabob's artillery. From all I could learn (for the apostate spoke very vehemently and with an almost incredible swiftness in Moors), Menotti, who had for years supplied the old Soubah with information respecting us and our designs, suddenly demanded from Surajah Dowlah that in the event of this place being captured a certain female should be allotted to him as a part of his reward. Finding the Muxadavad Durbar disinclined to increase their offers, he supported his request with threats, declaring that he would otherwise betray the Nabob's designs to our Presidency. On this Sinzaun visited Calcutta in disguise, as I understood, and arrived at the determination to carry off the lady himself, whereupon, so he alleged, Menotti sought to betray both him and their common design to us, trusting to obtain the object of his pursuit through the gratitude of the chiefs of our factory. At this point of his discourse the accuser directed at Menotti a gross taunt that appeared to sting him to the highest pitch of indignation, for drawing a stiletto that he had contrived to conceal about him, he flung himself upon Sinzaun with such fury, despite his chains, that it seemed impossible to part 'em. But the renegade wearing a shirt of mail under his Moorish vest, the blow was fruitless, and Menotti was dragged from his prey, when the Soubah, who was prodigiously incensed that such an attempt should be made on his officer in his presence, cried out to the guards to fall upon him, and he was cut to pieces in the twinkling of an eye. Can you wonder at my seriousness, gentlemen, after beholding so shocking a spectacle?"

The gentlemen vied with each other in expressions of horror, but what does my Amelia think was the state of mind of the three persons that knew who was the unhappy creature alluded to as the object of the rivalry of these two traitors? My poor father groaned aloud, while I sank down by his side overcome with terror, and Captain Colquhoun opened his vest and showed me the butt of a pistol, which, indeed, was the greatest comfort that he could have offered me at that moment. But the next there came an even greater alarm to rouse us from our stupor of fright, for Lieutenant Bellamy pushed his way through the crowd to us with—

"There's several Moors of high rank crossing the parade, gentlemen, and they say that one of 'em is Sinzaun."

"Crouch down where you are, madam," says Captain Colquhoun, "but get a glimpse of the fellow if you can. It may be that our alarm en't needed. And, gentlemen, not a word of Miss if your lives be the forfeit."

There was five hundred *bercundauzes*, or gun-men, drawn up on the parade facing us, with their matches ready lighted, and a strong guard placed over us, with another on the stairs leading to the bastion, and some of these men brought torches, which they lighted from the matches of the *bercundauzes*, for it was dark under the varanda where we were, the sun being near its setting. Presently the party of Moors of whom the Lieutenant had spoken came to the front of the varanda, feasting their eyes, I suppose, on the wounded and worn-out men that had opposed them so long. But one of them suffered his eyes to rove keenly over the whole body of prisoners and their surroundings, and although I had never before seen him but in a masque, I knew him at once. Then he spoke in French to the only other female that was escaped, the wife of one of the sea-officers named Carey, and a fine handsome young woman, though country-born, and his voice was that which I had last heard from King Lewis at the Masquerade.

"And are you, madam, the only lady that has the honour of having taken part in this resolute defence?" he asked her.

"Why, indeed, sir, there was another," she said, "but I han't seen her for some time now."

Once again did the wretch's eyes search the place, while I crouched behind the gentlemen, half-dead with fear, but he went away disappointed. It was now dark, and the Musslemen, by which is meant all the Moors and Moguls among the enemy, sung a thanksgiving to *Alla*, which is their name for the Deity. Seeing them thus occupied, Captain Colquhoun turned round to me.

"Was that man he whom you feared, madam?"

"Alas, sir, he was!"

"Then he won't be satisfied with his search, and if the prisoners are marched out on the parade, he must find you. If only we had any disguise at hand——"

"Oh, dear sir, pray kill me, or if that be wicked, disfigure me in any way you will, sooner than I should fall into his hands."

"Hush, child; I had sooner save you from him and death both. Would it be possible, I wonder——? Do me the favour to take down your hair, madam."

I could not guess what he intended to do, but I obeyed, wondering, and the Captain combed my hair back with a pocket-comb, and tied it with one of the ribbons I had taken off, like that of a youth.

"The lack of powder will excite no remark, after our five days' uneasiness," he muttered to himself. "Put your cap and fallals into your pocket, madam, lest they would be picked up and excite suspicion. Pray will one of you young gentlemen oblige Miss with a hat? Mine is hugely too large."

Lieutenant Bellamy at once lent me his own hat, and tied a red silk handkerchief round his head, to give himself, as he said, a piratical air, such as might strike terror into our gaolers.

"Now has any of the seafaring gentlemen a watch-coat, or anything of the kind, with him?" asked the Captain.

"Why, look ye, sir," says one of them, "we are fair roasted already with the heat. What should we want with watch-coats?"

"Will this serve your turn, Captain?" cries Mr Eyre, bringing forward a great travelling-cloak. "I thought it might be of use if we were forced to lie to-night in the open, or on a stone floor, but pray consider it your own if it's to advantage Miss in any way."

"You're a friend in need, sir," says the Captain, taking the cloak and wrapping it round me from the chin to the feet, so that not an inch of my white gown was anywhere visible. It happened most fortunately that I was not wearing a hoop, having laid it aside because it incommoded me in my care of my papa, so that I might very well pass for a boy in the dim light. The heat of the cloak was stifling, of course, but think, my dear, what was at stake!

"The prettiest young fellow in Calcutta!" says Mr Fisherton, who had been watching the transformation.

"Young gentleman," says Captain Colquhoun sternly, seeing me shrink back, "is this the time for jests? Sure respect for the lady's feelings should withhold you from such a freedom, if your own sense of fitness won't do it."

"On my honour, sir," cried the young gentleman, "I sought but to cheer Miss with an assurance of the completeness of her disguise, so pray pardon me, madam, if I caused you pain."

"You must stand here, madam, among these gentlemen and away from your papa," says the Captain, leading me out of the corner. "Gentlemen, I need not ask you, I'm sure, to stand close round Miss."

There was no time to answer, for the Moors having finished their devotions, there came a Jemmautdar to summon Mr Holwell to another audience of the Nabob, and as soon as he was gone some one standing in the front of the varanda called out that Omy Chund was coming. Presently the wicked old man, his usual sleek and spotless aspect somewhat marred by his week in prison, but wearing the Nabob's *seerpaw*, a rich dress of gold gingham, over his Gentoo garments, mounted the steps of the varanda, attended by two or three Moors.

"Gentlemen," he said in his own tongue, his cunning little eyes wandering over the mass of prisoners, "I am come on an errand of compassion. They tell me that the daughter of my good friend and patron, Fahrein Saeb, is among you, without any female attendance, and I have obtained leave from his Highness the Soubah to carry her to my own house and entrust her to the care of my family. I need not assure you that this offer springs solely from my respect and affection for Fahrein Saeb's memory, and that the lady will enjoy perfect safety and honourable treatment at my house until it be possible to restore her to her friends."

No one made any answer to this humane and affecting declaration, and Omy Chund walked along the varanda looking at the prisoners, and tarrying so long before Mrs Carey that her spouse, persuaded there was designs abroad against his wife, bade him go on quickly or he would knock him down the steps. Still not finding the unhappy creature he sought, Omy Chund told the chief Moor that was with him to desire the prisoners to sit down, which we did, I in the midst of the knot of gentlemen who shielded me. I could not be thankful enough that I had never met Omy Chund face to face before this day, for although his eyes rested upon me, he failed to recognise me in my disguise, and his aspect grew more and more sour.

"Who's that on the bedstead in the corner?" he says at last suspiciously.

"Why, Omy Chund," says my papa, raising himself up with Captain Colquhoun's help, and speaking in an agreeable rallying voice, "I fear you've forgot your friend. Don't you recognise Fahrein Saeb?"

"Pardon, gracious sir," says the Gentoo, quite confused. "I had understood you was dead. You won't take it amiss if I say that for your sake I had even hoped it, since I could not look to save you in the same manner as your daughter. Pray, sir, where's the young lady?"

"Why, in a place of safety by this time, I hope," says Mr Freyne. "You should bid your friends the Moors keep better watch, Omy Chund."

The rest of the gentlemen laughed to see Omy Chund so confounded, and he, muttering angrily to himself, went down the steps again after one more inquisitive search among us. But when he was gone, the remembrance of the menacing language he had used provoked many enquiries and surmisings, which were only allayed by the return of Mr Holwell from his third interview with our conqueror, who, said the good gentleman, had pledged to him his word as a soldier that no harm should come to any of us. I was now seated again at the side of my papa, who appeared strangely drowsy, saying two or three times over that he was fatigued and would rest, and finally falling into a doze, undisturbed by the conversation going on around him. I remember that the good Padra recalled to our memories that it was the Sabbath evening, and that Mr Fisherton entered into an ingenious calculation to prove that, allowing for the difference of time, the afternoon church service was just about beginning at Whitcliffe in the county of Sussex, where his honoured father is the Rector. One of the other gentlemen objected to some error that he imagined in Mr Fisherton's reckoning, and they were disputing the matter very pleasantly, when some one called attention to the alarming progress of the flames in which the greater part of the factory was now wrapped, and which, though they had been kindled upon the first entrance of the Moors, seemed to have gained fresh strength with sunset. The buildings both to right and left of us were now burning, and the horrid notion was suggested that our captors designed to suffocate us in the flames, which was supported by the sudden appearance of several Jemmautdars and fellows with lighted torches, who went about examining all the rooms under the varanda where we were. The young gentlemen immediately declared for rushing upon the guard and seizing their scymitars, so fighting to the last, rather than submit to such a fate, but Mr Holwell, who went to question the Moormen, returned quickly to assure us that they had no such inhuman intentions, but were only seeking a place to confine us in for the night.

It appeared that their search was successful, for the Jemmautdars returning and joining our guard, which advanced towards us from the parade, ordered us to go into the barracks, which opened upon the varanda where we stood. This was better than we had expected, for these apartments had been specially built with a view to coolness, and the gentlemen began talking and laughing over their good fortune and the oddity of the situation, while I stooped over my papa to awaken him gently, lest he should be startled by finding himself moved, but I could not succeed in rousing him.

"Pray, sir," I cried, catching Captain Colquhoun's arm in a great anxiety, "come here a moment. I can't wake my papa."

"Why, what's this, madam?" says the Captain, turning round quickly; and he laid his hand on Mr Freyne's heart and brow, then stood up and looked at me with a countenance so full of pity that I found myself raising my hands as though to ward off a blow. "Dear madam, your father will suffer no more," he said. I stood with my hands upraised, staring stupidly at him.

"Your father has passed away in his sleep, madam," he said, with great gentleness.

"My papa dead?" I cried. "Then I'll die with him!" and I threw myself down beside the bed; but the Captain raised me instantly.

"Madam, your papa employed his last strength in seeking to secure your safety. Will you suffer that sacrifice to be in vain? If you remain here alone, you're lost. Sergeant, give Miss your arm on t'other side."

I had no power to resist, though I could read in the Captain's words that my papa's efforts to divert Omy Chund from his search for me had so exceeded his strength as to cost him his life, and I felt myself half-dragged, half-carried away by the two men. I remember that the Captain's sleeve was stiff, and that he winced when I first catched his arm. It did not then occur to me what this signified, but now I know that he must have been wounded, and that the blood was dried on his clothes.

We were now inside the barracks, where we had thought we were intended to remain; but the guard still pressed upon us, some presenting their pieces, others with their scymitars drawn, all forcing us on towards a door that stood open at the end of the place nearest the bastion. Seeing this, the sergeant who was supporting me on the left gave a great laugh.

"Why, 'tis naught but the black hole!" he cried, "and that's none so dreadful. I ought to know, for many a night I've passed there, though not many on 'em sober, I must say. So keep up your heart, madam."

"The black hole?" says Captain Colquhoun, in a voice of great apprehension. "Sure they won't attempt to confine us all there? The place en't but 15 feet square."[04]

But the prodigious efforts he made to turn back were fruitless, for those behind pressed us on, being themselves drove forward by the guards, and ignorant of the nature or extent of the place they were entering, jesting as they came, until all were inside, when the door was immediately shut, condemning a good hundred and fifty[05] unfortunate wretches to the most dreadful of deaths, for, so far as I know, I alone among the victims am escaped to tell the tale (and who knows whether this writing of mine may ever come into the hands of any that will make known our fate? since for very shame's sake the Moors must surely conceal the frightful truth). The chief thought of the unhappy beings who were the last forced into the room was to get the door opened again, but having no tools, they laboured in vain. Meanwhile, my two supporters dragged me through the crowd towards the two small barred windows opening on the varanda, the gentlemen making way with the most engaging politeness in answer to Captain Colquhoun's cry of "Room for the lady, if you please, gentlemen!" In the window nearest to the door Mr Holwell and two other gentlemen, both badly wounded, were already seated, clinging to the bars; but at the second, although the sill was occupied, my protectors succeeded in finding a place for me close underneath, where they guarded me with their own persons from those who would have sought to drag me away. Close beside me was poor Mrs Carey, whose spouse was supporting her with an equal resolution, and she addressed herself to me with a pitiful laugh.

"La, miss! so you was there after all? En't it monstrous uncivil of the Moors to confine us in such a place? I vow I shall swoon in a minute."

I had no chance to answer her; for at this point Mr Holwell began to speak to the prisoners, exhorting them by all they held dear, and by the ready obedience they had shown him in so many perils that day, to behave with calmness and moderation, and not make their situation worse by giving way to frenzy. Having succeeded in obtaining some semblance of quietness, the good gentleman, from the window where he sat, called to the guards outside, offering them huge sums of money if they would remove half the prisoners to some other chamber, and so wrought upon them that one of them, I believe, departed to consult the Nabob's pleasure in the matter. After this, different plans were suggested for lessening the closeness of the room. The gentlemen stripped off their coats and waistcoats (such of them as had 'em on), and sitting down upon the floor, used their hats for fans, being so closely wedged together that they could scarcely rise, and many that were weak with their wounds dying in that position through sheer want of strength.

But to the closeness of the atmosphere and the suffocating heat was now added a new torment, for all were seized with the most frightful thirst imaginable, crying out for "Water! water!" in a heart-rending manner. The Jemmautdar who had gone away was now returned, saying that the Nabob was asleep, and he durst not wake him; but being of a more humane temper than his fellows, this man ordered several skins of water (these serve as bottles) to be brought to the bars of the window where Mr Holwell sat, and the sight of this relief appeared to turn all the sufferers into maniacs, fighting with each other for the very smallest portion. The gentlemen on the window-sill, passing their hats through the bars, and bringing them back filled with water, did their utmost to supply every one; but the quantity thus obtained was so small, and so much was spilt, that few received as much as a drop. Nevertheless, the mere thought of water had so great an effect on me that I entreated Captain Colquhoun with tears to suffer me to leave my place and struggle towards the other window; but he refused me with the greatest sternness, saying that my only chance of life was here, and held me fast when I would have slipped away from him and the sergeant. And all this time the malicious wretches outside were holding lights close to the bars, that they might the more conveniently watch the fighting that took place over the meagre pittance of water, and gloat upon our agonies. Just at this moment, as I remember, poor Mr Eyre came staggering out of the struggling throng at the other window, and seeing us, paused in his design of seeking some quiet corner in which to expire.

"Why, Captain, how d'ye do?" he cried, with his usual good humour, "and Miss too, as I live! Good evening to you, good evening, madam!"

Such a greeting in such a situation seemed to me so comical that as the unfortunate gentleman went on his way I began to laugh, in a wild sort of style, and with no mirth in it, as you'll guess, Amelia, but stopped short when the Captain clapped his hand upon my mouth.

"For Heaven's sake, madam, be quiet!" he shouted in my ear, "or we shall have 'em all yelling like fiends in another minute, and en't we yet sufficiently humiliated in the eyes of the Moors?"

I had no strength to answer, and stood leaning against the wall, held up only by the efforts of the Captain and Sergeant Jones from falling among the bodies that were heaped upon the floor, when I should never have risen again. Mr Holwell was gone now from his place at the other window, but whether sunk down through weakness or dragged away by force I don't know, and most of the gentlemen and the wounded officers were dead, leaving only the common men, whose superior strength (and, I fear I must add, their hardness of heart in striking down those that stood before them) enabled them to hold by main force the points from which they could obtain a little air. I saw the crowd of struggling wretches in the light of the lamps held by the guards, I heard the cries, shouts, groans, prayers, imprecations, which ascended in a horrible confusion, but 'twas all as if I was in a dream. The only thing I could think of was that if I did not have water to cure my raging thirst I should die, but by this time I was beyond the power of calling for it. Presently I found the Captain shaking me and bidding me keep up heart, and learned that I had swooned on his shoulder, but the only answer I could make to his exhortations was to form with my lips the word "Water!"

"And you shall have it, madam!" he cried, with the only oath I ever heard him utter, and snatching the hat from my head (I had dropped the stifling cloak long before), he bade the sergeant support me, and plunged into the shrieking, striving throng. How he succeeded in obtaining the water I don't know, but presently I saw him returning, holding the hat high above his head, while on every side were frantic hands stretched out to tear it from him, and dying men grovelled at his feet, imploring him for the love of Heaven to spare them a little drop, but he fought his way through the press without heeding them. He had almost reached us, when several desperate creatures flung themselves upon him and tore him down, but not before he had hurled the hat towards me. The sergeant seized it, and dashed a few precious drops into my mouth, then relinquished it perforce to the frenzied crowd that rushed upon us. Of the Captain I saw no more. Alas, my dear! unlike King David of old, your Sylvia was base enough to drink the water that had cost the blood of the noble gentleman that brought it to her, and she owes to it, questionless, the preservation of her unhappy life.

The next thing I remember is a struggle for the possession of our window, in which the sergeant raised me in his arms and set me for a moment upon the sill, but only for a moment, for I was torn down in an instant, my clothes in ribbons, while a huge black man, a corporal of our garrison, planted himself in my place. With an extraordinary agility and strength the sergeant saved me from being trampled to death on the floor, and assisted me to stand up. But I was weary of the struggle, and death was the only thing I desired.

"Let me die!" I cried to the sergeant, "let me die quietly," and the worthy man, seeing the whole window now blocked so that no air could come through it, dragged me along by the side wall towards the platform at the back of the prison. On reaching it, we found the corpses piled there in heaps, and among them (oh, Amelia, I can scarcely write it) was good Mr Bellamy lying dead, his hand clasped fast in that of his dead son. Sure you'll think that I, who had that night been bereaved of the best of fathers, and had seen my esteemed protector struck down in trying to succour me, could have no sorrow left, but the sight of the venerable divine, by whose wise counsels I had so often benefited, and the gallant young gentleman with whom I had danced and talked and laughed, lying there dead hand in hand, overcame me all at once. Something seemed to break in my head, a great cry burst from me, and I fell forward upon that dreadful heap, and knew no more.

CHAPTER XIII.
CONTAINING THE EPILOGUE TO THE TRAGEDY.

(Part of a letter from Robert Fisherton, Esq., to the Rev. Dr Fisherton, at the Rectory, Whitcliffe, in the county of Sussex, taken from the Fisherton papers, by the kind permission of the present head of the family. From his monument in Whitcliffe Old Church, we learn that Robert Fisherton was only eighteen years old at this time.)

On board the Bombay frigate, off FULTAH, *July ye* 5*th.*

Ever-honoured and dear Sir,— ... As I have already related to you the course of the late melancholy events by which our flourishing factory was destroyed, and so many of the most considerable among the Company's servants there doomed to a frightful death, I will in this present letter go on to speak of the scarcely less mournful circumstances that followed upon that crowning point of the Moors' infamy. Sure, dear sir, when the full horrors attending the capture of Calcutta shall be commonly known, in every civilised region the tear of sensibility will bedew the cheek of virtue in pity for our miserable fate. I believe, sir, that 'twas from your lips your son once heard that affecting anecdote of the great Tuscan poet, that when he walked abroad, his fellow-citizens, noting his gaunt air and the horror dwelling in his eyes, shrank away from him, whispering, "There goes the man that has been in hell!" Ah, dear sir, your son has also been in hell, and like the famous Florentine, will surely bear in his countenance for the remainder of his days the shadow of the awfulness of that night.

Words would fail me were I to attempt to trace the passing of the horrid hours, which those only lived through who were prompt to avail themselves of the deaths of those around them to seize upon the points of vantage thus left vacant. My own escape I attribute to my having succeeded, in spite of all attempts to dislodge me, in maintaining a position at one of the windows, close to Mr Holwell. When this excellent man finally gave up all hope of life, and resigned his place, I still held to mine, and had the great happiness, in the morning, of finding our worthy governor still alive under the heaps of dead on the platform, and with the assistance of Mr Ensign Walcot, of conveying him once more to the window, where his deathly appearance was effectual either in touching the hearts or in alarming the cupidity of our guards, for they sent word of his plight to the Nabob, who returned an instant order for our release from that charnel-house in which we were confined.

Oh, dear sir, how can I paint to you the pitiable situation of the twenty-three unhappy creatures that crawled forth from the cave of death?

and that by a path that it needed full twenty minutes' labour on the part of the guards to clear for us through the thickly piled bodies of our friends. My reverend father won't, I am sure, think the worse of me when I confess that on finding myself restored to the air and the light of heaven I gave way to a flood of grateful tears, able only for the moment to realise the blessings of release. But this tribute to the weakness of nature once paid, I became sensible that the most affecting scenes were taking place all around me. Sure it must have raised even the most hardened cynic's opinion of human nature, to behold the eagerness with which ghastly wretches, themselves scarce able to crawl, made their way back into the den from which they were but just escaped, in search of some friend in whom the vital spark might not yet be quite extinct. One incident of this kind, the beholding of which affected me most sensibly, I must relate for the admiration and approval of the dear circle at the Rectory.

Lying where I had thrown myself on the wet grass below the varanda, I saw a man staggering feebly forth from the dreadful chamber, supporting in his arms a female form, which he part dragged, part carried into the air with him. Laying the woman on the grass, he felt her heart and wrist with a kind of clumsy respect and tenderness, and shaking his head, murmured: "Dead, poor young lady, quite dead! Poor lass! poor lass!" but instead of remaining beside the body, turned back, to my surprise, in the direction of our dungeon. A horrid suspicion here seized me, and I dragged myself painfully to the side of the female. Oh, my father, conceive my feelings! The body was that of Miss Freyne, the daughter of one of our most respectable public servants, who himself had escaped the torments of the night only by expiring from the severity of his wounds shortly before we were forced into our prison. What! (I hear my sisters cry) is this the Miss Freyne of whom your every letter has spoke for near a year, the beauty, the toast, the admired of all Calcutta no less for the high qualities of her mind than for the charms of her person? Such is, alas! the case, and no philosopher could ask a more moving example of the fleeting nature of earthly prosperity. The unfortunate lady lay stretched upon the ground, her arms extended in front of her, her face fixed in an expression of horror such as I have never seen equalled, and approaching nearer, I sought to throw over her a coat that I had catched up, designing to cover that once exquisite countenance from the rude assaults of the sun and the insulting gaze of the Moors. What was my delight and astonishment to remark a slight, a very slight, movement in the supposed corpse, the merest flutter of a breath, nothing more. Filled with pleased amazement that a being so delicate should have contrived to support the hardships of the night, I called out in much agitation to Mr Secretary Cooke (Mr Holwell having been dragged away to attend the Nabob)—

“Pray, sir,” I cried, “lend me your aid. There’s a spark of life yet in our esteemed Miss Freyne, I’m convinced.”

“Then suffer it to become extinct, sir,” was the dreadful answer I received. “The unfortunate lady’s cruellest foe could do no worse for her than recall her to life now.”

I took his meaning. Pray, pray, dear sir, never allow any of my sisters to come to India, nor suffer yourself to be persuaded to marry one of them to any gentleman that has his occasions in this accursed country! Sure you would be of my mind, had you beheld, as I did, the unhappy case of this charming young lady, who was to find that very beauty of face, and elegancy of shape and air, which had brought all Calcutta to her feet, suddenly turned traitors to her, and become her most dangerous foes.

“I see as how you’re right, sir,” said a voice behind us, and I found there, on turning, the same man that had brought Miss Freyne out of the prison, dragging another corpse with him. “When I heard Mr Fisherton call out as Miss was alive, I was fair dazed with joy for the Captain’s sake, thinking as how he’d not given his life for naught, but ’tis better for the poor maid to die than to be carried off by the Moors. There’s one poor creature they’ve got already.”

He inclined his head in the direction of an unhappy woman, the wife of a ship’s officer whose dead body we had discovered in the early morning when searching for Mr Holwell, who was in the act of being dragged away, more dead than alive, towards the quarters in which were imprisoned the Indian women that had been captured in the pillage of the Black houses. “If I had a pistol handy,” went on the worthy fellow, “it should go hard with me but I would rob those fiends of their prey.”

Alas! we had not a weapon among us, and the man turned again to the body he had brought out last, which I now saw to be that of Captain Colquhoun of the garrison, a most excellent upright person, and the only one of our senior military officers that had or showed any the least warlike capacity, and began composing the limbs as decently as he could, covering the countenance with his own handkerchief. The deep sighs that broke from him during this operation, and the tears that rolled down his cheeks, helped me to recognise him, which the changes wrought by the night’s suffering had prevented me from doing hitherto.

“Sure you’re the sergeant to whom the Captain was so partial?” I said.

“That am I, sir, the unhappy reprobate as has lost the best friend and the kindest commander ever a man had. Three times I was broke for drunkenness, and three times the Captain kept me from going to the devil, and helped me to work my way up again, and now he can't look after me no more."

The poor fellow's complaint was interrupted by the passing of a sad procession. Coming from the Governor's apartments in the Fort, which the Nabob had appropriated to himself, and taking the way to the gate, where a common *hackery* drawn by oxen awaited them, we beheld our dear and respected Mr Holwell, and with him Mess. Walcot, Court, and Burdet, all surrounded by a guard drawn from the command of Meer Mudden,[01] the Soubah's general of the Household Troops, and before them an Indian that carried a huge Marrato[02] battle-axe, with the edge turned towards the prisoners. Mr Cooke sat watching them like one stunned.

"Sure we have seen the last of Mr Holwell!" he said, heavily.

"You think he and the other gentlemen will be put to death, sir?" I asked him.

"Who can doubt it, sir? Han't you seen the axe?"

This fresh misfortune kept us sad and silent for some time after we had waved our mournful farewells to our unfortunate companions, but then our own guards began to call out to us contemptuously to be gone, for we that were left might betake ourselves wherever we would. But where were we to go? Our ships were dropped down the river, and in all Calcutta, where we had reigned like princes a week before, who was now so poor to do us reverence? Such were the questions that, with blank countenances, we asked one another, almost ready to confess that our dead friends, whose bodies were now being carried from that frightful prison to be flung promiscuously into the ditch of our unfinished ravelin before the east gate, had found a happier fate than ours. But our sad speculations were quickly forgotten in an event that revived our worst fears. The Jemmautdar in charge of our guard (a depraved wretch like most of his fellows) was examining the dead bodies before they were carried out, with the view of discovering such poor remains of personal property as had escaped the plunderers of the evening before and the struggles of the night, and securing them for his own use. Unhappily there catched his eye the glitter of a silver buckle on Miss Freyne's shoe, which was exposed by her torn gown, and he fetched out a knife to cut it away from the leather. So clumsily did the brutal mercenary do his sacrilegious work that the knife cut deep into the lady's foot, when, to my horror and that of Mr Cooke, a faint groan escaped her lips, while a convulsive shudder ran through her entire frame.

"Bravo!" cried the wretch, "the woman's alive, then! She shall go to Muxadabad. Sure his Highness will pay handsomely for a European female to add to his seraglio."

"Jemmautdar Saeb," says Mr Cooke, giving the fellow a polite title of respect, "let the poor creature die in peace. You see there's scarce breath in her."

"Nay," says the Jemmautdar, with a horrid leer, "she shan't die in peace, nor shall you carry her off to the ships under pretence of caring for her body. She shall live and come to Muxadabad, and bring me a fine reward from the Nabob." And turning to some of his company, he bade them fetch a palanqueen, while Mr Secretary and I looked on with anguish depicted in our countenances, and the rest of the gentlemen that survived added their earnest supplications to ours. But the wretch in whose hands lay the unhappy lady's fate proved as callous as he had before shown himself avaricious, and we were about turning away with heavy hearts, that we might not look on the carrying away into a detestable slavery of a young creature for whom we all entertained such high esteem, when we saw Omychund entering at the gate, accompanied with a moderate but genteel retinue of servants. I leave you to imagine, sir, what were our feelings when we saw ourselves forced to supplicate this treacherous Gentoo, to whose resentment and chicanery it is now a common belief among us that we owe all our sufferings, and who had lain in our prison until the day before, but it appeared to all of us that in him we beheld our only hope of securing Miss Freyne's release from the most dreadful of fates. Omychund advancing towards us with his *sewaury*,[03] we rose at his approach, and this low-*cast* shroff, who had never before approached a European without the most abject tokens of respect, nor ventured into the presence of one without removing his shoes, had the gratification to see six Britons greet him with the lowest bows they could bring themselves to offer. He greeted us with an air of unassuming benevolence, and testified by his countenance and gestures that he at once compassionated our sufferings and deprecated our respect.

"Pray, gentlemen," he said in his own tongue, waving his hands in a gracious manner, "don't do me so much honour. 'Tis only by the favour of his Highness that he who was the dust under your feet yesterday is now raised over your heads. I know what it is to be a prisoner, gentlemen, and my intercessions, joined with his Highness's merciful disposition, have been happily successful in ameliorating your situation. You have been already released from custody, but I'm happy to inform you that 'tis permitted you to remain in the place and attend to your occasions, and that you'll do me a favour if you'll all draw on me for clothes and provisions, as well as your lodging charges, for I can't forget in this day of prosperity how much I owe to the obliging good nature of your nation in the past."

If Omychund's debt to the British nation was to be measured by the depth of the humiliation he was now inflicting on us, it goes to show that the impression shared by Mr Holwell and the late Captain Colquhoun and others of our gentlemen, that for years he was only waiting his chance to revenge himself for being turned out of his employment under the Company, was justified, but now his tones altered, and his countenance assumed an air of the greatest horror.

"What!" he cried, "do I indeed behold Fahrein Saeb's daughter? Is it possible that the unhappy young lady contrived to elude my well-meant search last evening, and has paid for her lack of confidence with her life? Alas! alas! that an effort so kindly intended should have been received with such suspicion!"

"Omychund," says Mr Cooke, approaching him, "now is the time to show your friendship. Miss en't dead, but the Jemmautdar yonder swears that he'll carry her off to Muxadabad. Pray use your best efforts to change his mind. Offer him any sum you choose—even up to a *lack* of rupees. I'm sure there en't a lady or gentleman left of the inhabitants of Calcutta but would gladly join to pay it."

"Jemmautdar Saeb," says Omychund, when the fellow, on his beckoning, came swaggering up, "is it true that you're taking the woman there to Muxadabad?"

"Quite true," says the other, "and I shall give her to his Highness. The other woman will do for the Buxey."[04]

"But this is a great lady. She's Fahrein Saeb's daughter."

"So much the better," with another leer.

"I am told to offer you many thousands of rupees to let her go."

"His Highness will give me more for keeping her."

"Then will nothing tempt you?"

"Not ten *corores* of rupees. Not all the treasure that the accursed Holwell has buried and won't give up. The woman goes to Muxadabad."

"I feared it was useless, Saeb," says Omychund aside to Mr Cooke. "This is an extraordinary resolved villain. If only the chance of last night had not been lost!"

"But sure they won't have the inhumanity to carry the poor lady away without one of her own sex to attend upon her?"

"Ah, in that I can help you, Saeb. As it chanced, there met me in coming hither a worthy woman that asked alms of me, whom I had known in more prosperous days. She had served several European ladies as a waiting-woman, and saved enough to set up a small shop in the Great Buzar. This was plundered and burnt last week, and she is reduced to penury. I will send one of my servants to call her, and she shall wait on the lady to Muxadabad."

"But sure she won't adventure herself into the enemy's stronghold?"

"Indeed, Saeb, the prospect of gaining a position in his Highness's household will transport her with joy."

"Well, I hope she's to be trusted. Pray, Omychund, present her with ten rupees from me, and bid her be good to her mistress."

"And the same from me," said I. "And from me," "And from me," added the other gentlemen, and Omychund called his cash-bearer from among his attendance, and bade him count out the money. By this time the other servant was returned with the iya, an elderly Moorwoman well muffled in a blue cloth, and to her Omychund gave the rupees, with many good counsels, which she promised faithfully to observe, while all the time she was assisting to lift Miss Freyne, who was still insensible, though faintly moaning, into the palanqueen, and place her as easily as she might. When this was done, and the *checks* drawn, she followed behind the bearers, and they passed out of our sight. Dear sir, I am sensible that we seem to have played but a sorry part in this affair, and yet, what could we do? There wasn't a man of us but would have given his life cheerfully to save Miss Freyne, but all our lives together would not have been accepted in exchange for hers, although, as you shall see, there was one worthy fellow did actually sacrifice himself for her.

"See," cried Mr Cooke, as the Jemmautdar and his men left the Fort after the palanqueen, "the rascal is taking one of ourselves with him. Who is it? This is contrary to the Nabob's message of clemency, Omychund."

"Not so, Saeb," says the Gentoo. "His Highness desires European gunners, and this person has offered himself as one of 'em. I fear he has the notion that he will be permitted to attend on the young lady, but he'll soon be undeceived in this."

"Sure 'tis that sergeant of Captain Colquhoun's!" said I, and on a sudden impulse, started to run after the poor man and warn him of his mistake, but so weak and sick was I that I could not even reach the gate before I fell down helplessly. And thus, sir, was this poor faithful fellow trapped into entering the Nabob's service, in the vain belief that he would be suffered to watch over the safety of the lady of whom his late beloved commander was enamoured. That very day, as we learned, was he put on board the same boat as Miss Freyne and her attendant, which started for Muxadabad under the charge of the Jemmautdar and a strong guard. Of the other unfortunate lady we have heard nothing, but we know sufficient to wish that Miss Freyne had, like her, been consigned to the Buxey, Meer Jaffier. It seems that as our ships dropped down the river from Surmans, on beholding the fall of the Fort, they were hotly cannonaded by the Nabob's fortresses of Tannah and Buzbudgia, and under this fire the snow Diligence, on board of which were Mrs Drake and Mrs Mapletoft and two other ladies, besides Mr Labaume, a French officer of ours, who was badly wounded, and Mr Holwell's goods and money, in charge of his clerk, Mr Weston, run ashore. The four ladies were handed over by their captors to Meer Jaffier, who treated them with the greatest humanity, and ordering his secretary, Mirza Omar-beg, to take a swift boat, put the ladies and Mr Labaume into it, and despatched them, under the secretary's care, to the ships, where husbands and wives were happily reunited. It may be that the Buxey has used Mrs Carey in the like handsome and delicate fashion, but of this we have no news.[05]

And meanwhile, what of ourselves? my good father will ask. Indeed, dear sir, the sojourn in Allynagore (as the Soubah has renamed Calcutta, building a mosque or Mussleman temple in the very Fort itself), which was granted us through Omychund's intercession, was but short. For ten days we all lay sick of frightful fevers and the most painful imposthumes or boils, which broke out all over us owing to the foul atmosphere we had been in. I'll assure the dear circle that it afforded us little consolation as we lay abed to hear the rain pattering on the roofs and terrasses, rain which began on the night of our sufferings,[06] and which, had it come one day nearer its usual date, might have availed to save Calcutta. As soon as any of us were able to be about again, our troubles began anew, for the Nabob made Monickchund the Phousdar of Houghley governor of Allynagore. This man affects to rule with an iron hand (the Soubah being returned to Muxadabad), and on one of the sergeants that survived with us the horrors of our imprisonment celebrating his recovery by getting drunk and killing a Moorman, Monickchund turned all of us Europeans out of the place, under penalty of cutting off the nose and ears of any one he found there after sunset of that day, so that we were forced to make our way painfully to Fultah, a settlement of the Dutch on the Houghley River, where our ships were lying. This place is at all times very unhealthy, but the great number of persons now crowded together on board the vessels, and sleeping on deck without any shelter, exposed to the rains without so much as a change of clothes, has caused an extraordinary great prevalence of disease. The wisest course for the unhappy persons in this deplorable situation would questionless be to make the best of their way by slow stages to Madrass, in spite of the opposing winds, but Mr Manningham, who has good reason to dread the true history of his pusillanimous behaviour becoming known at that place, pointed out so forcibly to the President and Mr Frankland the inexpediency of such a proceeding, that they, being themselves in the like case with him, put an end immediately to the notion. This apart, I know my dear friends will rejoice to hear that the greatest kindness is shown by all on board the ships to us unhappy sufferers, and that many who have saved but little of their property share the scanty remnants with us.

The full history of the capture of the Fort was unknown until our arrival, although some partial reports had been brought in by blackfellows, and the utmost horror and amazement was excited by what we had to tell. Mrs Freyne has taken her stepdaughter's melancholy fate so much to heart that she has requested Miss Freyne's name may never again be mentioned in her hearing, but the young lady's chief female friend, Mrs Hurstwood, looks at the matter in an entirely different light. Repairing, at her request, on board the Dodley, where she is lying sick, I related the whole mournful affair to Mrs Hurstwood, when the lady astonished me by crying out to know whether there was none of us man enough to snatch a scymitar from the guards and slay her unfortunate friend. To this I could only reply, quite confounded, that I could not have ventured upon so terrible and resolved a measure but upon the lady's own urgent request, upon which Mrs Hurstwood mocked at me for preferring my punctilio to Miss Freyne's honour and happiness, and bade me depart and never enter her presence again. Happening to meet Mr Hurstwood this morning, he told me that my news had so grievously affected his lady that she had been seized with a fresh access of her disorder, in so much that the physicians despaired of her life, a moving incident that shows the falseness of those who contend that no true friendship can exist between persons of the female sex. But as to that which the lady found fault with me for not doing, I can't discern, even now, that I ought to have done it. I do entreat my dear father to unite his supplications to Heaven with mine, that my hesitation may be over-ruled by Omnipotence for good, even for that of the unhappy lady herself, and so assist to calm the troubled mind of, sir, your obedient son and servant,

ROBERT FISHERTON.

From Mrs Hurstwood to Colvin Fraser, Esq.

On board the Hon. Co.'s Ship Doddaly, off FULTA, *July ye 6th.*

SIR,—I send you these lines by the hand of Mess. Manningham and La Beaume, to whom is committed the melancholy task of announcing at Madrass the deplorable ruin that has lately fell upon our Calcutta factory. I make no excuse for addressing a letter to a gentleman that I know so slightly, and with whom my relations in the past have not been so friendly as I should have desired, seeing he had succeeded in inspiring such a tender interest in the bosom of my dearest friend. Mr Fraser don't need me to tell him that I was always of opinion Miss Freyne might do vastly better than marry him, and that in aspiring even to the honour of her friendship he was pretending to a favour much above his deserts. True, sir, and even at this present time I can't bring myself to feign otherwise, but I don't think so ill of Mr Fraser as to imagine he will let my whimsies prejudice him against the lovely and innocent creature in whose behalf I now demand his help. What (you'll say), I have changed my tune? Indeed, sir, I'll assure you that the change springs only from the need of the moment, and 'twill require a very exceptional behaviour on your part to induce it to become permanent. But I do need your help,—nay, I demand it, and this because there's no one else to whom I can confidently apply, and to whom Miss Freyne's fate is a matter of such proper concern. My spouse knows that if there's any question of attacking Muxadavad when reinforcements reach us, he must march with the troops to Miss Freyne's rescue (if he be forced to do no more than carry a fire-rock in the ranks), or he shall never again call Charlotte Hamlin his wife, but the unreasonable creature persists in considering me before my dearest Sylvia, and won't consent to take any present step that might interfere with his protecting me. Our excellent Mr Freyne is no more, and his lady is too much relieved to find herself suddenly liberated from the scandal that was beginning to threaten her name, and to believe herself the heir to all that her spouse has left behind him, to feign any interest in the recovery of her stepdaughter. Your cousin Colquhoun, the worthiest person of my acquaintance (you are aware of my opinion, that if you, sir, had possessed the Captain's disposition, or he your youth and prospects, I need have sought no further for a spouse for my Sylvia), is also dead, and the only person left to watch over the dear creature's fate is myself. The fearful news that my dearest girl had been carried into the most frightful and revolting slavery imaginable threw me at first into such a sickness that both Dr Knox and a Dutch physician from the factory here predicted my immediate dissolution, but, sir, I can't, I won't die, while my Sylvia needs a disinterested friend. If I can do no more than incite you to attempt her deliverance, I shan't have lived in vain, but I fear that I don't trust Mr Fraser sufficiently to die happy until I have seen him actually successful. Come, sir, I challenge you to undertake the task. You have declared that you love my incomparable Miss Freyne—or at least, at the end of a monstrous fine and flowery epistle of yours there was a postscriptum that the dear creature would not read to me, but to which her eyes returned ever and anon with a smile of sweet satisfaction when she thought I wasn't looking at her—what, pray, is your love good for? Hitherto it has been fertile in producing the most fantastical letter ever wrote out of a romance, and the most unhappy expedient for sparing your punctilio and testing your mistress's affection that ever set a gentleman and lady at cross purposes, but is it capable of anything more? You have confused and muddled your affairs in a style worthy only of a poet; is it possible to you to go to work like a man of sense to set 'em right? If so, let me see you throwing, for once, your prudence and calculation and worldly wisdom to the winds, and setting out to rescue Miss Freyne, if living, to avenge her, if dead. You'll observe that I don't condition with you to marry her if she be rescued. Your sentiments may have altered, and no man shall marry my Sylvia Freyne that would make a condescension of doing so. My house and my heart are always open to her; your part is only to restore her to the arms of, sir, your obedient servant,

CH. HURSTWOOD.

Three letters from Colvin Fraser, Esq., to Mrs Hurstwood.

THE TANK-HOUSE, MADRASS, *Aug. ye* 17*th*.

MADAM,—Your obliging favour is to hand, writ in language that I am sensible my former behaviour has but too well deserved. The just remarks that you have passed upon my usage of the dear lady whose name I scarce dare profane with my pen find a ready echo in the heart of the unhappy wretch that now addresses you. I dare not, madam, protest my love for Miss Freyne, but I'll hope to prove it. I have long been convinced that the happy issue hinted at for my affairs in my cousin Colquhoun's letter of April the 29th was not to be confidently looked forward to, for in that case what punishment would I have received for the sufferings inflicted on my charmer by my fault? But that my punishment should arrive through further sufferings on Miss Freyne's part—sure, dear madam, this is more than is just, for I had willingly endured any trials rather than they should come on her. When the news arrived here in the middle of July of the fall of Cossimbuzar, I was very urgent with Captain Latham and the Admiral to grant me leave to accompany Major Kilpatrick's detachment of 230 Europeans, which was despatched at once to the assistance of Calcutta, but I was strictly refused, both because it was intended very shortly to employ all our force in aiding the Nizam Salabadjing against Mr Bussey, who has established himself with a French garrison at Charmaul in the vicinity of Hyderabad, and also because it was the confident expectation everywhere that Fort William would easily beat off any army the Soubah could bring against it. In spite, however, of the cheerfulness of all around me, I remained in a state of the most cruel anxiety, although not anticipating news of such horror as reached us yesterday by the hand of Mr Labaume. Mr Manningham, whom you mention as also detailed to carry the awful tidings, chose to remain at Vizagapatnam, being apprehensive as to the sort of reception he might expect here when his cowardly behaviour became known, and indeed, I think the men would have beat him to death with their scabbards, or the ladies stabbed him with their bodkins, had he been within reach when they heard of his action in forsaking the defence, and going on board the ships with the women and Mr Frankland, after no more than a day's fighting. On his arrival, Mr Labaume was summoned to the consultation chamber, where he delivered his despatches to Mr President Pigot and the Council, and answered the questions showered upon him as to the reason and manner of this unparalleled calamity. Then, when the public men were satisfied, came the turn of those that had relations or private friends in Calcutta, and among them myself. I knew by the young gentleman's air when he saw me that he had ill news to convey, and like a man condemned to drink poison, that might begin by sipping delicately at the edge of the cup, I only approached by degrees the topic of my supreme concern. "What of my friend Jack Bellamy, sir?" "Dead, sir, and the Padra too." "And my cousin Colquhoun?" "Dead, like them, in the black hole." "And my good friend Mr Freyne?" "Dead of his wounds, sir." "And—and what of his daughter, sir?" "Alas, sir! she fell into the hands of the enemy, and was carried to Muxidavad." Such was the awful gradation of my misery, which made me burst through the crowd and rush into the open air, whither Mr Labaume followed me and thrust a pacquet into my hand. 'Twas your letter, madam, but indeed its incitements were not needed, although they served to impel me to a greater frenzy than I was in.

Scarce knowing what I did, I returned to the consultation chamber, and waited at the door until the Admiral had ended his conference with Governor Pigot and the Council, waylaying him as he came out, and demanding his leave to repair at once to Fulta in order to take measures for Miss Freyne's deliverance. What was my consternation when Mr Watson not only refused me very curtly, but looking keenly into my face, ordered me to return on board my ship at once. The habit of obedience assisted me to turn my steps in the direction of the strand, but once out of the Admiral's presence the thought of my dear angel's cruel fate overcame me again, and blotted out all recollection of the order I had received. Instead of seeking a shore-boat to go on board the Tyger, I turned aside to the ramparts, and there wandered about, I think, for hours, seeing that it was before sunset I had met with Mr Labaume. My whole soul was consumed with the thought of the miseries that the dear creature, whose humble servant I am proud to be, must have endured. An officer of the city watch coming upon me at last, recommended me to leave the walls, and finding that I was as though I heard him not, led me by the arm to the strand and set me in the direction of the spot where our boats from the ships are wont to land and embark their crews, with great peril from the surf. Wading along in the heavy sand, with no design nor intention in my mind for betaking myself anywhere, it seemed to me that I heard my name called, but

I could not discover from what point the voice came. Presently, however, I felt myself seized by the sleeve, and found that Billy Speke, son to the captain of the Kent, and the Admiral's favourite midshipman, was come running after me.

"The Admiral bids you attend him at once, sir," he said.

I followed the lad to the road, where I found Mr Watson standing beside his hackery,[07] which he had halted on catching sight of me. He was on his way home from the President's to the Tank-house, which is his residence while on shore. Looking at me with great seriousness, "What are you doing here, sir?" he asked me. "Did you repair on board as I ordered you?"

I could only look at him without a word, but I fancy he must have read in my countenance something of the torments I had been enduring.

"Come home with me," he said, with that benevolent air which has made him the idol of every man that has ever served under him. "You shall lie at the Tank-house to-night, and I will make your excuses to Captain Latham." With gentle force, he compelled me to enter the hackery. "You are very foolhardy thus to expose your health to these night airs, child, and I shall bid my surgeon look to you, for I don't desire to lose one of my most active officers before we sail to avenge our people at Calcutta. Pray, Mr Speke, contrive to perch yourself somewhere on this machine, and bid the driver go on."

"Oh, pray, sir," I cried, "is Calcutta to be avenged?"

"I believe so," said the Admiral. "Some of the Council were very urgent for sending only a small force, and keeping the rest to attack Bussey, but I have fought hard, and Mr Pigot is with me, to strip this place of every ship and every man we can send, and if I don't mistake, there will be a greater man than I on the same side after to-morrow. We have sent swift *cossids* to fetch Colonel Clive with all speed from Fort St David."

"Oh, sir, for Heaven's sake," I cried, "be so good as to overlook my disobedience, and allow me to make one of the force you send."

"Why," said our noble commander, "if I judged you by your behaviour to-day, child, I should put you under arrest for intending to desert, and punish you by leaving you here when we start for Calcutta. But it shall be overlooked, if you'll give me your word of honour not in any way to anticipate the departure of the force."

You'll guess, madam, with what gratitude and alacrity I gave the required pledge, knowing that with Mr Watson and Mr Clive in charge there would be no delay in despatching the relief. The Admiral was as good as his word, and entertained me at his house for the night, wishing me sounder sleep than I have enjoyed. I can't sleep, madam, for the fearful dreams that beset me, and I can't think calmly, for I am almost mad, so that I have sought to quiet myself writing to you. I am sensible now of a sort of drowsiness stealing over me, so I hope for some relief.

Pray, madam, how did you know that I writ verses? I have never confided the secret even to my adored Miss Freyne, hoping one day to surprise her with a poem worthy of her, and I am sure, madam, that you was never told it by your obedient, humble servant,

C. FRASER.

(*Written below the signature in another hand.*)

Rear-Admiral Watson has the honour to inform Mrs Hurstwood that Lieutenant Fraser has been seized with one of the malignant fevers of the country, but is receiving every imaginable care and attention at the Tank-house, and Dr Ives thinks tolerable well of his case.

THE TANK-HOUSE, MADRASS, *Sept. ye* 18*th.*

MADAM,—I am but now recovering from an attack of fever, the consequence, as I suppose, of the disorder of my spirits at the time I writ last. Alas that I should have so little that's comforting to tell! Mr Labaume will have informed you of the divided counsels and faint-hearted schemes prevailing at this place, and of the incredible obstacles placed in the path of the Admiral and Colonel Clive in their patriotic efforts to redeem the disgrace inflicted upon the British nation by the success of the Soubah's arms. Will it be credited in future ages that while a good portion of the Council thought only of sending to Fulta to fetch away the refugees there, and abandoning Bengal to the Moors and the French, Mr President Pigot, while ranging himself on the right side, desired to command the avenging force in his own person, though neither soldier nor seaman, and that Colonel Adlercron has over and over again brought matters to a deadlock by insisting on his right to the command, as being senior in his Majesty's service to Colonel Clive? Were it not that Colonel Lawrence, Mr Clive's ancient superior in the Carnatic wars, enjoys but poor health, we would questionless find in him another claimant to the honour. Lying, as I am, in the Admiral's own house, where I have received such continual and obliging kindness as could not have been exceeded in my own father's abode, I am in the way of hearing all that goes on from the gentlemen who visit me, full of indignation and resentment, as much almost against Colonel Adlercron and his intimates as against Surajah Dowlah. But to-day I have experienced a special honour, and been gladdened by the best news I could receive in my present unhappy situation. The Admiral came in just now to visit me, bringing with him a person in a military undress whom I knew to be Colonel Clive.

"And so this is the young gentleman that desires to avenge his mistress!" said the Colonel, when they had both spoke to me very condescendingly. "Well, I don't know but one thing that makes a man fight better than the desire of vengeance."

"And what's that, Colonel?" asked Mr Watson.

"Why, sir, the fanatic fury of a religious war. The man that believes himself Heaven's commissioned messenger don't dare allow himself in slackness."

"Sure, sir," said I, "my commission is also from Heaven, for the lady I desire to serve could in no way be distinguished from an angel."

"Well, you'll have your wish before long, I hope," says Colonel Clive, smiling at my warmth, yet not unkindly, "for I believe our difficulties are composed at last."

"Indeed," says the Admiral, "I can't tell how grateful I am that Mr Fraser has been laid aside all this while. My troubles would have been ten times greater had he been continually scolding me for delay."

"Indeed, sir, I have much for which to ask your pardon," I said.

"And you also may be thankful, young gentleman," said the Colonel, "for your sickness, for I hear the surgeon says that the disorder of your brain would without it have increased into madness."

But perhaps my greatest cause of gratitude, madam, is the frightful delay that has occurred, since the force has not been able to sail without your obedient, &c.

His Majesty's Ship Tyger, MADRASS ROAD, *Oct. ye 9th.*

MADAM,—At last I enjoy the felicity of assuring Mrs Hurstwood that our fleet leaves Madrass to-morrow, carrying with it Colonel Clive and his army. The continual delays interposed by the arrogant pretensions of certain unqualified persons have, alas! operated in a manner extremely opposed to the wishes of all concerned, so that whereas, by sailing when the news of the Calcutta calamity first reached us, we might have made the mouth of the Ganges in eight days, we must now consider ourselves fortunate to do it in as many weeks, which all adds to the cruel loss of time that has took place. I entreat you to believe, madam, that I am fully sensible of the deep anxiety you will lie under as to the progress of our campaign, since Mr Hurstwood has insisted on carrying you from Fulta to Madrass in hopes of procuring your recovery, and I leave this billet behind me to greet your arrival, and to assure you that I'll do my best to keep you acquainted of all that passes bearing any reference to the affairs of the lady who is our common care. You'll perhaps, madam, think me too cheerful in my anticipations, but (I don't know why) I can't bring myself to believe that my part in this expedition will be limited to avenging my adored Miss Freyne. Is it impious to suppose that Heaven would interfere to protect, even by miracle, a creature of such transcendent excellence? and in that case, might not mine be the inexpressible joy and honour of restoring the most adorable of created beings to the arms of the friend whose merits alone approach hers? But, madam, I won't raise your delicate spirits too high with these delightful visions.—I am, &c.

CHAPTER XIV.
TELLS OF A VOYAGE ACCOMPLISHED FROM SCYLLA TO CHARYBDIS.

From Miss Sylvia Freyne to Miss Amelia Turnor.

MUXADAVAD, *End of September* 1756.

At last I find myself once more able to take up a pen for the purpose of writing to my Amelia, but how vastly different is my situation from any that she has yet been made acquainted with! My last letter was scribbled on my knee in the chamber at Fort William where I sat watching by my papa's side, and was handed to Mr Hurstwood to be conveyed on board the ships. Whether it has ever reached my dear girl I know as little as whether her eye will ever rest on this. To write some account of what has befallen our factory and my wretched self is an exercise that offers me the pleasing prospect of a moment's forgetfulness of my present situation, and to write it in the form of a letter to my dear Miss Turnor is only just, in view of the compact entered into between us before we parted. To say that I have neither the means nor even the hope of advancing the epistle towards its destination might seem to pronounce it a sad waste of time to write it, but since the Moors (they say) preserve with the most scrupulous care imaginable any piece of written paper they may find, lest it should chance to bear upon it the name of *Alla*, it may happen that some scrap of this letter may yet reach the hands of my Amelia Turnor, and serve to shed a little light both upon the destruction of our Calcutta settlement, and upon the fate of the unhappy Sylvia Freyne. But if this is to be the case, I must set down in order the whole history of our calamities.

(*Here follows the narrative incorporated into chapter xii.*)

How long this merciful swoon lasted, which rendered me insensible alike to the horrors of the prison and the miserable deaths of my best friends, I don't know, but on recovering my senses I found myself laid on a native bedstead in an apartment which I took to be the cabin of a boat, since I could see the shining of water reflected upon the roof through the *checks* at the sides. The only other person in the chamber was a female wrapped in a blue cloth and seated in a corner. Rising when she found my eyes fastened upon her, I saw her to be an elderly Moorwoman, decently but poorly clothed.

"*Salam, Beebee*!" says she in Moors (which is as much as to say, Your ladyship's humble servant), approaching me with an air of great timidity and respect.

"Where am I?" I said, putting my hand to my head, for I was in the strangest state of mind, my dear, conscious that something terrible had taken place, but knowing no more what it was than if I had been dead. I remembered nothing; I suppose I could not have declared my own name had I been asked it. My eye fell on my clothes,—they were torn to rags, frightfully soiled, and stained with blood. I lifted my arms,—they were covered with bruises, and the knuckles and elbows grazed. My hair hung in a great mat, all rough and dishevelled, and I had the notion that there was something relating to it that I could not recollect. It had to do with my pocket, surely, and turning with difficulty, I pulled out a cap and a parcel of hairpins, tied round with two or three ribbons. Then I remembered everything—the Captain's disguising me, my papa's death, our being hurried into the black hole of the Fort, and the awful night that we passed in that horrid prison. Reaching this point, my spirits could no longer endure the recollections that came crowding upon 'em, and I burst into a passion of sobs and tears that seemed as if it could never cease, so that the old woman, who stood patiently by, became alarmed, and sought to quiet me.

"Alas, Beebee," she said, "why should a young lady of your fine prospects indulge yourself in such transports of grief? 'Tis true you have been roughly used, but you was fated to undergo a short trial, that it might bring you the greater felicity thereafter. Your slave has no such hope, and has lost more than you, but she bows to the decrees of fate."

"And is it possible," I cried, "that there's a human being on this earth more unfortunate than I? Pray, good woman, tell me your history, that I also may learn to endure my miseries with something of your philosophy."

"Indeed, Beebee," says she, "the tale's but a mean one to relate to a lady of your quality. Your slave was mistress of no more than a small house and a decent business in the Great Buzar, but she rejoiced in the company of her children and grandchildren. When the Nabob's army came, her shop was plundered, her house burnt, and her family slain or dispersed until she was left alone. In the morning, yesterday, she was weeping over the ruins of the beloved spot, when there came along a parcel of soldiers, who seized her also."

"Alas, my poor woman, you have indeed suffered!" I cried. "But pray tell me your name, that I may know how to call you."

"I am named Misery, Beebee. In the Buzar they call me Misery Bye."[01]

I could scarce restrain myself from crying out when I heard this ill-omened name, but fearing to hurt the poor woman, "Tell me, Misery," I said, "was you carried off to attend upon me?"

"Even so, Beebee. They said there was a servant needed to wait upon a young lady of very great birth, who was to be sent to Muxadavad for a present to the Nabob."

At these awful words the full horror of my situation became clear to me, and I fell into a frenzy, crying out that I was indeed undone, and that death was my only hope. Misery stood quiet beside me, save that once she seized my hands, fearing that I designed to dash myself against one of the beams in my madness, and when I was become a little calm, said very earnestly—

"Why this passion, Beebee? You are treated honourably, and you have a great prospect to look forward to. Instead of these rags you'll wear the finest gauzes and the richest silk and tinsel, your hair will be braided with gold, and such jewels as you have never even imagined will load your hands and feet and face and neck. Only lay aside this frenzy, which will but damage your beauty, and permit your slave to practise the arts with which she is acquainted for soothing your spirits and restoring the charming colour of which your troubles have robbed you, and I'll assure you that instead of the Nabob's being your conqueror, you shall be his. You shall have the finest palaces in India for a residence instead of your poor Calcutta houses, and you shall be the envy not only of all the ladies of his Highness's seraglio, but of all the women in Bengall, and rule the province and spend all its revenues if you will."

Was ever such a bare-faced proposition made before to a Christian Englishwoman, my dear—nothing less than that I should sell myself, body and soul, to this wicked heathen prince for money and jewels? I sat up on my bed.

"Misery," I said, looking at her with great sternness, "I have suffered you to speak this once, since you have never learnt better. But you must understand now that for a female that is a Christian and a Briton there could be no greater disgrace and wretchedness than to become the Nabob's slave, as you propose, were he ten times as great and rich as the Emperor of Delly himself. I can die, if it please Heaven so to decree, but I had rather die a hundred times over than purchase a dishonoured life by a weak compliance."

"Your slave is a poor ignorant Moorwoman, Beebee," she replied, "and don't understand such fine notions. What good would they be when you was dead? But it is fate, and it en't for your slave to complain that you design to slay her as well. She has but to submit."

"Pray," said I, but feebly, for the warmth with which I had spoke had wearied me, "how can my persistence injure you?"

"Alas, Beebee! your slave has incurred the displeasure of Ally Verdy Cawn Begum, his Highness's grandmother. Knowing that I was skilled in treating the sick, the Begum sent to me when I lived at Muxadavad for a medicine to cure a favourite slave-girl of some ailment. Unhappily the remedy fell into the hands of another slave—a rival of the young person in the good graces of the Princess—who mingled poison with it, and succeeded in effecting the death of the favourite. The unhappy event was attributed to me, and had I not fled precipitately to Calcutta, I had fallen a victim to the Begum's resentment. You are carrying me back to Muxadavad, Beebee, and what can I look for but death? If you enjoyed the Nabob's favour you might protect your slave, but resolved as you are to withstand him, there's nothing but destruction for both of us. But it is my fate."

She sat down again in her corner, and covered her head with her cloth, wailing to herself in a subdued manner, while I tossed and turned upon my bed, endeavouring to discover some means of saving the poor soul from sharing my destruction while maintaining my own punctilio.

"Misery," I cried at last, "there's no need for you to perish with me. The soldiers will surely permit you to walk on the deck, since you are their countrywoman, and you must seize your chance and slip on shore at some place we touch at. They won't even perceive your absence if you are prudent."

"Nay, Beebee," said she, with a dogged air, "I was carried hither to attend upon you, and I'll do it. If I am fated to die, die I must, but I won't abandon the lady I have the honour to serve."

And as though to show that the matter was put aside, she brought some water, and asked whether she should wash my face and dress my hair; but when this was done, and I found myself somewhat refreshed, she returned to her corner and her lamentations in the oddest and most resolved manner. I can't be quite sure how the time passed after this, for I had a great deal of fever, but in the intervals of my disease, if Misery were not waiting upon me, which she did with a curious sort of skilfulness that I found very soothing to my aching frame, I heard her still bewailing herself. This did not add to my comfort, as my Amelia will guess, indeed it perturbed my spirits extremely; but I could not see that I was called upon to sacrifice myself for the sake of this unfortunate woman, even though 'twas her unaccountable fidelity to me that kept her from saving herself. Also, I must confess, I had sometimes the notion that she was endeavouring to work upon me to play the infamous part she had proposed, through my pity for her, but in this I did her an injustice, as you'll perceive. I suffered more and more from the fever as the time went on, regaining my senses less frequently, and finding myself continually weaker, and this gradual decline served to suggest an expedient to Misery.

"Beebee," she said to me, as she tried to make me drink some sort of broth she had brought in, "your slave would fain offer you her counsel."

"Say on, Misery," said I, too weary to do anything but wish she would be silent.

"Since you was pleased to reveal your lofty notions to your slave, Beebee, she has thought about them very often, and it seems to her that she has devised a plan by which it might be possible for you to escape the Nabob."

"Why, then, tell it me," I cried, full of eagerness. "I could hear nothing better."

"Hush, Beebee. The soldiers or the boatmen might hear. If you'll permit it, your slave will approach her head close to you, and whisper. Well then, Beebee, we have now left Allynagore (as the Nabob has named Calcutta) four days, and to-morrow the Jemmautdar in charge of the boat looks to arrive at Santipore. Now in that place there lives a rich merchant, a Christian, but a very virtuous and charitable person, though an unbeliever." (So the Mussllemen call us, Amelia.) "This gentleman is a friend of the English, and made many intercessions to his Highness on their behalf when he marched against their factory, but in vain. If we could get speech of him, sure he would help us to escape the vigilance of the soldiers, and reach the shore, where he would receive us into his house and conceal us."

"But who is this person, Misery? and what claim have we upon him, that he should expose himself to so much risk and inconvenience?"

"He is called Mr George, Beebee, and he's of so charitable a disposition that he believes any person in distress to have a claim upon him."

"Sure he's the very friend we need," I said; "but how throw ourselves in this way upon a stranger? Is the gentleman a married man, Misery?"

"Not to my knowledge, Beebee," she said, somewhat doubtfully, but seeing my countenance fall, cried out suddenly, "Your slave is a fool, Beebee. How could she have forgot that Mr George is but lately married to a young lady of his own nation, whom he adores?"

"I'm glad to hear it," said I. "Well, Misery, can we get speech of him?"

"Any idle fellow on the *gott* would carry a message, Beebee, if you paid him for secrecy."

"Alas!" I cried, "I have nothing to pay him with. The plunderers took everything."

"Your slave was more cunning than that, Beebee. When the *louchees*[02] in plundering the Buzar stripped her of her jewels, she contrived to hide this," and she brought out from a corner of her cloth, where she had it tied up with great circumspection, a silver *bangul*, as they call a bracelet, set with corals.

"With this, Beebee," she said, showing me the jewel, "your slave will send a message to Mr George, desiring him to meet her in some retired spot. She cured his aged father of an ague some time since, so that he won't refuse her. Then she'll demand an asylum in his house for you, Beebee."

"But how shall we cheat the vigilance of the soldiers, Misery? They are perpetually on the deck, quarrelling and gaming, and must know that I have never offered to show myself. Are they also to be bribed, or how am I to slip past them?"

"No, Beebee. They would not accept of a bribe, for their business here is well known, and they would pay with their lives to the Nabob for their slackness. We must deceive 'em. They must think you dead."

I felt myself grow pale. "But how shall we manage that, Misery?"

"Why, Beebee, they have heard so much of your fever and weakness that it won't surprise 'em, and they can't be held to blame for it."

"But would you convey me to land in the night, Misery?"

"No, Beebee, for they would desire to know what was happened to your body. Your slave has a better plan than that. With a drug that she will administer to you, she'll make you resemble a corpse, so that you're carried out in broad daylight to be buried."

"In a coffin, Misery? And what of the physician, and the grave-diggers?" with an increasing horror, for, my dear, your foolish Sylvia's mind had flown back to the days when she read "Romeo and Juliet" by stealth with her Amelia, and she seemed to anticipate for herself the calamities that attended the personages of our great poet's tenderest tragedy.

"The Moors don't use coffins, Beebee. You would have your head wrapped in a cloth, and be carried on a bier. Nor do physicians prescribe remedies for women among the Moors, except very rarely. As for gravediggers, there won't be no need of 'em. A Christian would not receive here the burial of a believer, and 'twill be due to the piety of your poor attendant that your corpse en't tossed ashore on some sand-bank, but carried into the *jungul*," this is what they call a wood, "to be covered with branches. You see how easy it will be to practise for your recovery."

"Misery," I said, "I'll consent to this frightful plan, since your life is at stake as well as mine, except in one particular. I won't be drugged. I have resolution enough to remain motionless while I am carried on the bier, but I can't endure to be deprived of my senses."

"Do you perceive, Beebee, that the slightest movement will bring destruction on your slave and also on Mr George?"

"Yes, I understand, and nothing shall persuade me to move or speak. You can't think that I would sacrifice my only hope of escape, to say nothing of the persons that are befriending me."

"Be it so, Beebee. From this moment, then, don't speak above a whisper. You are dying, remember."

But indeed, Amelia, I had not felt so much alive since my misfortunes had commenced. The finding myself confronted with the possibility of an honourable escape, and freed also from those pangs of remorse that had beset me for Misery's sake, forbade me to sleep, and I must have passed hours in anticipating to myself every the minutest particular of the morrow's enterprise. But this excitement also worked well for Misery's plans, for towards morning it was succeeded with a heavy stupor, in which I lay as one dead. During this period of insensibility the poor woman contrived to effect a prodigious amount, for on my waking I found her seated on the floor beside me, not engaged in lamentations, but watching eagerly for my opening my eyes, in order to tell me of the success she had met with.

"Your slave has settled everything, Beebee," she said, so eager as not to wait for me to address her first. "There's but one thing fallen out different from what we planned, and that is, that Mr George is departed with his new-married lady to his house in Dacca, but his brother, Mr Gregory, who received my message instead, recognised in me the healer of his father, and will entertain us when we escape, and provide for our forwarding to Dacca, where you'll questionless be able to obtain shelter on board a Europe ship, lying hid in Mr George's house until the chance offer itself. The Jemmautdar and his soldiers believe you dead, for I departed so far from my duty as your attendant as to permit the chief rascal to peep in at the door, and see you lying stretched and stiff upon your bed, and he fancies that I landed when we reached Santipore merely in order to hire some *hallicores*"[03] (these are persons of low *cast*), "to carry away your body. In that he was right, Beebee, but those persons will be servants of Mr Gregory in disguise, and they will carry you to the Armenians' garden on the outskirts of the place, where they bury such Christians as die here. There a palanqueen will be in waiting, with relays of bearers, which will set off at once with you and your slave, to carry us to another branch of the river, where a boat will be ordered to be ready on which we may drift down the stream to Dacca. This will mean an increase of the length of our voyage, but my Beebee won't care for that, since 'tis to end in freedom."

"You're right, indeed. How shall I ever repay you, Misery, for your faithfulness to an unhappy alien, who can't even reward you with money?"

"Sure the applause of your slave's conscience will be her reward, Beebee. And now let your slave entreat you to speak no more, and to remain lying stiffly, as you was just now, lest any of the soldiers should be so profane as to peep in. The bearers won't arrive till sunset, and there's more than an hour to that yet. We must travel all night to reach the Dacca river."

"Tell me only one thing, Misery. How did the Jemmautdar take the news of my death?"

"Indeed, Beebee, he swore in an extraordinary manner at first, and cursed the day he was born; but on your slave's reminding him that the event was ordered by the decrees of fate, he became calmer, and is now engaged with his *hooker*."

Thus satisfied that the Jemmautdar would not be drove to any rash courses by my evasion, I turned my mind for the next hour to the business of remaining still; and, indeed, my dear girl won't know how vastly hard it is to lie perfectly quiet until she has done it knowing that the slightest movement may bring ruin not only on herself but on her humble friends. After a time Misery brought out a great parcel of cotton cloths, and wrapped me in them, over my own clothes, fastening my arms to my side, and swathing my head, in particular, so tight that I could neither see nor hear anything, nor scarcely breathe. Knowing that she took these precautions for fear of any rash or undesigned movement on my part I durst not protest, lest she should again urge upon me the drug (to which I was resolved not to submit, since who could tell into whose hands I might fall when in that state?), and resigned myself to enjoying only just so much air as would keep me alive. Presently I was sensible that the bedstead on which I lay was being lifted and carried along, and hearing sounds as though from a great distance, I guessed that the soldiers were passing their ribald remarks upon my funeral. Two angry voices that pierced even my wrappings I determined to be those of the Jemmautdar and Misery—she demanding, at first in an obsequious manner, but later with much warmth, some reward for her services such as might enable her to return to Calcutta; he declaring that she might be thankful to escape with her own life after her carelessness in suffering me to die. But in a break in their wrangling there reached me another voice, which must surely have made me forget my promise to Misery if I had been able to speak or move, for it cried out in English, "What, dead? Poor maid, poor maid! But one can see as how it's best for her." This English voice filled me with the strongest excitement, for I had heard no English spoken on board the boat, nor had Misery told me of any English person there, but after my first surprise I remembered my part sufficiently to make no attempt to stir. My bier was carried for some distance, passing, as I judged, through the town, and was then suddenly set upon the ground, when I was raised from it, and placed, as I guessed, in a palanqueen of the French or native style, which was immediately put in motion, even before Misery, who accompanied me, could begin to unwrap the cloths that swathed me.

"Now, Beebee, you're started on your journey towards freedom!" were the grateful accents that greeted my ear when she uncovered my head.

"Thanks to heaven and to you, my worthy Misery!" I cried. "But tell me, whose was the English voice that came so near to rendering our plan a failure by tempting me to move?"

"There was no Englishman there, Beebee, I'm positive," she said, shaking her head. "I had heard there was a country-born clerk a prisoner on the boat, who is being carried to Muxadavad because he's believed to know something of the money that his Highness failed to find in the Calcutta treasury, and it may be he was moved to cry out in English when he heard you was dead. I heard some person bawl certain words in a strange tongue, but knowing no English, I didn't recognise 'em."

"Would that we had been able to save him also!" said I, loth to think that any person of British speech should remain in the power of the savage Surajah Dowlah; but Misery pointed out to me that it would not have been possible for us even to release the unfortunate man from his bonds, much less to bring him to the shore. We journeyed all that night, the bearers travelling at a speed most unusual with them, and relieving one another at the proper intervals with an almost incredible promptness. Without this assurance that our progress was extraordinary rapid, my anxiety would have been extreme, and even as it was, my terror magnified every chance sound into a token of pursuit. However, at the break of day we arrived safe on the bank of a river, and there went on board of a boat that was awaiting us, Misery pointing out the superior convenience and elegancy of the lodging provided us to that we had left, notwithstanding its smaller size. The boatmen having with great civility enquired my pleasure through Misery, we put off at once, but during the four days and three nights that followed I don't think I slept once—indeed, the very fever that had seized me so often of late seemed to have lost its power. Nor must you think, Amelia, that this wakefulness was all due to fear, although I never ventured to show myself outside the cabin, and the approach of another boat, or even of a few persons on the bank, was the signal for an excessive alarm. I was conscious of a singular exaltation of spirit, owing to the marvellous manner in which I had been delivered from the thing that I had greatly feared (as the Scripture saith), and not even the remembrance that I should arrive at Dacca a friendless, penniless pensioner on the bounty of an Armenian household with which I had no acquaintance, could damp my ardour. I was delivered out of the hands of the Nabob, I was safe, and I could not in view of this crowning mercy think of the possible humiliations and difficulties that might await me. My soul was filled with gratitude to Heaven, which had made use of the poor pagan Misery as an instrument to save me, by means not only of the affecting fidelity she had exhibited towards myself, but also of the false accusation which had frightened her away from Muxadavad. And, moreover, had I been inclined to undervalue the mercies I had experienced, Misery herself would not have permitted me to do so, for she related to me perpetually the most appalling histories of the frightful torments inflicted on unhappy wretches who had refused to do the pleasure of the Nabob or the old Begum, so that I might know from what I was escaped, now that I need no longer fear that some such horrors were before myself.

After sunset on the fourth day of this our second voyage, our boat came to an anchor (if that's the proper phrase) off a large town, and Misery, congratulating me on being arrived at Dacca, besought the continuance of my favour when I should find myself again among Christians and safe from my foes, of which I assured her with the utmost warmth, as well I might, Amelia, might I not? A palanqueen, with a retinue of servants, was awaiting us, and we were borne along for a good distance, which served to impress me with a very lofty notion of the size of Dacca. At last we entered the courtyard of a house, as I could discern from the echo, and having stepped out of our machine, found ourselves standing in a varanda that overlooked a pretty extensive garden, in the midst of which was a pavilion or garden-house. I had hoped to be greeted on my arrival by Mr George's lady, but though there was a parcel of women about they were all servants, and Moorwomen to boot. I stood waiting in the highest state of expectation while Misery spoke aside with one of these, and returning to me, said that the garden-house had been set apart for my sole residence so long as I remained in the family, and that if I would repair thither, Mr George would do himself the honour of waiting upon me at once. My countenance must have displayed the amazement I felt.

"Sure it's Mr George's lady I ought to see?" I said.

"Mr George is a Christian, Beebee," says Misery, quickly. "He's acquainted with European gentlemen, and knowing their customs, was anxious to welcome you himself to his house, but if you desire it, your slave will send word that you don't choose to see him until his lady has received you."

"Why, no," said I, grieved to think of wounding this generous Armenian, who had undertaken such an incredible expenditure of money and pains for the sake of an absolute stranger, "since the gentleman piques himself on his acquaintance with our customs, and don't disapprove of 'em, I shall be happy to see him."

I walked with Misery to the garden-house, one of the Moorish females carrying a torch before us, and found the principal apartment on the ground-floor airy and agreeable enough, and very delicately ornamented with different-coloured marbles and strange devices wrought on the walls and ceiling. Glancing at these by the light of the torch, I heard a footstep, and turning, saw standing at the door a tall person wrapped in a cloak, who bowed deeply, but made no motion to approach me. Such humility and diffidence, on the part of one who had so vastly obliged me, filled me with shame, and I sprang towards him.

"Dear sir," I cried, throwing myself at his feet, "accept the heartfelt thanks of a poor creature that can never hope to repay you, but by her gratitude, for your extraordinary great kindness. Sure my generous host won't require my stammering tongue to testify to all the obligations he has laid me under, but will perceive that they're impressed for ever on my grateful heart."

"Fairest Clarissa, welcome to Muxadavad!" said Mr George in French, and throwing back his mantle, disclosed—oh, my dearest Amelia, pity me, imagine the agony of the moment—the features of the hateful Unknown, of the more hateful Sinzaun! I had fled from the Nabob to place myself in the power of this execrable, this odious and abandoned man.

The wretch had the assurance to try to touch me, and I fancy I remember endeavouring to push away his hands as I fell in a fit at his feet. The treacherous Misery succeeded in restoring me, but as soon as my eyes fell on Sinzaun I fainted again, and went from one fit into another as long as he remained near me. He departed at last, leaving a message for me with Misery to the effect that the alarm which seized me at the sight of him had caused him the most poignant anguish, that he desired nothing but my honour and happiness, and that he would make no attempt to force his presence upon me until I should choose to express a wish to see him. "If this be true," thought I, "I am safe from him for ever," but I could not bring myself to believe in the wretch's departure until, accepting with reluctance the support of my perjured attendant, I had tottered into all the rooms and varandas of the garden-house to assure myself that he was not there. Misery expressed the most excessive concern for my disorder, and would fain have piled oath upon oath to induce me to believe in her innocency of the wicked device by which I had been duped, but I cut her short very sharply. I could not suffer the creature to please herself with the notion that she had hoodwinked me a second time, and the assurance of this made the wicked old woman bewail herself most sadly, even while she entreated me to drink a syrup of fruits which she offered me, and lie down to sleep. I am almost certain, Amelia, that the foolish creature had mixed with the syrup some narcotic drug, I hope with no worse design than to make me sleep and perhaps ward off the attack of fever she foresaw, but if this was so, she compounded her dose badly, for instead of sleeping I was never so wide awake in my life. At last I could lie down no longer, and feeling a prodigious desire to walk in the open air, I slipped on my gown again, and stepping over Misery, who lay on the floor wrapped in her cloth, went out into the garden. There was dark clouds gathering, for this was the season of the rains, when excessive wet alternates with burning sunshine, but the moon was shining almost as bright as day, and as I walked about among the untidy beds of flowers, all as variegated and confused as possible, and no symmetry anywhere, I considered of my situation.

Now that I was at length undeceived, it seemed to me incredible that I could ever have been taken in by so complicated a plot. I remembered that only the night before I had remarked to Misery that the boatmen appeared still to be rowing against the stream, and not drifting with it, as she had assured me would be the case, and that she had answered this showed we were now close to Dacca, which stood upon a third branch of the river. Not knowing the situation of Dacca, I had accepted her explication easily, and the reward of my credulity was to find that the palanqueen which had carried me from the river at Santipore had brought me back to the same stream higher up, so that I was arrived cheerfully at the spot I most dreaded in all the world. The wicked art of the whole design, and the pains taken to make me imagine myself acting altogether on my own motion, amazed me the more I thought of them, but I perceived quickly that I owed the cruel deception to the necessity of deceiving not only the Jemmautdar (if indeed he was deceived at all), but the Nabob and his people, and also my own nation. Should that poor country-born clerk that had cried out in English on seeing me carried forth have speech with any European on the way to his captivity, he would inform him of my death, and all enquiry concerning the miserable Sylvia Freyne would be at an end.

This consideration awoke in me the resolve to undo the injury I had done myself in consenting to appear dead. If I was ever to be saved, or even if my friends were ever to know my true fate, I must needs discover some means of opening communication with them. But how was this to be? I was a prisoner in Muxadavad, in the power of the wicked Sinzaun so long as I remained where I was, at the mercy of the Nabob or any of his abandoned soldiery if I left the house. Our factory at Cossimbuzar was destroyed and the gentlemen there dispersed, and the foreign factories had shown themselves too friendly to the Nabob to give me any hope that they would help me. The only expedient that I could devise was to throw out into the street pieces of paper containing some account of my situation, confiding in that superstitious reverence of the Moors for handwriting which I have mentioned before, and trusting that Heaven would guide these frail messengers to a suitable destination. I was the more encouraged in this last hope because there was nothing in any way deceitful or untrue about this plan, and I was now ashamed to think that I had anticipated and claimed the Divine assistance in a design so full of falsehood and deceits as that by which Misery had secured my escape from the custody of the Jemmautdar.

But now there faced me this new difficulty; how was I to obtain writing-implements? If I had anticipated my misfortunes I should questionless have had the prudence, like Pamela, to conceal some pens and paper about me, but as it was, I had lost even my tablets and pencil. The only piece of paper I possessed was Mr Fraser's letter, which I had carried in my bosom ever since receiving it, and I had nothing at all with which to write. But the dreadful necessity of my case proved to be the mother of invention, for remembering some old story I had read of prisoners that wrote to their friends in their own blood, I drew my hussy[04] from my pocket, and plunged a blade of the scissors into my arm (I could not do such a thing now, Amelia, but that night I seemed to be raised above myself). Then with a bodkin dipped in this horrid ink I wrote twice over on the back of the letter:—

"I am not dead, but in the power of the wretch Sinzaun, at Muxadavad. Help me, any Christian that may read this, for the love of God, or at least tell those escaped from Calcutta where they may find the unhappy Sylvia Freyne."

When this was wrote, and dry, I turned to the letter and read it through again, as though I had not long known it by heart, then tore off the post-scriptum, which I could not let go. To tear the dear sheet seemed to be to tear my own heart, but I forced myself to do it, and folding each piece small, wrote on it in the best Moors I could manage: "Take this to any hat-wearer (so they call Europeans), and he will give you ten rupees," only, as I can't write the Indian character, I was compelled to do it in ours, and I don't know whether a Moor would be able to read it. After securing the precious post-scriptum again in my bosom, I hastened through the garden to a set of stairs that I had noticed led to the house-roof on the side by which we had entered, and found to my delight that from this roof I could look into a street. Here I threw my two missives, one from one end of the roof and one from t'other, and returned with failing steps towards the garden-house. Whether the effect of the drug was passing off, or my fever was coming on, I don't know, but I was sensible of nothing but a supreme melancholy and listlessness and a most devouring thirst. My eyes failed me, so that I could not find my way back to the garden-house, and as I crept along, feeling my path with my two hands, I seemed to be no longer in the garden, but once again in the black hole at Fort William. "Water! water!" I cried in a voice of despair, as I had done there, and as at that time the words appeared to be echoed by voices of agony all around. I felt sure there was water to be had, if I might only reach it, and I was fighting my way, as I believed, through the struggling crowd, when I found my progress suddenly stopped. It was in vain that I struggled, for Misery was holding me fast, having pounced out upon me just as I reached the edge of a great tank or artificial pond of water, and was rating me like a slave that had run away.

"I saw you try to stab yourself, Beebee," she cried, "and when you was frightened at the sight of the blood, I saw you go to the roof and try to throw yourself over twice. I was close behind you. I knew you would come here next, and I hid and waited. Do you think I don't know that you want to kill yourself, and bring down Meer Sinzaun's wrath on your slave, because you hope to punish me? I fear you'll get your wicked will by dying of fever from this night air, but I'll see at least that you don't drown."

I struggled with her again, but in vain, for I could not recall the word for *drink* in Moors, and all I could utter was an entreaty to be allowed to reach the water, which she was resolved I should not do. Thus, still struggling, she forced me back to the garden-house, where, seeing me try to reach the water-jar, she perceived at last what I wanted, and pouring me out a draught, induced me to return to the bed which I did not leave again for two months, as near as I can tell. I have quite lost count of days since the beginning of this sickness, but by noting the time when the rains ended, I am come to believe that this is now the month of September, the month in which, a year ago, I landed at the Calcutta Gott. Ah, my dear, what crowds of recollections rise in my mind when I make this calculation! Sure there never was a poor creature that in so short a space of time endured such complete vicissitudes, nor found herself, after them, in so helpless and cruel a situation. And all these misfortunes I have lived through, if I may say so, several times over, since, while my fever lasted, my disordered brain continued to present me now with pictures of my life in Calcutta, and now with visions of the days (ah, blessed time!) when, with my Amelia, I passed my hours contentedly in alternate tasks and simple pleasures, and dreamed as little of my brief exaltation as of my subsequent fall from being Queen of Calcutta to being Sinzaun's captive. But always when I was enjoying a moment's pleasure in these charming visions, the sight of Misery, or her voice speaking in Moors, or even a glimpse of the strange devices on the walls of my abode, would carry me in a moment to the trials of the siege, the horrors of the prison, or the dread that seized me when I heard Sinzaun's greeting, and so I must live over again all my adversities.

It was when I was somewhat recovered, the fever only gaining the mastery of my intellects for a part of the day, that Misery came one evening to say that Meer Sinzaun desired to wait upon me. Words fail to describe the horror that seized me at the sound of that dreadful name. I would have sought to flee and hide myself, but wanted the strength to move, and even with holding up my hands to ward off the sight of the wretch I fell back upon my bed fit to expire. Misery scolded me very heartily for what she called roundly my silly foolishness, but brought word at last that Meer Sinzaun would speak with me through the curtain that hung over the door, and would not attempt to penetrate behind it. It was some time before I could succeed in calming my apprehensions sufficiently to listen to the wretch, but when I began to understand him he was passing from compliments and condolences to tell me that he was about to attend the Nabob on his campaign against the Phousdar of Purranea,[05] and that he trusted to find me restored to health on his return.

"But, madam," he went on, as though he had apprehended the joyful confusion that arose in my mind at the prospect of his absence, "you won't be left unattended here, I'll assure you. My steward, a very worthy person, in whom I repose the utmost confidence, will wait upon you twice a week, and receive any orders you may desire to give him through this curtain. He knows you only as a ward of mine called Nezmennessa Beebee,[06] a Mogul damsel of quality from the north, and you'll find him as ready as I am to indulge you in any reasonable matter. But is there nothing that Clarissa will permit me to gratify her in before I depart? Won't she believe that her Sinzaun's whole fortune is at her disposal?"

At once, to shame the wretch, I asked for writing-implements.

"Why, madam," he said, "indeed you shall have 'em. Clarissa desires to divert herself with writing to the charming Miss Howe, I suppose? I can't undertake to forward your epistles, indeed, and I fear you'll also want the means, but at the least I shan't suppress 'em, and since I am unfortunately ignorant of English, I can't even take pleasure in the reading them."

I was at my wits' end to imagine how this cunning man could reconcile it with his plans thus to give me the chance of making my situation known to my friends, but I need not have feared for his schemes.

"There is, however, one restriction that I must lay upon you, madam," he continued, when I had expressed my gratitude, "and that is, I can't have this indulgence abused. There must be nothing more of this sort." He handed a paper round the curtain to Misery, who brought it to me. Oh, my dear! it was one of the billets I had writ with my blood, imploring help. I was speechless, after the first exclamation of horror, and he went on: "That, madam, was picked up in the street by one of my servants, and handed to me. I can't read the English, but its purport I can guess by the ink employed in writing it, and the words in Moors, which I have made out, though Clarissa will pardon my saying there's no Moor that could do it. Now, madam, you can't deny that in bringing you here, however much against your will it may be, I have at least saved you from the Nabob. Suppose this paper was carried to any Moor that could read English, or some European anxious to curry favour with Saradjot Dollah" (so he called the Soubah, in the French fashion), "you would at once ruin me, and destroy yourself. Is that Clarissa's design? I think she'll admit she has been honourably treated here, and I'll assure her that anything she pleases to demand shall be at her service within the hour. Is that a reason for bringing about the destruction of her adorer? You may write what you will, madam, but I must have your word that you won't use my ink and paper in compassing my ruin."

"I'll promise you that, sir," said I, somewhat ashamed. "You may count the sheets of paper when I've done with 'em, if you will. But I can't promise you that I won't try to escape if any English come to Muxadavad."

"Any English!" he said. "I fear, madam, you don't appreciate the unhappy situation of your countrymen at this time. The few left in Bengall are cooped up in the Dutch bounds at Fulta, and are dying like flies with the unhealthiness of the place. As soon as they can find ships to carry 'em to Madrass, away they'll go, so I would not have you rely on them for deliverance."

"Indeed, sir, I have given up relying on any power but that of Heaven."

"That's since you found yourself at Muxadavad instead of Dacca, I suppose, madam?" The profane wretch actually said this, Amelia. "Perhaps you'll be pleased to add to your prayers a petition for the success of his Highness's arms against the Purranea Nabob, and in especial for the safety of your humble adorer? If I should fall, Saradjot Dollah would be my heir, and should we both perish, then Sucajunk would be master, and in either case Clarissa might find that she had changed her gaolers for the worse."

Could anything, my dear, exceed the coolness of this hardened reprobate?

CHAPTER XV.
WHICH RECOUNTS THE TRIALS OF A DEVOUT LOVER.

Letters from Colvin Fraser, Esq., to Mrs Hurstwood.

H.M.S. Tyger, off FULTA, *Dec. ye 20th.*

MADAM,—I take this chance to acquaint you that the fleet is now at length arrived in the Houghley River, after a voyage so tempestuous that it might well be imagined the devil and all his angels were gathered to oppose our progress, distrusting our object. Being thwarted in our course from the very day we sailed from Madrass by the prevailing north-eastern *munsoon* and the currents setting from the north, our only means of fetching Bengal was to steer across the bay and back again, thus reaching our journey's end crab-fashion. In this tedious style, then, and afflicted by continual rough weather, we pursued our voyage, passing over first to the coasts of Tannasery[01] and Arracan, then tacking to the westward until we were in the latitude of the sands at the eastern mouth of the Ganges, next making our way with the help of the tides to Ballisore Roads (losing in this manœuvre the Cumberland and Salisbury, which took the ground off Cape Palmeiras), and finally reaching the mouth of the Houghley, where we were welcomed in the name of those refuging at Fulta by Mr Watts, late of Cossimbuzar, and Mr Becher. There we might still be at this moment, owing to the danger apprehended by the pilots in navigating the great ships over the shoals called the Braces before the spring tides came, but this difficulty was surmounted with great spirit by Captain Speke, who had been several times before in the river, and taking the Kent across in safety, the other vessels followed without mishap. So protracted has been our struggle with the opposing forces of nature, that all on board the vessels were placed on strict rations both of meat and drink, and the supply of rice failing entirely, a considerable number of Colonel Clive's Tellinghy[02] soldiers actually succumbed to starvation, being forbid by the rules of their religion to touch the salted meat served out to them.

The Kent and Tyger arrived off this place five days ago, but 'twas not until to-day that we were gladdened by the sight of our consorts, with the exception of the Cumberland (which, though she and her sister in misfortune have been got off, can't continue her voyage, and carries back to Vizagapatnam with her 250 of the Colonel's white troops) and the Marlborough, which has on board the greater part of our stores and nearly all our field artillery, but parted company with us, being a slow sailer, in a storm off the Negrai's. Besides the two great ships and the Salisbury, therefore, Admiral Watson has under his command only his two frigates and the fireship, with the two Indiamen used for the transport of the troops, while Colonel Clive's army amounts to no more than 900 Europeans and something over 1200 Seapoys. Major Kilpatrick's force of 230 Europeans, which, as you know, madam, was despatched from Madrass to the help of Calcutta as soon as the news was received of the fall of Cossimbuzar, has suffered so grievously since its arrival in August, from the necessity of taking up its quarters in swampy ground, because there was no room on board the ships, that a full four-fifths of the men are dead, and of the rest not more than ten are fit for duty. This heavy loss is partly compensated by the enrolment of seventy volunteers from among the Calcutta refugees, the most active of the gentlemen belonging to the factory; but, better than this, we possess in the justice of our cause and the reputation of our two commanders a guarantee of success and of the favour of Heaven upon our enterprise. Already the Admiral has sent letters, couched in terms of great severity, to Monickchund, the Soubah's governor of Calcutta, demanding redress for the wrongs done to the Company and its servants, and nothing is heard on every side but conjectures as to the answer that will be received.

Nothing but conjectures is heard in the fleet and army, I should say, for (will it surprise you, madam, knowing the gentlemen?) all the members of the Bengal Council that are escaped have no time to think of anything but their own punctilio, without it be the property they lost in the fall of the place and the means of recovering it. Mrs Hurstwood mayn't have heard that Mr Drake, finding the sour looks he met with and the remarks passed upon his conduct in deserting the Fort vastly galling to his high spirit, has posted in every public place in Fulta an advertisement desiring that it may be pointed out to him where he failed in his duty, and what more he could have done that he did not do. This was wrote after a laudable prudence had caused him, with his friends, to assume three months ago the style of Governor and Council of Bulrumgurry (that poor mean place being the only spot of ground left to us in Bengal), in the fear of offending the Nabob by aspiring to be still in possession of Calcutta. True, our colours are now hoisted just outside the Dutch bounds at Fulta, but Mrs Hurstwood will already be certain that so resolved a step was not taken until the arrival of the fleet. 'Tis some consolation that Mr President's fantastic manifesto was replied to by a young gentleman named Dash, whom I have met at Calcutta, and who acquainted the world in writing that while he durst not risk his place in the Service by accusing the Governor without a mandate from the Company, he was prepared to justify all that had been said if he were called upon. There's one matter, however, in which Mr Dash attacks the Presidency, where I can't follow him, and this is the advancing Mr Labaume to the rank of captain in the Company's army. Who should better deserve the elevation than a foreigner who fought on our side with so much spirit and devotion, and was only saved from the dreadful fate of the rest of the defenders by being carried to the ships mortally wounded, as was thought? And yet Mr Dash, who don't think it necessary to declare the time or manner of his own leaving the Fort, finds fault with Captain Labaume's advancement because he is a Papist! He believes, questionless, that all Papists should be warned to fight on t'other side.

Mr Dash's most fervent supporter in this matter is Mrs Freyne, who champions with uncommon zeal the cause of my old adversary, Mr Bentinck. This gentleman's exploit, in quitting the Fort full twelve hours before even the President and the chief military officers, has not yet been properly recognised by any step in rank, and 'tis whispered that the Council stand too much in awe of Colonel Clive to bestow this merited promotion. In this case, the lady will find it necessary to turn the artillery of her charms on the Colonel, since (so says wicked rumour) though not altogether inconsolable on good Mr Freyne's account, she en't minded to bestow herself on a gentleman that han't got his company. I went some days back to pay my respects to Mrs Freyne, but the mention of my name sent her into so violent a hysterical fit, as recalling to her all the cruel misfortunes she has suffered, that I thought it better to withdraw. I am not intending any disrespect to the lady, but I can't be sorry that she and my charmer cherished no extraordinary affection one for the other.

Dec. ye 21st.

The despatch of this pacquet, madam, leaves us still at Fulta, forced to listen to the vapourings of Mr Drake and his fellows, and unable as yet to follow the promptings of our spirits and advance against the Moors, no answer having been received to Mr Watson's epistles sent to Monickchund. There en't a man either on board ship or in the ranks but burns to avenge—oh, madam, what have we not to avenge? But why am I running on in this style and delaying to impart the news that has sent me to the writing of this letter as to the hardest task imaginable, since 'tis to quench in Mrs Hurstwood's bosom the hope which is already extinguished in my own? You guess, madam, questionless, what it is I have to tell, but my coward pen still refuses to set down the frightful truth in such a form that it may reach you. And yet I can't, I dare not, write on any other topic—how could I, indeed, when my whole heart and soul is filled with this one? Oh, madam, our beloved Miss Freyne is no more! Now I have wrote it, but the sight of the words brings no conviction to my mind. Sure such a blessed creature could not die, knowing that she must leave this world a desolation thenceforth to her adoring friends; the goodness of her heart would alone retain her here, in compassion of their need of her. But no; that bright spirit which was too pure and ethereal for these grosser regions is returned to its native skies, leaving us forlorn. Don't, madam, account me so churlish as to grudge to you the recollection of the affectionate friendship which was never broken by a quarrel, but figure to yourself the state of mind of the wretch who addresses you, when he remembers that the love which is his boast brought to its dear object nothing but fresh adversities and the increase of her unmerited misfortunes, and that it has now proved itself as powerless to save as it was potent to wound. Indeed, madam, I can't but admire the extraordinary course of my passion for Miss Freyne, which caused me to injure most deeply the creature I most adored, and which finds her removed from its reach just when there was a hope that I might in some measure redeem my past behaviour. The fault was wholly mine, indeed my bitter fault.

But why do I trouble Mrs Hurstwood with my useless lamentations, instead of presenting her with the melancholy history so far as I am acquainted with it? I was walking, madam, this evening on the esplanade of the Dutch factory here, when there met me Captain Labaume and another gentleman, who both turned aside and saluted me.

"Your servant, gentlemen," said I.

"Your servant, sir," says Captain Labaume. "I think you en't acquainted with my friend? Mr Warren Hastings, late of the Cossimbuzar factory—Lieutenant Fraser of the Tyger. Mr Hastings is possessed of certain news that concerns you, sir, which it is his painful duty to communicate."

"Perhaps, sir," says Mr Hastings, as the Frenchman bowed and left us, "you would prefer to turn aside into the gardens here, rather than learn in this public place what I have to tell you?"

I bowed, for when I tried to speak the words were wanting, and we turned into the Dutch Governor's gardens, where I stopped short and looked at the young gentleman, a person of very pleasing appearance. Sure no more agreeable messenger ever carried such heavy news as that which I read in his eyes before he told it. "You need not speak, sir," I said. "You're come to advise me of the death of the loveliest of her sex?"

"Sir," said Mr Hastings, "I can but pass on to you a message delivered to me. Near six months ago I was lounging one evening with my friend Mr Chambers on the *gott* belonging to the French house at Sydabad,[03] where we had refuged after the fall of our own factory. We were watching the boats that passed, too many of them, alas! laden with the spoils of Calcutta, and guarded by others with flags and music and all imaginable pomp. Suddenly, from the deck of one of these there rose up a man, almost naked but for a piece of a gunny bag that was wrapped round him, and with his limbs covered with the most frightful boils and sores. 'Sure, sirs, you must be English?' he cried, gesticulating towards us with his chained hands, and hearing a British voice, we hastened to the water's edge. The Jemmautdar in charge of the boat was come up when we reached it, and ordered the poor wretch, with blows and curses, to be silent, but we appeased him with a rupee or two, and obtained leave for the prisoner to speak. He informed us that he was a sergeant of our garrison here, and had suffered the torments of the Black Hole in company with his captain and a lady whom the Captain respected very highly. The lady being found alive on the morrow after the tragedy, was ordered to be sent to Muxidavad to the Nabob's seraglio, and this poor fellow, desirous of serving one whom his late commander had so much esteemed, accepted an offer to enter the Soubah's service in the hope of being permitted to attend upon her. In this pious wish, however, he was disappointed, for though on board the same boat, he saw nothing of her until—until—pray, sir, prepare your mind for grievous tidings—he beheld her corpse carried on shore for burial at Santipore. The fever that seized all those who survived the night of torment had proved too strong for her delicate frame, finding its work aided, questionless, by the anguish of spirit natural in such a situation as hers. The pious care of a poor Moorwoman, her attendant, procured the unhappy lady a grave in the garden belonging to the Armenians of the place—this, said our wretched informant, he was assured of by one of his keepers, more humane or less brutal than the rest, and he was desirous that the lady's friends should know it also. Mr Chambers and I divided the little money we had upon us between the poor fellow and the Jemmautdar, whom we sought to engage in his favour, and since then I fear the matter had almost slipped my memory, after I had once learnt from Mr Holwell in his captivity at Muxidavad that both the lady's father, and also Captain Colquhoun, whom he believed to be her humble servant, were dead. I did send word of what I had heard to Mrs Freyne, whom I understood to be at Fulta, but receiving no answer of any kind, my mind was soon busied again with the secret negotiations I was engaged in on the Company's behalf, and 'twas not until I fled hither when my dealings with the Seats were threatened with discovery, and learned by chance from Captain Labaume your melancholy history, sir, that I knew I could resolve any doubt of yours as to the unhappy fate of the lady in whom you claim so deep an interest."

I had listened to Mr Hastings's tale without any interruption but that of sighs and unconquerable groans, but now I could contain myself no longer. "And can there be," I cried, "a God above, when so transcendent a creature is permitted to expire miserably, without a friend at hand to close her eyes?"

"There's worse things than death, sir," says Mr Hastings, with a modest hesitation. "Perhaps we should rather give thanks that the amiable lady you adored was suffered to expire peacefully before ever reaching Muxidavad."

"I accept the just rebuke, sir, but—oh, sir, you never knew Miss Freyne. Had you enjoyed her acquaintance, though but for an hour, you would have thought the world bare without her. What, then, can you imagine to be that man's state of mind who was honoured with her particular regard?"

"Why, sir," cried the warm-hearted young gentleman, "I would have him thank Heaven continually for the happiness with which he has been blessed, and live to prove himself not unworthy of his dear mistress's favour."

"Your hand, sir!" said I, moved by his honest ardour; but, madam, 'tis cold comfort to pay to the memory of the dead those honours you had hoped to bestow on the living, and how much more when the fault is your own.

Dec. ye 23rd.

I may perhaps seem over-bold, madam, in continuing to trouble you with my unworthy epistles when the beloved link between us is wanting, but I believe my kind Mr and Mrs Hurstwood will excuse my presumption, remembering, in the goodness of their hearts, what state of mind I must be in, deprived as I am of the delicious hopes that have sustained me hitherto. That you, madam, was joined with your humble correspondent in a common admiration for our incomparable Miss Freyne, is reason enough for me to regard you as my sole remaining friend, and I can't doubt but Mrs Hurstwood's worthy spouse will allow me in this melancholy pleasure of reckoning with his lady how much we have both lost. There are at present but two thoughts in my distracted mind, the one to kill the Nabob, the other to fulfil the last pious duties to the mortal (alas that I must write it!)—the mortal remains of my charmer. True, the accomplishing the first won't restore her to me (any more than the finest tomb I might raise to her memory could do more than tempt Indian lovers to drop a tear on the spot where a Briton bewailed his mistress), but at least it would rid the world of the monster who is responsible for such a calamity's coming upon it. En't that a laudable object, madam? I entreat your opinion, for I have incurred the displeasure of my revered commander Mr Watson on this very matter.

The affair happened thus. I was returning this evening from a solitary ramble on the skirts of the town, engrossed with my own melancholy thoughts, when there met me a Dutch artilleryman, who offered to sell me an Indian scymetar he was carrying, which he had got (he said) some time back from a disabled Mogul that had been wounded in the Nabob's Purhunea campaign, and had no further use for it. The weapon pleased me, and paying the fellow what he asked, I carried it with me. Passing through the town, I met a party of officers from the Kent, among them Billy Speke, who exclaimed on seeing me carry a great sword naked in my hand, and asked me what use I designed to put it to.

"Oh, 'twill serve to kill the Soubah," I said, my mind still on the same topics.

"'Twill kill no one without it be sharpened," says one of the gentlemen.

"How do these fellows manage to fight with such a thing?" says another.

"Oh, sir, 'tis a most deadly weapon when bright and keen," said the first.

"Sure you would not compare it with one of our swords, sir?" asked the other.

"I vow, sir, you might find yourself hard put to it to maintain your ground against a person skilled in its use. Pray, Mr Fraser, if you en't in no haste to return to the Tyger, come on board with us, and let us have your scymetar sharpened, and convince this unbeliever by a pass or two that it's no toy."

I complied the more readily with this request that I remembered a message I had promised to deliver from our surgeon to Dr Ives of the Kent, and went on board with the other gentlemen in a shore-boat, when Billy Speke ran to find one of the armourer's mates, and brought him to us with his tools. While we stood round watching his work on the sword, the discourse turned, as might be expected, on fighting, and the officers of the Kent, in anticipating the progress of events, began to prophesy the capture of the Nabob's strongholds and the destruction of all his army.

"Do what you will with the army, gentlemen," said I, "but leave Surajah Dowlah to me."

"Sure, there's no one would dispute your right, sir," said one.

"Every seaman in the fleet will support you in the vengeance you seek," says another, "and will see you have a fair field for't."

"Will they?" says a voice that made us all turn round, to see the Admiral standing behind us, with a brow as black as thunder. "There's a seaman here, gentlemen, that will do nothing of the sort. What! do I find myself in command of a set of bloodthirsty adventurers, instead of British officers? Mr Fraser, how dare you import a private quarrel into your dealings with his Majesty's enemies, sir?"

"If I could forget the cause of that quarrel, sir, I would be the most abandoned wretch on earth."

"I don't ask you to forget either the quarrel or its cause, sir. Don't bandy words with me. Pray what's to become of your men and the King's interests when you are hunting for the Nabob all over a battlefield? You're here to uphold the honour of Britain by punishing the villains that have assailed it, not to seek vengeance for private wrongs—no, though your own mother had been slain by the Moors."

"But, pray, sir," Billy Speke ventured to say, knowing himself a favourite, "how is Mr Fraser to remember his quarrel without seeking to avenge it?"

"That's for him to settle with himself, young gentleman. All I can say is, that if I find him seeking vengeance, back he goes on board the Tyger and into irons, for neglecting his duty in face of the enemy. I would have you know, gentlemen, that you en't knights-errant, but persons under discipline, and that discipline I'll maintain. Is that the sword that's to kill the Nabob, Mr Fraser? Give it to me, sir—a heathenish weapon to do heathenish work, properly enough."

I handed him the scymetar, and he endeavoured to break it across his knee, but though it bent nearly double it resisted him. Catching up a hatchet that lay by, he smashed the sword on the grindstone with it, and threw the pieces towards me.

"Keep to your Christian sword, sir, and use it in a Christian manner. Fight when you find yourself compelled, but don't go out man-hunting. No," seeing me look abashed, "I en't displeased with you, though I was but a few moments back. I look to see you all do good service in a day or two, gentlemen. What? you han't heard? Monickchund refuses to forward my letters to the Soubah, saying 'twould be as much as his head's worth, and Mr Clive and I are agreed to move up the river as soon as we can get our stores aboard. There'll be no peace until Surajah Dowlah is well thrashed."

The Admiral left us, and the other gentlemen, commiserating me for drawing his displeasure upon myself, fell to talking of the projected advance, which (whatever Mr Watson may choose to say) can bring me no satisfaction but the gratifying of my revenge. That this sentiment is an unchristian one I can't deny; but how, madam, can I acquit the Admiral of encouraging my thirst for vengeance so long as it consorted well with his designs, and discovering its iniquity only when it threatened to oppose 'em?

But this remark is in itself an offence against discipline, and I'll say no more, merely laying the case before Mrs Hurstwood, and entreating her judgment upon it.

CALCUTTA, *January ye* 25*th*, 1757.

The extraordinary success which has greeted our arms seems, madam, to demand some record from me, that Mrs Hurstwood may be informed how signally the righteous enterprise on which we are embarked has been prospered by Heaven. But first, madam, permit me to say (lest you should suspect me of any design to glorify my own part in this campaign) that Colvin Fraser has not succeeded in slaying the Nabob, nor even in performing any notable feat of arms. Were the fame of his dear charmer dependent upon his puny efforts for its preservation, as the knights of the chivalric ages were wont to achieve their exploits in celebration of the beauty and merits of their mistresses, it would, alas! enjoy but a brief immortality; but since every man that beheld Miss Freyne must carry her image imprinted on his heart till death, her memory needs no assistance to maintain itself, although it may serve to glorify the feeble achievements of the man who unhappily survives her.

Our fleet, madam, sailed from Fulta on the 27th of December, and two days later cast anchor off the village of Mayapore, whence it appeared most convenient to undertake the assault to be made on the fortress of Budje Boodje. Here occurred the first of those dissensions between Admiral Watson and Mr Clive which, but for the interposition of Providence, must have jeopardised, if not destroyed, our expedition, Colonel Clive desiring that the troops should land from the ships in the immediate vicinity of the fortress, while the Admiral, foreseeing that Monickchund, who had been very busy strengthening the place, would have a great advantage in opposing their landing, recommended that they should march by land the ten miles from Mayapore. Colonel Clive at length yielding up his opinion, this was done; but the march having been over marshy ground much cut up with water-courses, and the labour of dragging the field-pieces and ammunition incredibly laborious, the troops, half-dead with fatigue, were permitted to rest themselves when they had reached the points from which the Colonel intended the assault to be made on the morrow. When our men were all asleep, Monickchund steals up with a prodigious force, having observed all Colonel Clive's dispositions, and attacks our bivouack so hotly that our troops, hastily aroused from their slumbers, gave way to a temporary panic. The field-pieces proving useless (owing to their being mounted on the wrong carriages, and having neither tubes nor port-fires), they were abandoned to the enemy, together with the buildings in which we had been encamped, and but for the extraordinary spirit displayed by Colonel Clive, who was himself labouring under a severe illness, the affair must have ended in a disastrous rout. The Colonel, despatching two platoons to attack the village now held by the Moors, drove out the enemy, though not without a heavy loss, and rallying his men, succeeded in chasing Monickchund and his cavalry from the field, thus winning a victory which was even greater in its moral than its material result, aided, as it was, by the Admiral's sailing up to Budje Boodje and engaging the fortress with the Kent alone, silencing the Moors' guns and opening a breach in the walls.

The first proof of the enemy's loss of spirit was seen the same evening, when a detachment of our seamen, being sent on shore in readiness to take part in the attack projected for the morrow, found the Moors so much cowed as to permit them to approach quite close to the walls of the place. Among these men (who had all, I fear, indulged somewhat freely in *grog*, which is a mixture of arrack and water, by way of celebrating Colonel Clive's victory) was one Strahan, a common sailor belonging to the Kent, who was more drunk than his fellows. He, scrambling over the parapet of the fort, where it was broken down by the Admiral's fire, found the place empty, but for a few Moormen seated on the platform of one of the bastions, and forthwith rushed upon them flourishing his cutlass, having first fired off his pistol and given three huzzas, crying out to his friends outside that he had taken the fort all by himself. Hearing the shout, first the rest of the sailors, and then the whole army, without waiting for either their officers or the Colonel's orders, rushed over the bridge and into the place, the foremost arriving to find Strahan hotly engaged with the Moors that were left (who took to their heels at this accession of force), and with his cutlass broke to within a foot of the hilt. So happy was the exploit of these drunken sailors, that 'tis with regret I must add that, the fort being in our hands and guards posted about it from among our own Seapoys, the seamen, mistaking them for the enemy, fell to fighting with 'em, and discharging their pistols, were so unlucky as to kill Captain Dougald Campbell of the Company's army, a very worthy person and a countryman of my own, who was come from Bulrumgurry to offer his services to Mr Drake at Fulta, and had accompanied the force.

Our next achievement was the capture of Calcutta, which held out for less than two hours against our cannon from the ships, the garrison firing only those guns that were already loaded. Monickchund had quitted Fort William even before our arrival, so great was his terror of Colonel Clive, and the troops he left were not concerned to improve upon his example, while the peaceable inhabitants, relieved from their oppressors, welcomed us gladly. Here again there occurred an unhappy dissension between our commanders. Admiral Watson, the place having surrendered to the fire of the ships, appointed as its governor Captain Coote,[04] who is in command of the detachment of Adlercron's Regiment[05] serving as marines on board the fleet. Mr Clive resenting this very seriously on his arrival, a hot discussion followed, Mr Watson even going so far as to threaten to turn his guns on the Colonel; but both gentlemen being equally zealous for the public good, the quarrel was quickly composed, through the mediation of Captain Latham, who is in a strict intimacy with both parties, by the Admiral's taking possession of the town himself and handing over the keys to Mr Drake. Yes, madam, to Mr President Drake. I think I behold your indignant countenance on reading this piece of news. As soon as the intelligence of our success was received by the other European factories, we were overwhelmed with congratulations from the French and Dutch, who proved themselves such broken reeds to the unhappy defenders of Calcutta in their extremity; but our leaders were prepared to overlook this former time-serving behaviour in return for their assistance in crushing the Nabob, and offered them an alliance. This they refused, however, the chiefs declaring that they had no power to conclude such a treaty without instructions, although they offered to preserve a strict neutrality between us and the Moors; but this not being considered worth entering into articles about, the Mynheers and Mounseers returned empty to Chinchura and Chandernagore respectively. Only two days later there reached us by way of Aleppo the news that war was declared against France last May, and I venture to say that the gentlemen are now regretting their precipitation in declining our friendship.

When this news arrived, madam, I was absent with the force which was sent against Houghley under Captain Coote, who, assisted by a body of seamen from the fleet, captured the place with slight loss on the 15th of this month, destroying the houses and magazines in order to strike terror into the Nabob, and obtaining plunder to the amount of 15,000*l*., although, as has since been discovered, the Dutch had taken all the Moors' most valuable effects under their protection, and hid them safe at Chinchura. In this capture of Houghley I had the good fortune to receive a musquet-ball right through my hat without injuring me in the least, but alas! I can't now take the comfort from this miraculous escape that I would have done five weeks ago. Returning from the expedition amid the acclamations of our fellows, we were in hopes to find the fleet already preparing to move up the river against Muxidavad itself, but discovered instead that our leaders were again divided in opinion, the Admiral desiring to press on immediately at all hazards, but Mr Clive, whose instructions from the Council at Madras bind him to return to that place by April, willing to come to an accommodation with the Nabob, sooner than drive to extremities the master of such vast armies. On this occasion 'twas the Admiral that yielded, finding himself opposed not only by Colonel Clive, but by Mr Drake and the Bengal

Council, who, fearing lest the French should unite with the Soubah against us, have sought to forestall 'em by obtaining his ear through his bankers Mootabray and Roopchund Seat. From what appears, however, the report of our successes has so much irritated the despot that no one dares to suggest making peace with us, and he is already marching from Muxidavad at the head of his army. Meanwhile, the Seats' agent or *vacqueel*, Rungeet Roy, is with Colonel Clive in the camp he has fixed at Cossipore,[06] in the direction of Chitpore, but beyond the Morattoe-ditch, while in the Nabob's attendance we have an agent of our own, a Gentoo banker of this place called Omichund, with whose name you, madam, may be acquainted. This man's interest in Calcutta, owing to the quantity of houses he owns here, makes him very desirous of peace, although he is so intimate with Surajah Dowlah as to possess his ear, and we who follow Admiral Watson are prodigiously apprehensive that he'll succeed in bringing about a settlement without any further fighting.

Meanwhile, madam, since our betters are all engaged with these weighty matters, time hangs somewhat heavy upon our hands. The Bengal gentlemen, it's true, can think of nothing but their own hard case, for while the Company's merchandise was found for the most part untouched in the Fort, all their private property is gone. Their houses are destroyed and their livelihood lost, while there remains a standing memorial of their humiliation in the shape of the mosque built within the very walls of the Fort by the Moors. 'Tis, perhaps, not wonderful that these gentlemen should be anxious for peace to be made, when they can fall to their money-making once more, but their conduct in the past forbids any excess of sympathy with their present situation. As for me, madam, I experience a melancholy pleasure in tracing the scenes associated in my mind with the memory of my lost charmer. The ruins of her father's abode, the chamber in the Fort where, detained by a more than filial devotion, she risqued, and as we now know, sacrificed her life in her tender care of Mr Freyne, are my daily resort. Captain Labaume and young Mr Fisherton have filled my gratified yet regretful ear with praises of her demeanour during the siege and in the awful events which succeeded it, and will it shock Mrs Hurstwood if I confess that in all my natural grief for my angel's loss I can't escape a sentiment of grateful pride that so glorious a creature would condescend to entertain a particular regard for Colvin Fraser?

CALCUTTA, Feb. ye 14th.

Oh, madam, I can scarce bring myself to sit down quietly and write to you, and yet this time it's no bad news that forbids me to proceed. What bad news, indeed, could I send to Mrs Hurstwood in any degree comparable with that contained in my letter announcing the death of her friend? And what joy, then, must inspire my pen when the charming task before me is to cheer the heart of the most faithful of women by reversing that announcement? Yes, madam, the news I have to communicate is the best, the very best—or if not the very best that our dear Miss Freyne's well-wishers could desire, at least so good that the delighted mind foresees immediately the best of all following it. Miss Freyne, madam, is living, and to Colvin Fraser has been vouchsafed the honour of attempting to restore her to her enraptured friends.

But how my pen hastens along now that 'tis dipped in joy! Pardon me, madam, for my disorderly method of procedure. And yet 'tis better to have uttered the charming truth, for to write of all the circumstances without letting slip the all-important fact until the right moment arrived, would be impossible to me. Oh, madam, the amiable Sylvia still lives!

But once again, to my sober history. During the latter part of January, after my last letter was wrote, the Nabob amused himself and us with sending an Armenian named Coja Petruce[07] backwards and forwards with feigned offers of peace, while the entire time he was advancing steadily with his army, burning, as he approached our bounds, the villages which acknowledged our authority, and at last passing our furthest outpost. Finding a parcel of *louchees* plundering within our boundary, the officer in command at Perins Redoubt stopped them with a sally, but the head of the Moorish army coming up, began to entrench themselves on t'other side of the rivulet. Colonel Clive, marching out from Cossipore with a considerable force, treated them to a slight cannonade, but returning at night to his camp, the main body came up and established themselves before morning, the Soubah sending word from Nabob-gunge, a hamlet about six miles off, that he desired deputies from the English to attend him and treat of peace. Mess. Walsh and Scrafton were the gentlemen chosen for this perilous office, and setting out in good time reached Nabob-gunge only to find the Nabob departed, discovering, moreover, that the perfidious prince had crossed Dum Dumma Bridge, and was actually encamped in Omichund's garden, within the circuit of the Morattoe-ditch. Our envoys, introduced by Rungeet Roy to the *duan* Roydoolub, were treated with great indignity, their persons being searched before they were admitted to the *durbar*, where they found Surajah Dowlah surrounded with a host of attendants, all huge and ferocious in appearance, and dressed out with thick stuffed clothes and prodigious turbands, in order to strike terror into the gentlemen. These, however, retained sufficient spirit to protest against the usage they had received, when the Nabob at once cut short their complaint by referring them back to Roydoolub. On returning to the tent assigned them, the deputies were warned by Omichund that the Soubah aimed only at keeping them in play until his cannon were come up, and with much presence of mind the two gentlemen, putting out their lights, as though they were about to wait on Roydoolub, went instead along the high road inside the Ditch until they came safely to Perins, and so to Colonel Clive's camp. Since no one could now entertain a doubt as to the hostile intentions of the Nabob, an action was determined upon, the Colonel's plans being precipitated by the desertion of all our servants and cooleys to the enemy, rendering it alarmingly difficult to obtain provisions.

Mess. Walsh and Scrafton arriving in the camp about seven in the evening, Colonel Clive, on hearing their report, repaired immediately on board the fleet, and asked and obtained from our brave Admiral the assistance of a body of seamen from the ships, designing to make an attack on the Nabob's camp and seize his cannon. At three o'clock the next morning, the fifth of this month, the expedition left the camp at Cossipore, an example of that extraordinary promptitude in dealing with an enemy which has gained the Colonel his reputation among the Indians. So poorly was our army furnished with the means of transport, owing to the Council's fears of offending the Nabob should they set on foot any warlike preparations, that it was necessary to employ men as beasts of burden. There was no bullocks, such as you, madam, know are commonly used in this country for the transport of artillery, and in all the army but one horse, which came with us from Madrass. The order of our march was first a body of Seapoys, then six hundred and fifty Europeans, both soldiers and volunteers, then another body of Seapoys, and lastly the guns, which were six field-pieces and a haubitzer,[08] all dragged by our gallant seamen, and with their ammunition carried on the heads of Lascars. A hundred artillerymen accompanied them, and the whole of the train was guarded by the remainder of the sailors, amounting to six hundred men, among whom was your humble correspondent. With the Europeans in front was Colonel Clive. Reaching the vicinity of the Morattoe-ditch, we found the huts and tents of the Nabob's camp scattered in a disorderly manner on both sides of it, and coming suddenly upon the enemy, drove in their advanced guard, who fired off their matchlocks and other arms and fled. One of their rockets chancing to strike the cartouch-box of a Seapoy, the consequent explosion caused a temporary confusion in our ranks, but this being alleviated, we advanced as best we might, for no sooner had daylight appeared than one of those thick fogs peculiar to this season in Bengal immediately enwrapped the entire scene, concealing us from the enemy and them from us.

Arrived opposite Omichund's garden and the Nabob's quarters, we were startled by the fog lifting suddenly and showing us a prodigious force of Persian cavalry, who had discovered us by the noise we made in marching, about to charge our line. But, as has often been remarked, 'tis in such alarming moments as this that Colonel Clive is at his best, and steadying the troops by his voice and example, they poured a volley into the horsemen at thirty yards' distance, which caused them quickly to scamper off. There being now no hope of surprising the enemy, we proceeded in a very warlike manner, directing a constant fire both of cannon and musquetry on either hand into the fog, which was descended afresh, but this bravado on our part was like to have led us into a serious disaster. Some distance in front of us was a causeway, where a road crosses the Morattoe-ditch, and this causeway was strongly held by the enemy, whom the Colonel designed to drive off, and having reached the inner side of the Ditch, to retrace our steps to Omichund's garden, and beat up the Nabob's headquarters. But our cannon continuing to fire when our leading files turned to the right to cross the causeway, killed several Seapoys, which cast the rest into a panic, and while Colonel Clive was rallying 'em the enemy opened a smart fire from two cannon they had mounted in a redoubt to the right of the causeway, which threw the whole battalion into great confusion, so that the notion of forcing the barricade was given up, and all pressed forward to reach the next bridge, that at the commencement of the avenue called Lol Buzar. The necessity of dragging the field-pieces along the ditches between the rice-fields caused us incredible labour, while we were now and again compelled to raise 'em up the banks and bring 'em into action, in order to keep off the enemy's horse, who were perpetually at our heels. A strong party held the bridge when we reached it, but giving way before our fire, we drove back also the horsemen pressing upon our rear, and gained our own territory, where the Colonel thought it well to give up the further prosecution of his design, in view of the prodigious fatigue to which the troops had been exposed, and we marched back to Fort William through the Lol Buzar. In fact, madam, we returned safely, though with considerable loss, having gained a victory in spite of our retreat, for the tyrannic and feeble-minded Surajah Dowlah was so deeply impressed by our performances that, hearing falsely that the Colonel had not lost a single man, and finding his own army much more disheartened than ours, he sent Rungeet Roy the next day to propose terms of peace.

But now for the affair which will make this indecisive battle for ever more memorable to Colvin Fraser than the most brilliant victory. I had been looking to the comfort of my men, who were permitted a rest and a mid-day meal at the Fort, and was expecting to receive orders to carry them on board the Tyger again, when there came up to me Lieutenant Carnac of Adlercron's Regiment of foot, whose acquaintance I had made on the expedition against Houghley.

"The very man I was seeking!" he cried. "Pray do me the favour to accompany me, Mr Fraser. Your presence is desired."

"And who may it be that desires it, sir?" said I.

"Why, certain very weighty persons, and for weighty reasons," says the young gentleman, passing his arm through mine with an agreeable familiarity. "It seems you have been consorting with traitors, sir, and you must justify yourself."

"Sure you're in very good spirits, Captain."

"Believe me, sir, I en't rallying you. You're needed to help clear up a strange affair. In seeking to find a way across the rice-fields this morning, I and some twenty of my men became separated from the battalion, and were brought up suddenly by coming upon two of the enemy's guns, mounted in a rude battery. The men in charge of 'em were as much astonished as we were, and for a moment we stood staring at one another with open mouths. Then one of the Moors recovered his intellects sufficiently to rush to one of the pieces, intending to discharge it by firing his pistol into the touch-hole, but before he could reach it, up jumps one of the men at the gun and fells him with a rammer, then turns upon the rest, and lays about him with such good will that he had 'em all drove out of the battery in an instant. Having chased 'em all away, he returns suddenly, and seeing us with our pieces raised, cries out in a lamentable voice, 'Don't fire, gentlemen, for the love of heaven! I'm a Briton like yourselves!' This confession inflamed the men so deeply, finding a European fighting on the side of the Moors, that they would have cut the poor wretch to pieces if I hadn't held 'em back almost by force, but he pointing out that he had saved us all from destruction by the enemy, they cooled a little, when he showed us further that he had loaded both guns up to the very muzzle with stones and rubbish and such a quantity of powder that they must sure have burst and destroyed all the Moors in the place had they been fired. This proving him to be well affected, we spiked up the guns and carried him back with us, since he desired to be confronted with Mr Hastings or any of the Calcutta gentlemen that survived the Black Hole, saying they could vouch for his honesty. Since we returned to the Fort, hearing some one mention your name, he demanded vehemently to see you, saying that he had news of infinite gravity to give you."

"Questionless the poor wretch is my cousin Colquhoun's sergeant, who was forced to enter the Nabob's service," said I, and attended the Captain into Colonel Clive's presence. No sooner had I entered than the unfortunate prisoner, who was standing loaded with chains while the Colonel interrogated him, sprang forward and cast himself at my feet.

"Thank God, sir, that you're come!" he cried. "I've thought every moment as how the General was going to order me out to be shot, but I don't care how soon he do it now. There's one thing been on my mind, and that's to give you this," and he pulled a small shred of paper from some hiding-place in his clothes. "Not being no scholar, I can't read all the words, but ever since I had it I've feared as how I'd led you and the other gentlemen into a horrid mistake, and perhaps ruined the poor young lady as I'd wished to give my life for."

I tore the paper from his hand, but the mist before my eyes forbade me to read it for a moment. Then I saw that on one side 'twas covered with my own handwriting. Madam, 'twas a part of the letter I writ to my dear Miss Freyne near a year ago from Vizagapatnam, that letter on which you have been pleased to rally me more than once. But on the other side—oh, madam, figure to yourself my sensations at the moment—were a few words scratched in a brownish sort of ink with some blunt instrument, scratched, as I could not doubt, by my charmer's own hand.

"I am not dead, but in the power of the wretch S ..." (this name is illegible, owing to the folding of the paper) "at Muxadavad. Help me, any Christian that may read this, for the l ... God, or at least tell those escaped from Calcutta where they may ... the unhappy Sylvia Freyne."

Was ever such an affecting billet handed to a lover before, madam? I am not ashamed to say that I found myself incapable of speech as, after pressing the message to my lips, I handed it to Colonel Clive, who demanded it with an impatient gesture, nor did it surprise me that the Colonel's face was moved when he read it.

"Wrote with the poor woman's own blood!" he said, as though to account for his emotion, and I started forward to reclaim the paper with a cry, for the notion had not occurred to me. To what alarms, madam, must the dear creature have been exposed before resorting to so dreadful an expedient for revealing her situation! "Wait a moment, sir," says the Colonel; "what's this? Something wrote in broken Moors—'Take this to any hat-wearer, and he will give you ten rupees,' but in the English character! How did the poor soul expect it to be read? Where and how did you get hold of this, fellow?" he asked of the prisoner, who was risen again to his feet.

"I had it of a Moorman, your honour, who said as how he had lighted on it in a street of Muxidavad, but he could not, or maybe would not, tell me the place. He kept it for a charm, but I chanced to have a leaf out of a printed song-book about me, that I had picked up among the spoils, which I gave him in exchange for it, telling him as how 'twas a more powerful charm than his. And when I had it, I did naught but look out for a chance of escape, that I might bring it to Miss's friends, but they watched me so as I couldn't nohow get away before to-day."

"Do you believe the man worthy of credit, Mr Fraser?" says the Colonel aside to me.

"Why, sir, how would I do otherwise?" I asked.

"You're a prejudiced witness, sir, I see. But since Mr Fisherton has testified to the man's motives in entering the Soubah's service, and Mr Hastings speaks of seeing him conducted by force to Muxidavad after the lady's supposed death, I think we need scarce doubt him. What do you say to returning to the Company's service, my man?"

"There's naught could please me better, your honour."

"Then be it so, and let me hear a good report of you in the future. Hark ye, sir," to me, "I thought at first of demanding the restoration of the lady from the Nabob as an indispensable condition of peace, but I en't so sure now that 'twill be the most prudent plan. Think the matter over, and let me know to-morrow what your judgment is. Till then I will say nothing to any one."

I bowed and withdrew, feeling a prodigious great surprise that Mr Clive should entertain any doubts on what seemed to me to be a matter of such simplicity; and finding Mr Hastings, who is serving as a volunteer in the European ranks, outside the place, I begged leave to attend him to his quarters, and laid the question before him, showing him the precious paper, though I would not trust it out of my own hands.

"How do you fill up the blanks in this message, sir?" said he. "Not the two latter, which are of slight importance, but the first?"

"Why, with the Nabob's name, sir. How else? 'In the power of the wretch Surajah'—sure 'tis as clear as daylight."

"It's possible," said he; "but why not the Nabob or the Soubah? Either term would surely come more readily to the pen. There's others beside Surajah Dowlah whose names begin with an S, sir. For example, there's Meer Sinzaun."

"The renegado?" I cried.

"No other. The fellow, as I have heard, piques himself upon his fine taste, and he might well prefer a European lady to the Moorish wenches. 'Tis but a notion of mine, but if you'll permit, we'll ask Captain Labaume and Mr Fisherton, who were well acquainted with the lady, if they know of anything that would argue any truth in it."

He called his Indian servant, who had remained faithful when his fellows deserted their masters, and gave him an order, while I kept silence, regarding the matter in this new and disagreeable light. Presently Mess.

Labaume and Fisherton entered the apartment, the former feigning anger at being summoned.

"I'faith, Mr Hastings, you're an insolent dog!" he cried. "How dare you send your commands to your superior officer, sir? I was but just sitting down to my dinner when up comes your blackfellow with, 'Hasteen Siab's compliments, and will the Captain Siab[09] wait on him immediately?' Sure you'll have to learn that you en't President of Bengal yet."

"Indeed, Captain, that's a lesson I shan't learn if my friends are so complaisant in pardoning my incivilities. But here's the reason for my breach of discipline. You've heard the joyful news of Miss Freyne's safety which our friend Mr Fraser has received by means of a billet from herself. Now there's something in the letter inclines me to think that the lady's present custodian en't the Nabob at all, but perhaps the apostate Sinzaun. Is't possible that he can have heard of her before the siege, and plotted to get her into his power?"

"Possible?" cried Captain Labaume. "Why, sir, to the best of my belief the fellow was so captivated by the report of Miss's beauty that he adventured his person in Calcutta itself for the sake of seeing her, and forced his company upon her at a masquerade. It's in my mind that he pursued her for some time with his solicitations, but poor Jack Bellamy could have told you more of that than I."

"And his knowledge lies buried in the ditch of the ravelin yonder," says Mr Hastings.

"But I can tell you more than that, sir," says Mr Fisherton. "When the Fort was taken, and before we poor wretches were drove into the Black Hole, Sinzaun came to scrutinise us, looking for Miss, as she believed. She testified such terror in view of the villain's efforts to discover her, that Captain Colquhoun assisted her to disguise herself in a man's hat and cloak, and she escaped notice for the time."

"This is as I feared," said Mr Hastings. "We can't doubt but the apostate has got the unhappy lady into his power by some device to hoodwink the Nabob. Now you perceive, Mr Fraser, why the Colonel thought best not to demand her release openly. Miss is hid in some spot known neither to us nor to the Nabob, but whence she could be quickly removed if enquiry was made touching her. To broach the topic would be to unite the Nabob with Sinzaun against us, and destroy all hope of liberating the captive. Your plan will be to despatch a secret agent to Muxidavad to discover where the lady is confined, and then to frame some means of effecting her escape. There's a parcel of Armenians and Moorish traitors would do the work for you, if you paid 'em high enough."

"Sure Omichund's the man," says Captain Labaume. "He has rogues enough in his pay to corrupt all India."

"Oh no, sir," cried Mr Fisherton. "Sure you can't know that the vile wretch sought to decoy Miss to his house by a promise of safety on the night of the Black Hole, acting, as every one present believed, in Sinzaun's interest. I fear this new misfortune is also of his hatching, since 'twas he had the woman fetched that was to attend upon the lady to Muxidavad, and though he feigned she was a stranger to him, I doubt she was his tool."

"'Tis well we know this," said Mr Hastings, "or we should questionless have applied to Omichund for advice and assistance, as in all other cases. We must find you another messenger, Mr Fraser."

"I thank you, sir," said I, "but if there's any art can smuggle me through the enemy's lines, I'll go myself to Muxidavad."

"There's none," said he. "No disguise could ensure your safety, sir, and you might not only fail to help the lady, but even endanger her."

"If there's any power on earth can get me into Muxidavad, sir, thither I'll go."

Mr Hastings and his friends shook their heads and lamented over my obstinacy, but as you'll hear, madam, there was assistance in store for me of which we did not dream. Had any one told us at that moment that after our march through his camp, which led to nothing, the Nabob would treat for peace, we would have laughed at him, and yet the treaty was signed only four days later, on the 9th. The Nabob covenanted with us that he would restore the plunder taken at the fall of Calcutta (this, which appears but a silly condition, the spoils being dispersed through a whole army, was insisted on by the Bengal gentlemen), permit the fortifying of the city and the erection of a mint, and allow the Company's *dustucks* to pass untaxed and unopposed in his dominions. He also restores the villages granted to the factory by the Emperor Ferokshere, and all the former privileges, from whomsoever obtained, asking in return an alliance offensive and defensive against all his enemies. Mr Clive replied to this by demanding liberty to attack the French at Chandernagore, but the Nabob answered cunningly enough that if the Colonel would oblige him by preventing Mr Bussey from invading Bengal from the Decan, and Count Lally's fleet, of the despatch of which he had heard, from attacking it by sea, there would be time to think about Chandernagore afterwards. The Soubah further asked for twenty English gunners for his artillery, and Mr Watts, the late chief of Cossimbuzar, to reside at his Court, believing him to be a meek sort of a person, destitute of guile, and both these requests have been granted. When the treaty was signed, the Nabob sent a present, comprising in each case an elephant richly caparisoned, a robe of honour, and an elegant jewelled ornament for the head, to Colonel Clive, Admiral Watson, and Mr Drake, presenting *surpaus* or dresses of state also to Omichund and Runjeet Roy, for their assistance in the negociations. The Admiral, who is hugely dissatisfied with the treaty, thinking it shame to make peace when the blood of our fellow-countrymen remains unavenged, refused to accept his present, but willing to show some civility to the noblemen that brought it, carried them on board the Kent and exhibited to them his lower tyre[10] of 32-pounders, of which they, returning, made a dreadful report to their master.

And what, Mrs Hurstwood will say, was Colvin Fraser doing all this time? He was waiting for his chance, madam, and he found it three days ago, when Mr Watts was but just started on his way to Muxidavad, taking with him Omichund and the gunners for whom the Nabob had asked, as well as Mr Ranger, whose name won't be unknown to Mrs Hurstwood, as commandant of the Cossimbuzar garrison. Colonel Clive was engaged in preparations, carried on with the greatest secrecy imaginable, for an advance against Chandernagore, to be undertaken without the Nabob's knowledge, when there arrived in the camp a venerable divine, newly come from England in one of the Company's ships, who brought letters of commendation to Mr Watts, as head of the Cossimbuzar factory, having left Europe long before anything was known of the melancholy revolution here. This excellent person, the Rev. Dr Dacre, is interested in observing the manners and studying the antiquities of the Indians, and has undertaken this prodigious journey at an advanced age in the hope of conversing with the learned among that people on their own soil. In place of being deterred by the terrible events that have transpired since his voyage was planned, the venerable man is solely eager to let slip no part of this period of peace, and desired to follow Mr Watts immediately on his way to Muxidavad, where he looks to obtain much enlightenment both from the Moorish *Imaums* and the Gentoo *Pundits*. Here, madam, was my chance, for I knew well that I could never have prevailed upon Mr Watts to permit me to be of his company, and therefore did not ask him. Guessing that the Admiral was devising some means by which Dr Dacre might be despatched up the river, I waited upon him in his cabin and asked his leave to visit Muxidavad in attendance upon the worthy divine. You would have smiled, madam, to behold Mr Watson's astonishment at my request.

"I think you forget, Mr Fraser, that you han't yet near made up the time you lost at the beginning of this cruise. There's not an officer in the fleet but could ask leave for such a jaunt as this with a better grace than yourself."

“Indeed, sir, if it were only a jaunt I desired, I would not venture to ask it.”

“What is it, then? Sure it can’t be true what I heard Billy Speke chattering about t’other night, that you still have a notion of rescuing the lady of whom you told me at Madrass?”

“That’s my hope, sir.”

“I had thought better of your sense, child. If the lady be still alive, sure you can do her little good by approaching her, and you may, by arousing the suspicion of her captors, bring about her destruction.”

“Trust me, sir, I won’t act rashly. If the lady have—have formed other ties, I’ll bow humbly to her discretion, and nothing will induce me so to act as to bring suspicion on her. But I must know if she’s satisfied to remain a prisoner.”

“You’ll embroil us afresh with Surajah Dowlah’s whole horde, to say nothing of risking your own life and losing sea-time, and very likely affronting Colonel Clive. No, Mr Fraser, I can’t have you go.”

I had expected this. “Then permit me to resign my commission into your hands, sir,” I said, laying it on the table before him.

“What, sir?” cried Mr Watson, with mingled grief and indignation, “are you serious? Do you know what you’re doing, with this expedition against Chandernagore close at hand? D’you know what will be said of you throughout the fleet?”

“I have considered that, sir, but the lady has no friend to attempt her rescue but myself. I am all she has to look to for help, and I won’t abandon her for the sake of my own advancement.”

“For the sake of your duty to his Majesty and the service, sir! D’you know you are a very foolish and wayward youth?”

“Since you tell me so, sir, I can’t but believe it.”

“You’re a foolish and wayward youth, sir, but I tell you this. If you had been willing to desert the lady in her extremity, Charles Watson would have took away your commission himself. That man’s no British seaman that would leave a woman a prisoner in the hands of the Moors. Take back your papers, child; I’ll make things right for you with Captain Latham. You shall carry despatches to Muxidavad from me to the Nabob, and you shall remain there as long as I can conveniently spare you, but I rely on you to do your business as speedily as may be. You will leave this on Tuesday by the boat that carries Dr Dacre.”

And that Tuesday, madam, is now to-morrow.

CHAPTER XVI.
CONTAINING THE MEMOIRS OF A CAPTIVE.

From Miss Sylvia Freyne to Miss Amelia Turnor.

MUXADAVAD, *End of October*, 1756.

Although I have finished the history of the misfortunes that brought me to this place, I yet continue to write, more for the sake of occupying my mind than from any hope that the letter will ever reach my Amelia. It has taken me a whole month to complete my narrative, for so weak was my hand in commencing that I could not manage above half a page a day, though now I can with little weariness fill the best part of one of the thick gilt-edged sheets of paper with which Meer Sinzaun has furnished me. But why make such a business of it? my dear girl will cry. Because, Amelia, I must find something to do, or I believe that the sufferings I endured before coming here, and the apprehensions natural to my present frightful situation, would drive me mad. Meer Sinzaun was wiser than I thought him when he permitted his prisoner to divert herself with pen and ink, for he don't desire (no more than Lovelace did) to find himself the gaoler of a wretch whose intellects are disordered. Figure to yourself, Amelia, that for near four months, which I have spent in this prison, I have seen no one but Misery and the two or three women belonging to the house, and now and then a gardener or other low-*cast* person in the distance, without it be that I get sometimes a stolen peep into the street through a small barred window in the upper storey, but only when Misery is absent, for she threatened me with having my one spy-hole bricked up when once she catched me indulging myself with a glimpse of the world. Shamefully though this wicked old woman abused me in the matter of bringing me here, I can't say but she is civil and respectful enough at most times, making her chief exception when she chances to find me praying. This she appears unable to endure, and makes a point of interrupting me, or of fidgeting about so as to disturb my thoughts. It seems to me that Sinzaun must have threatened her very severely in case I contrived to escape, and that she fears some miracle being wrought by Heaven to assist me. If the poor creature knew how often I have prayed in vain that I might die, sure she would experience no further alarm at the sight of my prayers; but, indeed, she is right enough in imagining that if I should ever effect an escape from this house it must be by means of a miracle.

Do you remember, Amelia, that day when the Rector's brother came to pay his respects to the gentlewomen at Holly-tree House, and discovered us all sitting round in tears, our needlework neglected, while Mrs Eustacia read aloud to us from the pages of 'Clarissa'? The good bluff gentleman, you'll recollect, sat for a while listening, with a snort or a "Pshaw!" at intervals, as though determined not to be moved, but at last, taking advantage of the moment when Mrs Eustacia herself had been forced to remove her spectacles, in order to wipe away the moisture that was gathered on 'em, he cleared his throat, and looking round very fiercely upon us, demanded what the mischief Clarissa meant by secluding herself in an obscure lodging at Hampstead, and thereby increasing the perils of her dangerous situation, instead of seeking out a magistrate at once and throwing herself upon his protection? You'll remember how we all cried out that the delicacy of her sentiments, her respect for the punctilio of her family, the fear of directing public attention to her own equivocal position, and a dread of finding herself repulsed, would all prevent a female of elegant feelings from taking so bold and resolved a step. "Then I hope for your own sakes, my pretty Misses," says the good gentleman, "that you'll none of you ever find yourselves in that poor girl's situation, or your delicate sentiments will land you in a worse trouble than mere public notice," and he stumped away with a prodigious determination.

But if he were here now, I think that good man would confess that I have not even Clarissa's chance of escape allowed me. My dear girl won't do me the injustice to suppose that I have sat down tamely to submit to any fate my captor may destine for me. No, I have made the circuit of the garden and the roofs which surround it times without number, seeking to discover some unguarded window or door, some outside staircase, or even some broken place that might afford me the means of getting outside my boundaries, but to show you with what lack of success I need only say that Misery don't even take the pains to follow me, now that she's satisfied I shan't throw myself over. She wraps her head in her cloth and falls asleep, taking occasion when she awakes to ask me, in the humblest style in the world, whether I have yet succeeded in finding a cranny to squeeze myself through? But even if I could elude her vigilance and that of the rest, and let myself down over the wall by any means, in what sort of situation should I find myself on the outside, in a country where women of quality never stir out of their own grounds but in a suitable conveyance and surrounded with armed servants? Without friends or money, knowing the language but imperfectly, what could your poor Sylvia do? Sinzaun was right when he said that she might well find herself in a worse captivity than this.

In fine, my dear Miss Turnor, I can't see the smallest hope of my escaping unless I can obtain some dye with which to stain my skin, and a trustworthy guide who would undertake to procure me the dress of a low-*cast* female, and convey me to one of the European factories near Cossimbuzar. But how hopeless does it appear to seek for such a person in a city where we Britons are now not only hated, but despised! Nevertheless, in the faint expectation of lighting upon some such charitable soul, I have sought to enter into conversation upon indifferent topics with each of the women of the house at various times, intending to broach my subject by degrees, but they all feign not to understand anything I say. Their stupidity must be assumed, Amelia, for if I spoke Moors as badly as they pretend, how could I make Misery understand me, which she does without the smallest difficulty? The truth is, my dear, that it's useless to seek to work upon people of this sort without you have money to offer 'em, and that I have not, and they know it. Had I command of sufficient sums, I believe I might be able to buy over even Misery herself, for I have seen her eyes sparkle with avarice when I hinted at the quantity of rupees my friends would pay were I restored to them. But alas! I have not so much as an *anna* to give her as the earnest of a reward, and Misery is a prudent soul, preferring not to do business save for money down.

But how then do I occupy myself, my Amelia will ask, in a place where there's no visitors, no diversions, no walking nor riding abroad, and no books? Indeed, my dear, I make the fruitless journeys I have described round the circuit of my prison, I observe the growth of the flowers and sometimes pluck a few, I write to my dear distant friend, and I work with my needle. Perhaps I have no right to say *my* needle, for you don't know the odd rules that these people have, all the sewing and embroidering being done, as a general rule, by men. To show you the difficulty I found to obtain this natural and necessary weapon of our sex, I must tell you something about my clothes. When I was first able to leave my bed, Misery had the assurance to bring a complete Persian dress for me to put on. You would have laughed, Amelia, if you had not been in my situation, to picture me wearing first a vest of thin silk, then a little velvet waistcoat ornamented with goldsmith's work, and a silk petticoat of red and green stripes—the stripes going *round* the garment, fancy, my dear!—and over all a cloth or veil of silk five or six yards long. Turning away in much displeasure, I bade Misery fetch me my own clothes, which she did with a good deal of grumbling. But alas! though they had been washed while I lay sick, they were so ragged and stained and shrunk that 'twas impossible to put them on.

"You are a Moorwoman now, Beebee," says the presumptuous Misery, "and of course you'll wear the Moorish dress."

"I en't a Moorwoman, and I won't wear a Moorish dress," said I, upon which the old woman had the insolence to mutter that since Meer Sinzaun furnished the clothes I might as well wear what he sent.

"On the contrary," said I, "I'll have 'em as unlike as possible to those he sent, that so I may forget the humiliation sooner. How dare you, woman, bring me these shocking gaudy colours, when you know I'm lamenting the loss of the most tender and deeply honoured of parents? Fetch me some decent black stuff, and a tailor to make a gown according to my taste, for I won't wear these things."

Finding me so angry, Misery became vastly submissive, as is her way when I assert my will, and entreated with tears that I would pardon my slave, for there was no such thing as a black stuff to be had in all Muxadavad, since none of the Indians wear this mournful hue, and that to send to any of the foreign factories for it would cause suspicion that 'twas a European desired so unusual a fabric.

"Very well," I said, "I en't unreasonable. You may bring me white or gray or purple, and I'll wear it, provided the tailor knows his business."

But at this Misery fell down at my feet again, and struck her head against the floor, lamenting that 'twas impossible to employ a tailor. He would demand a muster,[01] she said, and when he had my old gown given him, there would be no concealing that 'twas part of a European dress. This was true enough, and I resigned with some regret the notion of the tailor, for these men are extraordinary ingenious in copying any pattern given to 'em, and produce wonderful pieces of work with their rusty needles and scissors that scarce hang together at the rivet. "Come," I said to Misery, "you and the other maid-servants shall do the sewing, and I'll tell you what I wish done." But to hear the cry she raised, you would think she had never touched a needle in all her life, which I can hardly credit. Then, imagining that she had vanquished me, she sat up upon her heels with a smile of assurance to see me put on the Persian clothes. But this I was resolved not to do, for the dress would have been the very livery of slavery, implying that I laid down willingly the privileges of our own free and enlightened land to take up the wretched degraded existence of the Indian women. "Not at all, Misery," I said; "see that the stuff is got, and I'll do the sewing myself." At this there was another shriek of protest, but this time I was firm, and when next the steward came to the curtain to enquire my wishes, I demanded stuff and needles and thread. (My own needles were gone out of my hussy. I fear Misery knows more about them than she feigned to do.) The steward appeared to consider my request in the highest degree extraordinary, more especially when Misery had spoke to him for some time in the Persic[02] language, which I don't understand, but upon my recalling to him sharply his master's orders, he besought my pardon humbly for his hesitation and promised obedience. More, he asked me whether I was content with my woman, or if I found her saucy, and would prefer another, but to this I answered that she was well enough, and I desired no change. You perceive, my dear, I know that Misery is false to me, but with another I might be in doubt whether she was to be trusted or no, and so perhaps be led into rash confidences. My forbearance gained me much credit with Misery, who came to me afterwards and placed my foot upon her head, thanking me, in her usual insinuating, deceitful style, for my goodness in passing over her pert behaviour.

Well, Amelia, I had my stuffs fetched me at last, white muslin for gowns, and a sort of dark purple satin, very rich and thick, for a petticoat. You'll smile to think of your Sylvia setting up as a mantuamaker and milaner,[03] but I found the benefit of Mrs Abigail's instructions while at the school, and I don't think my work would disgrace me, even in England. But oh, my dear, the difficulties of making a gown where there's no such thing as lining or buttons or hooks and eyes, or even lace or trimming! I wish I could show my Amelia my wonderful devices of muslin frills, and ribbons made of strips of satin, and gold clasps used for buttons. But at least I have shown Misery which of us is mistress and which maid, and I have refused to be turned into a Moorwoman to please the taste of my wicked persecutor, who—

Oh, my dearest girl, I am in such a tremble I can't go on writing. Misery is just come to tell me that Meer Sinzaun is returned to the city with the Soubah after a wholly successful campaign against the Purranea Nabob, and that he'll do himself the honour to wait on me this evening. I think I had almost forgot the wretch; at least I never believed he would return so soon. What shall I do? what can I do?

Nov. ye 10th.

I have delayed, Amelia, to write you the history of my interview with Sinzaun, because day after day, whenever I thought of the wretch, I was seized with such a shuddering that I could not put pen to paper. But to-day I am resolved to do my utmost to conquer this weakness, since if the mere thought of Sinzaun in his absence make me tremble, in what condition shall I be the next time he chooses to force his presence upon me?

As soon as I could collect my thoughts after receiving Misery's announcement, I came to the desperate resolution to behave towards my captor in as easy and cheerful a style as I could assume, affecting to regard him merely as a charitable person that had saved me from the Nabob with the object of restoring me to my friends, and ignoring as the creations of a mind diseased all my terrors respecting him in the beginning of my fever. If I could play my part discreetly enough, this expedient might, I thought, procure me some short respite, and perhaps give time for help to reach me,—for surely, unless Britons were prepared to sit down tamely under the most shocking oppression and ill-usage, some attempt must soon be made from Madrass to redress our wrongs. With this in my mind, I prepared to receive Meer Sinzaun. Misery, seeing me, as she believed, resigned to my situation, fell in joyfully with my imagined compliance, and was so presumptuous as to weave in with my hair, as she dressed it, some flowers she had plucked from the garden. This bold device I quickly discovered, and punished the woman by compelling her to take out the flowers and comb my hair up tightly under my cap. At least the odious wretch should have no occasion to fancy that I had dressed myself fine to meet him.

Seated, at the appointed time, in the outer room of the garden-house, which I have taken for my saloon, I awaited the approach of my enemy. Presently I saw him crossing the garden, muffled very ingeniously in the robes of a Moorman of quality, which were drawn up about his face, but of these he disencumbered himself with great agility upon the varanda, and on Misery announcing him, entered my presence in a European habit of great magnificence, bowing in the most submissive manner. I rose and made him my best curtsey. "Your servant, sir," said I. (You must remember, Amelia, that all our intercourse was in French, since Meer Sinzaun don't speak English; and indeed I have reason to be grateful for the pains our good Mrs Abigail and Mrs Eustacia took to make us speak their own language with fluency and correctness.)

"Nay, madam, behold your slave at your feet," he replied, offering his hand to conduct me to the settee. His touch sent a shudder through my frame, but I did my best to conceal the repulsion with which he inspired me.

"Pray be seated, sir," I said, as he still stood before me in a humble attitude.

"Madam, your commands can't but be obeyed," he said, and seated himself opposite to me. For the instant I imagined—so complaisant was his tone—that my fears might after all be unnecessary, but stealing a glance at his countenance I perceived that here was still the old Sinzaun, the man that had got me into his power and meant to keep me there. To hide the despair that seized me, I made shift to speak.

"You are returned from your campaign, sir?"

"Yes, madam, and not only in safety but in triumph,—thanks, as I can't doubt, to your kind prayers on my behalf." Oh, Amelia, if you could have seen the horrid smile on the wretch's lips as he said this! "Or rather, permit me to say, 'twas the beneficent influence of my goddess herself that accompanied me in the fight, and preserved me from harm. Clarissa will deign to accept my poor thanks?"

I was almost choked by the wretch's assurance, but struggled on.

"You found the time pass agreeably, sir, I trust?"

"Agreeably enough, madam, but prodigious slowly. The charmer who knows where I had left my heart won't ask me why the days seemed so long. And now may I put the same question to Clarissa? Whatever answer she may please to make will content me, for though she be cruel enough to find the time of her adorer's absence pass quickly, yet she will but be recognising his devices for her entertainment."

"The time is always long, sir, when one is parted from one's friends." I said this with great seriousness, designing him to receive it as a rebuke for detaining me from my friends so long, but what was my horror and disgust when he bowed with his hand on his heart, crying—

"Oh, madam, you overwhelm me! A thousand thanks for your charming condescension! That Clarissa should miss her slave is indeed the height of bliss for him."

I clasped my throat with my hand, my dear, or I should have cried out, to see this wretch sitting there complacently to torment me. But I felt assured that he was endeavouring to drive me to some hysterical outburst that might display his power over me, and I resolved to disappoint him if I died for it. While he continued romancing for a moment or two, uttering all the extravagancies he could think of to rob me of my self-command, I recovered myself a little.

"You was so obliging as to furnish me with writing implements, sir, before you left," I said when he ceased, "and I must be permitted to show you that I have made no use of 'em such as you would disapprove. There were thirty sheets of paper in all, I believe. Here's the thirty still, though in part used," and I counted 'em over to him.

"Oh, sweet innocence!" he cried, "that combines the sprightly simplicity of Pamela with the majesty of the divine Clarissa! Sure my charmer never thought so meanly of her Sinzaun as to imagine he would call her to account for the indulgences he was allowed to furnish her? Thirty sheets that have been touched by Clarissa's fingers! Fifteen or so that bear the impress of her hand! Give me, madam, at least those blank sheets, that I may wear 'em next the heart where your image dwells. I would ask for one of those that are wrote on, but that I know they're too precious to be parted with, and I would not put my Clarissa's tender heart to the pain of refusing her adorer. But the blank sheets I must have."

"Oh, sir, would you deprive me of my sole diversion?" I cried.

"Deprive you, madam? Oh, this carping mercantile spirit don't become my Clarissa! You shall have two fresh sheets for each one that I take—will that lift the storm-clouds from my charmer's brow? How is it my star among women will so seldom permit her worshipper to bask in the light of her smiles? He don't deserve the indulgence, that he knows, but for the sake of Clarissa's reputation for clemency were it not well that she should show herself more complaisant?"

I gazed at him wildly while he uttered these words in a tone of tender reproach, gathering up the blank sheets the while. "Like Pamela's Mr B.," he continued, in a meditative style that checked the sobs which would otherwise have burst from me, "I can't find it in my heart to deprive my charmer of the pleasure she takes in writing, even though she use it to revile myself. To be sure, I can't read what she writes, and so improve my disposition, but then, no more can the thrice-happy being to whom it's addressed. How could I rob Clarissa of a diversion that pleases her, and can injure no one, even myself?"

I think the wicked man looked to see me fly into a passion and demand how he knew that I had wrote anything against him, but I reflected that he could scarce imagine I should deal with his name in my letters with any great tenderness, and that he had but made a guess at what they contained, and I said no more than—

"Sure you must be very well acquainted with Mr Richardson's works, sir?"

"Madam," he replied, "they are the study of my life. In the French translations, they are my greatest treasures, and I admire them continually more and more. I think I may say that there en't a virtuous sentiment, nor a neat touch of humour, that I could not give you chapter and verse for on the instant, in the whole three novels."

Is it not extraordinary, Amelia, that a person like this can actually take pleasure in such works as Mr Richardson's, whose whole course and tenor must be a standing rebuke to him? They say that the devil can quote Scripture, as indeed is proved by the Gospels, and this shows that evil beings will read good books without being improved by their study.

"And more," he continued, "'tis to the good Mr Richardson that I owe the honour of meeting the lady whose portrait he had surely drawn by anticipation in his 'Clarissa.' When, in the dress of our great sovereign, I penetrated unknown into the Masquerade at Calcutta, drawn by the fame of a certain lady's beauty that had reached me, I found myself attracted by one who seemed to me to be none other than Clarissa herself. 'Here, Sinzaun,' I said to myself, 'is a fellow-student of the books you reverence, one who has perceived what is the crowning-point of Clarissa's history, and has ventured to outshine all other beauties by the simplicity of her attire and the piteousness of her aspect!' Judge, madam, what were my feelings when I discovered my Clarissa to be the very being at whose shrine I was come to worship!"

"Alas, sir!" was all I could say.

"Yes, madam," he went on, "I have learned much from Mr Richardson. You won't find me falling into the error of Lovelace, and making use of barbarous force to constrain my charmer, while her mind and heart remain unsubdued. It is Clarissa's favour that I desire to gain; she must become mine by her own free consent. I can wait until she choose to oblige me, for I know she'll make me happy at last."

He spoke with so much confidence and security that I began to feel as they say birds do when a serpent approaches 'em, powerless to withdraw from the noxious influence, however heartily I hated it, wondering almost whether this man could force me in spite of myself to consent to become his. I broke the spell with a vast effort by asking him the day of the month, which he told me, and shortly afterwards took his departure, leaving me to spend the night in sobs and tears, and urgent prayers to Heaven to save me or let me die.

December ye 15*th*.

Since my last writing, Amelia, I have endured three interviews with Sinzaun. Such is the horrible cunning of this wicked man, that he don't present himself at regular intervals, nor inform me of his intended visit until a short time before he appears, so that I spend my whole time with the dread hanging over me of being suddenly confronted with him. This garden seems to be haunted with his image; the slightest footstep—even a shadow falling on the path—drives me into an agony of fear, and the wretch can't help perceiving, when he comes, the condition my terror throws me into. This alone would prove his cruel nature, that with all the respect and admiration he professes for me, until I'm sick of hearing it, he continues to force himself upon me with the sole purpose of tormenting the being he feigns to love. Indeed, he goes so far as to rally me upon my apprehensions, telling me once that my lofty courage recalled to him some personage of one of the French poets who declared that he feared God and had no other fear,—"a sentiment," says Sinzaun, "that I'll venture to commend to my Clarissa, since it describes so exactly her own absence of alarm." Oh, my dear, is it come to this, that my timidity is bringing a reproach upon the religion I humbly profess? And yet, who could avoid fearing this man? Sure to feel at ease in his presence would come near to sharing his evil deeds.

My dear girl will scarce credit it, but I am convinced that my persecutor entertains himself during his absences with devising fresh miseries for me. He comes to the house muffled in various disguises, and is at huge pains to explain to me that he runs an incredible risque of being tracked by spies, and that he can't set out to pay me a visit save when he has seen the Nabob engrossed in some new and delightful plan of wickedness. "Then," says he, "I fly on the wings of love to my charmer, confident that one short hour in her presence will stimulate my invention even to the point of devising fresh pleasures for Saradjot Dollah, such as may gain me a further audience of her."

"Indeed, sir," I said, "I can't but think it a pity that you don't attempt to lead the Nabob into the paths of virtue. In so novel a pursuit the Prince—and perhaps Meer Sinzaun also—would find a freshness and singularity far more agreeable than the dulness of the evenings you are so obliging as to sacrifice to the poor prisoner here."

"Dulness! sacrifice!" he cried, brushing away my suggestion lightly; "sure Clarissa must be seeking for compliments. I'm hugely grateful, madam, for your obliging thought, but I'll assure you that I amuse myself infinitely during these visits. I can't recall any occasion of my life on which I have been better entertained."

I can well believe it, Amelia. I never look at him if I can help it, for so great is the loathing with which the man inspires me that I can't bear to meet his eye, but when through inadvertence I have done so, I perceive in it a sort of sombre ferocity united with delight in my sufferings that makes me tremble. Can my dear Miss Turnor figure to herself the being forced to enter a tyger's cage for the purpose of diverting the tyger? Which would be the worse, does she think, this, or that the tyger should be so obliging as to exert himself to entertain you? I think she'll say that one is as bad as the other, and this is my case with Sinzaun. I suffer equally when he compels me to speak and when he speaks himself, for the man, my dear, is an atheist. I would not write this terrible charge, lest my indignation against him should have caused me to judge him harshly, if I had not heard it from his own lips, but he has assured me more than once that the one deity in which he believes is gain, and the one incentive that moves men is advantage. "I believe in my Clarissa," was the utmost I could get from him when I pressed him strongly on the point, and he added that his life had taught him there was no Providence, either to punish the evil or protect the good, but only a blind fate, out of whose unsteady dispositions the wise man must shape his own road to success. En't this cruelty indeed, to seek to deprive a poor creature of her faith in God just when she needs it most? But sure Meer Sinzaun has overreached himself in this, for I need not go far to learn of the existence of the devil, and to disbelieve in God on the devil's word would questionless be the extremest folly in the world. But having thus unfolded to me what he called the wise man's creed, which he said he had gathered both from European philosophers and from the sages of the East, Sinzaun went on to show its practical application, desiring to prove that there was no truth nor honour nor virtue in the world, any more than Divine justice nor providence, and proceeded to turn into ridicule the very books he had been praising to me a month before. I can but be grateful he don't know his Bible as well as he does Mr Richardson's works, for sure 'twas only ignorance, and not good will, made him stop short of attacking that. He cited instance after instance to prove that there was no virtue in goodness, and no reward for't if there were, and no shame in sin, nor punishment neither, and I could not hope to contend with him. You know, Amelia, I was always the one to be worsted in an argument. How I wished that my dear Mrs Hurstwood were present, with her ready tongue, to give the assailant as good as he brought, and to silence, if she could not convince him, whereas I could but sit quiet, or protest without hope of moving him, while he attacked everything in which the Christian believes. At last he took his leave, and summoning my courage, I said as I curtseyed to him—

"Permit me to say, sir, that I'm entirely at variance with the opinions you have chose to utter this evening."

"A thousand thanks for the assurance, madam!" was the wretch's reply. "My mind is inexpressibly relieved. I should be desolated if I thought my Clarissa shared those opinions I have indicated as my own."

As much as to say that he would prefer his mistress to remain a believer in Christianity, because she would then be the better wife to him! Oh, Amelia, how can anything that is said or done move such a man? I dread and detest him more and more, and my only comfort is based on his assurance that he would wait patiently until he had gained my favour. If he can wait, so can I, if he don't drive me mad first.

January ye 24th, 1757.

I have been favoured with several further visits from Meer Sinzaun, but to describe these miseries at length would be as unprofitable to my dearest friend as it would be painful to myself; yet of the last I must say something, for the pitiless wretch told me he must take leave of me for a season, since he was about to attend the Soubah into the neighbourhood of Calcutta, there to destroy the last remnants of British trade and enterprise in Bengal.

"Sure, sir, your prince has done more than enough for his honour already in that line," I cried, in an agony to see my countrymen still further threatened.

"Why, indeed, madam," he replied, "if there had been only your brave Calcutta gentlemen, Mr Drak" (so he pronounced it), "and his two chief friends, in the matter, we had been contented to leave them alone. The persons who deserted their posts and connived at the destruction of their factory in order to satisfy their enmity against their unfortunate colleague, Mr Holwell, might well have been suffered to remain at Fulta, subsisting on the charity of Omy Chund and the French and Dutch factories, until they could be taken off and carried to England by their ships arriving this season. But there was a certain restless troublesome fellow named Clive, who may be known to you by reputation, at Madrass when the news of the fall of Calcutta reached there, and this pestilent wretch has proposed to himself to establish the British again in Bengall. Sure the beginning of his enterprise can't have given him much hope for its ending; for, embarking with all the forces he could command on board of the fleet lying at Madrass, he set forth in the worst season of the year, with the result that the whole of the ships was destroyed by storms, and but a few score of men, with Mr Clive himself, escaped in boats and landed in the river."

"Oh, sir, what is it you say?—all the fleet destroyed?" For you know, Amelia, who is serving on board Admiral Watson's fleet, if Sinzaun don't.

"All, madam, so far as my information serves. Whether the Admiral or any of his officers and men are among those saved by the boats, I can't of course say. But I should judge by his actions that Mr Clive is alone. What do you say, madam, to his being kindly received and used by his Highness's garrisons at Tanners and Buzbudgia, and taking advantage of their hospitality to make an attack upon them by surprise, inflicting some loss, though but a trifling one?"

"Why, sir, that if Colonel Clive acted so, he must first have perceived treachery on the part of the Moguls." But to myself I added, "If this man can tell me a tale so manifestly false respecting Colonel Clive, he may be deceiving me also with regard to the fleet."

"If that's so, madam," replied Sinzaun, "I'm sorry for the poor gentleman, for you must see that even a warrior of such renown can't be permitted to defy his Highness in this style in his own province, and his Highness proposes to prove this to him shortly. But there's more trouble in store for poor Mr Clive, for he has committed the grave military error of neglecting his base of operations. For this adventure in Bengall he deprived Madrass of all its troops, ignorant that Mons. Bussy was leagued with Salabatzing[04] against the place, and that our new great fleet under Lally wasn't far off.[05] I fear Britain will lose more than Bengall by his rashness."

"Alas, alas!" I cried, with tears.

"I have the greatest respect, madam, I'll assure you, for Mr Clive, and it shall be my endeavour to see that his life is spared and himself put safely on board of a ship bound for England. These Indians will questionless desire to see him led in fetters and rags through the streets of Muxadavad, as was done six months ago with Mr Holwell and his companions, but he shall be saved this if I can compass it."

"Oh, sir, is it true that good Mr Holwell was used in this barbarous fashion, and exposed to the insults of the citizens, after enduring the miseries of that terrible night?"

"Why, yes, madam. Poor Mr Holwell was hardly used indeed, being sacrificed first to the pique of his colleagues, and then to the resentment of Omy Chund, whom he had left in prison when he took command of Fort William. You may chance to have heard it said that Omy Chund never forgives, and he had old grudges also to avenge, and so the four gentlemen found it who were sent here after the fall of Calcutta. There's a gay young spark belonging to your Cossimbuzar factory that would say the same, I think. Being permitted to refuge with the Dutch, Mr Hastings thought fit to abuse his Highness's clemency by stirring up his subjects to revolt against him; but a whisper from Omy Chund,[06] to whom he had opened his designs, warned Saradjot Dollah, and sent the young intriguer flying to join his friends at Fulta. A most useful worthy fellow is Omy Chund, and I myself have good cause to be grateful to him. But this brings me to the object of my troubling my charmer with a visit to-night. Will Clarissa permit me to make preparations for our union when I return from Allynagore?"

"Our union, sir?" I stammered.

"Why, yes, madam, that delightful event which has shone like a beacon before your adorer throughout these long months. What! did Clarissa wrong her Sinzaun by imagining that he purposed to keep her immured within these walls, remote alike from the society and the enjoyments of her sex? No, madam; permit me to seek a priest at Chandernagore, and bring him with me on my return (you see my care for your punctilio—I offer you no Moorish marriage), and Clarissa shall discover what delights can be offered for her acceptance by the man she has so infinitely obliged. A palace instead of this rustic abode, such clothing and jewels as no queen in Europe could show, a place and credit second only to that of Ally Verdy Cawn Begum herself, and the eternal adoring devotion of her attached Sinzaun."

Now why was it, Amelia, that I could not refuse this proposition at once? "Oh, sir, you overwhelm me——" I faltered, with my eyes on the ground.

"Nay," replied my suitor, "Clarissa has certainly misjudged me. Did she imagine that I destroyed Calcutta merely that I might keep her a prisoner?"

"You destroyed Calcutta, sir?"

"Why, yes, madam, though I would have spared it had you deigned to listen to my vows, as I expressed in the first chitt I writ you." I remembered the billet I had read aloud to my dear papa and Captain Colquhoun, and shuddered. "Had Clarissa yielded to my entreaties, could I have done less than spare her countrymen for her sake? My influence thrown on the side of clemency, instead of into the opposite scale, would have turned his Highness from his purpose, or at the least I could have delayed the march by some accident to the artillery, and so given time for the rains to begin, which would have saved Calcutta. But since Clarissa remained obdurate, I could do no less than destroy the place whose capture meant that I should obtain possession of her."

"But, sir, you could not—oh, I don't know what I am saying—my head is in a whirl—'twas the merest chance——"

"There was no chance at all, madam. My plans were all concerted with Omy Chund. Who prevented you from going on board the ships with t'other women? Omy Chund, through his servant. Who raised the panic that drove Mr Drak to fly before the time he had intended? This same servant. Who was prepared to protect you against his Highness's soldiers by asserting my authority? The fellow again. Who suffered you to slip through his fingers that night, but redeemed his fault nobly the next day by sending an agent of his with you as your attendant? Omy Chund himself. Sure Clarissa can't talk of chance now, any more than she can pretend to mistake my design in thus making myself master of the being I adored."

Was ever such a cruel coil of deceit and trickery wound about a poor creature, Amelia? If you could know the horrid feeling of helplessness that seized me in face of this man's plottings! Oh, my dear, your Sylvia is a sad coward. She durst not look the perfidious wretch in the face, and declare her hatred at once of his proposition and himself. Instead, she had recourse to a miserable equivocation that darted into her mind.

"Sir, you can't but be aware that 'tis only seven months since I lost the best of fathers. What have you seen in Sylvia Freyne to make you think so meanly of her as that she would outrage all the laws of decorum and filial piety by listening to a proposal of marriage in such circumstances?"

For one instant, my dear, the man was taken aback. "I declare, madam, you're cleverer than I thought you!" was in his eye, and the unhappy fool before him rejoiced. Then he said, "I accept the rebuke, madam, and Clarissa shan't be troubled again with my ill-timed importunities for the present, unless there's any reason for infringing her pious punctilio in her own interest."

He left me soon after, and for three days I have been in a continual terror lest his departure should only be a pretended one, meant to throw me off my guard. But I have seen and heard nothing of him, and the steward assuring me to-day that the Soubah had left Muxadavad with his army, I begin to feel that I may look forward to a short period of peace.

Februaryye 21st.

Sinzaun is returned, Amelia, bringing such tidings as have reduced your unhappy Sylvia to the lowest depths of despair. Immediately upon entering the saloon he acquainted me that Colonel Clive, after a gallant resistance, in which he was nobly supported by his troops, had been forced to surrender, and was now in captivity until some Dutch or other European ship could be found to convey him to England, while the last traces of British influence in Bengall were now destroyed. As if this grievous news, putting an end to any extravagant hopes that might have crept into my mind, were not enough, my persecutor must needs add a keener edge to my suffering by saying—

"Will it please the amiable Clarissa to learn that she had some hand in this overthrow? I was told by one of the captive British officers that 'twas the knowledge of Miss Freyne's carrying-off by the Moors that had played a principal part in inducing her generous countrymen to attempt this rash expedition in the vain hope of rescuing her."

Was not this an excess of cruelty, Amelia? Not content with bringing about the destruction of Calcutta, I must involve in my misfortunes the forces of Madrass and our great, our only commander on Indian soil. Blame me, my dear, if you will, but I think you'll scarce wonder that the impulse seized me to unite my unhappy fate with that of the sneering wretch seated opposite me, and draw down upon him some of those calamities which seem to follow every one with whom I have to do. Almost as the thought crossed my mind, Sinzaun remarked, with great deliberation,—

"If I cursed the unfortunate Mr Clive a month ago for tearing me from the side of my charmer, I have some hopes of finding reason before long to bless him. The Soubah has been pleased to appoint me a mission to visit Mons. Bussy, who is advancing hither from the Carnatic, and welcome him in his triumphal course. Now in this agreeable jaunt I shall be accompanied with my own tried troops, and no one can question my actions. I see that Clarissa's health is suffering from her close confinement within these walls, and perhaps she may find the prospect pleasing of a journey that would carry her through the most charming region of Bengall, in the company of a man that would spare no pains to make it enjoyable to her. The past can't be undone, but if Clarissa will relax her prohibition, and suffer her adorer to seek the priest he spoke of, it may be that she'll find it easier to banish from her mind the sad images which can't but cloud at present the spirits of a creature of so much sensibility."

Sure it must have been that Providence in which he affects to disbelieve that directed Sinzaun's tongue to the mention of the past at that instant, thus recalling my mind from the shocking scheme of vengeance that had presented itself to me to a frightful question which I had been led to ask myself during his absence.

"Before I answer you, sir," I said, "permit me to ask you a question. You have acknowledged making use of Omy Chund's servant to keep me in the Fort at the time the rest of the European females escaped. You know by what means he effected your purpose—by bringing word to me of his finding my father wounded to death in one of our outposts, when the gentlemen who had last seen him declared that he was well and unhurt. Was this, sir, a part of your plan? Did you bring about the murder of my father in order that you might carry into execution your designs against his unhappy daughter?"

I stood up and regarded him, and his eyes fell before mine, but he sought to speak with his usual lightness of tone. "If Clarissa seeks to hold me responsible for all the deeds done by my agents, I fear the record will be but a black one," he said. "Can she imagine that her adorer would desire to raise his hand against one dear to her? The Gentoo fellow had his orders given him to carry out, but the means of doing so were left to himself."

"Enough, sir!" I said. "Hitherto I have thought you might not be guilty of this crowning infamy, but now I am persuaded that you suggested if you did not order it. And in return for the murder of the father you seek to obtain the hand of the daughter! The reward may be but a poor one, but it's beyond your reach. I will never become your wife, sir—never, never, never!"

"I think you will, madam. This display of heroics don't displease me, even without the entertainment it affords. One can allow some degree of passion to the last female of your nation in India."

"The last female of my nation in India, sir?"

"Why, yes, madam, the last. You en't aware that when Mr Clive had forsook Madrass, Mons. Bussy swooped down upon the place by land, and Count Lally by sea, finding it an easy prey. Bombay was already fallen into our hands, and the smaller factories were dealt with by a detached squadron. The few English that survived these misfortunes have been embarked in their vessels and despatched to their own island. Britain don't own a foot of Indian soil to-day—save for a huge quantity of graves. And is this the moment for Clarissa to use these bitter reproaches to her adorer, whose faults are all to be set down to the excess of his passion for herself? She'll deign him a gracious answer?"

"The same answer, sir, as if she were the last female of her nation in the world—never—a thousand times never!"

"We shall see, madam. I think you en't yet fully acquainted with Sinzaun's disposition. Don't consider it presumptuous if he tell you that when he returns from his journey you'll plead to be allowed the favour he now offers you;" and he departed, leaving me more dead than alive.

The last female of our nation in India, Amelia! Is there any use in leaving these records of her fate, when there's no one can read them or convey them home? Perhaps some future age may bring them to light, and I won't destroy them. Do you remember my name in your prayers daily, my dear friend, as I do yours, and as we promised to do when we parted? If you knew at this moment that your Sylvia's earnest prayer was for death, would you have the humanity to join your petitions with hers? If you truly loved your poor girl you would, for death is now her only hope. Clarissa died, you'll remember, but I am so frightfully strong, and—I am the only female of our nation left in India.

CHAPTER XVII.
IN WHICH GREEK JOINS GREEK.

From Colvin Fraser, Esq., to Mrs Hurstwood.

THE ENGLISH HOUSE, MUXIDAVAD, *Feb. ye 28th.*

Being now arrived at Muxidavad, madam, I take up my pen to fulfil my promise to keep Mrs Hurstwood informed of the progress made towards the release of her incomparable friend. But first, lest I would raise too high the anticipations of my kind correspondent, let me say that the three or four days I have spent in this place have brought nothing but disappointment, both private and public. We can't obtain any news of Miss Freyne, and our natural enemies, the French, have sought the aid of the inconstant barbarian, to whom Mess. Watson and Clive taught so lately a needed lesson, to defeat our plans for their overthrow. Mrs Hurstwood won't have forgot that, either in my last letter or in that before it, I writ that Colonel Clive had demanded permission of the Soubah to attack Chandernagore, but met with a temporising answer, which neither accorded the desired liberty nor refused it. The Colonel, taking advantage of this ambiguous quality of the Nabob's reply, continued his preparations for the enterprise with all the speed and secrecy imaginable, considering it of prime importance to break the power of the French in Bengal before they could seize the moment of his returning to Madrass to attack our weakened factory, and ten days ago he crossed the river with his army.

But now begun a din indeed! The French writ urgent letters to the Nabob, which reached him at Augadeep,[01] a village some forty miles south of this place, imploring his protection against the wicked and rapacious British, and so it was, that all his favourites concurred with their entreaty. Monickchund feared that in the event of our succeeding with the French we would fall to remembering that he had possessed himself of a huge portion of the spoils of Calcutta, and request of him to disgorge it, Coja Wasseed, who manages the French trade, was naturally loath to lose his office, and the Seats, to whom the Sydabad factory is indebted in the extraordinary sum of thirteen *laacks*, were drove near distracted by the prospect of seeing themselves deprived of the hope of regaining it. Hence, when Mr Watts arrived at Houghley, he learned through Omichund, who travelled with him, from the Phousdar Nuncomar,[02] that the Nabob had sent two of his servants, Seen Bawboo[03] and Montra Mull, to Chandernagore with a present of a *laack* of rupees, and had ordered the Houghley garrison to render the French every assistance in the event of an attack by us. This last peril was averted by the address of Omichund, who was able to bring Nuncomar over to our side by a bribe of 12,000 rupees, but on reaching Augadeep, Mr Watts discovered that to attack the French at present would only serve to precipitate a conflict with the whole army of the Soubah. The weak prince received our agent with the most violent demonstrations of displeasure, nor was it until Omichund had sworn on the foot of a Bramin, as the most solemn oath he could take, that the British had no ill designs, that Surajah Dowlah would consent to await even an explication from Colonel Clive. Urged by Mr Watts' recommendations to prudence, the Colonel withdrew his troops, writing to the Nabob a friendly letter to assure him of our regard for his wishes. Thus the affair came to an end for the present, but with what humiliation for us and triumph for our enemies Mrs Hurstwood won't need me to tell her.

As to Mr Watts, who shares to the full the Colonel's suspicions of the French, I can't but think his disappointment would have killed him, had he not found so much to be done in repairing our damaged influence at the Court. When I reached Muxidavad, he was still smarting under his defeat, and while receiving Dr Dacre in the most handsome manner, showed signs of desiring to avenge a portion of his wrongs on me. He could not well refuse me a lodging, since I carried the Admiral's despatches, but all his words and looks exhibited the most undisguised hostility, in so much that he failed even to invite me to his table on the evening of our arrival. My revered Mrs Hurstwood will understand with what apprehension I viewed this enmity on the part of the person to whom I looked most for help in discovering my beloved, and with what resentment mingled with resolution I obeyed a summons the next morning to Mr Watts' closet.

"Be seated, sir," says the good gentleman, throwing a fiery glance at me. "Pray, sir, what are you doing in Muxidavad?"

"I am the bearer of Mr Watson's despatches, sir."

"Sir, I know that, but it don't give you any more right here."

"I protest, sir, you're using very strange language towards me."

"The Admiral is behaving monstrous strangely towards me, sir. I put my neck in a noose by coming here, endeavouring to serve the Company by my long experience of these Indians and my knowledge of their politics and customs, and he must needs spy upon me by means of an insolent Scotch——"

"Stop, sir, pray, before you utter words that I'll be under the necessity of resenting. Permit me to say that you're entirely mistaken in Admiral Watson's design. True, he has honoured me with the carriage of his despatches, but only as the cloak to an errand of my own. He had no desire to spy upon you, sir, far less to interfere with your arduous labours here."

"I'm infinitely obliged by your remarks, sir, but they're contradicted by Mr Watson's choosing to send his letters to the Soubah by another messenger than myself."

"Indeed, sir, there's no question of my delivering the despatches in person. I hope never to meet the Soubah save on a battlefield. I am instructed to hand the letters to you, to be delivered as you see fit."

"That sounds fair enough," says Mr Watts, regarding me with something less of suspicion, "but I should still be glad to know the reason of your presence here, sir. A *cossid*, or good Dr Dacre himself, might have served to bring the letters."

"Why that, sir, is the very matter I desired to unfold to you. May I hope you'll treat it as confidential, whether you approve it or not?"

"I hope, sir, you en't come here to get us into trouble with any wild notions? But pray open your mind to me."

"I am here, sir, on the behalf of a lady who survived the fall of Calcutta only to become a prisoner to the Moors. She contrived to throw out from her prison a paper, from which it has been gathered that she's in the hands of the renegado Sinzaun, somewhere in this city, but we know no more than that."

"And you hope to rescue her? Young sir, take the advice of a man that has seen more of the world than you, and let the lady alone. Whether she be a willing or a reluctant captive, you can do her no good."

"If you had the honour of the lady's acquaintance, sir, you'd know that no weak compliance would make of her a willing captive. If for any reason she believe it her duty to remain in captivity, I hope I won't persecute her to leave it, but if she be detained against her will, as I can't doubt, I would be lacking in every manly quality if I suffered her to pine in vain for a deliverer."

"You talk very fine, sir, but what do you purpose to do?"

"Why, sir, with your kind permission, I hope to remain here, and do my utmost first to discover the lady, and then to devise means for releasing her."

"Indeed, sir, it's well you're speaking to me in an unofficial manner. Do you perceive that you're gravely purposing to place all our lives in jeopardy? This Sinzaun is very great with the Nabob, and any attempt to interfere with his women would lead to our destruction. Are you minded to rush upon your death?"

"At least not until I have rescued the lady, sir."

"And why then, sir? But pray give a thought to me and to the other gentlemen here, and also to the Company's business in our hands. Sure you must see I can't permit you to raise a hornets' nest about us, and cause the ruin of the interests committed to my charge, which are those of the British nation?"

"Nay, sir, I don't desire to jeopardise your endeavours by any rash action of mine. I am seeking your advice in the hope of attaining my end in a secret manner. You don't need to tell me that on any inkling of my business reaching Sinzaun he would at once convey the lady to some distant place beyond our power to discover."

"Come, sir, I see you're a person of sense. But tell me, has Sinzaun any reason to believe you interested in the lady?"

"To the best of my belief, sir, he has none, and I'm sure the lady won't give him any."

"That's better, for I was beginning to think you had destroyed any hope of success by showing yourself in these parts. But, as it is, we may be able to do something. Since returning to Muxidavad, Sinzaun han't appeared outside his abode, under the plea of illness, but my spies give me to understand that the Nabob has despatched him on a secret errand to Bussey. No, sir, don't assure yourself of success too soon. You must make no appearance in the affair, but remain in this house, or attend Dr Dacre to view the sights of the city, as though you had no design in hand. For a European lodging here to set on foot enquiries regarding a woman in native custody would be to excite the town against us, and endanger our lives. You must employ some Indian as your spy, who may worm himself into an intimacy with some hanger-on of Sinzaun's, and so discover whether your belief be well grounded. As for finding such a person, Omichund will do the business for us."

"Pray, sir, don't let Omichund have any hand in the matter. 'Twas he betrayed the lady into Sinzaun's power."

"What, sir? make no use of Omichund? Then, indeed, you must do your business for yourself as you choose, for the fellow has all our lives in his hand, and would imagine himself betrayed if we employed any one else. You may have heard that he never forgives, and I don't pretend to desire such usage for myself as he brought on poor Mr Holwell."

"But pray, sir, what am I to do? As a man of honour, you can't bid me leave the lady to perish, and to appeal to the enemy for help would be a strange piece of folly."

Mr Watts thought for a while. "Look ye here, sir," said he; "since you have approached me in my private capacity, and as a person of honour and sensibility, I can't but choose to advise you. You have seen my Tartar servant, Mirza Shaw[04] Buzbeg—unfold your history to him. Being a Musselman, he goes in and out among the townspeople as one of themselves, and he is faithfully attached to my service, since I did him a benefit eight years ago at Patna. I believe the old rascal has a wife in the city—maybe two—and women might be useful in finding out such things as you desire to know. Strike a bargain with Mirza Shaw, but don't let him drive you too hard—though that's a caution I need scarce offer to a gentleman of your nation—and set him to work. You may find him slow, but don't let your impatience lead you to take any steps for yourself. If you get into any difficulty, I can give you no help—nay, I must if necessary disown and punish you, for my first consideration is my business here. The Calcutta gentlemen think fit to point the finger of scorn at me, because, say they, I surrendered Cossimbuzar without firing a shot, when twenty-four hours' resistance would have saved Calcutta, and Surajah Dowlah has asked for me here because he believes me a mild-spirited person, harbouring no resentments. So be it. Mr Clive and Mr Watson may fight if they choose, but when the Soubah's power is broke, 'twill be thanks to William Watts as much as to either gentleman."

"Indeed, sir, your boldness in returning here has been much admired."

"And not without reason, sir. There was one of my young gentlemen in the Cossimbuzar factory—Hastings is his name—who thought he would rise upon my downfall, and earn eternal gratitude as the destroyer of Surajah Dowlah. Refuging with the Dutch at Calcapore[05] after the troubles, he begins to plot with the Seats and others against the Nabob. That's all very well; but my young conspirator can't conceal his importance in having devised an actual plot, and by some indiscretion lets the affair come to the Soubah's ears, when at once we have excursions and alarms, exit Mr Hastings from Muxidavad, and enter one more fugitive at Fulta. I think better of you, sir, than to expect you to follow such an example, but I hope you perceive I can take no official notice of your errand here, nor can't afford to protect you should you incur the Soubah's resentment."

I assured Mr Watts at once of my confidence in his kindness and my prudence in making use of it, and proceeded to come to an agreement with the Usbeck Tartar by whom the good gentleman is so oddly attended. This is a shrewd fellow enough, and agreed willingly to act as my correspondent in the city, testifying a prodigious antipathy for the man Sinzaun, as an apostate that had encouraged the Nabob in his debaucheries, and introduced him to other vices than those native to the country. While waiting for any discovery of Mirza Shaw's that may afford me a chance of action, I have made bold to offer my services to Mr Watts to assist him in the huge quantity of writing that falls to his lot, which has tended still further to conciliate his kind opinion towards me. Mrs Hurstwood has been pleased to rally me more than once upon my style in writing, but I hope she'll grant now that I am putting it to the best use in thus placing it at the disposal of my country, and saving Mr Watts' time, since both he and Omichund are incessantly occupied in attempting to gain over the Nabob's intimates to our party. Ramramsing Rajah, the head of the spies, has been bought over entirely to our interests, but the rest still tend to the side of the French, although Mr Watts, with undaunted boldness, is now sending letters to Colonel Clive recommending him in the most persuasive manner to advance against Chandernagore without considering the lives of those at this agency.

March ye 20th.

I have now been near a month at this place, but alas, madam! as yet I have nothing to report as regards any success in the enterprise in which Mrs Hurstwood's heart, no less than my own, is engaged. Mirza Shaw assures me positively that there's no person of British birth in Sinzaun's household, nor can he discover that such a one has at any time been a member of it. The conclusion to which we are driven is that the villain has concealed the dear sufferer in some mean and remote part of the city, desiring to possess his prize without fear either of the greed of the Nabob or the jealousy of his own seraglio, and the Tartar is now devoting his efforts to discovering such a retreat. But this is an endless task! you'll cry. Indeed, madam, it is sufficiently appalling, but I would search Muxidavad house by house sooner than leave Miss Freyne to languish in captivity.

But if my private chronicle be destitute of events of any moment, this en't the case with public affairs, which indeed have beset us round with so many threatening waves that we are like to find some difficulty to keep our heads above water. The first event that disturbed the current of our politic dealings with this Court was the news that arrived immediately after the despatch of my last letter, that the Mogul Emperor's great city of Delly had been captured by an army of Pitans and Afguhans[06] from the north, which plunged the Soubah into the most abject fear imaginable. Apprehensive lest the Pitans would next proceed against his own rich province, he sent for Mr Watts, and besought the aid of the English against this common foe, promising to pay Colonel Clive a *laack* of rupees a month if he would but defend him with his army. Almost at the same time came news from Calcutta of the extraordinary obstinacy of the French at Chandernagore in their negotiations with us, by which they may, indeed, be said to have rushed upon their own destruction. Willing to oblige the

Nabob, and at the same time to provide for the safety of Calcutta when he should be forced to return to Madrass, Colonel Clive had proposed to the French that a strict neutrality should be observed in Bengal between the armies and fleets of the two nations, in spite of the war in England and the Carnatic. In this measure Mr Watts concurred, suggesting that the observance of the treaty by the French should be guarantied by the Seats, to whom they are so deeply indebted, and the Colonel, in order to secure the guarantie without offence, requested the Soubah to undertake it, which he did.

But when matters were adjusted thus far, the French fancied it a good chance to refuse suddenly to conclude any treaty at all, alleging that nothing they might promise would bind their head factory at Pondicherry, which is true enough, as all agreed when they remembered the breach of faith committed eleven years back at Madrass, when Mr Dupleix chose to destroy the town which his own Admiral had admitted to ransom. The recollection in itself was sufficiently sinister, but when the news came that Salabadjing, owing to our failure to support him in the Carnatic, and the diversion of our forces for the recapture of Calcutta, had been compelled to receive Mr Bussey again into favour, and hand over to him the provinces of Masulipatnam, Ganjam, and Vizagapatnam, thus bringing him within two hundred miles of Fort William by way of Cuttack, we could not doubt but the French were preparing a blow against us, and amusing us with negotiations while they collected their troops. On this our commanders lost no time in preparing to anticipate the threatened danger, Colonel Clive writing to the Nabob that he was advancing with his army to assist him against the Pitans, and halting on his way at Chandernagore, while the Admiral, who would not yet consent to act without the Prince's leave, wrote him a letter in a very moving style, pointing out not only the presumption of the French in invoking his name as the guarantie of a treaty they had no power to conclude, but also the delay of his own subjects in fulfilling the terms of the Calcutta agreement, and threatening him with ruin and destruction if these were not performed punctually and at once. This epistle was carried to the Nabob by Mr Watts, who, finding the Prince very apprehensive alike of the Pitans and the English, took occasion to represent the ingratitude of the French to him very forcibly, wringing from him at length a permission for the attack upon Chandernagore. Of this signal triumph we were apprised by the good gentleman himself on his return from the Kella,[07] which is the Soubah's palace here.

"This, gentlemen, is the first nail in Surajah Dowlah's coffin!" he said, laying a pacquet on the table before Dr Dacre and myself. "In less than two days Colonel Clive and the Admiral may proceed to attack the French."

"But have you succeeded in gaining the Soubah's leave, sir?" I asked him.

"He gave me a grudging assent, sir, and foreseeing that it needed but the next comer to induce him to reverse it, I applied at once to the *Huzzoor Nevees*,[08] whom I had already secured by means of a genteel present, and had him write the letter of permission in a proper style, and seal it with the Soubah's ring. The *cossid* is now making ready to start, and the pacquet will reach Admiral Watson in thirty hours or so."

"But en't I to carry the letter, sir?" I asked, for the Admiral had desired my return as soon as there should be any hope of attacking the French.

"Why no, sir. Would you have me lose all my pains? You can't travel near so fast as one of these fellows, and the passing of a European would set the whole riverside agog. 'Twould be surmised that only a pacquet of prodigious importance could demand such a messenger, and if the friends of the French didn't detain you, at least they would delay your progress."

"But I have Mr Watson's orders, sir."

"I vow, young gentleman, you'll drive me to lock you up, for stir from here you shan't. Don't be afraid; I'll assure the Admiral that you're too useful for me to spare you, and if you lose the fight, at least you won't be further parted from your mistress than you are."

This consideration went some way to reconcile me to my absence from the battle I anticipated, but I can't deny, madam, that I have been in a perfect fever since the *cossid* left, torn one way by my duty to the Service and t'other by my affection for Miss Freyne. I am forced even to envy Dr Dacre, who remains calm amidst all the alarms surrounding us, thinking only of the *Pundit* with whom he is studying the *Sanskerreet*[09] language, or of the venerable Moors whom he visits for the purpose of questioning them on their religion. Our situation is the most precarious imaginable, for only a few hours after the despatch of the letter there arrived another from the Prince, forbidding any hostile action in the most peremptory terms, which Mr Watts sent off with as little speed as he dared employ, and we understand that the Soubah is perpetually despatching messengers of his own, bearing menacing letters, to the Admiral and Mr Clive, while he has ordered Roydoolub to march with his army to the support of the French. It is our fervent hope that these discouragements will arrive too late to deter our gallant commanders, who may be trusted to have acted at once upon Mr Watts' motion.

March ye 31st.

Our patriotic anxieties have been happily relieved, madam, by the arrival of Mr Scrafton, of the Company's Service, on his way to Dacca, bringing news of the glorious triumph of our arms in the capture of Chandernagore, which surrendered eight days ago to Admiral Watson. Our success was not without alloy, being attended with a very heavy loss of life and great damage to the ships, while a parcel of French took advantage of the respite allowed for considering the terms of surrender to slip out and make their way to Sydabad, their factory near Cossimbuzar, where Mr Laws[10] has 'em concealed. So stubborn, indeed, was the enemy that we would scarce have been able to subdue them before Colonel Clive had drawn lines of investment about them on the land side, had it not been for the assistance rendered by a deserter named Mr Terrano,[11] who upon some affront received from the *Directeur*, Mr Renault, came over to us, and pointed out to the Admiral the only channel for the ships to pass up the river, which the French had blocked by sinking six vessels there, besides mooring two great booms across the stream with chains. In spite of this advantage the passage was so dangerous that the Kent, which suffered most, has been condemned, being an old vessel, and is fallen down to Calcutta to be broke up, while only one officer on board of her escaped unwounded, poor Billy Speke, among others, sustaining an injury that is like to be mortal by the same shot that wounded his father, the Captain.[12] My own ship, the Tyger, came off somewhat more lightly, although among the wounded was Admiral Pococke, who, arriving at Culpee in the Cumberland from Madrass, and finding the action imminent, was so resolute to take a share in it that he came up the river in his long-boat, and hoisted his flag on the Tyger, to the excessive mortification of Captain Latham, who saw himself cruelly deprived of the honour of fighting his ship. As for the army which the Nabob sent by Roydoolub to the assistance of the French, it was detained at Houghley by the address of our friend Nuncomar, who persuaded the commander that Chandernagore would be fallen before he could reach it. The letters sent to forbid the attack, arriving after that which permitted it, were treated by the Admiral and Colonel Clive with unconcern, a treatment accorded also, as we hear from Mr Scrafton, to Mr Drake, whose speech at the council held before starting on the expedition was so hesitating and contradictory that no one could make anything of it, and on the Colonel's suggestion it was unanimously voted that the President's opinion was no opinion at all.

And what (I am so vain as to imagine I hear Mrs Hurstwood cry), what of the few British left in Muxidavad at a time when their countrymen were thus defying the wrath of the tyrant? Indeed, madam, I think you'll agree that the protection of Heaven was extremely manifest in our case, for in the midst of the raging fury of the Soubah over the news there arrived two pieces of intelligence that recalled to him his need of our protection. By means of a private messenger (his favourite Sinzaun, as we understand), he learned that Mr Bussey, who was universally believed to be marching to the support of Chandernagore, had been compelled to turn back in order to put down the troubles which were arisen, as soon as he turned his back, in that part of the Decan where the French pretend to domination. At the same time the news came that the Pitan army, having made an alliance with Balagerow,[13] the Maharattor general, was marching upon Behar, and in this extremity the Soubah dissembled his indignation at the capture of Chandernagore, and writing insinuating letters of felicitation to the Admiral and Colonel Clive, reminded them of their promise to assist him, and went so far as to restore a portion of the Calcutta spoils of which he had dishonestly retained possession. Nothing could exceed his obliging behaviour to Mr Watts, which he extended also to Mr Scrafton, who, being admitted to a share in the plans of Mr Watts and Omichund, was glad to find himself introduced at Court, that he might the more readily observe the demeanour of the Prince and his attendance. With such excessive affection for the British has the Soubah been filled during these last few days, that hearing from Omichund, who attends his Durbar regularly, that there was in our house here one of Admiral Watson's officers, whom he had not seen, he chid Mr Watts for his negligence, and bade him bring the gentleman to pay his respects to him, in order that he might show favour to the servant of his dear friend, the *Armiral Dilleer-jing-behauder*,[14] for so they call Mr Watson, meaning the Courageous in Battles. This demand was very disagreeable to Mr Watts, who had been rejoicing in that my desire to keep out of the Nabob's sight jumped so well with his own wishes, but he signified his compliance with a feigned air of readiness, and warned me not to let my temper get the better of me in my intercourse with the Soubah. Mrs Hurstwood will be at no loss to imagine my feelings in prospect of being confronted with this monster in human form, but since I was warned that my refusal might bring destruction upon the agency, I prepared, though with a vastly poor grace, to attend Mr Watts to the Kella, and am but now returned from the visit, which I will endeavour to describe to you, madam.

On entering the Palace we passed, before reaching the Durbar, through three great courts, each filled with a multitude of soldiers and attendants, and so came into a pretty flower-garden, planted with two rows of trees, and having channels of water running between the borders. At the end of this garden was a terrass, where the Durbar was held, and at the foot of the steps we were constrained to leave our shoes, and to make a salute in the Moorish style, by lifting our hands to our heads from the ground. On the terrass was a sort of square porch, open in front to the garden and on one side to the river, where the roof was supported on pillars hung with flowered muslin, which was caught up with cords and tassels of gold and silver. On the other two sides the walls were covered with shining white *chunam*, and ornamented with small niches, very regularly placed, while the floor was laid with fine mats, and on the wide sopha[15] was spread a carpet of three thicknesses of muslin. In the midst of this sopha sat the Nabob, his elbow resting on a cushion of brocade. He is a person of middle height, very black for a Moor, his eyes lively and piercing, and his countenance bearing an air of frankness. On his head was a little cap, his vest was of flowered muslin, and his Moorish trowsers of cloth of silver. On his left hand sat his brother Merzee Mundee[16] cross-legged on the carpet, and on his right, but at a greater distance, Roydoolub, Meer Mudden, and five or six others of his great men, the one nearest to him being a person of a dark and forbidding countenance, who pleased me even less when he smiled, which he did whenever the Nabob turned towards him, than when he wore a serious air. All this I had leisure to observe while the Nabob seated Mr Watts on his right hand, with me beyond him, and exchanged with him many compliments in the Persic language, addressing him as his dear friend Watch Siab, without having recourse to the interpreters who stood behind.

Oh, madam, you can't fancy the sentiments that possessed me as I looked upon the man to whose tyrannic fury and insatiable avarice I owe it that my dear Miss Freyne has been torn from her paternal abode and is at this moment a prisoner among these pagans! As I regarded him the impulse seized me to spring upon him and threaten him with instant death unless he restored me my beloved; but even as I laid my hand on my sword I remembered that he might conceivably know nothing of the matter, and that such an outburst might warn the true criminal if he were present. I endeavoured to turn my glance from the Prince to the officers and guards that stood on either side, but he remarked the motion of my eyes, and said something to Mr Watts with a laugh.

"His Highness desires to be informed whether you're always so serious of aspect, Mr Fraser," says Mr Watts, giving me a private sign to make some civil reply, but this was beyond my power. I could only utter a confused word or two, but my chief was more ready than I. "I'll tell him that you belong to a nation that was never known to smile," he said, and spoke in Persic to the Nabob. While all the assembly was laughing to see me put out of countenance, the person that sat next me, and whose countenance I distrusted, leaned forward and said something smiling.

"Meer Sinzaun says that you come like a thunderstorm," says Mr Watts to me. "He felt cold as soon as he caught sight of your gloomy countenance."

"Pray tell him that thunderstorms bring worse things with 'em than cold, sir," said I, wondering no longer at the dislike I had felt.

"Are you mad?" says Mr Watts, hastily. "Sinzaun is aiming to make his Highness believe you possess an evil eye." Turning to the Nabob, he told him, as I learned afterwards, that though I bore a surly air I was well versed in military affairs.

"Aye," says the Prince, "I would I had a regiment of men of his nation. If they were all as tall and as sour-looking as he, they would frighten away the Pitans by their looks alone," and every one laughed at his jest. Shortly afterwards the officers of the guard appeared before the terrass to make *salam*, as they call it, each man at the head of his company, and after this Mr Watts took his leave, the Nabob bidding him farewell in the most obliging manner, but Meer Sinzaun testified by his looks the same dislike for me that I had conceived for him.

April ye 30th.

Alas, madam! I have still no news to give you of our adored Miss Freyne. It appears almost incredible that the minute enquiries and researches of Mirza Shaw should not have produced the slightest result, but so far he can tell me nothing, though once or twice of late I have observed about him an air of mystery that has made my heart leap with groundless joy. My sole comfort is that Meer Sinzaun has again been absent from the city, as we are assured in a sufficiently strange manner. Colonel Clive having demanded of the Nabob to give up Mr Laws and the fugitives from Chandernagore, the Prince sent them away as though to go to Patna, telling the Colonel that he had banished them from his dominions, but despatching to them secret instructions, as we learn, to proceed no further than Rajamahol.[17] They passed through Muxidavad in military array, as we ourselves beheld, having with them no less than thirty small carriages and four elephants, and Sinzaun questionless accompanied them, since we hear from Coja Wasseed that he saw him pass through Ballisore, taking with him a present of an elephant and divers jewels from the Nabob for Mr Bussey.

You'll guess, madam, that this evasion points to a change in the Prince's attitude towards us; and indeed the retreat of the Pitans from Delly, coupled with the Colonel's demand for leave to attack the Sydabad factory, placed us for a time in the most imminent danger, which may be said still to continue. Finding himself no longer in need of our protection, the Nabob took occasion, on hearing that Colonel Clive had despatched a force in pursuit of Mr Laws, to give way to the most violent transports of rage, in which he drove our *vacqueel* with ignominy from his presence, and threatened Mr Watts with death either by beheading or impaling, unless we made peace with the French or withdrew immediately to Calcutta. Mr Watts met these menaces with the greatest calmness and resolution, refusing both of the Nabob's conditions, and obtaining leave from the Presidency to send down the treasure and effects of the agency to Calcutta in view of a fresh outbreak of war, since the Soubah has ordered Roydoolub and his troops to advance to Palassy,[18] which is on the way to Calcutta from here. Considering that a rupture was now inevitable, the Colonel sent Captain Grant with forty Europeans and some Tellinghys to Cossimbuzar, with several boat-loads of ammunition concealed under rice, but these were stopped and turned back at Cutwah without being able to reach us. In this melancholy and mortifying situation Mr Watts has displayed the utmost resolution and intrepidity, attending every day at the Durbar (for when he did not appear there the Nabob sent for him to come), and supporting the insults of the ungracious tyrant with all the temper and calmness imaginable, although they have preyed so sadly upon his mind that he could not have persisted in his task but for the consolation imparted by the kind letters of Colonel Clive and the Admiral. These gentlemen have themselves suffered under the waywardness of the Soubah, Colonel Clive receiving from him in one day as many as ten letters, wrote in the most opposite styles, the whole of which he has answered suitably to their contents, and with all the punctuality and complaisance in the world. At last the Nabob, perceiving, apparently, that he was alienating those who might be of service to him, changed his behaviour suddenly, and sending for our *vacqueel*, presented him with a *serpau*, summoning Mr Watts also to his presence and caressing him, seeming to consider that this condescension should atone in full for all his insulting behaviour.

But this last outbreak of the inconstant Prince has persuaded all that have to do with him that there's no confidence to be placed in any of his assurances, and this sentiment has now spread from the British to his own courtiers, whom he has used with the utmost arrogance, heaping insults upon the Buxey, Meer Jaffier, who married his great-aunt, fining Monickchund and throwing him into prison for stealing a portion of the Calcutta plunder, placing his worthless favourite Moonloll[19] over the head of Roydoolub, and keeping the Seats in a perpetual apprehension lest he may deprive them suddenly of their wealth. Questionless, the youthful tyrant has prepared his own destruction. A week ago Mr Watts was approached by a Mogul named Godar Yar Caun Laitty,[20] who commands 2000 horse in the Soubah's service, but is entertained by the Seats to protect them in case of danger, and was acting now upon their motion. This person, opening his mind to Omichund, who was sent to confer with him, proposed that when the Soubah, who was about to take the field at Patna against the Pitans, had started on his campaign, the British should assist Roydoolub and the Seats to seize Muxidavad, and immediately make

Yar Caun Laitty Nabob, in return for which he would enter into any engagements we pleased. Almost before Mr Watts had imparted this notion to the Presidency, there comes also the Armenian Coja Petruce, bringing the same proposition from Meer Jaffier, and he having so much larger a force at his command Mr Watts inclines to him.

As though to prevent any sentiment of compunction on our part for thus plotting against him, the Nabob has thought fit to exhibit again the utmost hostility towards us. In place of removing his army from Palassy, as Colonel Clive requested him, he has patched up a peace with Meer Jaffier and sent him there with reinforcements for it. At the same time, having heard from his spy Mooteram the absurd report that in spite of his stopping Captain Grant's detachment at Cutwah, we had half our army concealed at Cossimbuzar, he sent a mob of servants and troops to search the factory, but they found there only forty Europeans, of whom twenty were the artillerymen that were lent to him in February. More than this, we learn that he has wrote to Mr Laws requesting him to remain with his men at Boglipore[21] as his guests until he sends for them, and that he is despatching Sinzaun afresh to Mr Bussey to promise him twenty *laacks* of rupees if he'll come to his assistance, while he has stopped with stakes the entire breadth of the Cossimbuzar River at Sootey, twenty miles below this place, with the design of preventing the passage of our ships, of whose armament he cherishes the wildest notions, although they could never come up so far. Thus, madam, we are placed between an infuriated despot and a parcel of timid conspirators, all afraid the one of t'other, Meer Jaffier refusing to trust Omichund and the Seats jealous of him, while Yar Caun Laitty may at any moment revenge himself for being set aside by revealing the whole affair. ...

Madam, I must add one word to the end of this letter. We have hope at last. Mirza Shaw has just approached me with an air of the utmost secrecy, and informed me that last night he tracked Sinzaun in disguise to an obscure house on the outskirts of the city, where, as he learns from the gossip of the neighbourhood, he entertains a lady whom he has given out as his ward. She is called Nezmennessa Beeby, but she is very white, and wears an outlandish dress, so that they believe her a woman either of Persia or Cashmere, and Sinzaun talks with her through a curtain with great respect. So cautious is the fellow that no one in the vicinity knows who he is, but they believe him to be a slave-merchant, who intends a most delicate gift for the Nabob. Oh, madam, picture to yourself the horror of the situation! What's to be done? We can't be sure that this lady is Miss Freyne, and to rescue the wrong captive would but plunge us in fresh difficulties. How to obtain a sight of her, open communication with her—above all, how to release her? But of that I can say more when the Tartar has conducted me to-night to view the house.

May ye 23rd.

I am conscious, madam, that you'll be justly indignant with me for leaving you so long in suspense after the affecting news contained in my last letter, though indeed I have put off writing from day to day in hopes to find something certain to communicate to you, but in vain. On the night after my letter was despatched, Mirza Shaw attended me to the house of which he had spoken, both of us wearing the Moorish dress, and we traced its extent and examined the outside walls, which are high and in good repair, and (as is common with the houses here) destitute of any openings by which a secret entrance might be effected. The only means that suggested itself to me for scaling them was a ladder of ropes furnished with a hook at one end, which might be thrown over the summit of the wall, and catching there afford us an ascent, but the Tartar objected very pertinently that without knowing who was to be found on the other side of the wall we might well terminate our lives and our hopes of rescuing Miss Freyne at once in our first attempt. Other expedients we discussed, without finding any that commended itself to our prudence, and we left it at last that Mirza Shaw was to linger in the vicinity of the house, and representing himself as a *boxwaller*,[22] insinuate himself into the confidence of the servants, and so perhaps gain access to Nezmennessa Beeby herself, or at least discover who she may really be.

This prudent decision has met with an incredible want of success, and I fear that had it not been for the threatening posture of public affairs your correspondent, madam, would have brought the entire enterprise to destruction by rushing hastily upon some solution of the difficulty. But events of importance have followed so close upon one another, and Mr Watts has found it needful to make such constant demands upon my humble services as scribe, that even the question of Miss Freyne's release has been occasionally driven from the forefront of my mind. Nine days ago Mr Watts arrived at an agreement through Coja Petruce as to the treaty to be made between Meer Jaffier and the British, the Buxey assenting to all our demands, but repeating his entreaty that Omichund should not be informed of the affair. In this Mr Watts endeavoured to content him, but the old Gentoo had already been told too much to render it possible to keep him in ignorance, and was also anxious to know why no favourable answer was to be given to Yar Caun Laitty, whose proposals had at first been so warmly entertained. Finding that the disclosure could not be avoided, Mr Watts at length unfolded to him the compact with Meer Jaffier, which has roused in Omichund an implacable hatred, since he could not fail to perceive that the explication was only extorted by necessity. This passion he gratified immediately by threatening to disclose the entire scheme to the Nabob, unless the possession of one-sixth of that Prince's jewels, and a huge *dussutary*[23] besides on the rest of the spoils, were secured to him by the treaty. This Mr Watts was unable to promise on his own authority, but, soothing the traitor with agreeable words, referred the matter to the Select Committee at Calcutta, while Omichund took occasion to exhibit that wild prodigality of deceitfulness in which he takes delight. Obtaining access to the Nabob, he informed him very circumstantially that he had discovered a plot between the English and Mr Bussey, who were about to unite their forces with the object of hurling him from the throne. Absurd though such a notion is, it commended itself to the Nabob, who rewarded Omichund by ordering the repayment to him of a sum of money which he had lent so long before as almost to have lost hope of receiving it again, and this was an ample satisfaction to the wily Gentoo, although Surajah Dowlah was undeceived almost immediately by the arrival of the news that Mr Bussey, far from allying himself with us, was reported by advices from Ballisore to be five days' journey this side of Cuttack, marching against us with 700 Europeans and 5000 Seapoys.

Immediately after this, Mr Scrafton arrived suddenly from Calcutta, bearing a letter that had been delivered to Colonel Clive by a stranger Gentoo known to none of the gentlemen there, and giving his name as Govindroy.[24] This letter purported to be from the Maharattor leader Badgerow,[25] offering the Colonel an alliance for the purpose of crushing the Nabob, and it fell in so pat with our desires that no one could consent to accept it as genuine, all conceiving it to be a trick of Surajah Dowlah's to entrap us. In this difficulty, Colonel Clive took the courageous step of sending the letter to the Nabob as a proof of our good faith, but he designed to reap the additional advantage from Mr Scrafton's journey of establishing communications with Meer Jaffier, who had proceeded unwillingly with his army to Palassy after the Soubah's feigned reconciliation with him. In this, however, Mr Scrafton was anticipated by the Nabob's spies, who (whether guessing his intention or not I can't say) turned him back and forced him to take the straight road, but the Soubah, receiving the letter, appeared much moved by the confidence reposed in him by the British, and also by the affecting remonstrances on his late unfriendly behaviour addressed to him by the Colonel, so that he ordered Meer Jaffier with his army to return to Muxidavad. But the unsteady Prince is now too late in this last change of front.

Of the course which the Council at Calcutta have thought fit to adopt with regard to Omichund's unjust demands I can't speak with certainty, but I fear I have a very fair notion of it. Four days back a messenger of the country brought to Mr Watts the treaty drawn up and signed by the

Council, ready for presentation to Meer Jaffier, and the good gentleman enlarged to Dr Dacre and myself with a good deal of merriment on the clauses which had been added at Calcutta, stipulating for donations of money, in excess of the sums named in restitution of last year's losses, not only to the army and the fleet, but also to each member of the Council. There was no mention of Omichund's name, which surprised me, but before I could remark on the omission Omichund himself was announced, when Mr Watts immediately doubled up the treaty and thrust it into his breast.

"Be so good as to pass me that *lol coggedge*,[26] Mr Fraser," he said, indicating a red paper that had been in the same pacquet with the white one he had just concealed. Glancing carelessly at it, I perceived that 'twas another copy of the treaty, but with a clause added, in which I saw Omichund's name.

"Sure there's something wrong here, sir," I said, looking at the list of signatures; "I could swear that Admiral Watson never writ his name in that style."

"Have I asked your opinion on the matter, sir?" says Mr Watts.

"Why, no, sir; but the hand is far liker Mr Fisherton's than the Admiral's."

"You'll oblige me infinitely if you'll hold your tongue, sir," said Mr Watts very angrily, as Omichund was brought in.

I did hold my tongue, for the business was none of mine, but I can't help being persuaded that Colonel Clive and the Council have devised some plan for hoodwinking Omichund with a false copy of the treaty, which they have not dared to ask the Admiral to sign. There's something ironically suitable, questionless, in the old deceiver's being thus deceived; yet I can't but regret that a body of Britons should voluntarily decline to his pagan level in order to get the better of him. The device, whatever it may be, succeeded so far that he departed satisfied; but he has since exhibited fresh apprehensions, and Mr Watts is doing his best to induce him to return to Calcutta with Mr Scrafton, under colour of removing him out of danger, but this kind solicitude is perpetually defeated by Omichund himself, whose avarice forbids him to leave Muxidavad until he has recovered certain further sums due to him, thus continuing from day to day our anxiety as to his intentions.

Mr Watts, meanwhile, continues with the greatest coolness imaginable to attend the Durbar, as though he were not in danger of being denounced as one of those who are plotting to dethrone and kill the Nabob, and is received with varying favour. Since the visit I described to you, madam, I have not attended at Court, but while waiting upon Mr Watts to the Kella, have remained in one of the anterooms until his business was finished, and there I have to-day met with a notion that I hope to employ for the rescue of our dear Miss Freyne. Waiting among the Nabob's inferior courtiers, I observed that some of these were passing the time by listening to a person that appeared to be relating an improving history of some sort. Mr Watts' *mounshy* being with me, I invited him to interpret what was said, and this the story-teller took as an extraordinary great compliment, and told his tale with an eye to me, pausing between the sentences in order to leave the interpreter time. I'll own that I was not a little disappointed at first with the narrative, which contained none of those wonders that the Easterns are wont to import into their romances. To be brief, madam, it concerned a vizier that had robbed the king his master, and was sentenced to be imprisoned without food or water in the topmost apartment of a lofty tower, there to starve to death. But happening to possess a faithful wife, the lady came by night to the foot of the tower, and desired, weeping, to know how she might gratify her unlucky spouse. "Why, my dear," says he, "you may save me if you will." The lady on this dried her tears, and requested the vizier's commands. "To-morrow night," says he, "bring here a beetle, some butter, a skein of silk, a ball of twine, and a long and stout rope, and I'll show you how to employ 'em." The lady came punctually the next night, bringing with her the desired articles, and at her spouse's direction placed a small lump of butter on the head of the beetle, and fastened the end of the silk about its body, setting the insect on the wall of the tower as high up as she could reach. The beetle, discovering by the odour of the butter that there was a feast in the neighbourhood, which it judged to be somewhere in advance of itself, crawled up the side of the tower, led on perpetually by the fallacious delight, and came at last into the hand of the vizier, who unfastened the silk from its body, and desired his lady to attach the end of the twine to that of the skein. Pulling up the silk, he then obtained possession of the twine, by the means of which he next drew up the rope, and, fastening it to a pillar of his apartment, descended the tower in safety. This conclusion was much applauded by the audience, and I desired the *mounshy* to make my compliments to the narrator, which appeared to gratify those who stood round, though it had surprised them prodigiously to guess to what a degree the fellow had really obliged me.

In order that you, madam, may understand my gratification, you must know that Mirza Shaw and I have been seriously disturbed this three weeks by the difficulty of throwing a rope (of a size sufficient to be safe to descend by) from the ground to the roof of a house without making such a clatter as to rouse the whole neighbourhood, even though we had succeeded in opening communications with Miss Freyne. The notion of a grapnel we have been forced to relinquish, owing to the tumbledown and uncertain state of the parapets even in the best houses here, which might involve us in a serious catastrophe should the wall break away. But with the new plan suggested by the tale I had heard it seemed to me that I saw my course marked out, and I opened my mind to the Tartar as soon as we were returned to the house and I could catch him alone. He did not accept my proposition with that eagerness I had anticipated, but I perceived that this was because he was piqued that the suggestion did not come from himself.

"Sure you've forgot the situation of the place, Siab," says he. "The sight of two men carrying such a paraphernalia will rouse the whole quarter against us."

"Why, as to that," said I, "we must have the rope of silk, and I'll wind it round me under my coat."

"If you look to see your Beeby touch a beetle with her fingers, and fasten a rope so as 'twill be safe, and then consent to descend by it, you're a rash man, Siab."

"The lady will forget her feminine fears in such a case," said I. "We must trust her to fasten the rope safe, and as soon as that's done I'll ascend it and lower her down."

"But think, Siab. You've caught your beetle, let us say, and started him on his journey up the wall. But all beetles may not be charmed by butter, or even if he be, a beetle travels but slowly. For us to remain in an attentive posture outside a house in a frequented place until he had reached the top, would infallibly lead to our seizure by the Cotwal, even if we had not a crowd to observe our doings."

This was, indeed, a grave objection, and one that I could not get over, since 'twas not reasonable to suppose we could control the motion of the insect to our liking. The place stands in a pretty crowded part of the city, and we could not hope the neighbours would permit us to play at house-breaking for several hours uninterrupted; while even should they prove so complaisant as to do this, their very observation would be fatal to our design. I was altogether taken aback, and stood staring at Mirza Shaw. Suddenly a notion entered my head, suggested by the narrow streets that surround on all sides the English house, on whose roof we were standing.

"Are you well acquainted with the lanes about this house of Sinzaun's, Mirza Shaw?"

"Seeing that I have lately spent the best part of my time there I should be but a dolt if I were not, Siab," he answered.

"Then have you observed whether in any of them there's an empty house that might be hired? It must be a large house, as high as Sinzaun's or even higher, and it must face it."

"I don't say but there might be such a place found, Siab."

"Then hire it this very day. Tell what tale you choose, and come to me for the money."

"Ah, I perceive your honour's meaning." Mirza Shaw put on a thoughtful air. "But a beetle won't walk from roof to roof on the air, Siab."

"No, but we'll do without the beetle, and make our task the easier. Trust a seaman to throw a ball of twine safe across the gap."

"But that would make a noise, Siab, if the Beeby did not catch it."

"But a ball of woollen yarn would not, and would serve as well to pull the twine across as the Vizier's skein of silk, if 'twas paid out gently. Go and hire the house, Mirza Shaw, and I'll perfect my plan. I have in my head the hint of a device for the lady's rescue."

June ye 8th.

At length, madam, the day is arrived on which it's possible to make a serious endeavour to open communications with Miss Freyne, and since the attempt can't take place before nightfall, Mrs Hurstwood won't be surprised that I have taken refuge in writing to her to escape from the tumult of my own too eager thoughts. There's another reason also why I would set down the events of this last week, and that is, that in case our lives, Mirza Shaw's and mine, should fall a forfeit to the audacity of our attempt, or that a general catastrophe should tear from us the fruits of victory by means of the destruction of the entire agency, Mrs Hurstwood may be assured that not the will, but only the power, was wanting for the rescue of her friend.

At the extreme end of last month the importunities of Mess. Watts and Scrafton prevailed on Omichund to allow himself to be transported from the city. The business of obtaining the Nabob's permission he effected by feigning to claim from the Prince on behalf of the British the huge sum of money he had promised if they supported him against the Pitans, whereupon he was drove out of the palace with ignominy, and commanded to quit Muxidavad immediately. Yet when this had been happily accomplished, and the journey begun, the aged miser succeeded in evading Mr Scrafton at the first halting-place, and returned to scrape together some further petty sums that were owing to him, though he continued the journey later in the day. His departure relieves us from some anxiety, though not from all, for Mr Scrafton writes that he shows himself perpetually troubled with suspicions and apprehensions, and Coja Petruce tells Mr Watts that Omichund has wrote to bid him prevent matters coming to a head until he has assured himself that his ill-gotten gains are faithfully secured to him.

Since getting rid of Omichund, our chief concern has been with the treaty, which had then been signed only by the British. Meer Jaffier returned to the city on the 30th, in obedience to the Nabob's order recalling him with his army from Palassy, but he was received by Surajah Dowlah with so much contumely that he retired at once to his own palace in the south part of the city, which he placed in a posture of defence, and summoned his friends to join him. Four days later Roydoolub, returning with his division, examined the treaty in concert with Meer Jaffier, and raised difficulties with regard to the sums of money allotted in it to the British, which he declared the whole contents of the treasury would not suffice to furnish. Being promised, however, by Mr Watts the entire management of the affair, and a genteel *dussutary* for his pains, the worthy *duan* overcame his scruples, and in conjunction with Meer Jaffier signed the treaty four days ago. On the very day this was done, the Nabob, not because he was acquainted with it, but merely to gratify his feelings of enmity, and as though to stifle any remorse that his kinsman might have been entertaining, removed Meer Jaffier from his office, setting up Coja Haddee, a favourite of his own, as Buxey.

Although the treaty was now signed, it was not yet complete, for Meer Jaffier had still to swear his resolution to observe it, but there was difficulties in the way of his doing this. Meer Jaffier durst not quit his palace, nor durst he receive a visit there from Mr Watts, even had Mr Watts been prepared to brave the suspicions of the Nabob so far as to go thither, while no confidence could be reposed in any inferior person as a witness of the solemnity. In this strait Mr Watts displayed an intrepidity such as few would have credited him with possessing, for confiding in the fidelity of his servants and the manners of the country, he entered three days ago a covered palanqueen, such as women of distinction are wont to ride abroad in, and caused himself to be carried through the city and into the inmost recesses of Meer Jaffier's seraglio, where that nobleman, placing one hand upon the Alcoran (the accustomed pledge of the Moors' falsehood), and t'other upon the head of his son Meerum,[27] took an oath to observe the compact. And here I must remark upon the extraordinary zeal and resolution with which Mr Watts has conducted all this business, which is the more wonderful when his readiness to confide in and submit to the Nabob in the surrender of Cossimbuzar is recalled. That the animadversion excited by his behaviour on that occasion has stimulated him to prove it untrue may well be believed, yet how seldom do we behold an error in judgment or a moment of timidity thus courageously repented of! Would that this gentleman's superior, Mr Drake, had shown any signs of retrieving in a similar manner his far greater fault, instead of bending all his energies to the amassing of wealth by the efforts of others, whom he yet has not sufficient spirit even to support in their designs!

But I have wandered from my mention of Mr Watts' intrepid journey, from which he returned safely, and which brought to me such a confirmation of my hopes as served to repay me in full for all my arduous labours for Miss Freyne's release. For Mirza Shaw, coming from attending his master in his dangerous passage, approached the varendar where I sat.

"Siab," he said, "Nezmennessa Beeby is the Beeby you seek."

"What!" I cried, "have you spoke with her?"

"Nay," said he, "but it chanced that as we passed the house to-day one of the *gwallers* that was bearing Watch Siab's palanqueen slipped and fell, and the rest raised a great talk and shouting. There's a small barred window high in the wall just there, and when I glanced at it I saw a woman looking out. She was very white, and she wore a head-dress such as the Beebies of Calcutta wear."

"Heaven be praised for this certainty!" I cried. "Did the lady make any sign to you?"

"Nay, Siab; how should she know who I might be? She disappeared from the window suddenly as I looked at her, and your honour's servant saw no more."

"But wait, Mirza Shaw. Was the lady in good health? How did she look?"

"Why, Siab, she appeared pale, as the European Beebies always do. I can't tell if she was ill, since I never saw her before."

And this cold-hearted rascal had beheld my beloved, yet could tell me no more of her than this! Pity me, madam, seeing me so tantalised. But this en't the last of my trials. Yesterday Mr Watts despatched Omar-beg, a Moorman, an officer of Meer Jaffier's, to Calcutta with the treaty (I fear I would be right in saying the two treaties, the white and the red), but announced to us his purpose of remaining at Muxidavad until the last extremity. Dr Dacre is still here with us, and we have just been joined by Mr Ranger, whose occupation is now gone, since the garrison of the Cossimbuzar factory, which was reduced at the end of April to no more than a corporal and six European soldiers besides the *bucksarries*, has now been wholly withdrawn by Colonel Clive's orders, and the men are on their way to Calcutta. My pleasant friend refused to accompany them, being determined, as he says, to be in at the death, which will be his own, indeed, as much as ours. Mr Watts has desired us all to be ready on the shortest notice to take flight, or at least to remove to Maudipore,[28] a country house that he occupies two miles to the south of Cossimbuzar, whence we may seek to refuge at Calcutta. This order has filled me with apprehension, for what's to be done if Mr Watts desire to send us away before we have released Miss Freyne? and work as hard as we may during the hours of darkness, the Tartar and I have not yet been able entirely to complete our preparations. Worst of all, Miss Freyne has no knowledge of 'em, for Mirza Shaw has in vain endeavoured to obtain access to her in his disguise as a pedlar. The women of the house, even, I believe, her own attendant, will come and examine his wares, but he can't get sight of the lady. And now the Nabob, who has shut himself up in his castle of Herautjeel, in the midst of the city, is exchanging menaces with Meer Jaffier, whose fortified palace is separated from his by the river, and it's expected that the Prince will shortly call up his army, and open upon our friend the pretender with his cannon, when Mr Watts will questionless order us out of the city....

I had wrote thus far, madam, when Mirza Shaw, who has been spending the night in the house we have hired facing Sinzaun's, came to me a few minutes back with what seemed a piece of rag in his hand.

"This, Siab," he said, "was thrown out to me just now from the window where I saw the Beeby t'other day. Hearing a slight noise, I looked up and perceived one edge of the grating move a very little way, just enough for this to be pushed out. I beheld no one, for I was too close beneath the window."

He presented me with the rag, which I found to be a handkerchief with a stone tied up in it—this to give it weight, as I suppose. The letters S. F. were worked very finely in one of the corners, but on the stuff itself were traced rudely in blue thread the words, "Save. Quick." The sight almost deprived me of my senses.

"Wretch that I am!" I cried. "We are too late."

"Nay, Siab," says Mirza Shaw. "The Beeby's there still, though she may be exposed to a sudden peril. We may questionless save her yet."

"But what do you imagine this danger to be?" I asked him.

"Why, Siab, I think Sinzaun is about to give her to the Nabob."

I sat down again, sick at heart, remembering that the Soubah's parasite, Moonloll, had gained his position by handing over to the Prince his own sister, a young lady who was reported to be the most delicate figure in the world. Sinzaun might well be put to it to surpass such a gift as this, but he has the means ready to his hand in our beloved and unhappy sufferer.

"Mirza Shaw," I said, suddenly, "you and I will forestall him yet."

"So be it, Siab. I have finished the ropes and the basket, and I will fetch you as soon as it's dusk."

"No," I said; "the lady must be warned as we designed, or we may miss her in the darkness. I'll go to our house in a *dooley*."

For you must know, madam, that my disguise for going about my business with Mirza Shaw is no other than the outer garment of a Moor-woman, veil and cloak in one, which covers me from head to foot, concealing even my eyes with a netting. This passes well enough in the dusk, but in daylight I fear that so strapping a wench might excite more attention than would be desirable, so that the privacy of a *dooley* was needed for my conveyance. Mirza Shaw required no second bidding. He departed to find a *dooley*, while I sought to curb my impatience by finishing my letter to you. Sure there never was a *dooley* so hard to find. The rascal must have been gone a whole day. No, there he is returning. Madam, I trust you are remembering in your prayers this enterprise of ours, and your obedient, humble servant,

C. FRASER.

CHAPTER XVIII.
PROVING THAT THE DAYS OF MIRACLES ARE PAST.

From Miss Sylvia Freyne to Miss Amelia Turnor.

MUXADAVAD, *April ye 29th.*

For more than two months, Amelia, I have been free from the oppression of Sinzaun's presence, and have not taken up my pen, having nothing to record. Not that my persecutor's errand to Mons. Bussy has occupied the whole of this period, for I am assured that he has visited the house more than once, and that Misery has spoken with him, but he has been so gracious as not to force himself upon me. I wish I could believe that this abstinence sprang from any desire to show me kindness, but I am convinced it is designed to make me sensible that I am in disgrace. Indeed, since even the steward has ceased to pay his weekly visits, and the women of the house refuse to permit me to speak to them—running away if I come near—I think Sinzaun must desire to force me into a compliance with his wishes through the mere dulness and emptyness of my lot. One poor black girl there was—a Hobshee or Habashy, as the inhabitants of Abyssinia are called here—in whose grotesque countenance I fancied I could detect the signs of a greater humanity than her fellows possessed, and endeavoured accordingly to awaken her compassion, although I got no further than to tell her I was a captive like herself. I fancied she sympathised with me, but when I looked for her next, hoping to advance in my purpose, she was not to be found, and Misery, on my asking what was become of her, would do nothing but laugh in the most horrid, unfeeling style. Since that time, also, the other women have avoided me with this extraordinary care, making off as soon as I approach them, as though fearing punishment if they listened to a word from me. Were the disgust I feel towards my gaoler less deeply rooted, I'll own I think he would succeed in bringing me to compliance, for what could be more painful to a rational creature than to remain pent up between four walls, seeing and conversing with no one but Misery, and deprived of every semblance of occupation? But however calculated may be his designs, he shan't induce Sylvia Freyne to entertain her father's murderer as a suitor for her hand.

But perhaps you'll say I am relinquishing hope too easily, in thus choosing deliberately to sink into imbecility (as appears but too likely to be my fate) instead of making some attempt to escape. Why, Amelia (I can't help writing to my dear girl as though she were ever likely to receive this letter), where should I, in my present unhappy situation, take refuge, even if I were once outside these walls? Do you remember that there's not a person in India would be willing to shelter me; or, if willing, would not be deterred by fear of Sinzaun and the Nabob? And how should an unhappy creature, that has already contributed to destroy her country's settlements here, have the assurance to involve any other community, as that of the Armenians or the Prussians, in her misfortunes? But even to do this further mischief I must find means to leave this house, and how? Misery, the only creature I speak to, and that will speak to me, is impenetrable, incorruptible. Do I try to move her on the grounds of mercy or forbearance? "Beebee," she cries, "you talk very fine language—too fine for your slave to understand." While if I seek to appeal to her in the name of religion, she will shut her eyes and begin to chaunt, "There's no God but *Alla*, and Mahomet is his prophet!" until I am gone away from her in disgust.

I have but one faint semblance of hope, and that's very much akin to despair. Now and again I hear the servants talking of some enemy that's invading Bengall, and seems to be driving the Soubah's forces before him. This invading army they call by the name of the *loll addama*,[01] which means the red men, and speak of its leaders only by the titles of Saubut Jing and Dilleir Jing Bahadre, or the Tryed and the Courageous in Battles. From which side it comes I can't say, for the only time I have heard anything certain of its advance was more than a month ago, when one of the other women called out to Misery that the red men had captured the city of Farashdanga, and made Zubdatook Toojah[02] and his army prisoners; but I don't know where this city may be, and the name of the chief man I never heard before. Should these red men continue to succeed in their campaign, and go so far as to seize Muxadavad, I might perhaps find a chance of safety,—not that there's any reason to anticipate a change of gaolers to be an improvement, but that in the confusion of the moment I might be able to elude the vigilance of Misery and the rest, and slip out of the house. But this is only foolishness, for so far from the red men's taking Muxadavad, they seem to have retired, or at least made no further advance, since the capture of Farashdanga, and my hopes have sunk with their fortunes. And to-night, says Misery, Meer Sinzaun will attend me here.

April ye 30th.

Well, Amelia, I have received my last warning, and the next interview with which my gaoler favours me is to bring me my last chance. Oh, how I wish that all were over now, and that I had not this perpetual tormenting apprehension besetting me continually! For I don't even now know the worst; I can but guess at it.

Yesterday evening Sinzaun presented himself at his usual hour, some time after sunset. Approaching me with an air of assurance he sought to kiss my hand, but this I was able to prevent, trusting the repulse might inform him of my temper towards him without entering upon a controversy. This hope appeared to be fulfilled, for he opened his discourse by apologizing for the length of time he had absented himself from my saloon, remarking that he had undertaken several journeys to Mons. Bussy and other French officers in the interval. But having finished his excuses, he changed his topic on a sudden.

"When Clarissa's humble servant last had the satisfaction of beholding her, it may be that he approached with too much precipitation the subject which is nearest to his heart," said he, "and that the passion which possesses him rendered him oblivious of the usual proprieties. But although he may adore Clarissa without asking to know more of her than that she returns his affection, it en't reasonable to expect the same of her. Know then, madam, that the individual who is so happy as to find himself at your feet is a son of one of the highest families in France, and in that favoured country enjoys the style of Count of St Jean, which the pagans here corrupt into Sinzaun. Certain youthful excesses on my part, coupled, perhaps, with too ardent a love of political activity, induced my family to set before me the alternatives of the Indies or the Bastille. As a young person of spirit I chose the Indies, and at Pondicherry should have reaped, I don't doubt, much fame and glory, had not adverse circumstances again conspired to drive me from my post there. Having had the misfortune to kill another officer in a duel, I was challenged afresh by his brother and father-in-law, of whom I killed one and wounded t'other. All three were persons of consideration in the place, and it appeared desirable that I should quit it. The cause of the duel it's unnecessary for me to explain to a young lady of Clarissa's penetration. Your charming sex, madam, are answerable for many miseries that afflict their adorers—but I don't desire to cast blame on any one. I left Pondicherry somewhat hastily, and not finding it desirable to attempt to take service with any of our allies in the Decan, made my way to Bengall, where Ally Verdy Cawn was glad enough to engage my help in his struggle with the Morattoes, and I rose before long to a situation of confidence in his army. Perceiving, however, that the old Soubah had not long to live, I made my court to his grandson, and succeeded in establishing myself in the favour of Saradjot Dollah, to whom I was so happy as to render considerable service in the measures he took for assuring the throne to himself on Ally Verdy's death. 'Twas in this employment that I fell in with the unlucky Genoese Menotti, who might still be alive and wealthy had not Clarissa's virtuous example seduced him to leave off his evil ways and desire to marry and live honestly. But I won't speak hardly of one to whom I owe the felicity of this moment——"

The wretch paused, and regarded me with his evil smile, as if expecting me to speak, but I have learned to endure a prodigious amount without contradicting him, and he went on—

"Of the consequences of this acquaintance I don't need to speak, for the unhappy man contrived to oblige me in the most extraordinary manner while endeavouring only the opposite; but I desire to reassure my Clarissa, whose apprehensions I have observed with regret, as to the future. Some persons, madam, having rose to the position I now occupy in the Soubah's favour, would bend their minds to the task of supplanting him and obtaining the Soubahship in his stead—nay, there are some plotting to do so at this moment. But such en't Sinzaun's ambition. His eyes are fixed on Paris, not on the Indies. To present this potentate as the ally and vassal of France is my aim, and in constituting myself at once his protector and his servant I perceive the means to attain it. By winning his battles for him——"

"Against the *loll addama*, sir?" I asked him, moved by I don't know what impulse. To my surprise he gave a huge start.

"Pray, madam, what do you know of the *loll addama*?" he cried, with an oath.

"Why, sir, I have heard the servants talk of 'em, that's all."

"I'm glad it's no more, madam. Their doings en't for Clarissa's ears. Yes, the *loll addama* are among the enemies to be defeated, questionless. Well, then, having made myself a position here, I intend it shall serve me in Europe. You know something, madam, of the frequency of revolutions in these countries, and you'll guess that any wealth I may possess en't locked up in houses or lands. No, 'tis all invested in precious stones, such as neither kings nor great ladies can resist. When I make my appearance at Versailles as the embassador of the friendly Saradjot Dollah, bringing with me gifts that may well seem unsurpassable to those that don't know the East, is there any fear that the amiable follies of my youth, whether in Paris or Pondicherry, will be remembered against me? No, the Court will be at my feet, grovelling there in the hope of picking up a diamond or two, and I shall be a greater man than the great Mons. John Laws himself. But to me the keenest delight will be the introduction of my little Puritan Clarissa into the great, the polite world."

"Sir," I said, my voice trembling, as he glanced at me with an odious air that was at once gallant and malevolent, "pray be so good as to leave me out of your designs. I am neither fitted nor eager to take part in them."

"Why, that's my great inducement, madam," he cried. "So long as I have had the honour of Clarissa's acquaintance, it has been my perpetual entertainment to perceive that she never thought with me on any single topic. Had she displayed an accommodating temper I might soon have wearied of her, but how can I tire of observing the pains that so agreeable a young lady takes to disoblige me? And if I find the diversion so much to my taste here, what will it be when my charmer becomes acquainted with the life of Paris? Her frequent blushes and her ready tears, and the speaking eyes in which I can read every thought of her innocent heart as in a book, will all be so many additions to my delight in returning to my ancient home."

Oh, Amelia, if you knew how I hated the man as he said this! It makes me writhe (there's no other word for it), to be forced to submit to the degradation of listening to such words from him. You'll wonder, perhaps, to hear me say that I could wish he did indeed cherish for me the affection he pretends. But then, my dear, I might have some hope of moving him by my entreaties—for true love, they say, will take part with the beloved object in opposition even to its own desires; but how can I hope to make any effect upon a wretch that owns he seeks but to divert himself by tormenting me?

"So, then," the odious creature proceeded, "when Clarissa consents to make her Sinzaun happy, she need not fear a life of perpetual seclusion here. While we remain in Bengall, 'twill, alas! be necessary for her to conform when abroad to the usages of the country, but within the walls of her house she shall enjoy the most complete freedom, and when we reach France, the more liberty she demands the better shall I be pleased."

"Oh, sir!" I cried, and, unable to bear more, threw myself at his feet, choking with sobs, "pray don't mock me in this cruel manner. I have done you no harm. If this poor face has catched your fancy, it en't by my good will; but if you have any kindness for the unhappy creature you say you love, let me go—suffer me to return unharmed to England."

"Won't my dear unreasonable one understand," said the audacious, catching my hand and seeking to draw me towards him, but this I resisted, "that if I had designed to let her depart to England, all the trouble and pains I have been at would have been thrown away? Don't she perceive that for all I have done and spent for her I must have a return? Must I be so harsh as to inform her that if I mayn't attain my ambition *for* her, it must be *through* her?"

"I don't take your meaning, sir," I faltered. Could the man intend to sell me for a slave? "I have friends in England who en't wealthy, but would impoverish themselves without a murmur to reimburse you any expenses to which you may have been put, if that's your condition."

"Oh, no, madam, Sinzaun en't a trader. Nothing could please him better than to have the happiness of winning your affections, but he has a foolish prejudice against using force to compel 'em, and piques himself upon his genteel treatment of you. But there's others that don't share this prejudice, and he might find himself forced, in his own interest, to resign his concern in you to them. Pray don't suspect him of the vulgarity of employing menaces. He seeks no bride but one that comes to him of her own free will, for he don't desire that either here or in Europe his Clarissa should proclaim herself his only upon compulsion."

"At least, sir, let me know what I have to fear," I groaned.

He smiled. "Why, no, madam; that's my affair. You don't choose to give me a favourable answer to-night, perhaps? No? then we'll leave the matter until our next meeting. I can't advise you to continue to resist me, for I have so much interest in you as makes me deplore the notion of putting you to any inconvenience, and i' faith, I see no hope for you if you persist in your present frame of mind. You have, I believe, learned something of my disposition since coming to Muxadavad, and you won't suspect me of going beyond my intentions when I say that in justice to myself I must soon abandon this struggle in favour of a more certain good. Believe me, I can't but pity your obstinacy, and you'll remember this too late."

May ye 17*th.*

Sinzaun is departed again upon an embassy to Mons. Bussy, carrying with him, so Misery tells me, a gift of two *lacks* of rupees from the Soubah to the French leader. So long as he is absent I may hope for a respite, but he can't now be away much longer. For some days I have had the thought of seeking to discover from Misery the fate that he designs for me, but this morning it chanced that she approached the matter herself, by asking me whether I would give her my hussy when I left this place.

"Why, Misery, you can't sew," I said. "What will you do with scissors and needles?"

"Oh, they'll be useful in other ways, Beebee. Europe goods are stronger and more delicate than country-made, and your slave has served you faithfully for close upon a year."

"But I've no thought of leaving this place," I said. "Whither should I go?"

"Why, Beebee, to the Killa. Meer Sinzaun destines you for the Nabob."

I shivered, for the same thought had come to me several days before. "How do you know this, Misery? Has Meer Sinzaun told you?"

"How should Meer Sinzaun tell his doings to his slave, Beebee? I have guessed it a long time, and I'm making ready to go my own way."

"Then you purpose to forsake me, Misery?"

"Indeed, Beebee, if I saw any signs that you'd accept your lot, and be content to win the favour of his Highness, I would never be separated from you, but since you seem to be as obstinate as ever, I won't risk my head. I have provided for my escape, and now that Calcutta is built up again, I shall return to my old trade and seek customers among the ladies there."

"But is Calcutta built up again? By whom?"

"Why, by the Moors, of course, Beebee," very hastily. "Do you think the Moorish ladies don't value the services of the Mother of Cosmetiques as much as the English Beebees?"

"Oho, so you was the Mother of Cosmetiques, Madam Misery?" I cried, remembering the part the woman had played in my former history.

"Yes, Beebee, your slave is she," with a sort of proud humility. "If you would have suffered it, she could make you so beautiful! Even now, if you'll invite her to attend you to the palace, she'll engage that there shan't be a lady to compare with you. His Highness——" she saw my angry gesture of silence, and dropped her fawning tone. "Well, I have neglected my trade for a year to attend on you, Beebee, and now I must return and take it up again. I only hope you won't be sorry that you've so often spurned the counsel of your poor Misery."

"For that you must blame the badness of the counsel," said I, pretty coolly, for I disliked the woman's assurance in presuming to advise me; but she leaned forward as she sat at my feet, and raised her eyes to mine in the most entreating style imaginable.

"Oh, Beebee, suffer your slave to say a word. If you have indeed been resolved all these months to repulse Meer Sinzaun in the hope of finding yourself presented to the Nabob, let your slave share in your triumph. This is what Meer Sinzaun believes of you, for how else could you have resisted his constant assiduities? and 'tis this makes him so angry, and well it may, for he's dying for love of you."

"If you can't speak truth, my good woman, at least try to talk sense," said I, and tearing my gown from her hold, left her, for I was prodigiously vexed to find that she had devised all this scene in Sinzaun's interest, and was seeking to bend me to his will lest, forsooth, he should misconceive my motives! You'll agree with me, Amelia, that Sinzaun's opinion would be the last in the world to weigh with me in considering any matter of right or wrong.

June ye 5th.

I have a strange thing to tell my dear girl this evening. Happening to be in the house for greater coolness during the heat of the day, I found myself not far from the small barred window of which I have spoken before, and hearing a great uproar and noise of voices in the street, went to look out. Below me was a palanqueen attended with several servants. One of the bearers had chanced to fall, and received some hurt, and the rest were scolding and consoling him by turns, while the palanqueen rested on the ground. As I watched, one of the *checks* was withdrawn a little way, and a face looked out. It was the face of a European, Amelia, an Englishman, if I don't mistake—an elderly person of respectable appearance. That was all I could see, for the servant that seemed the chief over the rest—a Moorman, but with a turbant such as the Tartars wear, having the *puckery* twisted round a high pointed cap instead of a small round one—pulled back the *check* with an extreme haste and violence, and rebuking the bearers for their confusion, bade them take up the palanqueen again. Hearing Misery approaching, I durst not remain at the window, but at least I had gained something on which to meditate. There's one Englishman, then, left in India—a prisoner, questionless, from the secrecy and severity with which he was secluded, but not used apparently with any great harshness. Sure he might help me in some way, if only I could get speech of him. But how to reach him, since I am secluded at least as rigorously as he? I have passed my time to-day devising a thousand plans, all suggested by this extraordinary event, for opening communications with my fellow-captive, but since he don't know of my existence, nor I of his place of confinement, and since I can neither leave this house nor find a trusty messenger, I have been forced to reject my designs one by one, as each more wild and extravagant than the last. And to-night, as Misery is just come to tell me, Sinzaun purposes to do himself the honour of paying me a visit. Oh, Amelia, this unfinished sheet may prove to contain my last farewell to you.

June ye 7th.

My sentence is pronounced, Amelia, and your poor friend is now like no one so much as the criminal in Newgate, who knows that the day is his last. I was still writing the words with which my letter of yesterday closed, when I became sensible that there were eyes regarding me, and looking up, I found Sinzaun standing in the doorway. The start I gave on seeing him there almost overturned the smoky native lamp by the light of which I was writing, but I saved it in time to prevent the destruction of my papers, while he complimented me on the assiduity I showed in keeping up a correspondence with my friend. I put up my writing implements hastily, my sole anxiety being to bring the hateful interview to a close, and for this once Sinzaun appeared inclined to second my efforts.

"May I take it that Clarissa has done me the honour to turn over in her mind the proposition I submitted to her at our last meeting?" he asked.

"I have considered of the matter carefully, sir."

"And may I hope she'll condescend to make me the happiest of men?"

"I'm sure, sir, I wish you happiness, but I won't marry you."

"No, madam? and yet I offer you such advantages of wealth, situation, dress, and jewellery, as would tempt the gross of women."

"None of these, sir, can break down the barrier caused by the measures you thought fit to take to get me into your power."

"You take a vastly high tone with me, madam. I could almost fancy I had been so unfortunate as to lay siege to a heart already occupied by some happier rival." He looked curiously into my face, but I summoned resolution enough to appear unmoved, not knowing to what further trial he might be about to subject me. "Can it be that the fortress had surrendered before my arrival to one of those gay young gentlemen that fluttered about Clarissa at Calcutta?"

"Sir," I said, "all this is beside the mark. Pray believe that I must refuse to marry you were you the only man in the world."

"And that's final?" he cried, springing up and seeming to tower above me. "Then on your knees, madam! Unsay those words, and ask my pardon for 'em, or"—and he swore a horrid oath—"by this time to-morrow you'll be in the hands of a man that will take no refusal from you. I saved you from the Nabob once, but not for this. Unless you'll pleasure me, you shall pleasure him."

"I am a weak woman, sir, and if you deliver me by force to the Nabob I can't hope to resist. But yield to you by my own will I won't."

"What!" he cried, sneering, "you'd have me employ force, as a salve to your conscience? But I won't gratify you, madam. You'll marry me of your own free will, or go to the Killa."

"Then Heaven's will be done, sir."

"What—you expect deliverance from this dilemma that I've set before you? What friend have you in the world that can assist you now?"

"None, sir—except God."

"And you have never appealed to God until this moment? He has not left any prayer of yours unanswered? You anticipate seriously a miracle of deliverance after a whole year in which your God has done nothing for you? Fie, madam! the days of miracles are past—even if you believe they ever existed."

"My duty remains the same, sir."

"Very well, madam. To-morrow night—no, the night after. To-morrow the Nabob has ordered a great fight of wild beasts for the diversion of the Court—two nights hence, I'll offer the Nabob an entertainment at this house, and Clarissa will assist me in providing it. That is, unless I should receive a message from her to-morrow. After that, 'twill be too late."

Oh, how I prayed last night, Amelia, that it would please Heaven to give the lie to this man's jeers by permitting me to expire before morning! But morning is come, and I still live.

June ye 8th.

I can't tell how the hot hours of yesterday passed, my dear friend. I was too wretched to write, even had I found anything to make known to you. I roamed restless through the apartments here, or sat crouched in a corner, murmuring that God had cast me off and left me helpless before the cruelty of my enemies. At night, as I tossed upon my bed unable to sleep, there came to me a thought, but whether from a good or evil source I can't pretend to guess. Does my Amelia remember a sentence that our good Rector at home once cited in describing the character of the excellent and devout Athanasius? It pleased us so much that when we were writing out our recollections of the sermon the next day we were so bold as to ask the Rector to give it to us exactly, that we might copy it into our commonplace-books, and he told us it was wrote by the Judicious Hooker. Comparing the situation of Athanasius with that of his adversaries, this learned author spoke of the uncertainty that existed "which of the two in the end would prevail; the side which had all, or else the part which had no friend but God and death, the one a defender of his innocency, the other a finisher of his troubles."

"Alas!" I cried, as the words returned into my mind, "but what of me, since God will neither defend my innocency, nor permit death to finish my troubles?"

"Why," said a voice in my mind, "seek death, since death won't come to you."

The notion was plausible enough, and I had soon formed a plan. From a certain spot on the varanda I had often observed that 'twould not be difficult to climb upon the roof of the garden-house, which is fantastically ornamented with a cupola and many small towers. There, I determined, would I conceal myself before the Nabob's arrival, and perhaps it might please Heaven to keep my persecutors from looking for me in that place. If so, well; but if not, there was the tank, washing the very walls of the pavilion, and to plunge myself into the water from such a height could scarce fail to bring me the death I sought. Do you blame me, Amelia? Then I hope you may always continue to do so, for that will show that my dear girl has never found herself in my desperate situation.

This frightful resolution taken, I fell asleep, and (such is the effect of coming to a decision, however shocking) was able in the morning to contemplate my affairs with something more of coolness and composure than yesterday. Misery and I were banished early from the pavilion into the house, for the *mollies* were busy setting rows of small earthen lamps everywhere in the gardens, in readiness to illuminate them at night in the Indian style, while other men were preparing a feast in the garden-house—all seeming as though they made ready for my execution. This was the thought in my mind when, passing up the stairs with Misery, I catched sight through the window of the man in a Tartar dress whom I saw two days ago in attendance upon the English prisoner. He had some fruit in his hand that he seemed to have bought from a street-hawker, and entering into the house facing this one, he shut the door upon himself. Oh, how this sight rekindled the hopes that I had persuaded myself were all extinct! How I blamed myself that I had not kept watch at the window more constantly, and so discovered that the man frequented, or perhaps inhabited, that house, or even, it might be, that 'twas there the prisoner was confined, for then I might have prepared some means to catch their attention. A written paper might not tell anything of my history to the Tartar, but finding strange characters upon it he would questionless take it and inquire of the prisoner what they could signify. Then I remembered that although the man was gone into the house, 'twas not necessary he should remain there always. He might come out at any moment. Misery had left me, and I ran to my writing materials, intending to prepare a small billet that I might push through the grating. But even as I laid hands on the pen and ink, I recollected the promise I had made to Sinzaun not to use in endeavouring to escape the writing implements with which he had furnished me. Here was a dilemma indeed. "Sinzaun has proved himself unworthy of credit and of the remorse you experienced towards him," said that voice which had spoken to me in the night. "Nay, but that makes no difference in my duty," said I. "But sure you never thought to prevent yourself escaping when you gave the promise," said the voice. "If promises were to be kept only when they were easy, and broke whenever we found them press hardly upon us, they would be fine things!" said I. "Will you perish on a point of honour?" says the voice. "Not if I can be saved otherwise," said I, taking the handkerchief from my pocket. In my hussy I had a needle threaded with the purple silk I had used for sewing at my petticoat, and before Misery returned I had worked roughly on the cambrick, close to my cypher in the corner, the words "Save. Quick." If Sinzaun's words were true, and my history as well known as he declared, I thought the prisoner would be at no loss to perceive who it was that demanded his aid. How he was to help me I did not know, but at least this one hope of safety should not be lost.

Misery departing again before very long, I broke off a loose piece of stone from the wall, and tied it in the handkerchief, lest it should flutter in the air as I threw it out, and then flying to the window tried to thrust the little bundle through the grating, intending to hold it by one corner until the Tartar appeared again. But the holes were too small to permit it to pass through, and as I tried in turn to break the stone smaller and to force the grating aside, I saw the man come out of the opposite house and begin to lock the door behind him. The sight drove me to desperation. With my scissors I began to chip out the mortar that held the grating in its place, and when both the points broke off I picked at it with my nails. The blood ran down my fingers as I worked, but just as the Tartar was turning away from his door the edge of the grating moved. I had not thought I was so strong, but I twisted it aside far enough to thrust the handkerchief through. It rolled down the window-ledge, then struck against some inequality or projection, and stopped. I thought I should have screamed, for the man was now out of sight, having crossed the street to gain the shade cast by our wall, but I forced my hand through the gap I had made, and succeeded in giving the tiresome missive a push that sent it safely over the edge. I could not tell whether it had reached the proper person, but I had enough to do to pull the grating back to its place and hide the traces of my doings before Misery came back. I was bathed in sweat and trembling with fright, and my wounded hands alone would have betrayed me had my Abigail's sharp eyes catched sight of 'em, but I was able to huddle them up in my gown, pretending that I was tired after my wakeful night, and desired to rest, and so threw myself upon my couch and waited.

Misery sat down opposite to me, and smoked her water-pipe very contentedly for I don't know how many hours, until one of the other women came to tell her there was that *boxwaller* again at the door, that had visited the house before, and called her to come and see his wares. None of these Indians can ever resist the delight of chaffering over a bargain, and away went Misery, her anklets clattering. No sooner was she out of sight than I, who had been enduring her presence in a tumult of eagerness and impatience that I can't attempt to describe, nor would my Amelia appreciate it if I did, sprang up from my bed, and catching up a piece of rag, began to bind up my hands, standing at the window as I did so. Opposite me was a similar window in the other house, and as I threw a glance across the street it seemed to me that there was something white behind it. Looking more intently, I perceived that this was the white wrapper of a Moor-woman, who was lifting her hand and making vehement signs to me to go up to the roof. My dear girl will judge that I did not delay, but as I reached the top of the stairs I saw something thrown, which struck the stones with a hard sound. Running to it, I picked it up, to find that 'twas only a piece of plaster from a wall, to my great disappointment. The parapet was too high to permit me a view over it, but I was doing my utmost to raise myself so as to peer over its edge, when something soft came over it and struck me in the face. Astonished, I seized it, believing it at first to be nothing but a common ball of worsted, but soon perceived an edge of white paper peeping out. In an instant I had the worsted unwound, and was reading the billet, which runs thus:—

"Be at this same spot as soon as it's dark this evening, and watch for a second ball of yarn, which wind up gently until you find a piece of twine in your hands. Pull that in also, and there will be a rope at the end of it. Make this fast securely to some solid body, and wait for your friends. Be secret and speedy, but feel no alarm. You will yet be saved."

I had only time to glance at this delightful message when I heard Misery returning, and thrust it into my bosom with the yarn as the old woman came up the steps to look for me. Her discourse on the folly of exposing myself to the sun at such an hour I endured with becoming meekness, and laid myself down again, with my face turned away from Misery. A new thought was come to me. The writing of the billet, though hasty and careless, appeared familiar. Scarce daring to credit the notion, I compared it, on the first opportunity, with the precious post-scriptum belonging to Mr Fraser's letter, which has never left me night or day, and I could not doubt but the same hand had wrote both. Picture my feelings, Amelia! So far from finding myself alone in India, there was close at hand, and at large, the very person I would have chose to be there! You'll wonder to find me calm enough to write this, but indeed, if I had not my writing to occupy me, I believe I should go mad with joy, or at least arouse Misery's suspicions by my transports. My smarting fingers are stiff, but my heart is so light that the pen fairly flies over the paper. Misery believes I am making my will, or so she told me just now. My will, Amelia! But oh, my dear, think—if Heaven had answered my impious and undutiful prayers last night, I should have lost this happiness. I was repining against the prospect of the most charming day that has ever opened to me! And moreover, while

I have been murmuring that God wrought no huge and signal miracle to save me, I have overlooked the constant succession of miracles that has preserved me thus far—my being brought out alive from the dungeon at Fort William, the plot of Misery and Sinzaun, my fever even, and all those exactions of the Nabob that have kept Sinzaun perpetually occupied in going to and fro with messages for Mons. Bussy, instead of remaining here to torment me, not to speak of the extraordinary crowning mercies of to-day!

MOIDAPORE, *June ye* 10*th*.

Oh, my dearest friend, I have the strangest, the most charming and perplexing news to tell you. You can't be more surprised to hear than I am to write it. I give you my word, I scarce credit it myself. But how my pen is running away with me! I *will* be orderly; I won't, after my usual fashion, impart to my Amelia the end of the history first and then proceed to turn back to the beginning.

Well, then, my dear, where was I? Oh, yes; I was writing to my sweet girl in Sinzaun's house in Muxadavad, with my hands all swathed up in rags, and it was only two days ago. Only two days! But I am wandering again. Back to your proper course, Miss Sylvia Fr—ah, well, I mean my good Sylvia—and recount your tale in a methodical style from its earliest original. That day of anticipation came at last to an end, Amelia, and at sunset Misery went as usual to gossip with the rest of the servants at supper, and also, questionless, to watch for the coming of the Nabob and Sinzaun. She had done her best to induce me to put on the Persian dress she had brought me long before, alleging that 'twould render the Nabob more kindly disposed towards me; but when I told her roundly that was the very last thing I desired, she gave up her attempts, and was so good as to leave me alone. My Amelia will find no difficulty in picturing with what delight I gathered my papers together, and tying them into a pacquet, with two or three garments (all the baggage I possessed!), hastened up the stairs to the roof, and waited there while darkness came on. Never, it seemed to me, had night been so long in falling—never had the people in the streets been so late in seeking the decent shelter of their abodes. At last I heard the Cotwal, who is the head of the city watch, pass with his constables, and knew that he was clearing the streets of belated passengers, so rendering them all the safer for my escape!

As soon as the watch were fairly passed out of the vicinity, I heard something soft fall close beside me, and on picking it up, found it to be the promised ball of worsted, which I began to wind up very gently and delicately, in the most horrid fear lest I should break it. But 'twas not long before I felt a knot, and the twine came to my fingers instead of worsted, and when I had wound that for a little, I found the hard end of a stout rope in my hands. You won't be surprised, my dear, to hear that I found no little difficulty in securing this rope, having no experience in such matters; but I twisted it round and round the stone pillar that stood at the head of the stairs, and fastened it with as many and as tight knots as I could devise. Then, guessing that my friends on t'other side would look for some signal from me, I pulled the rope smartly three times, and waited, breathless. Presently the rope began to creak and strain, as though it felt the weight of some heavy body, and almost at the same moment I observed that my knots appeared to be slipping. In a frightful agony of fear I threw myself on the rope, kneeling upon it and gripping it with all my strength, scarce able to believe that it was not sliding through my fingers. I heard more creaking, and then all on a sudden there stood on the parapet a huge tall figure in the dress of a Moorman, and I'll assure you I had screamed if I could have uttered a sound.

"Are you there, madam?" says a voice that I knew, though it was but a whisper.

"Here, sir!" I answered; "but I fear this rope en't safe."

The man let himself down softly from the parapet, and undoing my knots, fastened the rope again in the twinkling of an eye, with so much art that the harder he pulled the firmer the knot became. Then, leaving the rope, he dropped down at my feet, and seizing my two hands covered them with his kisses, in which, as I can't help fancying, there was mingled not a few tears.

"Oh, dearest madam, do I behold you at last?" he said.

"Dear, dear sir," I murmured, shaking from head to foot, for his warmth deprived me of all my self-command, "pray—oh, pray—this kind, this obliging behaviour—indeed I can't support it—I had given up all hope—I fear I shall swoon."

"No, that you must not do," said Mr Fraser, rising and supporting me in his arms. "Forgive me, dear madam, for agitating you to such a degree with my transports of joy. But I know my dear Miss Freyne won't endanger the lives of those that are come to save her by yielding to a feminine weakness at this moment. Compose yourself, madam, and let me bring you across the gulf."

Drawing me to the parapet as he spoke, he clambered up it with an extraordinary agility, and having seated himself at the top, turned and held out his hands to me. I don't know whether I climbed or whether the gentleman pulled me up, but I reached the ledge of the parapet in some way, only to shrink aghast from the next stage of the journey. The means of accomplishing this was nothing more nor less than a basket, Amelia—a shallow sort of car made of wickerwork, hung on the rope by its handles, and swinging at the side of the house over the black chasm of the street. Do you wonder that I shuddered?

"Oh, dear sir, I can't," I cried; if it be possible to cry out in a whisper.

"Oh, pardon me, madam, you must," says Mr Fraser. "Only permit me to lower you into the basket, and if you remain perfectly still you'll be drawn across in absolute safety. I worked myself across with my hands on the rope."

Was this said to remind me what danger he was braving for my sake? I don't know, but if it was so I had deserved the rebuke. I thought of Sinzaun and of my desperate resolves of the night before, and took shame to myself for my cowardice. Mr Fraser was holding the basket steady with his left hand, and, extending the right to me, I found myself somehow or other in the machine, but how I don't know, for I was not sensible of having moved—indeed I felt powerless to do so.

"Keep quite still," says Mr Fraser with a cheerful air, perceiving, perhaps, that my trembling imparted a rocking motion to the basket; and making a low hissing sound, I found myself drawn along the rope by a cord attached to one of the sides, while Mr Fraser moderated the speed by means of one that he held. I suppose I was not left swinging in this way between heaven and earth for more than a minute, but it might have been a life-time, and when I reached the parapet of the house opposite, the Tartar who stood there was forced to lift me out of the basket as though I had been an infant, before he sent it spinning along the rope back to Mr Fraser.

"Why don't the young Saeb come?" I heard him murmur to himself in Moors, when he had placed me safely on the roof itself, and stood waiting, as I guessed, for the signal to pull the basket across again. Still he waited, and still no signal came, and in a prodigious agitation I clutched at the man's foot.

"Why does he delay? Have they killed him?" I gasped out.

"They won't kill the young Saeb so easy as that," he growled, without looking at me, his eyes still fixed on the house I had just left.

"Oh, if they have taken him, let me go back and give myself up instead!" I cried; but the man shook me off, and bade me roughly be silent.

"Here he is!" he muttered at last, and almost as he spoke Mr Fraser appeared on the parapet, having crossed as before, without giving the signal.

"I fear I alarmed you, madam," he said, breathlessly; "but at the moment when I was about to leave the roof, I heard a slight jingle of ornaments, and, glancing towards the stair, saw a woman creeping away. To allow her to give the alarm would have been fatal to our hopes, and I sprang upon her like a wild cat. She was old, but she fought fiercely enough, and 'twas more than a minute before I could get her gagged and bound with strips of her own cloth. She was more frightened than hurt, I fancy; but I trust I han't inconvenienced any friend of yours?"

"Oh, sir, 'twas my woman Misery, the second worst of my enemies," I said, almost sobbing, as Mr Fraser paused in unfastening the basket from the rope, and looked at me.

"Why, then, save that she's a woman, I could wish I had used her worse," said he, cutting the rope, and so leaving it to hang down from the side of Sinzaun's house. "Is she likely to be soon discovered, do you fancy, madam?"

"When Sinzaun brings the Nabob to the feast he has prepared, which may be at any moment. Oh, dear sir, take me away,—save me; don't let me be dragged back to slavery after enjoying this one taste of liberty!"

"Why, no, madam; we'll carry you to the Agency at once, and there you're on British ground. Put this on over your clothes," and he handed me just such a white wrapper as the woman had worn who had directed me through the window at noon, and who I now perceived must have been himself in disguise, "and we'll set out."

While speaking, he and the Tartar had been excessively busy in hacking to pieces the basket and other traces of their occupation that lay about; then Mr Fraser took up my pacquet of papers, and the Tartar led the way down the stairs and so through a passage and two doors into the street. Do you realise, Amelia, that I had not stood in a street for near a year? 'Twas that time, also, since I had walked any distance, and the Moorish slippers I wore were not the easiest of foot-gear to walk in. Seeing my difficulty, Mr Fraser offered me his hand, and though the Tartar grumbled at the civility, as being inconsistent with our disguise, we held each the other's hand for the whole distance, to my great comfort, under the cover of my veil. Stealing along thus in the darkness, with the Tartar going first to watch for any danger, and choosing out the narrowest and darkest by-ways for us to pass through, we saw at a distance a glare of lights, and heard the sound of music and shouting.

"Sure his Highness is on his nightly rounds," says the Tartar.

"The Nabob? Then he's going to Sinzaun's house—for me!" I murmured, and would have fallen, had not Mr Fraser supported me.

"Courage, madam! We'll reach the Agency before he can discover your evasion. Which way, Mirza Shaw?"

"This way," said the Tartar, and led us down a lane and into an open doorway, where we stood and trembled, for although our party might have hoped to pass the Cotwal, with the help of a suitable present, as two respectable Moormen guarding some relative to her abode, we knew that the Nabob and his loose companions were accustomed to maltreat any unoffending person they met, and only to release such an one, after loading him with shocking insults and the most degrading injuries, with the loss of all the property he might have about him. But the riotous rabble passed the end of our lane without discovering us, though they turned their lights into most corners in the hope of catching sight of some crouching wretch, and when they were gone we left our concealment and hastened on, Mr Fraser cheering me with the assurance that we had not now far to go. The words had scarce left his mouth, when the music, which had been dying away, became on a sudden louder again in our ears.

"Some one from the house has met 'em and given the alarm," says Mr Fraser.

"Pray leave me, sir, and save yourselves," said I. "You have done your utmost."

"Pray, madam, what do you take me for?" he asked.

"Here's the door," said the Tartar, who had been groping with his hands along a wall, and Mr Fraser whistled softly. The door opened, and I was hurried inside, and into a sort of closed shed filled with packages.

"Pray, madam, be so good as to rest here for a moment, while we acquaint Mr Watts of your arrival," says Mr Fraser, and I was left alone in the dark.

(Miss Freyne's next letter appears unfortunately to have been lost.)

CHAPTER XIX.
IN WHICH A KNOT IS TIED.

From Colvin Fraser, Esq., to Mrs Hurstwood.

MUXIDAVAD, *June ye 8th, Evening.*

My pen, madam, ought by rights to be dipped in joy, since it has the charming task of announcing to the most faithful of friends that the dear sufferer, in whose fate she and I have experienced a joint concern, is now safely restored to the society of her countrymen, and that no long time will, I trust, elapse, before she hastens to Calcutta to embrace her Mrs Hurstwood. This agreeable news, you'll say, should stimulate me to impart it in fitting terms, but to tell you the truth, madam, I have begun this letter already three times over, for I can't satisfy myself in communicating the rest of my intelligence. 'Tis not only that I lack the fitting words for so tremendous an announcement, my heart fails me in imagining Mrs Hurstwood's scorn and resentment on hearing of my presumption; yet I would cheerfully brave even these did my mind supply me with terms appropriate to my situation, but rather than degrade the occasion by my poverty of speech, I'll leave my news untold. In short, madam, I can't write; my heart is too full. My revered and obliging friend Dr Dacre will take up the task I have abandoned, and permit me to subscribe myself, Mrs Hurstwood's most obedient, humble servant,

C. FRASER.

From the Rev. Dr Dacre to Mrs Hurstwood.

MUCKSADABAD, *June ye 8th, Midnight.*

In obedience, madam, to the urgent entreaty of my young friend Lieutenant Fraser, I venture to intrude myself upon the notice of Mrs Hurstwood, confiding in that sprightly and indulgent temper of which none can be ignorant that have been in company with the gentlemen whom she honours with her acquaintance—a favoured band in which it is my earnest desire to be numbered at the earliest possible period. In the joyful confusion of mind which is the natural accompaniment of Mr Fraser's present situation, he has been unable to direct me in any way in the task I have undertaken, and I purpose, therefore, to follow the extremely just precedent which I understand him to have established in his former epistles to Mrs Hurstwood, and relate the events of this evening in their proper historic order. If, in so doing, I should lay myself open to that reproach which has been recorded against old men by my honoured friend Mr

Samuel Johnson, that they too often grow narrative in their age, and weary where they hope to please, let my fair correspondent be so gracious as to ascribe the fault to the respectful awe in which I stand of her, and not either to my subject or my ill-will.

Seated this evening, madam, upon the varendar here with my obliging host, Mr Watts, I took occasion to remark upon the absence of the two young gentlemen, Mr Fraser and Mr Ranger, neither of whom I had seen since early morning.

"Mr Ranger I sent to Maudipore on an errand as soon as it was cool," replied Mr Watts, "and I heard him come in a while ago. As for the Lieutenant, he's engaged on his own business, but what that is I don't know, nor do I ask it."

"What's this noise of shouting and singing that I hear approaching?" I asked him. "Sure there's no idol-pagoda so close as that?"

"No, 'tis but the pagans holding one of their *tamashes*, or as like as not the Nabob is taking an evening walk with his intimates. One of my correspondents in the Durbar brought me word to-day that Meer Sinzaun's influence with his master is on the wane, and that he was endeavouring to re-establish it by presenting him with some very choice entertainment this evening at a house he has on the skirts of the town. Questionless the Prince and his favourites are now on their way thither. If there was the faintest touch of spirit in Meer Jaffier, he would sally out and capture Surajah Dowlah when he's passing through the streets with all this riot and noise, but the fellow has no more enterprise than any *bawboo*. However, provided the Nabob don't pay me a visit, there's nothing to trouble us in his nightly perambulation."

"Am I mistaken, or is the noise stopping before the gate?" said I.

Mr Watts raised himself on his elbow to listen, just as Mr Ensign Ranger approached us from the direction of the gate, having the liveliest contempt imaginable depicted upon his visage.

"Sir," says he to Mr Watts, "there's Rajah Moneloll[01] at the gate, with a whole rabble of *louchees* at his heels. They say there's a slave-girl—a country-born wench—missing from the seraglio, and demand to know whether she has took refuge here. I have assured 'em of the contrary, but they require to see you."

"See me they may, but they won't find the door opened to 'em," said Mr Watts, turning towards the gate, whither we were accompanied by Mr Fraser and the servant Mirza Shah, who had just joined with us. We found

Moneloll very particular in his enquiries, though he offered no reason why the wench should seek refuge with us.

"I have told you that she en't here," says Mr Watts at last. "The only woman in the place is the *chokeydar's* grandmother, and she's near a hundred years old, but if you're desirous to see the old lady, I'll have her step this way."

This handsome offer raised a laugh, but the favourite represented that the Nabob would be better satisfied if his men were permitted to search the house in order to assure themselves of our innocence.

"Then I fear his Highness won't be satisfied," said Mr Watts, "for no one enters this house to search it but over the bodies of these gentlemen and myself, and for that you'll have to answer to Saubut Jung Behader."[02]

"Why do you feign to take my jest for earnest, Watch Siab?" says Moneloll, with an air of reproach, and withdrew with his followers.

"Because it would have turned to deadly earnest when once these fellows had laid hands on the treasonable papers I have in the house," said Mr Watts to me in a low voice.

"They're setting guards to watch the house, sir," says Mr Ranger, "so as to allow no one to enter unperceived."

"This might have been serious a week ago," said Mr Watts, "but now——"

"Sir," said Mr Fraser on a sudden, "I must ask your pardon for correcting what you said a moment back, but the lady that Moneloll seeks is in the house."

"In the house, sir? Where?"

"In the godown at the back of the courtyard, close to the small door, sir."

"And you choose this moment, sir, when all our lives hang upon a thread, and spies among our servants are watching not only our motions, but our looks and words, to embroil me with the Nabob for the sake of a half-*cast* wench?"

"Sir! the lady is she of whom I told you, who survived the fall of Calcutta."

"Pray, Mr Fraser, remember I warned you that I could not listen to any account of your aspirations in coming here. Still, you have set the affair in a better light, and kept me from handing the woman back at once to the

Nabob, as I was about to do. But if I may presume to ask it, what's your object in bringing her here?"

"To procure for her your protection, sir, and the means of rejoining her friends."

"And this when every foot of the way to Calcutta swarms with enemies! Perhaps you en't aware, sir, that to-morrow you're to repair to Maudipore with Dr Dacre and Mr Ranger, in order to be ready should I be compelled to quit Mucksadabad suddenly. Pray, is the lady to go with you or remain here with me? How, pray, do you hope to convey her to Calcutta? Sure you had better have left her where she was."

"Had I done so, sir, I would be the most calculating coward that ever breathed."

"Say you so, indeed? Come, sir, what's your relation to the lady?"

"I honour and esteem her infinitely, sir."

"Pray, are you her humble servant?"

"That's the position to which I aspire, sir."

"Well, will you marry her to-night?"

"To-night, sir? But I han't asked her."

"That's an omission can quickly be repaired. Will you do it?"

"But, sir, such haste—indecent haste—her friendless situation—she would feel her delicacy outraged by the mere suggestion——"

"Oh, we won't press you, sir. Mr Ranger, you're acquainted with the lady. Will you assume the office of protecting her?"

"With all my heart, sir, this very moment."

"Sir!" cried Mr Fraser to Mr Watts. "Jem!" to Mr Ranger.

"Why, what a selfish cur art thou, Colvin!" cried the young gentleman. "A true dog in the manger, and sullen at that. Because the poor girl don't find favour with thee, would'st have her lose all chance of a kind spouse?"

"Put up your sword, sir," cried Mr Watts angrily to Mr Fraser. "How will you quarrel with Mr Ranger for obliging me where you refuse? Have you anything to say against him?"

"This, sir," said Mr Fraser, standing and confronting Mr Watts very stiffly. "Shortly before the fall of Calcutta I received a letter from my cousin Colquhoun, with whom you was acquainted, saying that in response to my urgent desire expressed to him, he was setting on foot a treaty of marriage between Miss Freyne and myself, but beyond adding that she had offered no opposition to the match, he told me nothing of her temper towards me. The troubles that followed brought the negotiation to an abrupt conclusion, so you'll perceive I can't tell how I stand with regard to the lady."

"I'll promise you this, at least," says Mr Ranger; "I won't run off with your mistress before your eyes, Colvin."

"Pray, sir, be silent," says Mr Watts. "Am I to understand that you're willing for the completion of the treaty, Mr Fraser, if the lady be the same?"

"Why, yes, sir, with all my heart. But how approach the subject without seeming to the lady to presume upon such slight service as I have been able to render her? She is the very soul of delicacy, and to be lowered in her eyes would be intolerable to me."

"Give me your hand, Mr Fraser!" says Mr Watts, warmly. "You're a youth of spirit, and I honour your scruples. You shan't have this odious task forced upon you. I will myself approach the lady on your behalf, and take her mind in the matter."

I have never, madam, seen a young gentleman with so astonished an air as Mr Fraser. "But, sir," he stammered, "the haste will be the same."

"My good sir," says Mr Watts, "I'll assure you the lady shall be told that you're about to be forced to the altar at the sword's point. I'll swear to her that you'd wish to delay the ceremony for ten years if it could be compassed. In fact, to satisfy you I'll intimate to her that you marry her but to oblige me. What, en't this enough?"

"Sir, sir!" cried the unfortunate young man, and stopped, unable to say more.

"Come, sir," said Mr Watts, "trust me to guard both the lady's punctilio and your own. Her father was one of my most intimate friends, and I desire nothing but good to his daughter. If she's reluctant to have you, I'll say no more, but if you're both willing, why delay? Come, doctor, you shall add your persuasions to mine."

Taking the lantern which the Tartar brought him, Mr Watts led the way to the godown, leaving Mr Fraser a lively image of despair, and his friend plying him with mocking consolations. Mr Watts unlocking the door, we passed into the warehouse, and discovered a female form seated on one of the bales. To you, madam, who enjoyed for so long the felicity of being continually in company with Miss Freyne, I need not express the sensations with which my friend and myself beheld the extraordinary loveliness of this young creature, more especially when we remembered the affecting situation in which she was placed, as she rose and saluted us with an air of modest dignity that added, if that were possible, another to the many graces of her aspect.

"Your servant, gentlemen," said she.

"Madam," says Mr Watts, "your most humble servant. My old comrade Hal Freyne's daughter don't, I hope, hear for the first time the name of William Watts? This here is my friend Dr Dacre, a learned divine and most ingenious author."

Miss Freyne curtseyed again, in acknowledgment of my host's too partial mention of myself, but methought her eyes rested with a more assured confidence on Mr Watts, who (worthy man!) experienced, as I thought, some embarrassment in fulfilling the task he had chosen, but in this I was to find myself mistaken.

"Doctor," he said, turning to me, "you was right and I wrong."

"Indeed, sir, this handsome acknowledgment——" said I, altogether ignorant of his meaning.

"Yes, indeed. I thought the young gentleman's fears uncalled-for, but now I'm inclined to believe him rather presumptuous than modest."

I began to understand. "He seemed to me to carry himself very properly, sir."

"But in face of so much beauty, sir! Why, Prince George himself would have good cause to tremble in the presence of such a lady. The assurance of these young fellows is prodigious! I'm unwilling to prejudice the foolish youth in the eyes of a person he reveres so highly, but I must confess I should be glad to see his arrogant pretensions suitably rebuked."

"Sure, sir, you're too hard," I said, while Miss Freyne turned her eyes in bewilderment from one of us to the other. "The young gentleman displayed a very proper sense of his own unworthiness as compared with the lady, and after all, he has done his best to serve her."

"A plague on his services, sir!" cried Mr Watts. "Is it to be endured that the mere risque of finding himself dismissed the navy, together with a paltry five months' residing and working here for Miss Freyne's release, should inspire the coxcomb with the notion of possessing a claim on the lady's gratitude?"

Here Miss Freyne interrupted us. "Sir," she said, with the most charming blush imaginable, "I can't help guessing that you speak of Mr Fraser. I trust I han't been so unfortunate as in any way to injure his prospects in life through the generous ardour that impelled him to attempt my release?"

"Why, madam," says Mr Watts, pushing his wig on one side, as one greatly perplexed, "this is the fact of the matter—though indeed, if I didn't know that Miss Freyne's wit and discretion are reported to exceed, if possible, her beauty, I should not venture to lay it before her. I can't deny but Mr Fraser is in bad odour with his superiors, and runs some risque of being put on his trial for desertion, owing to his exceeding the time allowed him here by the Admiral; but as I said just now, any man should count himself honoured in being permitted to run some risque for Miss Freyne's sake."

But here I thought that Mr Watts was gone too far, for the unfortunate lady fell back against the goods behind her, as pale as death. "Alas!" she murmured, "must I involve yet another in the miseries I bring on all concerned with me—and this one my brave deliverer?"

"Nay, madam," cried Mr Watts, "the young gentleman is of opinion that you may compensate him if you will for any risques to which he may have been exposed. But, as I was saying, who could expect Miss Freyne to sacrifice herself for such an insignificant person?"

The lady's face was whiter than before. "Sacrifice myself? I offered that very thing, but he refused," she breathed, so low that we could scarce hear her, "and now he sends to ask it of me! No, sir," she cried out suddenly, "'tis unpossible. You must have mistook him. He could not be so base."

"Why, madam," said Mr Watts, in extreme surprise, "I have said that I think the young gentleman presumptuous, but I can't see that there's any baseness in asking you to be his."

"What! is that all?" she cried, and immediately fell to laughing and weeping in a style that I found vastly alarming. "I thought you was telling me that he desired I should give myself up again to Meer Sinzaun, sir."

"Oh, madam," said I, "indeed you wrong the young gentleman."

"I know I do, and I'm an ungrateful wretch!" she cried, still sobbing.

"Well, madam, 'tis in your power to make him full amends," said Mr Watts. "May I inform him that you have no objection to marry him to-night?"

"Sir!" cried Miss Freyne, drawing herself up with all the dignity in the world.

"Why, madam, here are you in extreme need of a protector, and out yonder is Mr Fraser, languishing under the conviction that he's offended you beyond pardon in hinting at his desires by my lips. Here also is Dr

Dacre at your service. If this be the right moment for exhibiting severe justice towards the man that loves her, I'm convinced Miss Freyne will show it; but if it's possible for mercy to override punctilio, then I believe she has sufficient greatness of mind to lay aside the privilege of her sex, and make Mr Fraser happy without tormenting him further—unless," added Mr Watts with great anxiety, "you have already, madam, entered into any engagement of marriage that would forbid this?"

"No, sir, I am happily free. Refusing Meer Sinzaun's addresses, he desired to revenge himself by resigning me to the Nabob; but from this frightful slavery I was rescued—by Mr Fraser. I hope, sir, you don't expect me to agree with you in the remarks you was pleased to pass on the gentleman just now? I have such a confidence in him, and I am so deeply indebted to his kindness, that I could not hesitate a moment in making him happy, as you are obliging enough to call it, if I could believe it really for his advantage. But this extraordinary haste—my desolate situation—the want of the merest necessaries of life—" the lady looked at her gown, and blushed again; "and also—— But pray, sir, if Mr Fraser's feelings are so deeply engaged, why don't he approach me himself on the matter? Sure you'll agree that he owes me the compliment of declaring his own wishes and enquiring mine?"

"Why, madam, the poor young gentleman is in so sad a state, from apprehension of his own unworthiness and your deserved severity, that I refused to allow him to plead his own cause, lest he should do himself less than justice. And that reminds me, we are prolonging his agony with the most exquisite cruelty. Madam, you'll consent?"

"Oh, sir—oh, Dr Dacre, you are a clergyman—advise me. I don't desire to be unkind, but——"

"Why, madam, I can but advise you to follow your own heart."

"And that," says Mr Watts, "Miss has been good enough to show us already. Come, doctor, let us inform Mr Fraser of his good fortune. Madam, I'll attend you again in a few minutes."

"Sir—Mr Watts!" I heard Miss Freyne cry, but my host shut the door behind him.

"I think you'll say I know how to humour the ladies as well as the Indians, doctor?" he said to me, very complacently, as we came to the house. "Come, Mr Fraser, your mistress consents to make you happy. Go and get ready, sir."

"But, pray tell me, sir—she en't offended?"

"Be thankful for what you've got, sir, and ask no questions."

"Don't be too curious in your enquiries, Colvin," says Mr Ranger. "Come at once and get rid of that undress of yours. I must have you wear your uniform to be married in."

"Stop, Mr Ranger!" cried Mr Watts. "Have you forgot that we must keep this wedding a secret from the servants? What will Mr Fraser's boy say to see him in full dress?"

"I vow, sir, I had quite forgot it; though, indeed, most of the servants are gone to their houses for the night. But sure, sir, you won't forbid me to oblige our friend with the loan of a ruffled shirt, and the merest sprinkling of powder? Why, the lady might cry off from her bargain if she discovered the true colour of his hair!"

This having the desired effect in inducing a smile on Mr Fraser's serious countenance, Mr Ranger led away his friend in triumph, while Mr Watts and I disposed the room as orderly as we might for the marriage. Presently the two young gentlemen rejoined us, demanding earnestly what was to be done for a ring? Incredible though it may appear, not one of us was provided with this essential feature of the ceremony.

"Has no one so much as a signet-ring?" cried Mr Watts. "Come, Mr Fraser, sure you possess one with a coat-of-arms on it, to show the noble house from which you're sprung? I never knew a Scotchman yet that did not carry with him so convenient a testimony to his ancestry."

"Any small article of the required shape will serve," said I, observing that Mr Fraser appeared to regard this jest as a reflection cast upon his nation. "I have known the handle of the church-key masquerade as a ring."

"Why, then, we need make no further trouble," said Mr Watts, taking a seal from his watch chain, and unfastening the ring that held it. "This will about fit your lady's finger, Mr Fraser, and she'll be able to say that she was married with the seal of the Cossimbuzar factory. I'll have some goldsmith make me another."

"Sure, gentlemen, we are keeping the bride waiting," says Mr Ranger. "Pray, Dr Dacre, lend me a prayer-book, and let me be clerk. As the lady has no bridemaid, Mr Fraser won't need a brideman, but some one must deliver the responses."

Having a second prayer-book with me, I was able to oblige Mr Ranger, and Mr Watts departed to fetch the bride. I had observed that Mr Fraser was wearing an extraordinary resolved air, and as soon as the lady appeared he stepped forward to meet her, saying very earnestly as he took her hand—

"Madam, the happiness you offer me is so extravagantly great that I scarce dare accept it, for I can hardly believe that you would condescend to bestow it of your own accord. Pray, madam, don't think I desire to press you unduly. If you have any doubt of my sentiments towards you, or hesitate to honour me by confiding yourself wholly to my affection, say so, and I will hint no more of marriage, but swear to convey you safe to Calcutta and restore you to your friends, if it cost me my life."

"Will you assure me on your honour, sir, that you desire this marriage?" The lady raised her eyes, and regarded him earnestly.

"Why, madam, 'twould make me the happiest man on earth," he stammered, meeting her glance with a sort of modest resolution which I thought one of the prettiest things I had ever seen.

"I thank you, sir. I have had my answer, and there's yours," and she placed her other hand in his, an action that transfigured Mr Fraser's face with delight. But Mr Watts, declaring that the lady was anticipating the service, and seeking to supersede him in his duty of giving her away by doing it for herself, took her hand again to conduct her where I stood, and I proceeded with the office in a low but distinct voice, the Venetian blinds being drawn to prevent any of the servants catching sight of what was going on, and the Tartar keeping guard in the varendar, armed with a sword and buckler. I observed that Mr Fraser made the prescribed answers in a clear tone, instead of merely bowing, a careless custom of this *æra* that has nothing to excuse it, and the lady also could be heard without much effort.

"Come, sir, salute your lady," said Mr Watts, when the service was over, compassionating the bashfulness of the married pair so far as to refrain from commencing the usual indecorous struggle (which a politer age will sure abandon) for the first kiss from the bride. "What, will you put a public affront upon Mrs Fraser?" for the bridegroom offered only to salute the lady's hand. "Well, sir, fools make fortunes, and wise men spend 'em," and Mr Watts saluted her cheek very gallantly. I won't deny that I put in my claim for the parson's fee, or that Mr Ranger exceeded his duty as clerk by demanding one also, but 'twas Mr Fraser observed that his bride was trembling, and hard put to it to restrain her tears. With a delicacy that I had scarce expected in him, he led her to a seat and begged her to compose herself, while Mr Watts, bustling about with a great air of mystery, brought out a bottle of champaign.

"Here," he said, "this is my last bottle. I was reserving it against the day Colonel Clive enters Mucksadabad, but now we'll drink Mrs Fraser's health in it. At least the liquor won't be wasted if our schemes miscarry. Put on a brighter countenance, doctor, or I shall congratulate myself in having foiled you in a design to run off with the lady yourself. I don't wonder you have a shame-faced air."

"Why, indeed, sir," said I, following with his humour in the hope of bringing a smile to Mrs Fraser's face, "I should have been sore tempted but for the remembrance of a remark of my friend Mr Samuel Johnson. Asked whether he regarded it as expedient that a young divine should make a runaway match with the object of his affections, 'Why no, sir,' he cried, 'for who should then perform the ceremony?' Sure that would have been my case also."

Perceiving my design, as I can't help believing, the lady smiled slightly, but Mr Watts took advantage of her cheerfulness to dash her spirits afresh. "Our next business, Mr Fraser," he said, "will be to devise some plan for getting your lady safely out of the city."

"Sure, sir," said I, "the Moors would not venture to lay hands on the wife of a British officer?"

"I would not recommend Mrs Fraser to ride out openly and put the matter to the test," says Mr Watts, "since even if they were disposed to respect a British officer's wife, what could be easier than to make her his widow?"

"Oh, sir!" cried Mrs Fraser, starting up from her seat.

"I don't purpose to assist 'em to do it, madam. I should fancy 'twould be quite possible to smuggle you out dressed as a boy."

The lady blushed deeply, and was silent, but her spouse interposed—

"Pray, sir, oblige us with some other expedient if you can. That you name is excessively repugnant to Mrs Fraser's feelings."

"I'll take Beeby Fraser in a palanqueen openly through the city and out at the gate," put in the Tartar, "if she'll wear a *notch*-girl's dress."

"Who asked you to speak, Mirza Shah?" cried Mr Watts angrily, while a deeper crimson spread itself over the poor lady's face.

"Sir," she said to her husband, "I'll submit even to this frightful degradation, if it be necessary for your safety and that of these gentlemen, but I know you'll spare it me if you can."

"I'll ride out with you openly, madam," he answered, "before you shall be forced to it."

"It appears to me," said I, "though I speak with some diffidence, that we might hope to put in practice successfully a device mentioned by several ingenious authors. Cleopatra, on being denied Cæsar's presence, caused herself, we are told, to be conveyed into his apartments concealed in a bale of carpets. Without for a moment resembling Mrs Fraser to the too-notorious queen, I think it might be possible to conceal her, when we quit the city to-morrow, among those wadded quilts we use for mattresses."

"Now, doctor, you talk like a man of sense!" cried Mr Watts. "Your device spares the lady's punctilio, and avoids endangering her spouse. Are you prepared, madam, to submit to a certain measure of inconvenience for the sake of freedom?"

"Indeed, sir, I am," she replied.

"Why then, Mr Fraser and Mirza Shah shall carry out the affair. But remember, sir, your lady is Mirza Shah's care on the journey, and not yours. If you was perpetually hovering about the baggage, the simplest Syke could not fail to discover your secret. Doctor, we owe you many thanks."

Pray, madam, don't take it ill in me thus to conclude my epistle with my own praises. Mrs Hurstwood won't misunderstand me, I'm convinced. The having served her friend, however slightly, will commend to her kindness her most obedient, humble servant,

JNO. DACRE.

(The preceding letter, as well as those written by Mr Fraser, was transcribed, as is afterwards explained, by Mrs Fraser, and sent with her own to her friend Miss Turnor, by whom they were preserved. The curious fragment which follows may be found in No. 17 *of the thirty large MS. volumes containing Dr Dacre's miscellaneous remains. As no transcript of it has been discovered among the Johnson papers, it is probable that the letter was never sent.)*

From the Rev. Dr Dacre to Saml. Johnson, Esq., M.A.

MAUDIPORE, *June ye* 13*th*, 1757.

MY DEAR SIR,—You will questionless experience some surprise to receive a communication from me out of my usual order, and dealing with none of those important matters to the elucidation of which my present journey is directed, and the surprise will be increased when you are good enough to examine the enclosed Pastoral Piece, belonging to a species of composition never yet attempted by me. It has so chanced, however, that the necessity of inditing to an elegant and virtuous lady an epistle in a somewhat more lively style than ordinary, has inflamed me with the desire of turning to the improvement of others the history of two young persons in whom I have conceived a paternal concern. Remembering my honoured friend's design of composing at some future period a second series of papers similar in their treatment to his immortal 'Rambler,' I have ventured to compile this little anecdote for his acceptance, disguising slightly the names of the persons affected, and adhering with the utmost strictness to the just rules he has propounded for the writing of Pastoral. I had, I'll own, some notion of following the precedent set by the erudite Sannazarius, and presenting my personages as fishers instead of shepherds (and this in relation more especially to the gentleman, who pursues the maritime calling); but the recollection of the arguments which you, my good sir, have directed against this innovation, quickly dissuaded me, for how should one whose chief passport to favour, even in these distant regions, is the fact that he is the friend of Samuel Johnson, oppose himself to the erudition of his preceptor? In one point, sir, I'll confess you will discover me to have forsook your example, and this is with respect to the introduction of the scenery and products of the East. The bird of Paradise, I am informed, is not a native of Indostan, nor does it utter any song worth mentioning, while the oak and the primrose are not to be discovered among the spice-groves of these countries.[03] To enter into a discussion of the subject would be impertinent in a work of the imagination, and I have therefore contented myself with citing such natural objects as I required, without describing them. Any criticisms that my honoured friend may be so kind as to offer will be welcomed by his most obliged, obedient servant,

JNO. DACRE.

The Exacting Lovers. A Pastoral.

Colin and Silvia were two young persons who appeared to all their acquaintance to be formed for each other. His mind was something of a gloomy cast, while she was possessed of a sprightly turn of humour; he was apt to be overbearing in his air, and she was endowed with that easy softness which is the most admirable characteristic of her sex; his disposition was of the sort that is on the watch for slights, hers inclined her to believe anything of her friends rather than that they were intentionally unkind. The chain that bound their lives in one was forged out of a long series of affecting incidents, which it is not convenient to include in the present tale. It will suffice to say, that Sinzonius, the tyrant of a town adjacent to the pastoral region in which Colin and Silvia fed their flocks, captivated by the beauty of the lovely maid, carried her away to his stronghold, proposing to himself to keep her immured until she consented to his desires. This execrable project was foiled by the resolution of Colin, who, assembling hastily his brother-shepherds, took advantage of the tyrant's absence to release the imprisoned fair. Such a service, in the estimation of all around, entitled the rescuer to the highest recompense that Silvia could bestow, and attended with a numerous throng of swains and nymphs, the youthful pair betook themselves to the temple of Venus, where they plighted their eternal vows amid the acclamations of all present. There being among the ministers of the temple, however, a spy in the pay of Sinzonius, this fellow hastened to inform his patron of what he had witnessed, whereupon the haughty prince vowed to be avenged upon those who had so successfully defied him, although he did not venture to attack them openly.

In a commodious cave that extended into the mountains overhanging the vale in which Colin and Silvia had fixed their modest abode, resided a venerable and pious hermit named Damœtas, who had beheld with a paternal satisfaction the establishment of their humble household. Living remote from the converse of men, he had not become sensible of the alarming menaces of Sinzonius when, quitting his rugged solitudes, he repaired one morning to the smiling plains beneath for the purpose of enquiring into the welfare of his youthful friends. His progress was frequently interrupted by the respectful greetings of the shepherds he passed, who, leaving their pastoral avocations, hastened to implore his benediction; but arriving at length in the vicinity of Colin's hut, what was his astonishment to discover in the youth, who lay stretched on the turf in an agreeable glade, a prey to the liveliest manifestations of grief. The garlands were fallen unheeded from his locks, and his sheep wandered at will, unrestrained by his idle crook. Profoundly affected by the sight of such extreme melancholy, Damœtas made haste to ask him how he did, and whether all was well with the amiable Silvia.

"Alas, Damœtas!" sighed the unfortunate Colin, "my imagined felicity is no more. I find myself shipwrecked when I fancied I was arrived in port."

"Unhappy youth, unfold your sorrows to me," said the sympathising hermit. "Have wild beasts attacked your flock, or is the herbage parched with drought?"

"Such misfortunes as these," replied Colin, "would be trivial to that which is befallen me. My adored Silvia repents already of her condescension."

"Is it possible?" cried the hermit; "she repents that she plighted her vows to you?"

"That, my kind patron, is Colin's unhappy case. You will bear me witness that I felt my happiness too extreme to continue, and it is already eclipsed. I have become sensible that 'twas not, as I dared to hope, the return of my own affection, but that obliging softness of temper which distinguishes my charmer, that induced her to be mine. A mere rude shepherd, I felt myself infinitely unworthy of so much beauty and virtue, but I fancied that the continual society of my beloved girl might in time elevate me nearer to her. But when I find her regarding me with apprehension, if not with aversion, what hope can I cherish?"

"Pray, good youth, inform me what has led you to this mournful conclusion."

"Indeed, Damœtas, I discover in my Silvia such a fixed melancholy as affects me inexpressibly. She beholds me depart in the morning with tears, and welcomes me with tears when I return at night, while coming upon her suddenly I have several times found her weeping. Add to this that she avoids my caresses, and won't permit me to enjoy her company in peace even at our frugal meals, but is for ever rising to peer round the corner of our hut, or among the trees, as though she anticipated the approach of some enemy, although I have assured her repeatedly that there's none in the vicinity. Whence can this uneasiness proceed but from aversion for her Colin? But even worse than this is the passion she displays for serving me and anticipating my desires (in all but the matter I have most at heart), such as the merest slave might exhibit. This morning only I bade her be seated, and told her with some sharpness that 'twas for me to serve her, when she cried out with tears that this was the sole recompense she could make me for the horrid injury she had done me."

"And this injury—what do you understand it to be, Colin?"

"Oh, sir, what can it be but the permitting herself to listen to my addresses, merely in order to oblige her friends? I don't deny but she hoped to oblige me as well, her grateful spirit estimating far too high the slight service I had rendered her, and indeed, my sentiments towards the dear creature are such that I could be content with being allowed to serve her, in the hope of bringing her in time to regard me with affection, but for the thought of the wrong I am inflicting on her in keeping her bound to a spouse she abhors."

"But you have made no attempt to enquire of your Silvia whether you have judged her aright?"

"Oh no, sir; how would it profit me to hear the dreadful truth confirmed by the lips of the woman I adore? No, I won't pain her by exhibiting what she has made me suffer. I may serve her better than that."

The good hermit folded his hands upon his staff, and looked fixedly at Colin. "Rash youth," he said, "what are these wild dreams in your mind?"

"There are none, Damœtas, but if in the strife with Sinzonius' forces an arrow should penetrate to this sad heart, my charmer would once more be free."

"I don't, I won't believe," said the hermit, "that she desires her liberty. Accept my counsel, Colin. Meet your Silvia always with a smiling and affable countenance, consult her wishes, and disregard her melancholy, which may be dissipated when once her spirits are recovered from her imprisonment. If you don't succeed in banishing it, at least you won't have added to it."

"Alas, Damœtas, this is mournful counsel for a man not three days married!" sighed the unhappy shepherd, and resumed his melancholy musings, to which the hermit sorrowfully left him. Continuing his journey, Damœtas arrived presently in view of Colin's rustic cot, which was seated on a gentle eminence, commanding a charmingly diversified prospect. Here he discovered the beauteous Silvia, who had thrown herself weeping on the ground in the delicious shades of the grove, paying no heed to the whispers of the balmy gale, nor to the music of the rill that murmured beside her. Hearing the approaching footstep, however, she sprang up from her lowly couch.

"Oh, sir, what of Colin?" cried the lovely nymph. "Is he safe?"

"I left him but now in perfect safety," replied the good Damœtas. "But what ails the fair Silvia, and why is she concerned for her Colin's safety?"

"Oh, sir," she replied with tears, "I think I have not enjoyed one easy moment since hearing of the menaces uttered by Sinzonius. I can't endure that Colin should be out of my sight, and yet when he is with me I am tormented with apprehensions of beholding him murdered before my eyes, and it is I have brought this danger upon him. Thoughtless and wicked damsel that I was, I consented to unite my own evil fate with his, forgetting the misfortunes that are come upon all connected with me."

"But sure Silvia was acquainted with this when she consented to oblige Colin?"

"Alas, sir! I forgot it, as I have said, for the moment, transported as I was with joy to think that I might hope to render him happy. But 'twas a deceitful hope. Colin has already learned his mistake."

"Has he discovered that his Silvia can't make him happy?"

"Alas, sir, yes! I have observed his uneasiness grow continually these two days. He has questionless determined that his poor Silvia en't worth the perils that the possessing her involves. My tears distress him, and I seek to hide them, but my apprehensions I can't conceal, and they tease him excessively. If I had but the assurance of his affection I could be happier, but the cup of my misery is filled by the thought that he was persuaded by his friends to take pity on me owing to my desolate situation. This very day I sought to express to him something of the distress I experience for the wrong I have done him, when he answered me very shortly that we had both made a mistake, but that 'twould do no good to weep over it."

The hermit, now become fully sensible of what the tragedians call the irony of the situation, was at some loss how to proceed, but said at length—

"In that remark, as I can't deny, Silvia's spouse was justified. I would have her dry her tears and meet Colin with a cheerful countenance. Let her dress herself in her best——"

"Ah, sir, I have but this one gown," said the lovely girl. How will this pastoral simplicity be despised by the ladies who read these pages!

"True," said the frugal Damœtas, "and 'tis a credit to Silvia that she can say so. But at least she may welcome her spouse in a cheerful style, and abstain from vexing him further with her tears. Did she entreat of him any explication of his unkind remark? It may be she misunderstood his words."

"Alas, sir, how could they be mistaken? Their meaning was too plain."

Finding himself again at a loss, Damœtas remained for some moments plunged in thought, until the notes of a melancholy strain discoursed on a shepherd's pipe heralded the return of Colin, which Silvia, absorbed in the violence of her grief, had not observed. Rubbing his hands merrily, the venerable hermit went forth to meet the mournful youth, and leading him into the cot, presented him to Silvia.

"In the glade," he said, "I met with a shepherd who was inconsolable because the nymph he worshipped did not return his affection, and in this hut I find a young woman refusing to be comforted because her adored spouse don't love her. Perhaps they may console one another."

"Is't possible?" cried one. "'Twas all my fault!" cried t'other, and they embraced with all imaginable tenderness, while the good Damœtas went on to say—

"Indeed, I can't but declare you both in the wrong. You, Colin, erred in permitting your gloomy constitution to persuade you of your wife's aversion for you, and in neglecting to enquire particularly into the truth; and you, Silvia, because you suffered your apprehensions to blind you to the care of that Providence which has so often assisted you in the past, and to go far to alienate the affection of your spouse. Learn then, both of you, to be wiser in the future."

In this strain Damœtas continued for some time to improve the occasion, until, perceiving with regret that his auditors were so profoundly engrossed in each other as to be altogether unconscious of his exhortations, he withdrew, and left them alone.

CHAPTER XX.
WHICH DESCRIBES A STRATEGIC RETREAT.

From Mrs Fraser to Miss Amelia Turnor.

CULNAH, *June ye 15th.*

I have amused myself not a little, my dear friend, during this last few days, in picturing the manner in which my Amelia would receive the astonishing news contained in my last letter, which I was so eager to place in her hands that I writ it in scraps, as the time offered, at Moidapore, and despatched it the night of last Saturday (the 11th), by a *cossid* that was carrying an epistle from Mr Watts to Colonel Clive, and called at the hunting-lodge for any private letters the gentlemen might wish to send. 'Tis true I have been inclined to repent of this precipitancy, for since arriving at the army we have heard a rumour that the fellow, being pursued by *decoyts* or highway robbers, lost in his flight some of the missives with which he had been entrusted. Still, I can't bring myself to believe that the epistle in which I acquainted my dear girl of all the incidents (whether alarming, affecting, or comical) of my marriage, and of the misunderstanding that, but for the interposition of good Dr Dacre, might have wrecked for ever my happiness with my dear Mr Fraser, could be the one of all the rest to go astray. Should it prove to have been thus ill-advised, I fear my Amelia must be the sufferer, for I could not bring myself to write that letter again.

At Moidapore, which is a country-house situated about one *coss*, or rather over two miles, to the south of Cossimbuzar, we spent in all five days, a period during which I was apparently as much a prisoner as when in Sinzaun's house, but with how great a difference! Carried into the place rolled up in a bundle of mattresses (believe me, my dear, I could have imagined myself again in the Black Hole, such was the heat and the want of air on my journey), I had allotted to me the *Ginanah*, or women's part of the house, with an agreeable small garden on which it looked; and here I remained without my presence being so much as suspected by any of the domestics, with the exception of the gentlemen's body-servants, who, being honest fellows, and continually employed about the house, were admitted into the secret. Of the anxious kindness shown me by Mr Fraser I need not speak, for the generosity of his mind is abundantly testified by the history I gave you of our first quarrel, if quarrel it may be called, which was so productive in misery at the time, but yet has something droll in it. The consideration of the other two gentlemen displayed itself in the most engaging manner, as my Amelia will perceive when I tell her that I had not to resent a single free remark from Mr Ranger, and that Dr Dacre was so obliging as to translate for me on the spot all the quotations from the ancient authors that he happened to employ in his discourse. What can I say more? As long as our stay lasted, my spouse and Mr Ranger occupied themselves during the morning and evening principally in hunting, which was necessary to give colour to their removal to the place; and your Sylvia found plenty to do in cutting out and making up from the stout cotton cloth of the country a riding-dress for herself, which Mr Watts had warned her she might need at any moment; while Dr Dacre, pursuing his studies with the most philosophical composure in the world, was so polite as to read aloud to her occasionally certain extracts from the work he is preparing on the relation of the Sanskerreet to the classical tongues, to cheer her labours.

During this blessed period we were not left entirely without news from the outer world, for Mr Watts despatched a messenger to us on some pretext or other once a day. The first of his messages was that which awoke in your foolish Sylvia's bosom all the apprehension which her Fraser misread so unfortunately. It acquainted us that Sinzaun had accosted him that day in a very affable style at the Durbar, asking his pardon for Moonloll's attempted invasion of the night before, and saying he was certain the female who had escaped was not at the Agency, for he had found a clue to her presence in a different part of the city, and expected to recover her immediately. To this Mr Watts had added: "I can't doubt but this complaisant address was designed to throw me off my guard, to the end that Monsieur Sinzaun, who has satisfied himself that Mrs Fraser was not of the party that rid to Moidapore, may find opportunity to introduce his spies into this house. His bribing some of the servants is merely a matter of time, and when by this means he has discovered that the lady en't here, he will divine that we have succeeded in overreaching him, and will turn his attention to Moidapore. When that happens, gentlemen, look to yourselves."

On the day after this alarming letter came a second to say that Aumebeg, an officer of the Buckshy Meer Jaffier, with whom Mr Watts has covenanted to turn traitor to the Nabob, was returned from Calcutta, whither he had gone to convey the treaty between his master and the British, bringing the news that the secret of the alliance had got abroad, and was the common talk of the soldiers at that place and Chandernagore. The wicked old Gentoo, Omy Chund, of whom my Amelia has heard before, having played a leading part in obtaining the treaty, had become alarmed that his advantage was not sufficiently regarded in it, but his apprehensions were pacified (I fear, by what Mr Fraser hints to me, in some not over honourable manner), and he was content to do no more than watch over his interests by accompanying Colonel Clive and his army when they marched against Muxadavad. Since this might take place any day, Meer Jaffier had sent to warn Mr Watts to make his escape, but the good gentleman was resolved to maintain his position until the last extremity, and, if possible, until he had permission from Colonel Clive to leave it. All this time the Nabob and Meer Jaffier, shut up in their respective castles within the city, were making preparations, the one for defence and t'other for attack, and exchanging such bloodthirsty menaces as might well terrify those who heard as well as those who received them.

Last Monday was the day on which our fears arrived at a climax, and our fortunes at a crisis. As soon as the heat of the day was over, Mr Ranger, who was gone to the stables to tell the grooms to have the horses ready for going hunting that evening, found an old woman of one of the gipsy tribes in the compound. On his tossing her the piece of money for which she begged, the crone requested to see his hand, and told him his fortune so accurately as regards the past, and so flatteringly as regards the future, that he was most extravagantly delighted, and carried the old creature to the house, where he summoned Mr Fraser and Dr Dacre, who submitted their hands to her inspection with an equally agreeable result. Mr Ranger's kind concern for my entertainment next caused him to suggest to Mr Fraser that he should bring the old woman into the Ginanah, that she might tell my fortune also. Always ready to consult my pleasure, and grown now somewhat secure through our continued safety, Mr Fraser came to propose the visit to me, suggesting that I should wrap myself in my Moorish veil, so that the sorceress might not know me to be a European. The notion of admitting this stranger did not commend itself to me, but seeing my spouse so eager, and attributing my reluctance to a foolish shyness springing from my long seclusion, I begged of him to bring her in. I could not doubt her possession of the powers to which she pretended when, after examining my hand very minutely, she informed me that I had of late passed through many trials, hinting not obscurely at their nature, and that I had been married only a few weeks, perhaps even days. To test her further, Mr Fraser asked her whether I had any enemies, to which she made answer that my safety was menaced by a very great person, but that I might rest easy, for his plots against me should not prosper. To this she added further prophecies, such as awoke in Mr Fraser an extraordinary delight, and he carried her out in great good humour. Returning to me, he remarked on the woman's having contrived to bite the coin he gave her, in order to test its goodness, although she appeared to possess no teeth to speak of. "I observed the marks," said he.

"Sir," I cried, a frightful conviction seizing me, "the woman was Misery in a disguise, and with her teeth blackened."

"What! the hag that betrayed my beloved girl to Sinzaun?" cried Mr Fraser, catching up his sword, and ran out, calling to Mr Ranger to accompany him. But although they searched high and low, and questioned the servants closely, they could find no trace of the sorceress, and returned disappointed, cursing their own credulity.

"How will my dearest life forgive me for bringing her into this new peril?" said my spouse, with the kindest, most melancholy air imaginable. "But at least the hag prophesied the downfall of her own schemes," he added, seeking to cheer me.

"'Twas but to throw us off our guard, I fear, sir. Relieved from dread of Sinzaun, she looks that we shall grow careless. But, oh, dear sir," and I catched hold of Mr Fraser's two hands, "if we are indeed exposed to that wicked person's attacks, let me alone be the sacrifice. Believe me, 'twould add infinitely to my affliction to know that I had endangered others."

"I fear, Mrs Fraser," says my spouse very solemnly, "you forget sometimes that you're married. How otherwise could you coldly propose that I would resign my wife to that lawless villain? Or perhaps you are good enough to intimate that you prefer him to me?"

"Oh, sir, sir!" I cried; and Mr Fraser embraced me with the most obliging tenderness.

"My foolish girl knows now what I'll think if I hear her say that again," he said, and went away to consult with Mr Ranger on plans of defence. But as it chanced, their valour proved unnecessary; for their council was interrupted with the commotion caused by the arrival of a palanqueen, out of which stepped Mr Watts, very cheerful and sedate, while among the servants attending on him was Mirza Shaw Buzbeg, riding a very fine horse of his own. The palanqueen and bearers Mr Watts sent back to Cossimbuzar, saying that he was going hunting with the gentlemen, and would carry them thither with him for supper, which (as he bade them remind the cooks) must be on the table without fail at the hour he had named. Coming in then among us, and rubbing his hands very complacently—

"Come," he said, "the hour is arrived, gentlemen, and Surajah Dowlah's knell has begun to toll. Meer Jaffier sent to me this afternoon to entreat that I would leave the city, since a rumour had reached the Nabob that Colonel Clive was advancing from Calcutta as far as Chandernagore with his troops. You'll guess that I was not catched unprepared, for I think 'twould be scarce kind in me to permit Surajah Dowlah to add to his crimes by compassing all our deaths. Leaving the city house in my palanqueen, I betook myself to Cossimbuzar, as I have done pretty often of late on pretence of business, and ordered the servants there to have supper ready against the time I should bring you back with me, gentlemen; but I fear that supper will be cold indeed before we return to eat it. Pack up your falbalas, madam; you have prepared an equestrian habit as I recommended you, I hope? To horse in half an hour, gentlemen! The beasts are in good condition, I trust?"

"Sure, sir," I heard Dr Dacre say, as I returned into my own apartment, "you can't intend to ride the whole distance to Chandernagore? Have you forgot we have a female of our party? Mr Fraser consulted me as to your intentions, and I assured him that you was but proposing to ride as far as some point on the river where we might obtain boats. You won't contradict me, I hope?"

"Why, look ye here, doctor," cried Mr Watts, "no man knows better than I do that the length of the journey and the extreme heat of the season will make this adventure of ours excessively fatiguing and not a little dangerous, but our lives are at stake. One of my reasons for lingering on in the city longer was that I was in hopes of hearing from Colonel Clive that he desired our retreat, and had provided boats to meet us on the way. But since he han't chose to be so considerate, we can only trust that the rumour which has alarmed the Nabob is true, and that we shall find the army on the march to Muxadavad. The Colonel knows our danger, for Aume-beg tells me that it has several times been reported in Calcutta that I had been seen slain, and my head set on a pole, and I don't doubt but he'll help us if he can. As for the lady, if I know anything of her, she'll share our hardships without whining or peevishness, and prefer 'em to the alternative of remaining here. And pray, gentlemen, do me the favour to get ready at once. I may be pursued even now."

The words were not out of Mr Watts' lips when the other gentlemen scattered each to his apartment, and Mr Fraser, lifting the *antiporta* of reeds through which I had heard all their conversation, came to me.

"My incomparable girl must show the stuff she's made of to-night," he said, with as great an air of cheerfulness as he could command. "We will have a long hard ride, but I know she'll do her best to support it for her Fraser's sake."

"Indeed, dear sir, I'll endeavour not to disappoint you," I said, the tears coming into my eyes at the kind and flattering style in which he spoke. Truly, my dear, I can conceive nothing that would grieve me more than to disappoint the dear gentleman in any particular, though I fear I shall never attain to the high ideal he has so obligingly formed of me. My Amelia would, I am convinced, discover a perpetual fund of amusement in the mutual dread which Mr Fraser and I entertain of losing each other's good opinion. I must tell her that so many years spent on shipboard have rendered my spouse an adept in what he prefers to call *making things fast.* His apartment at the Agency made me laugh, for everything that could by any means be packed up, put away, rolled up or hung up, had been so treated, until the place looked as bare as my hand. Observing my surprise, Mr Fraser told me that he liked to have things shipshape; and when I asked him whether he anticipated a flood, in which the whole house might sail gaily away, he looked at me as though I had displayed a design to attack his nation. It needs a woman, my dear, to diffuse that air of elegant disorder without which the finest apartment has an uninhabited air. To our sex alone does it belong to be easy without being untidy; for if men dispose things neatly they become also stiff. But seeing that Mr Fraser piques himself on his neatness, I allow him to do as he pleases at present, and to devise all manner of expedients for stowing everything away, until even the water-jar is furnished with a sort of rack on the wall. And here at Moidapore, when I had put on my riding-dress, he showed me a device of his by which my little bundle of clothes (containing my only gown, Amelia) might serve me for a cushion when I rode behind him, and was so pleased with his contrivance that I could not find it in my heart to rebuke his ingenuity by asking him what he thought the gown would look like when I wore it next. En't I a pattern wife, my dear?

"Alas, alas!" cried Mr Ranger, when I joined with the rest of the party, "sure the shade of good Mr Addison must wander distressed to-night. His fairest disciple has forsook him, and adopted the equestrian habit he detested."

This was said because I was forced to complete my riding-dress with a laced hat and undress frock of Mr Fraser's, suiting very well with my skirt, which is of a dark blue colour, but giving me (I can't deny) something of the air of the young ladies rebuked by Mr Spectator for aping men. Indeed, I think I should figure very passably in Hyde Park, unless the mode has altered since I left England.

"Don't tease the lady, sir," says Mr Watts. "She has acted like a woman of sense in dressing herself so as to attract as little attention as possible to our party. She might pass for a man at a very short distance."

If this was said to comfort me it failed of its effect, but I said nothing as we walked out through the garden to a spot remote from the servants' quarters, where the horses were waiting, each with its groom, called a *syce*, who can keep pace with his beast for several hours, even when the speed is very great. The Tartar, who had seen to the security of all the straps and buckles, was already mounted, and several dogkeepers, holding greyhounds in leashes, were present to give our evasion the air of a simple hunting-party. Having mounted (Mr Fraser had devised a sort of side-saddle for me, with the aid of a stirrup fastened over a peg) we rode out gently to the southward for some miles, feigning to be very eager in the search for antelopes or game of any kind, but displaying the utmost care not to fatigue the horses. Mr Ranger seemed to find this leisurely progress very wearisome, for he began presently to rally Mr Fraser on his appearance in the saddle, diverting himself with various odd comparisons respecting sailors on horseback. This mockery I should have found very annoying had I believed it to be well grounded, but Mr Fraser was accustomed to riding in his early youth, and has never neglected the accomplishment when on shore, so that he acquits himself with as much elegance as any gentleman need exhibit, and was able to endure Mr Ranger's raillery with the greatest complaisance. The young gentleman was so good-humoured as not to turn his attention to me, or I should have been less happy than my spouse, not having mounted a horse for over a year, but riding gently over level ground I found myself easy enough. Having started on our ride when it wanted about an hour to sunset, we had gone over six miles before darkness began to come on, which happens very suddenly in these countries, and Mr Watts drew rein at the summit of a slight eminence.

"See here," he said to the dogkeepers, "we don't seem to discover any game, so 'tis scarce worth while to keep the dogs out longer. Take 'em back to Moidapore at once. The gentlemen and I will ride quietly round by Cossimbuzar, and sup there before returning, and we'll hope for better luck another evening."

The dogkeepers obeying without any reluctance (for the Indians have a great fear of the darkness, both on account of wild beasts and of evil spirits), Mr Watts called upon us to follow him, and rid smartly down the further side of the rise.

"A moment back," he said, "before it was grown so dark, I catched sight of two men coming from the south, and if they en't wandering *juggies*[01] they're *cossids*."

We came upon the men before long, for it seemed that they had perceived our figures against the sky upon the hill-top, and directed their steps towards us. One of them was known to Mr Watts, who cried out to him to say where he had left Colonel Clive, to which he replied that 'twas at Chandernagore, but that he was only halting there for the night on his march to Muxadavad. This news served to raise all our spirits, which the *cossid* observing, he increased the effect by delivering to Mr Watts a letter which he had carried concealed in the folds of his turbant (for so scanty is the clothing of these swift messengers that they have no other place in which to deposit the missives with which they are charged), and which caused our leader infinite delight.

"Good!" he cried. "Here's the Colonel's letter desiring me to quit Muxadavad and join him with all possible speed. He will send forward boats with a military escort to the point where the Jelingeer[02] River meets this from Cossimbuzar, which will cut a fine slice off our journey, and he looks to have reached Culnah before we meet him."

Bidding the *cossids* continue their journey to the factory and refresh themselves there, Mr Watts saw them out of sight and then turned to us.

"Now, my good friends, our real work is to begin. Madam, allow me to assist you to dismount. Mr Fraser will put his saddle on your horse, and you'll find it best to ride behind him. Mirza Shaw will lead t'other nag, and you can change to it again half-way. Are your pistols charged, gentlemen, and your swords loose in the scabbards? We may have to fight our way to-night—indeed it's scarce probable we shall escape without a tussle with the blackfellows—and in such a case all will hang on our being able to ride 'em down before they see how few we are."

Almost as soon as Mr Watts had finished speaking, the saddles had been changed and Mr Fraser was mounted again, when Mr Ranger helped me to spring up behind him, and we started afresh, moving cautiously at first, but soon quitting the road and striking to the left. Here the country for a prodigious distance is uninhabited, and covered with thickets of an extraordinary denseness, along the skirt of which we rode at the utmost speed of which our beasts were capable, still maintaining a southerly direction. My dear, I have no inordinate desire, I hope, to establish myself as a heroine, nor to indulge in any extravagant descriptions of that night's sufferings, but since I contrived at the moment to refrain from any expression of the miseries I endured, in order not to incommode my kind protectors further, I may, perhaps, be permitted to confide them to the faithful bosom of my Amelia. Oh, my dear girl, the heat, the dust, the rough paces of the horse when we passed over a tract of hard parched ground, the thirst, the constant alarms, and worst of all, the sounds! Do you know what it is to *hear* the heat, Amelia? Don't think my intellects are disordered when I tell you that I heard it come rolling up like huge waves. I imagined it to be thunder until the gentlemen had assured me positively there was none. Then the sounds of the horses' feet multiplied themselves into the tramp of an immense army marching upon us, or there was a continual roar, such as might be made by a whole mighty river pouring over a precipice, and from the thickets we skirted came shrieks and groans and cries, which I was told were due to night-birds and wild animals, but which sounded at once more alarming and more mysterious from the uncertainty with which they reached the ear. These terrors did not, of course, attain their greatest height immediately. During the first part of the journey Mr Watts astonished us all by the gay good-humour with which he encountered the situation. Whenever we slackened speed for a rise in the ground, he would break into such agreeable and rallying discourse as made us forget our discomforts. The skill and temper with which he had braved the Nabob's threatenings and disarmed his suspicions, while at the same time plotting with his courtiers for his overthrow, formed his chief theme, as though, like the great Roman commander, he would have banished our fears by reminding us that we were in company with himself and his fortunes. Again, as though the sudden removal of the heavy anxieties under which he had laboured so long had left him as careless as a boy, he would set to rallying one of the other gentlemen, as when we stopped once that Mr Fraser and I might transfer ourselves to the fresh horse, and I sat panting on the ground while the saddles were changed.

"Come, doctor," he cried, in answer to a Greek quotation from Dr Dacre, "confess that you're cherishing a grudge against me at this moment for dragging you away from your books. I'm persuaded that in your heart of hearts you'd prefer to die with your dear classical authors rather than be saved without 'em. The blackfellows will make a fine bonfire of them, I'll warrant you."

"Indeed, sir," said the doctor, with something of a guilty air, "I must confess I would not trust the Indians with any of my treasures."

"Would not, sir? Pray what does that mean? I have observed your horse flagging very painfully—sure your saddle-bags are prodigious hard, and your pockets. Oh, doctor, doctor! can it be that you have loaded the poor dumb beast with the weight of your library—and you a *burra Padra*?"

"Only the most precious volumes, sir, I'll assure you."

"The cruelty's the same. Come, doctor, pitch 'em all out. Lighten the ship, as Mr Fraser would say. Will you exhibit less strength of mind than his lady, who was content to bring the smallest possible package with her?"

"Ah, sir, Mrs Fraser had no more to bring," said the poor divine with a deprecating air, which made Mr Watts laugh heartily. But having alarmed Dr Dacre sufficiently, he was good-natured enough to relieve him of the weight of one or two of the books, and Mr Ranger doing the same, the doctor's horse displayed a good deal more vivacity than before. On starting on our journey again, Mr Watts changed our course, remarking that we must have rode over twenty miles since parting with the *cossids*, so that there were thirty miles at least between us and Muxadavad, and 'twas now safe to turn our steps westward, and seek to come upon the river. Horses and riders were now alike fatigued, and even Mr Watts appeared to lose his cheerfulness as we rode on through the night, with the poor *syces* still keeping close to the heels of their beasts. Occasionally there was an alarm that a village might be near, when the Tartar, who was considered to possess the most perspicuous eye of the party, would ride forward alone and return to report his discoveries, but we succeeded in avoiding almost entirely the habitations of man, although, to speak truth, I could almost have welcomed the being taken prisoner, if it had signified that I was at liberty to leave the horse and throw myself on the ground. Longing only to be still and to slumber, it caused me the extremest agony to be borne along in this unceasing motion, afraid to indulge the drowsiness that tormented me lest I should lose hold of Mr Fraser's belt and find myself dashed to the ground. My dear Mr Fraser lost no opportunity of endeavouring to raise my spirits, praising my endurance in the kindest terms (oh, had he but known that I could barely keep myself from crying out to him for mercy's sake to stop the horse and suffer me to rest!), and cheering me constantly with anticipations of arriving shortly at the boats, but I fear he met with but slight response. I felt as though all the strength I possessed was needed for maintaining my hold, and yet I must have been able to speak, for on a sudden I found Mr Fraser addressing me with great concern.

"Why, what's the matter, sir?" I asked him, as he checked the horse.

"You cried out that you was forced to let go of your hold, my dearest life."

"I didn't know it, sir," I said, and laughed, and my voice had so droll a sound that I laughed again, "but indeed I can't wonder."

"Don't get light-headed, child," said my spouse, sharply. "Hold the bridle for me a moment," and when I reached forward and obeyed him, he unbuckled his sword-belt, and slipping it off, fastened it round himself and me both, so that I could not fall even though I loosed my hold. This occupied but an instant, but Mr Ranger came riding back to see what had detained us, and was very merry with Mr Fraser on his riding with his sword out, as though at a review. After this I must believe that I fell asleep in spite of the awkwardness of my position, for when the horse stopped suddenly I should have fallen off had it not been for the belt. As it was, I slipped helplessly from the beast's back when Mr Fraser unfastened the strap, and should have fell to the ground if Mr Watts had not catched me.

"Come, madam, keep your heart up," says the good gentleman. "We have made huge progress, and met with the most marvellous good luck throughout."

"How, sir?" I asked him.

"Why, we have encountered no enemy nor wild beast, there's light enough to see our way, and the rains en't begun, as they might well be, since last year they commenced so late. Figure to yourself what our flight would have been with rain falling, and the entire country a swamp!"

"Come, my dear, you must rest while we halt here," says Mr Fraser, while I endeavoured with my confused brain to picture the situation suggested by Mr Watts, and I resigned the attempt thankfully, lying down on the cloak my husband had spread for me on the ground, and suffering him to cover me with another. I must have fallen asleep immediately, for I dreamed that Mr Fraser came and looked at me very earnestly, but without speaking, and then went away, and waking, I found that he was gone. In the obscurity of the grove in which we were, I could discern the figures of Mr Watts and Dr Dacre, wrapped in their cloaks and stretched upon the ground; at a little distance were the *syces*, crouched upon their heels close to the horses, and Mirza Shaw, with his scymitar drawn, stood guarding his master with the most extreme vigilance, but my spouse and Mr Ranger were not to be seen.

"Where's Mr Fraser?" I cried out to the Tartar, sitting up in my place, but it was Dr Dacre that answered me.

"Why, madam, your spouse believed you asleep. He's but this moment gone forward with Mr Ranger to ascertain our position. There was some talk of a force of the Nabob's horse encamped in the village ahead of us, and blocking our way to the river, and Mirza Shaw has wounded his foot with a thorn——"

"But you've sent him into the midst of the enemy? Sure they'll murder him!" I cried, but Mr Watts, waking, silenced me roughly.

"Be quiet, madam, and pray let other people rest if you won't do it yourself. Mr Fraser's in no such terrible danger. If he's the wise man I fancy him, the enemy will have no chance so much as to catch sight of him."

Mr Watts fell asleep again at once, but I could not follow his example. The desire for sleep, which had tormented me so long, seemed to have left me, and a hundred horrid visions took its place. I saw Mr Fraser discovered, tracked, pursued, seized, tortured, slain, in all the circumstances that my apprehensive mind could suggest, and even the most ordinary sound that reached me was the signal to start a fresh train of horrors. I was a prey to the most cruel, the most poignant anxiety, and at the same moment to the liveliest remorse, and this because I had not awaked when Mr Fraser came and regarded me, thus losing what I persuaded myself was his last farewell. The shocking selfishness, which had caused me a year ago to destroy my dear Captain Colquhoun in obtaining for me the water that cost him his life, I saw repeated now in the insensibility I had shown to the presence of the person to whom I owe everything, and my heart was almost broken with the thought of such unparalleled ingratitude. Trembling all over with apprehension, I sat leaning against a tree, listening for a distant shot or shout that might confirm my worst fears. Presently Mirza Shaw, catching sight of me, limped across the glade to recommend me in a low voice to lie down.

"Is it near morning yet?" I asked him.

"Why, no, Beebee; only a little past midnight."

"But sure we must have been riding a dozen hours at least."

"Less than six, Beebee."

"Why, how long is it then since Mr Fraser started?"

"Twenty minutes, Beebee."

"But that's not possible. I have been listening for him for hours."

"Not so, Beebee. He has scarce had time to reach the village yet, much less to return to us. Beebee Fraser need not fear for him."

This was excessively consoling, questionless, but it failed to calm my fears, and I sat and shuddered until there was a rustling of the bushes, and the two missing gentlemen crept back safe into our midst. Mr Watts, awake at once, questioned them eagerly, and they told him they had reached the village, which is named Augadeep, and found the Nabob's force encamped on both sides of the road, but all fast asleep and without a single sentinel, after the manner of the Indians in war, so that they believed it possible to ride straight through them undiscovered, and reach the river on the further side.

"And so we will!" cried Mr Watts. "Wake up, doctor. The Retreat of the Ten Thousand will be naught to ours. Straight through the enemy's camp!"

The *syces* began saddling the horses again immediately, Dr Dacre arose with a good deal of sadness, and unwound himself from his cloak, Mirza Shaw put up his sword and led up Mr Watts' beast for him to mount, and Mr Fraser approached softly the spot where I was, intending to awake me gently.

"What, my dear, awake? and I recommended you to rest!" he cried.

"Excellent, sir!" cried Mr Watts. "You might have been married ten years, Mr Fraser."

"Save that then he would scarce have looked for his lady to obey him, sir," says Mr Ranger; but I paid no heed to their raillery.

"Oh, dear sir," I cried, throwing myself into Mr Fraser's arms, "how could I sleep when I imagined each instant that you was fallen into the enemy's hands?" and the remembrance of my frightful imaginations overpowering me, I burst into a passion of tears and sobs, which I endeavoured in vain to check.

"My dearest creature," said Mr Fraser at last, "these transports will endanger all our lives if you don't moderate 'em. Come, that's my brave girl! But you en't fit to ride any further to-night."

"Pray, Mr Fraser, do you purpose settling down for life in this patch of *jungul*?" cried Mr Watts, who was waiting impatiently. "No man can sympathise more heartily with your lady than I do, but delay will mean her destruction as well as ours."

Mr Fraser made no further protestation, but when Mr Ranger approached to assist me to mount, he gave him a sign, and together they lifted me to the saddle before my husband, so that he could hold me with his left arm, and still have his right at liberty. Mr Watts murmured a little, representing that in the event of a fight Mr Fraser would find himself sorely encumbered, but he was good-humoured enough, and we rode out of the wood. Before we had gone very far, Mr Ranger declared that we were approaching Augadeep, and the speed of the horses was checked. The road was happily deep in dust, so that there was no sound made, and we approached the village in dead silence, the ashes of expiring watch-fires alone showing where the Nabob's troops were encamped. And now I am about to record a confession that will force my Amelia to despise me, but not more heartily than I despise myself. As we passed between the watch-fires to right and to left, there came upon me the most horrid temptation imaginable to shriek aloud. I tried to reason with myself, in vain; I felt that I must scream, although I knew that all our lives would be the forfeit. Sure it was a heavenly inspiration that saved me, for I seized my handkerchief and stuffed it into my mouth with all my strength. "At least there'll be no sound now, even if I should scream," I said to myself, and then I must have swooned, for I knew no more until I found myself laid flat on a pile of cloaks in a small boat, with Mr Fraser endeavouring to force some spirit between my teeth. I wondered in a foolish sort of style whether he would succeed in getting it down, but never thought of assisting him in any way, even by opening my mouth, until he ceased his efforts and turned with a hopeless air to Mr Watts, who, with a pistol in one hand and t'other on his sword, was watching the black men that were rowing.

"'Tis too late, sir!" said Mr Fraser, heavily.

"What's too late, sir?" I asked him, finding my tongue all of a sudden, and Mr Watts broke into a loud laugh, which he sought anxiously to check.

"Why, the dram, madam. Here has your spouse been tearing his hair and vowing you was dead, and he your murderer. Pray why did you try to throttle yourself? That had more the air of suicide."

"I—I was afraid of crying out, sir. But where are we, and where are all the rest?"

"Why, madam, we are rowing down the Cossimbuzar river, as fast as these rascally *dandies* will take us. The Padra and Mr Ranger are in another boat, but since we could find no more than two, and there was no room for the horses, Mirza Shaw refused to abandon his nag, and preferring the beast to his master, remained behind with the *syces*, undertaking to save the whole caravan. Pray, Mr Fraser, keep an eye on that *mangee* there. I doubt he's purposing to run us aground."

"Now, my dearest life, I must have you try to sleep," said my kind spouse, making at the same time a threatening motion towards the helmsman, as Mr Watts desired. "My good girl won't be alarmed, knowing her Fraser is close at hand?"

"Why, no, dear sir," said I, and composed myself to sleep upon the cloaks, as though this strange situation were the most natural thing in the world. It seemed I had slept but a moment, when I was awaked with a great sound of cheering and huzzaing, and saw that we were arrived at a point where two rivers met, and off which there were lying several large boats. On board of these boats was a number of Europeans (whom I judged to be soldiers by the clothes they had hastily catched up), and these were all testifying their delight in seeing us by excessive shouts of joy. It needed no telling that we had met with the guard sent by Colonel Clive to greet us and bring us to the army, and there was little delay in rewarding the Indian boatmen who had done us such good service against their wills, and sending them about their business, while we were taken on board the Colonel's boats. My Amelia will set me down as a sad lazy creature, but I'll confess to her honestly that no sooner had I laid myself down in a cabin than I fell asleep again, and slept—how long does she imagine?—why, my dear, for twelve hours! Your idle girl never woke once until the boats reached Culnah at three o'clock in the afternoon, and I can quite believe she would have slumbered again after that but for the agitating news that reached her. Mr Watts has since rallied me more than once upon this feat, and says there's not a European in India but would gladly purchase the secret of sleeping so well in the hot weather, though I doubt they would scarce choose to earn their slumber by riding from Moidapore to Augadeep. But what, you'll ask, was the agitating news that I mentioned?

Why, my dear, while I was eating some breakfast at four in the afternoon on board the boat, in comes Mr Fraser, who had gone on shore with Mr Watts to pay his respects to Colonel Clive, with an air of huge triumph.

"The Colonel made particular enquiry how you did, my dearest life, and desired his compliments to you. He also requested the honour of your company at his table to supper this evening if you feel sufficiently restored."

"Oh, dear sir—sup with Colonel Clive! But I have no gown."

"Why, madam, where's that thin white thing you wore at Moidapore?"

"That muslin? 'Tis a simple rag, sir, nothing more, and all in the most frightful creases."

"'Twill but set off my lovely girl's face all the better. Come, dear madam, you wouldn't have me disoblige the Colonel? He showed me extraordinary kindness before I set out on my quest for my lost mistress, and I would wish him to see her now she's found."

"Oh, if you desire it particularly, dear sir——" Did you ever know a young woman more sweetly obliging than your Sylvia, Amelia? How otherwise could she have consented to appear at the table of the first general of the age in a horrid limp muslin gown without a hoop, made by her own hands, and a cap hastily fashioned (yes, my dear, I'll own it) out of one of her spouse's pocket-handkerchiefs? But there was no other ladies present, so that at least no comparisons could be drawn to her disadvantage, and the gentlemen were all in undress, as was, indeed, only proper at an entertainment held in a captured town in the middle of a campaign. Distinguished with the most flattering civilities by Colonel Clive, who came himself to the gate of his quarters to hand her out of her palanqueen, and set her at his right hand during the meal, won't you give your girl some credit, Amelia, that her head was not turned? But I must not leave my dear friend in ignorance of one fact that should surely have prevented the lightest mind from being uplifted by the elegant kindness of the Colonel. Among the officers and others that were invited, and whom Colonel Clive presented to me, were Mr le Beaume, now a captain in the Company's army, and Mr Fisherton, who is advanced to be the Colonel's secretary. When you remember, Amelia, the scenes in which I last beheld these two gentlemen, Captain le Beaume carried wounded into Fort William after the batteries had been abandoned, and Mr Fisherton in that place of horror, the Black Hole itself, will you wonder that they both approached me without a word, and that their feelings came near to overcome them when they touched my hand? Those who stood round were sensibly affected, and I needed but a little encouragement to give way to the melancholy recollections that thronged upon me. This the Colonel had not observed, for he was searching among those present for one whom he did not appear to find.

"Where's Captain Grant?" he said at last. "I hoped to present all your old friends to you, madam, and you must have been well acquainted with him."

"Here, sir, at the lady's service," said a gentleman wearing the dress of Adlercron's Regiment.

"No, not you, Major," says the Colonel. "'Twas Captain Alexander Grant of the Bengall Service I was seeking, an old acquaintance of Mrs Fraser's."

"The Captain sent his most humble apologies, sir, but he's indisposed this evening," says Mr Fisherton, and his eyes chanced to meet mine. You know in what posture I saw Captain Grant last, Amelia. Perhaps it en't to be wondered at that he should shrink from meeting the woman whom, in his eagerness for his own safety, he had refused to turn back to save. Something of this I think Colonel Clive must have read in our faces, for he muttered angrily to himself as though he had remembered something suddenly, and brought forward another gentleman, whom I recollect seeing once or twice at Calcutta, although he belonged to the Cossimbuzar factory.

"Mr Hastings, madam," said the Colonel. "Like Mr Fraser he's a new-married man,[03] but unhappily he han't had the foresight to bring his lady with him on this campaign, when Mrs Fraser and she might have exchanged confidences and allayed each other's fears."

Mr Hastings replying very genteelly that he hoped before long to have the honour of making his wife acquainted with Mrs Fraser, we went to supper, I being placed, as I said, on Mr Clive's right, with Dr Dacre on t'other side. The Colonel conversed continually with me in the most agreeable manner, asking me whether I had seen much of the army yet, and what I thought of his *loll pultun*?[04] This is a regiment of Seapoy soldiers which he has clothed and drilled like Europeans, thus giving them a much more martial air than our old *buxerries*, who were dressed after the Indian fashion in the long breeches called *panjammers*,[05] a *cabay* or vest, and a turbant. I told him that I had observed a number of these men as I passed through the place on my way to his quarters, and been much pleased with their air of neatness and discipline, and then, his words recalling to me that old mystery of Misery's and the other servants respecting the *loll addama*, I ventured to inform him with what awe and submissiveness the Indians were watching his progress, counting it to be of little use opposing him.

"I hope Mrs Fraser is so obliging as to share this persuasion of theirs?" said he.

"Why, yes, sir. How could I look to see a cause so good as ours permitted to suffer defeat at the hands of such a wretch as the Nabob?"

"Pray, madam, is it the case in your experience that Providence always awards the victory to the most deserving side?"

"Alas, sir, no! But I can't bring myself to believe that so great a commander as Colonel Clive would have been brought to Bengall merely to add another trophy to the blood-stained laurels of Surajah Dowlah."

"I thank you, madam, for the thought, which comes in pat enough with one that has occurred to me before. There was a young fellow of my acquaintance once that was sunk to the lowest depths of melancholy. He was poor and proud and in debt, and had not a friend that he could call his own, for besides being of a sad unsociable temper, there was a petulant roughness about him that alienated his acquaintances and outraged his superiors. The severities of this climate, added to his misfortunes, so affected the lad that he resolved to put an end to his existence. There was a loaded pistol at hand, and he placed the muzzle to his head, and pulled the trigger. The piece missed fire, but he was not to be put off. After examining the condition of the charge, he pulled the trigger a second time. Again it missed, and the youth, wondering at this unaccountable failure, determined that he must be intended for some great work, and laid aside the thought of self-destruction. I was that young fellow, madam, and it has seemed to me more than once that the liberation of Bengall may be the task I was destined for."

"Oh, sir, what cause has Britain to thank Heaven that your rash resolve was frustrated!" I cried. "Sure you can't now entertain a doubt of your ultimate success, for which all you have yet achieved is but a preparation?"

"Do you know what are the odds against us, madam? Do you know that this army which is called mine is held together only by the memory of my past successes? One disaster and my officers will recollect that their general was bred a clerk, and failed as a writer, and the Tellinghies will forsake the standard of the man whose luck is gone. For myself, madam, I may say without boasting that I have sufficient courage and patience to retrieve a disaster, if I may but retain the confidence of my friends. But to find myself forsaken by those on whose fidelity I had relied, to meet contempt where I had once inspired respect, and distrust where I looked for loyal confidence, that would be intolerable to me. To renew acquaintance with the miseries of my early Madrass days after having tasted of success and public favour, this I could not support—and the pistol is at hand now as then."

"Oh pray, dear sir, don't tempt Heaven a second time to alter its designs."

"Why, madam, have I not told you that so long as I am sure of my friends I can go on boldly? and I thank Heaven that's the case at present. But how solemn and serious is this discourse for so joyful an occasion! Sure it's very unkind in Mrs Fraser to tempt me into such melancholy recollections and confessions."

"May I venture to ask a favour of you, sir?" I saw Mr Clive desired to change the subject.

"Any favour Mrs Fraser asks is already granted. But perhaps I can guess what it is. You would have leave, madam, for your spouse to quit the army when we advance from hence, and attend you at once to Calcutta—en't that it?"

"Why, no, sir, I was about to entreat you to find some situation for Mr Fraser in which he may contrive to take part in the battle you expect."

"What, madam! tired of him already?" cried the Colonel; but seeing me covered with confusion and my eyes filled with tears at this unkind remark, he testified extreme penitence, and begged me to explain my desire more fully.

"Indeed, sir, I can't help being sensible that Mr Fraser lost his share in the taking of Chandernagore by his concern for my safety, which detained him at Muxadavad, and I would not be the cause of depriving him of this also."

"Why, madam, I thought there was but one woman in the world, and she my own wife, that would extend any sympathy to the concern a man has in his calling, but now I see there's another. I'll promise you to find a post for your spouse, if I have to make him Lord High Admiral of my fleet of rowboats."

"But, sir, you've only heard half my request. You'll permit me to accompany him?"

"Oho, madam, is that it? A battlefield's no place for women."

"Oh pray, dear sir, don't send me away from him. Picture the miserable apprehensions I should be under for his safety. Indeed I'll give no trouble."

"Will you be contented to remain with the sick and the baggage when the army marches out to fight, madam? Otherwise I'll have none of you."

"Oh yes, sir, provided you won't leave me too far behind."

"Madam, I'm not to be conditioned with by non-combatants. If I see too much of you, I'll send you down the river again under a guard. Our good Mr Watts is minded to accompany the army[06] and see the coping-stone set on his labours for the liberation of Bengall, and you'll be under his orders. Mr Fraser, I need volunteers for the artillery, sir, since I was forced to leave Lieutenant Hay and near all his seamen to garrison Chandernagore. What do you say to giving us the advantage of your sea-experience? Your lady tells me she won't let you out of her sight, but I hope we may be able to oblige her without losing your services."

"Indeed, sir, I'll be only too much honoured in being permitted to place myself at Colonel Clive's disposal." Mr Fraser's face was so full of delight, Amelia, that I felt rewarded for my sacrifice. After all, one must do one's best to oblige a man that's so ready to oblige you, and at least I shan't be parted from him.

This letter is frightfully long, Amelia. I wrote a good piece of it at Culnah, where the army remained until the 16th, and went on with it at Pultee, where we halted that night and part of the next day, while Major Coote with a portion of the army went forward to receive the surrender of the fortress of Cutwah, which had been promised by the governor of the place, although he thought it expedient to make some slight show of resistance. After a little firing the garrison retreated, leaving Cutwah, with a vast quantity of grain and considerable military stores, to us, and none too soon, for yesterday the rains began, and the army, who had spent the night in their tents, were forced to seek refuge in the houses of the town. I am finishing my letter in a commodious apartment of the fortress, overlooking the river Agey,[07] while all around preparations are making for the next advance. On the day of our reaching Culnah, Mr Watts despatched a messenger to our ally Meer Jaffier informing him of his safety and of the approach of the army, while almost at the same moment there arrived from this nobleman an Armenian, called Cojah Petroos by the Europeans and by the Moors Aga Bedross, to entreat Colonel Clive to hasten his advance. (I must not omit to say that Mr Watts' servant, Mirza Shaw, arrived safe on the 15th, with the *syces* and all the horses, which, having contrived to find another boat, they had swum across the river, holding them with the bridles lengthened.) From Muxadavad the Colonel hears that on learning of Mr Watts' evasion the Nabob exhibited the most abject terror, and breaking off the attack he was about to make on Meer Jaffier's castle, humbled himself so far as to seek a reconciliation with him, and received his oath of allegiance, which has caused some apprehension here. Elated with this triumph, Surajah Dowlah has wrote in terms of defiance to the Colonel, and though hindered by a mutiny of his troops, which was only appeased by the distributing among them a vast sum of money, is about taking up his ancient position at Placis,[08] a spot where he has a hunting-lodge, some fifteen miles from here. He has summoned Mons. Law and the other fugitive French to join him from Bogglypore, and Sinzaun and the rest of his countrymen that are with him already have shown the first taste of their quality by plundering and burning the Cossimbuzar factory in their rage at Mr Watts' escape. I write on June the 20th. What happened a year ago this day I need not remind my Amelia, but sure it's strange enough that the avenging of Calcutta should arrive at a time so closely joined with its fall.

CHAPTER XXI.
SHOWING HOW CALCUTTA WAS AVENGED.

CUTWAH, *June ye* 23*rd.*

Once more, my dear, I am left solitary, and as of old turn to my Amelia for consolation. My dear Mr Fraser quitted me early yesterday morning, and proceeded to Placis with Colonel Clive and the army, and here in the fort at Cutwah there remains a meagre company, awaiting with an incredible eagerness and anxiety every morsel of intelligence that may reach them. Nor is this apprehension excessive in view of the situation. We Britons, as my Amelia knows, are said to be too prone to undervalue our enemy, and that this is so is questionless Colonel Clive's opinion, although he himself offers no example of the fault. He has no fear, I heard him say two days ago, for a favourable result of the approaching battle, if every man of his force do his duty and his Indian allies keep their promises, but a single piece of carelessness or treachery may prove the ruin, not only of the army, but of the entire British cause in this region of the world. With another commander this unflattering estimate of the future might be expected to damp the spirits of the soldiers, but so great is their confidence in Mr Clive that they are sensible of no resentment even for his implied doubt of them, and are resolved to support him to the utmost of their power. The Indian allies are less to be trusted, I fear. Immediately after I closed my letter to you on Monday there arrived from Muxadavad the messenger despatched by Mr Watts from Culnah to Meer Jaffier, declaring that he had been received with distinction by that nobleman in private and assured of his fidelity, but that on the entrance of some intimates of the Nabob's, Meer Jaffier changed his tone immediately, while his son Meerham threatened to have the messenger put to death for a spy, uttering the most extravagant menaces against the English should they venture to advance towards the city. This unaccountable behaviour, coupled with the ambiguous epistles brought by Meer Jaffier's own messengers, startled Colonel Clive and induced him to waver in his design of advancing, insomuch that on Tuesday he summoned a council of war (the first, so Mr Fisherton tells me, that he has ever held) to determine whether to go forward against the enemy at once, or to strengthen this fortress of Cutwah and maintain ourselves here until the rains are over. To the great scandal of all the officers, the Colonel, instead of taking the opinion of the youngest gentleman first, and so through all the members until his own turn came as president, began by giving his own vote for delay, in which he was followed by the majority, although Major Coote and a few others spoke stoutly on the other side, the Major declaring with great warmth that he would rather abandon Cutwah and retire at once to Calcutta than give the Nabob the triumph of shutting up our army here. However, the council broke up, after doing nothing but invite the Raja of Burraduan to join the army with any reinforcements he could command, and the officers dispersed with the most dissatisfied air imaginable. The Colonel, whose ordinary resolved aspect was changed for a dejected and uncertain look, shunned the company of the other gentlemen, and as I sat at my window in the tower which has been assigned to us for an abode, I saw him wander away into a grove of trees near. He must have spent over half an hour in solitude, when up comes Mr Watts to me and demands to know whether I had perceived which way the Colonel went. After directing him, I ventured to hope that he was the bearer of good news.

"Why, yes, madam," said he. "Here's a *cossid* just come in with a message sent from Meer Jaffier by word of mouth, and containing very satisfactory assurances. It seems he's honest after all."

"Pray Heaven you may get the Colonel to believe it, sir."

"Indeed, madam, you can't desire it more than I, since my credit hangs on Meer Jaffier's honesty. I know Mr Clive would have chose to advance had he been acting alone, but our valiant Calcutta gentlemen, and the excellent Quaker in especial, have worked hard to imbue him with their own fears, so that he can't resolve to risque a second destruction of the factory. Yet he's excessive uneasy to find himself hanging back for the first time in his life, and I would lay a *lack* of rupees that he's seeking some good argument that would justify him in going forward. I hope to supply him with it."

And Mr Watts departed to seek the Colonel, finding him, as we learned afterwards, seated under a tree, and plunged in a gloomy meditation. What arguments were used I don't know, but presently, watching eagerly from my window, I saw the two gentlemen returning in company, both wearing a determined and confident air, and Colonel Clive's eyes, which are the keenest I have ever seen, full of the most unbending resolution. Meeting Major Coote, the Colonel exchanged a few words with him, and no long time after Mr Fraser came leaping up the stairs to my room to tell me that the army was to commence its advance at daybreak on the morrow.[01]

"And am I to ride, sir?" I asked him; "or will it be possible to proceed by boat?"

Mr Fraser turned his face aside. "Why, my dearest life," he said, "considering this frightful weather and the danger from the enemy, I fear——"

"Oh, dear sir, you would not leave me behind?" I cried. "Sure the Colonel promised——"

"But my beloved girl won't press that promise to an extreme when she knows how much it would add to her Fraser's anxiety? She'll do him the favour to believe that 'tis only his concern for her makes him entreat her to remain here under good Dr Dacre's care, and I think she'll oblige him by consenting to stay behind."

The tears were in my eyes. "Dear sir, how could I bring myself to refuse a request which you are good enough to express in such a charming style?"

"Nay, dearest madam, your complaisance in gratifying me would make me ashamed to ask a favour if I did not know that it caused you a pleasure to grant it," said Mr Fraser, but perceiving that what he had said might be taken in two different styles, he came and embraced me kindly, begging me with the utmost earnestness to remain behind at Cutwah, where the sick were to be left under a small guard, and not to insist upon exposing myself in the neighbourhood of the battle. I could not refuse to oblige him, having once consented, and that's the reason, Amelia, why I am writing to you from my tower in the fortress, instead of accompanying my spouse to the field.

At sunrise yesterday the army began crossing the river, but the transit was not accomplished until four in the afternoon. By this time Colonel Clive had received another reassuring letter from Meer Jaffier, stating that the Nabob was encamped with his army at a village called Muncarra, some little way to the north of Placis, and suggesting that the Colonel should march thither to attack him. The march was at once commenced, the boats carrying the camp equipage being towed against the stream, and the troops making their way along the bank, although, thanks to the inundation caused by the heavy rain, they were forced to plod through water up to their waists. The rain fell continuously almost the whole of the day, driving me from my station at the top of my tower, whence I had hoped to view a great part of the march, since it commands a vast extent of country, and I passed the weary hours in unravelling lint and sewing bandages for the surgeon here, although the damp weather has made my needles and scissors almost useless with rust. The need I felt of occupying my mind made me work so prodigiously hard that when I asked the doctor this morning whether he had anything more for me to do, he laughed, saying that he had already sufficient dressings to bandage the whole army from head to foot, and thus rejected, I fell back naturally into my old habit of making my Amelia the depositary of my anxieties. Indeed, my dear, I don't know what can be better, in such a situation as mine, than a faithful friend like yourself, unless it be the practice I have always pursued of writing to her constantly.

But my dear girl must not imagine that I have been left to pine, uncheered by any scrap of news, since daybreak yesterday. My dear Mr Fraser was so good as to despatch me a billet this morning, wrote with infinite difficulty in the most unpropitious circumstances. Reassuring my anxious mind by declaring that he has suffered no inconvenience from the discomforts of the march, he says that a halt was called soon after midnight in a grove of mango-trees close to the Nabob's seat of Placis, and that in this grove the troops encamped in the greatest comfort imaginable. (I fear this is only said to console me, Amelia, for you must remember the rain and the floods.) The sound of drums and other barbaric instruments was clearly to be heard from the enemy's camp a mile distant (for on hearing of the Colonel's advance from Cutwah, Surajah Dowlah had at once quitted Muncarra and marched to confront him), but this served rather to soothe than to disturb the grateful slumbers of our wearied army.

At daybreak the Nabob's army moved out from its entrenchments and disposed itself in the form of a crescent, as though designing to enclose our troops altogether, with the aid of the river, while Meer Sinzaun (oh, my dear, think what it is to me to hear that dreadful name again!) with four guns and his forty vagabond Frenchmen took post on the lofty banks of earth surrounding a tank that commanded the mango-grove. In order to reply to their fire, Colonel Clive posted two hovitzes[02] and two field-pieces at some brick-kilns in advance of the grove, and lest the enemy should imagine him alarmed by their approach, brought his army out of its shelter, and drew it up in order of battle, his left resting on the Nabob's hunting-lodge. The centre of the line was occupied by the European troops in four divisions, next came three field-pieces on either flank, Mr Fraser being in charge of one of those on the right, and at each extremity of the line a body of Seapoys. The battle began by the Frenchmen's discharging one of their cannons, which did some damage, and our artillery replying, the action became general, although we were at a huge disadvantage owing to the lightness of our guns. Having endured a heavy cannonade for about half an hour, and finding his losses considerable, the Colonel retired his troops again into the grove, leaving a small detachment at the brick-kilns and another at Placis House, and 'twas at this moment of disappointment and mortification that Mr Fraser wrote his letter to me. Having with the rest of the officers of the train besieged the Colonel in vain for permission to carry all the guns forward to the advanced posts, and finding himself compelled to crouch down among the troops behind a bank to avoid the enemy's fire, my spouse sought to mitigate his impatience by scribbling in pencil the history of the morning, which he had leave to despatch about half-past nine by a messenger that Mr Watts was sending back to Cutwah. The brilliancy of the spectacle presented by the enemy seems to have affected Mr Fraser a little disagreeably when compared with the travel-stained and wretched aspect of our own men, for he remarks somewhat bitterly on the magnificent display of elephants all covered with scarlet cloth and embroidery, of horsemen with drawn swords glistering in the sun, of heavy cannons drawn by vast trains of oxen, and of countless standards waving in the breeze—all this show being employed by Surajah Dowlah to conceal the badness of his cause. The dear gentleman closed the letter in somewhat better spirits, however, for our retreat having animated the enemy to an extreme degree of vivacity, they were advancing their guns with a great air of boldness, and Colonel Clive had just given orders for holes to be made in the banks of earth surrounding the grove, through which our field-pieces might be fired.

There, Amelia! 'Tis now two in the afternoon, and this pencilled chitt, which reached me about an hour back, contains the latest intelligence we possess. All the morning I have spent at the top of the tower, with every man of our sick garrison that was strong enough to climb so high, watching for messengers, and listening to the distant sound of cannon brought to us on the wind. At noon the rain began again, and drove me indoors and to my writing, and so far as we can discern, forced the cannonade almost entirely to cease. I had no notion that a battle took so long to fight, had you, Amelia? I have wrote this letter with all the minuteness possible, for the sake of filling up the time; how, I wonder, shall I spend the weary hours still before me, until this battle, which is to decide the fate of Bengall, if not of India (not to speak of your poor girl and her beloved Fraser) be ended? Happily the rain is almost ceased again, and Dr Dacre, who has established himself as a vigilant guardian over me, gives me hope of being allowed once more on my watch-tower.

Half-past six o'clock.

Joy, Amelia! we are victorious. Colonel Clive has justified the confidence of his troops rather than his own misgivings, and Calcutta is avenged upon the cruel barbarian who destroyed her a year ago. A breathless messenger, mounted upon a horse that he had ridden almost to death, arrived a few minutes back and brought us the news, although his errand was to demand the despatch of certain stores immediately to the surgeons accompanying the army. It appears that the cannonade begun by our guns in the morning after Mr Fraser closed his letter to me, was successful in keeping off the enemy, and that Meer Modin,[03] one of the Nabob's generals, and the only one among 'em that was truly faithful to him, was slain. The rain that commenced about noon spoiled the enemy's powder, while ours was kept under shelter and dry, and the semicircle of Moorish troops was observed to be retiring within the entrenchments where they had passed the night. Even before this, however, Surajah Dowlah, panic-stricken by his fears and by the death of Meer Modin, had mounted a swift camel, and forsaking his army, fled to Muxadavad. It had been agreed between Colonel Clive and his officers that no advance against the Nabob's camp should be made until night; but seeing the Frenchmen isolated at their tank, Major Kilpatrick could not resist pushing forward to dislodge them, without any orders from the Colonel, who was snatching a brief repose in the hunting-lodge. On being informed of the movement, Colonel Clive hastened out in much displeasure, and reproved the officer smartly for his independent action; but on receiving an apology from him, sent him back to the grove to fetch up the rest of the troops, and placed himself at the head of the detachment, with the determination to bring matters at once to an issue, and not encourage the enemy by a second retreat. Seeing the resolution with which the English advanced, Sinzaun withdrew his force from the tank, and planted his cannon in a redoubt at the corner of the Nabob's entrenchment, in readiness for the final assault.

All this time, says the messenger, our commander's spirits had been perturbed by the perplexing behaviour of a portion of the enemy's troops, which, being under the orders of Meer Jaffier and Yar Cawn Latty, should, in accordance with the engagements entered into by those chiefs, have changed sides during the battle, a manœuvre for which the amplest opportunity was offered by their position in that part of the half-circle nearest our posts and furthest from the Nabob's entrenchments. Far from taking this step, however, Meer Jaffier, whether moved by timidity or by the affecting entreaties addressed to him by the despairing Surajah Dowlah, did not even embrace the chance afforded him by the retreat of the rest of the army to separate himself from it, but advanced his troops with such a menacing air against our position in the grove that if his designs were amicable no one could have credited it, and a force was detached to hold him in check. Meanwhile Colonel Clive, having reached the tank abandoned by Sinzaun, planted his guns on its banks, and began a brisk cannonade on the entrenchment, following this up by an advance to a second tank and a piece of rising ground nearer still. The fire was replied to by Sinzaun's field-pieces and a strong force of matchlockmen, the cavalry also offering several times to charge, but being drove back in disorder by our guns. At last the Colonel, perceiving that Meer Jaffier's troops were moving off the field without attempting to support those in the entrenchments, recognised that he was secure from an attack in the rear, and prepared for the concluding effort. A strong detachment was sent forward from either flank to attack Sinzaun's redoubt and a hillock near it, the main body following more slowly as a support. The hillock was gained without a shot fired, and the redoubt abandoned by Sinzaun with only a little fighting, our forces entering it at five o'clock precisely. The exact issue of these last movements our informant was unable to describe to us, since he had been despatched by the surgeons to bring up the additional stores before the final attack was made, and only beheld it from a distance, checking his horse for a moment that he might see its success, and bring the news of the victory to us at Cutwah. Nor was he able, again, to furnish us particulars of the safety of any special person, save that he had seen Mr Fraser working his gun unhurt when he quitted the tank, although there were more killed and wounded in that situation than during all the rest of the day. It was commonly reported, said the man, that Colonel Clive would press on with his troops immediately the battle was concluded to the village of Doudpaur,[04] where he had promised to meet Meer Jaffier, so that I must resign myself, I suppose, to a further separation from my dear Mr Fraser; but I can support that with more equanimity, since I am tolerably assured of his safety.

CUTWAH, *June ye 24th.*

Alas, my Amelia! I began to rejoice, or at least to feel satisfied, too soon. Having finished writing to my dear girl, I descended to the lowest room of the tower, intending to join Dr Dacre at supper, but even as I entered the apartment the good divine stood forward as though to turn me back, and I saw that he was talking with a man in the dress of a common soldier. I could not doubt what was the matter.

"You're come to tell me Mr Fraser is hurt?" I said to the soldier.

"Why, no, madam," said he, and it seemed to me that I had heard his voice before at some very frightful moment of my life. "I was bid to bring you his honour's loving duty, and to tell you as how there wasn't truly nothing wrong with him."

I turned to Dr Dacre. "Oh pray, dear sir, don't torment me. What is happened?"

"Indeed, madam, there's so little happened that I had hoped to keep it from you until morning. Our good Mr Fraser has received a bullet through the thigh, but the bone en't injured, and save for the loss of blood he'll suffer little inconvenience."

"But I must go to him, sir. You'll help me to start immediately?"

"What, madam?" It was the surgeon left in charge of the sick here who came in behind me. "Go to your spouse to-night? and I had believed you a woman of sense! Pray what do you think you could do for him? Nothing but vex his mind and tease his doctors, I'll assure you. He'll come down in the boats to-morrow, and if I find you are to be trusted I'll let you have him to nurse."

"I'll assure you, sir, whatever you may find, you won't keep me from Mr Fraser's side!" I cried, dashing away my tears.

"Pray, madam, look at me," says the surgeon, gruffly. "Have I the air of being a man of my word, or not? 'Twill hang upon your behaviour whether I suffer you to approach your spouse. Why, you're shedding tears, madam! Was you purposing to weep over Mr Fraser? He don't want to be wept over, but to be kept quiet and cheerful, and that signifies that you'll take a good rest to-night, and eat your meals in a proper style, for if you don't, I'll have your good man brought into hospital and you shan't come near him. Remember, I must have your word for it in the morning that my prescription has been followed."

The surgeon went out, leaving me speechless by reason of his coarse and unfeeling language, and Dr Dacre, perceiving my agitation, said with great gentleness--

"Come, madam, our friend's counsel is sound enough, if rough. If you'll take your supper, this honest fellow here will join us, and tell us something of the manner in which Mr Fraser met his wound."

"Aye, madam," said the soldier, seeing me look eagerly at him, "I was by his honour's side all day at his six-pounder, first in the grove and then at the tank, and when he got leave to join the storming party I followed him again. We was climbing over the front of the redoubt before the Frenchies scuttled out at the back, and one on 'em, an ugly, black-looking fellow, stood his ground and called out something in French to his honour, who sprang forward in a fury to shoot him, but as he fired, a musket-ball passed through his leg, and his pistol went off as he fell, without doing any harm to the Mounseer. The fellow laughed, and turned to walk off, as cool as you please, but Mr Fraser catched hold of me (I was run to lift him up, as you may guess, madam) and cried out, 'Kill him, Jones! kill the villain that dares to slander my wife. 'Tis Sinzaun himself, the renegado!' There was a man of Adlercron's fell dead just beside me, and I catched up his piece and charged it, and fired twice at the villain, but missed him both times. His honour, seeing me stamp with rage, guessed how 'twas, and presently, 'Take this, Jones,' says he. 'Questionless the wretch bears a charmed life.' 'Twas a silver button cut from his coat that he held out to me, and I charged the piece with it instead of a bullet—for you know, madam, as how a silver bullet is good against all sorts of wicked charms. Sure enough it brought him down, and I cried out to his honour that he was done for. 'Well done!' says he, and faints away, and I carried him back to the doctors. But when I went to look for the villain's body, I found as how the other Mounseers had carried it off, so as I can't be certain he was dead, but I do believe it, madam."

"I know you now," I cried. "Sure you're Captain Colquhoun's sergeant!"

"Yes, madam, and proud to do a service to the Captain's cousin and his lady."

"Can I say better of you than that you're worthy of your Captain, Sergeant Jones? Though you don't mention it, I can't doubt but you saved Mr Fraser's life by carrying him so promptly to the surgeons."

"Come, my dear madam," says Dr Dacre; "instead of exchanging compliments with this worthy man, why not give him some supper and join him in the meal? That will refresh him and sustain you."

To please the good divine I consented to sit down to the table, but you'll guess that I could scarce swallow a morsel, although the sergeant made an excellent supper, offering profuse apologies for what he fancied his unfeeling behaviour, which indeed I could well pardon, since after fighting all day he had obtained leave to ride fifteen miles to apprise me of my dear Mr Fraser's situation. As soon as the meal was over I excused myself, and returning to my own chamber, did my best, after offering for my husband's recovery the most earnest supplications that gratitude and affection could suggest, to put in practice the second part of the surgeon's prescription. But a person of my Amelia's sensibility won't be surprised to hear that my sleep was perpetually broken with fancied alarms, and that I was haunted with the image of Mr Fraser lying prostrate and bathed in blood, and dying at a distance from me.

The morning brought with it something more of cheerfulness, and having satisfied the surgeon of my earnest endeavours to obey his commands, he was so obliging as to consent to "turn my spouse over to me" (that was his odd phrase) for nursing, and to add that if I would but keep a smiling face he would be better off than in the hospital. The boats arrived about eleven o'clock, and by taking advantage of an interval of fine weather the wounded were brought on shore in comparative comfort. Even to my dearest friend I can't describe my feelings when I beheld Mr Fraser carried in helpless and frightfully pale. The wound had been of such a nature as to produce an extraordinary effusion of blood before the surgeons could attend to him, and he was in a condition of extreme weakness, although his concern for me enabled him to wear a cheerful countenance and rally me on my too evident alarm and apprehension.

"I have a chitt here for you, madam," he said, as soon as I had assisted the surgeon to make him as easy as possible, "and I desire you'll read it in my presence."

I opened the billet he presented to me, and regarded it incredulously, unable to believe that after such a day of fighting, in the interval between deposing one prince and setting up another, Colonel Clive should have found opportunity to write to me.

"The Colonel gave it to me in the evening, when he came to visit the wounded," said Mr Fraser, "saying that he knew you would not regret my losing a share in the plunder of Muxadavad provided you had me again."

"Sure the Colonel's a discerning person," said I, and read the billet aloud:—

"MADAM,—I am fully sensible that by this time Mrs Fraser is heartily repenting her heroic conduct of t'other night, and wishing that she had carried her spouse in her train to an ignominious safety at Calcutta, but will she permit the horrid wretch that has led him into danger one word of excuse? Our victory, madam, I don't hesitate to say, we owe chiefly to the excellent working of our artillery, in which Mr Fraser took a principal part. Without Mr Fraser our fire could not have been so effective; with a less effective fire we could not have won the battle, *ergo*, Mr Fraser's presence with us was necessary to the victory. If Mrs Fraser declare she would have sacrificed her country's interest to her spouse's safety, such a sentiment from her lips will surprise none more than her most obedient, humble servant,

ROBT. CLIVE."

Do you wonder that this letter will be preserved among my most precious treasures, Amelia? Sure I perceive now how it is that Colonel Clive's soldiers cherish so great an affection for him, since he can write with such affable condescension to a silly girl who was playing at being heroical without knowing what the part demanded of her. That he should have cheered my dear Mr Fraser's weakness with kind words of praise for his services is no cause for surprise, but how few persons in his high situation would have cared to dry the tears of an anxious wife!

CUTWAH, *July ye 5th.*

It is now near a fortnight since the battle of Placis, Amelia, and my dear Mr Fraser, I am thankful to say, continues to make good progress. By the way, in looking over these papers of mine, my spouse insists that I have spelt the name of the battle wrong, since the Indians, who should surely know their own language, call it Palassy. But I tell him that Colonel Clive, in dating his billet wrote to me, spelt it Plassy, while Mr Watts, than whom no man knows more of this country, writes it Plaissy, so who shall decide? You'll wonder, perhaps, that I should submit my correspondence with my Amelia even to my husband's eyes, but I think my dear girl won't grudge him the entertainment he is pleased to find in what I write, for which he has made me to-day the prettiest return in the world. Going to fetch out my papers but now, I found among them a copy of verses addressed to myself, and soon perceived that they were of Mr Fraser's own composing. You know, my dear, that in the old days at Calcutta there was many such tributes offered me, but none of them, be sure, ever gave me one-tenth of the pleasure of this one. Not even for my Amelia can I bring myself to copy out this charming piece. Perhaps Mr Fraser may favour me in the future with some verses of a less intimate nature, but these must remain sacred to her for whom they were wrote; happy, thrice happy creature that she is! Will it surprise you, Amelia, to learn that your Sylvia's only fear is lest she be too happy? You must not fancy she can ever forget the horrors of the past year, nor the frightful deaths of the persons she honoured and revered the most; but in her marriage there's nothing wanting to render her felicity absolute. Indeed (I fear you'll laugh at this), all this past fortnight my dear Mr Fraser has shown himself so patient, so uncomplaining, that coupling this behaviour of his with the extraordinary consideration he has displayed towards me since our wedding, I have been terrified lest he should be about to be torn from me, and it gave me the greatest pleasure imaginable when he began to grow restless and irritable, and to chafe at the inaction made necessary by his wound. True, the verses he writ were designed as an atonement for this impatience, but I can't tell you how vastly glad it made me to find my spouse still the Colvin Fraser of old days.

But how I am running on, when I purposed only to tell you of Mr Fisherton's visit last night. Despatched by Colonel Clive from Muxadavad to this place, in order to arrange certain matters, of which more hereafter, he was so obliging as to sup with Mr Fraser and myself, and describe to us the concluding scenes of that tragedy of retribution which the Colonel has just brought to a close. Meeting Meer Jaffier at Doudpaur on the morning after the battle, our victorious commander accepted with the utmost complaisance the halting excuses of his ally for his equivocal behaviour of the day before, and having saluted him as Soubah of Bengall, despatched him at once to secure Muxadavad, whence the wretched Surajah Dowlah succeeded in escaping on his arrival. Meer Jaffier having established himself in the possession of the city, Colonel Clive followed him thither, and attended with a numerous train took up his quarters at the palace of Moraudbaug.[05] The next day he proceeded to the Killa, the whole population of Muxadavad assembling in the streets to gaze upon him with awful respect, and there placed Meer Jaffier upon the *musnet*, complimenting him with a *nuzzer*,[06] or friendly tribute, of a hundred gold *mohrs*, an example which was followed by all the nobles that stood round, in token that they acknowledged him to be the Nabob of the province. The grateful barbarian, desiring to acquit himself of his obligations to the English, waited the next day upon Colonel Clive, and entered into engagements for the punctual payment of the sums which he had already promised in relief of the distressed inhabitants of Calcutta, and as a compliment to the gentlemen of the Council and others, and this scene Mr Fisherton described to us very particularly, saying—

"And now, madam, I am come to a point that can't but be especially grateful to you, since it concerns the punishment of a villain at whose hands you have suffered not a little in time past. On the Colonel's entering the apartment where he designed to receive the Soubah's visit, old Omy Chund, with his usual bustle, pushed forward among his attendants, but not finding himself received with any distinction, withdrew in something of a pet to another part of the hall. You may not be sensible, madam, that this white-haired traitor was expecting to pocket the monstrous sum of twenty *lacks*, which he imagined himself to have secured as the price of his not betraying to Surajah Dowlah our confederacy with Meer Jaffier. The Soubah having entered and been received with the usual courtesies, the business on which he was come went forward, the treaty signed between us and him being produced. When various matters had been arranged, Omy Chund, who had again joined with the party in his eagerness to lay hands on his imagined wealth, cried out with an air of stupefaction, 'But it was a red treaty I saw!' 'Yes, Omy Chund, but this is a white treaty,' says Colonel Clive; then to Mr Scrafton, ''Twill be as well to undeceive the fellow.' Upon this Mr Scrafton, approaching the deluded Gentoo with no particular tenderness, and having in his hand the treaty wrote on red paper, which he supposed secured his claims, said, 'Omy Chund, you have been deceived. This *loll coggedge* is a forgery.' It took some time before Omy Chund could be brought to believe that in the genuine treaty his name did not so much as appear, and that he stood to gain no more by our victory than the other Gentoos of Calcutta; but being at last persuaded of his misfortune (when the resentment and indignation expressed in his countenance bars all description), he appeared suddenly bereft of his intellects, and was assisted out of the room by his attendants, remaining still, as we understand, in the same deplorable situation."

"But, sir," I cried, "you confound me! Is it possible that an assemblage of Britons, of Christians, should have conspired to delude this wretched pagan with a forged instrument? Sure the Colonel—sure Mr Watson—would never——"

"Indeed, madam, the notion was the Colonel's own, and all the other gentlemen attached their names to the red treaty without a spark of hesitation, save only the Admiral; and understanding that, though he demurred to take an active part, he experienced no repugnance to the affair, I took the liberty of adding his signature."

"Pray, sir," cried Mr Fraser with great warmth, "don't try to drag Mr Watson into your plot. If I were not persuaded that he'll disavow with indignation the infamous use you have chose to make of his name, I would throw up my commission sooner than serve under him again."

"Why, sir, he may disavow it and welcome, if he'll support his disavowal by withdrawing also from the benefits secured to him by means of the treaty as the officer in command of the squadron, but he won't."

"Pray, sir, don't judge of a seaman's honour by that of your most high-minded Colonel."

"Sir, I have suffered your injurious language to myself, but when you see fit to attack my generous patron in my presence I must resent it with my——"

"Pray, young gentlemen," said Dr Dacre, "remember there's a lady present, and leave Colonel Clive and the Admiral to settle their own shares of the matter. But come, Mr Fisherton, have you no compunction for your own part in this deception?"

"Not the slightest, sir. Even were I not persuaded that I had obliged the Admiral by relieving his conscience from the odium of signing the false treaty, while he retains the benefits it secured him, I have no pity for Omy Chund. You was not in the Black Hole, sir. Omy Chund contrived to bring about the miserable destruction of Calcutta in revenge for his own fancied wrongs, and 'tis no thanks to him that the happy issue of Mr Watts' negotiations han't been frustrated again and again. He practised for the death of Mr Holwell, and he was the instrument to betray Mrs Fraser into the hands of the vile Sinzaun. Sure the lady's spouse should be the last person in the world to find fault with me for the joy I experience in having assisted to punish the double-dyed traitor."

"Sir," said Mr Fraser gruffly, "I don't dispute the justice of the punishment, but only its means. Believe me, 'twill be a lasting blot on Colonel Clive's fame that he and those with him consented to enrich themselves while depriving their confederate of his share of the spoils."

"Are you pointing at me there, sir?" cried Mr Fisherton.

"Nay, sir, I don't doubt but the 50,000 rupees allotted you were worthily earned otherwise than by your dealings with the treaty."

"However they were earned," says the young gentleman, with something of a sigh, "they'll be well spent. Every *anna* but what I need for the most pressing necessaries shall go home to my family. 'Twill furnish marriage portions for my sisters, place my brothers out in life, and relieve my honoured father of his cruellest anxieties. I'll assure you, gentlemen, that at least the money shall be better employed than if Omy Chund had received it."

And turning resolutely from the topic, he described to us the miserable end of Surajah Dowlah, who, escaping in disguise with one of his favourite women and a single servant, was recognised by a *facquier* whose nose and ears he had ordered to be cut off a year ago, when on his march against the Purranea Nabob, and being seized and brought back to Muxadavad was murdered secretly by emissaries of Meer Jaffier's son Meerham. So surely have the crimes of this wretched prince brought their own punishment! Of Sinzaun nothing certain can be learned. There's a rumour of his being still alive, but if so, he's a fugitive in the Berbohm[07] country, with the rest of the Frenchmen that escaped from Placis, and have failed to join with Mons. Law, who is refuging at Patna, whither Major Coote was to start to-day with a sufficient force to bring him and his soldiers in as prisoners. The first instalment of the treasure due to the inhabitants of Calcutta as a compensation for their losses of last year is to be paid over to-morrow by Raja Doolubram, who has been set over the Muxadavad treasury, and it is to be sent down the river at once, when Colonel Clive is so good as to suggest that Mr Fraser and I should take advantage of the chance to travel by one of the boats carrying it, which will ensure both our comfort and safety.

At Mr Hurstwood's House, CALCUTTA, *July ye* 12*th*.

Once more, Amelia, I date my letter from Calcutta, after a voyage which has been one long triumph, owing to the precious freight of our fleet of boats. No less than a hundred of these were required to convey the Muxadavad treasure, which was packed in seven hundred chests, and guarded by a strong force of troops as far as the town of Nudiah.[08] Here the vessels were met by the boats of the squadron, and thus attended, with flags flying and bands of music playing, we sailed on to Calcutta, where the entire population, overwhelmed with delight at this extraordinary accession of wealth, gave way to the most extravagant rejoicing, and testified the utmost esteem and affection both for one another and for those in authority. Of these affecting demonstrations Mr Fraser and I were not witnesses, for an urgent letter from my dear Mrs Hurstwood had entreated us to land at Chitpore, and take breakfast with her at a *bungulo* or country-seat that Mr Hurstwood has lately bought. I found myself welcomed with tears of joy by my Charlotte, who appeared unable to make enough of me, and piqued me not a little by telling Mr Fraser roundly that much as she valued him, 'twas solely for my sake, and if he had any business in Calcutta, the day was his in which to do it, for she promised herself the pleasure of hearing my history from my own lips, and his interruptions were not desired. My dear spouse, knowing that I can't endure to hear his punctilio slighted, even in jest, laughed at me for my vexation, and declared he had suffered far worse things from Mrs Hurstwood, offering to prove it by one of her letters, which had been effectual, he said, in making him less ready to take offence than he had once been, since 'twas impossible to speak of him in less flattering terms, which he had yet endured meekly at her hands. Having seen him depart in a palanqueen, for his wound is now so far recovered that he is able to sit up, though not to walk, my Charlotte and I set to work to exchange a year's confidences. Figure to yourself, my dear girl, the prodigious task! If I had more to tell, Charlotte's kind expressions of sympathy and her eager questions gave her full as large a part in the conversation, although she insisted that I should recount all my tale before she would consent to impart any news of her own. When at last all was told, I demanded of her with indignation how she could find it in her heart to put a slight upon a person that had behaved with the courage and generosity Mr Fraser had shown, at which she laughed.

"Why, child," she said, "your zeal for your spouse charms me, I'll assure you. I vow I must reward it by letting you see the letters he wrote to me during his search for you. 'Tis no breach of confidence, for he has promised to show you mine. Come, there's the precious pacquet, which you may study in your palanqueen as we ride home, for I won't have a moment of our talking-time wasted to-day."

I leave you to picture, my Amelia, what your Sylvia's feelings were on reading these charming letters, every page in which breathes the respect and affection with which her spouse is kind enough to regard your unworthy friend. I am determined to obtain Mrs Hurstwood's leave to copy them out for myself, so that in case I am ever so base as to be in danger of forgetting how infinitely Mr Fraser has obliged me in the past, I may read them and be overwhelmed with shame, and I will contrive to grant my Amelia the privilege of reading them also. Those utterances in them which may appear extravagant, she'll pardon as the evidence of the too-partial kindness entertained for her Sylvia by the writer, for indeed I could not bring myself to leave 'em out. Something of this sort I said to my Charlotte when we were arrived at Mr Hurstwood's house, and she received it in her usual contradictory style.

"Indeed, child, I'm glad you're pleased. As for me, I took no pleasure in your Fraser until he left off writing letters."

"I am sorry my spouse annoyed Mrs Hurstwood with reports of his search for me."

"I'm sorry to see Mrs Fraser petted about nothing. Why, child, when I received Dr Dacre's letter announcing your marriage, and Fraser's incoherent scrawl saying that he could find no words in which to write, I was satisfied at last that the fellow loved you as he ought. So long as he could talk about his transports, even to his mistress's near friend, I could not repose in him the confidence I desired."

"Sure you're a person of vast authority on matters of love and marriage, madam."

"Questionless, my dear. Han't I set the fashion for Calcutta in weddings for many a long day? A surprise-wedding lends a charming touch to an evening party."

"But sure there have been no weddings here of late?"

"No weddings? Why, there's been little but weddings. You forget that a whole parcel of widows have required to be furnished with spouses."

"Sure you can't mean that the widows of the gentlemen who perished last year——?"

"But I do mean it. I don't desire to startle my Sylvia, but there's some things she must know."

"You'd have me understand that—that—Mrs Freyne——?"

"Precisely. Mrs Freyne is entered upon a second matrimonial experiment."

"And the happy person favoured with the transfer of her affections?"

"Come, child, I can't have you sarcastic. It don't become a young woman of my Sylvia's charming disposition. The favoured suitor, my dear, is Captain Bentinck, who got his company through the entreaties of the Presidency when he was left to undertake the defence of Calcutta on Colonel Clive's going to the war."

"She could scarce have insulted my papa's memory worse than by such a choice, made in such haste."

"Indeed, my dear, there was no haste, I'll assure you. The full year and a day—not a moment less—did Mrs Freyne wear her weeds to the admiration of the whole town, and 'twas in the evening of the 21st of last month she was married. Perhaps you would not say that this proved her a model of inconsolable constancy, but indeed she was thought to be extraordinary strict. Why, Mrs Campbell, who married Mr Hastings just before the hot weather began, only lost her Captain at the taking of Buzbudgia in January. She, I grant you, wasted no time. But I vow there's no need for you to regret Mrs Freyne's action, for you'll have the less to do with her. I thought I had best warn you of the affair, as you're about to meet her to-night."

"Sure my Charlotte will never ask me to do anything so repugnant to my sentiments."

"Your Charlotte does ask it of you. To tell truth, my dear, I have played a little trick on Mrs Bentinck. Shortly after her marriage she came with the solemnest face in the world to ask me whether I had not resigned all hope of seeing you again, since a year was past without any news of you. I had just received the news of your wedding, and made no scruple of assuring the lady that I was persuaded my Sylvia Freyne was no more, when she departed comforted, and is now wearing mourning for you. You perceive my plot?"

"Oh, my dear, don't attempt anything dreadful. I have no desire to alarm the lady into fits, or perhaps madness."

"There's no fear of that, child. 'Tis your papa's property Mrs Bentinck was concerned for, and that she can't hope to keep now you're returned. Sure you can't desire me to break the news to her gently? Is it to be announced as joyful or melancholy? If she learn it on a sudden, she can decide for herself. And now come to dress."

In Mrs Hurstwood's hands I feel myself a child, and when she desired me to wear one of her gowns, which she had had a tailor alter during the day to fit me, I obeyed her with all the meekness imaginable. I can't tell you how strange it appeared to me to put on a dress of ceremony once more, and I thought I had never seen anything so charming as the white satin petticoat and gown of white gauze sprigged with gold that my Charlotte had chose for me. When I was dressed, she came into the room with her hands full of crimson flowers.

"You look well enough, child," she said, "but you han't sufficient colour left to carry off a dress all of white. Besides, you was married more than a month ago, and we can't have you look too like a bride. So sit down, and let me adorn you."

I sat down as she bade me, and she fastened her red blossoms in my hair and in the bosom of my gown, then turned me round and told me in her impudent style that she thought I might pass tolerably for a boarding-school Miss just arrived from Europe if I would but keep that Fraser of mine from following me about everywhere. Having succeeded in making me angry, she informed me that I should find my adored spouse in the saloon, as indeed I did, with his wounded limb laid on a couch. It seemed to me that there was a slight gloom on his countenance, but he drove it away when I joined him, and we were talking over the events of the day when Mrs Hurstwood entered the apartment, bringing with her my stepmother and Captain Bentinck.

"This is the dear friend I desired to present to you, madam," said my Charlotte, with an air of extraordinary sweetness. For the instant I feared Mrs Bentinck's falling into a fit as she regarded me with consternation, but she recovered her coolness by a prodigious effort.

"I hope, miss," she said to me, with an air of grave rebuke, "your conscience tells you that you're a suitable object for Mrs Hurstwood's kindness?"

"Indeed, madam, my dear Mrs Hurstwood has always been too partial to my faults."

"Perhaps you han't considered, miss, that what we have heard of your adventures" (yes, Amelia, she went so far as to use that term) "will scarce entitle you to be received again in Calcutta. I had thought better of you than to expect to find you imposing on Mrs Hurstwood's good nature. Sure a humble retirement would befit you better."

Mr Fraser had raised himself angrily to speak when Mrs Bentinck made use of the horrid word *adventures*, but Charlotte gave him a signal to keep silent. Now she spoke with the greatest coolness in the world.

"Sure, madam, you must mistake my friend for some other person. This is Mrs Fraser, the wife of the gentleman yonder, with whom your spouse has, I believe, some acquaintance."

"Questionless he has married her in hopes of her papa's money," says Mrs Bentinck, as though she spoke to herself, but so loud that we could all hear.

"Madam!" I cried, very hotly, "Mr Fraser married me at a moment when all that he could hope for was to share the perils that menaced me."

"I fear, sir," she continued, as though I had not spoken, "you'll be disappointed to hear that Mr Freyne's wealth was by no means so great as was commonly supposed."

"Why, then I'm rightly punished, madam," says Mr Fraser, with infinite cheerfulness.

"And of what there is," she cried, vexed by his coolness, "not an *anna* that I can keep my hands on shall go to the creature you've married."

"Any remarks you may be pleased to pass upon my own conduct, madam, I'll be charmed to listen to, but I permit no one to insult Mrs Fraser in my hearing."

"Come, come, my dear," says Captain Bentinck, "there's been enough said. Mr Fraser and his lady will questionless pardon your natural agitation after such a start as you've had, and I need not say I shall be glad to meet the gentleman or any person he may please to appoint for the discussion of business."

"Oh, forgive me, sir!" cried his lady, making him a curtsey. "I had forgot you would scarce choose to meet Mr Fraser a second time at the sword's point."

"Madam," said the poor gentleman (I did truly compassionate him at the moment, Amelia), "I'm sorry to disoblige you, but if you'll be so kind as leave this matter to Mr Fraser and me, there'll be all the more hope of a peaceful settlement."

"And that signifies that you'll see your wife despoiled for the sake of the saucy creature there. Would that I had married a person with a spark of courage or manly sentiment in him! Well, sir," turning to Mr Fraser, "I perceive you'll have reason to bless the Captain's easy temper, but I wish you joy of what you may get. You've found your lady obliging enough when you was all she had to depend upon for entertainment, and she owed her precious life to you from day to day, but wait and see how she'll use you in Calcutta, when she has plenty of money and trains of admirers, and her dear Mrs Hurstwood to support her in all her whims. I fancy the spouse of the lovely Sylvia will find himself less important with his lady than he'd desire."

Sure some malignant spirit must have prompted Mrs Bentinck thus to foster the misgiving that I had discerned in Mr Fraser's mind already that day, but he answered her coolly enough—

"Since any kindness Mrs Fraser may please to show me is beyond my deserts, madam, I'll trust to be always grateful for it."

Disappointed of the effect she had hoped to produce, the lady left us with a disdainful air to join with the rest of the company, in order to receive whom Charlotte had been compelled to depart, hugely to her annoyance, and Captain Bentinck following her after a few civil words, I found myself for a moment alone, so to speak, with Mr Fraser. I could not resolve to lose this chance.

"Oh, dear sir," I said, very earnestly, "have I deserved this lack of confidence at your hands? Can you think so meanly of the creature you have so infinitely obliged as to imagine that the possession of any advantages would alter her carriage towards you? At least do me the favour to test my abiding gratitude, and if you find it wanting, recall me to a sense of my duty. I'll assure you it shan't be necessary to upbraid me twice."

"Why, what a bear I must be," cried Mr Fraser, "to have drawn this affecting appeal from my beloved girl! Indeed, my dearest life, if I looked sour on parting from you this morning, 'twas but the thought of a whole day spent without you, or if I answered that saucy lady less warmly than I felt, 'twas because I feared to give her cause to cry out on me as extravagant. That's my wretched pride again, you'll say. Well, so it is, and I'm more ashamed of it than ever in my life before. Won't my charmer extend me her pardon?"

"So long as I know I have your confidence, dear sir——"

"So long as my Sylvia pleases herself, let her know that she can't disoblige her Fraser. His confidence she must always possess."

I was made happy by hearing this, but none the less was I thankful not to have delayed making my appeal, for, knowing as I do my dear Mr Fraser's cast of disposition, I tremble at the prospect of the least interruption of the happy understanding between us. You'll own, Amelia, that I have some experience of the gloomy pride that possesses him when he imagines himself wronged, and to give him cause to display it would break my heart.

"Come, come," cried Mrs Hurstwood, coming up to us just as Mr Fraser had kissed my hand, "I can't suffer these public endearments now that you're returned to polite life. You must learn to carry yourselves towards each other with the indifference of persons of fashion. Besides, I want my Sylvia here, to present an old acquaintance to her. I'll find a consoler for Mr Fraser in a moment."

She carried me into the next room in a prodigious hurry, and bade me seat myself upon an ebony couch, then brought in no less a person than Admiral Watson, who walks now always with the aid of a stick, and bears traces in his countenance of the distemper from which he has suffered since almost his first arrival in Bengall.

"Now here, dear sir," says Charlotte, "is the beloved friend of whom I spoke to you. Pray did I exaggerate her charms in describing 'em?"

"Even Mrs Hurstwood can't perform the impossible," said the Admiral, bowing. "Her portrait I must pronounce to have fallen far short of the reality."

If I was puzzled by this introduction, and by the look my Charlotte cast at me as she departed, as though recommending me to do my best to gain Mr Watson's favour, I was worse perplexed by the good gentleman's conversation, for I soon learned that he imagined me to be a stranger to India, only newly landed from Britain.

"I fear Admiral Watson's memory en't so strong as his kindness," I said at last, after acknowledging several genteel compliments, "for I had the honour to meet him at Madrass near two years ago."

"Oh, madam," and the Admiral laughed, "'tis strong enough to recollect that Mrs Hurstwood has been known to play tricks upon her acquaintances, and I fear her lovely friend en't ashamed to copy her."

"Sure her trick was to make you believe I was newly from home, sir."

"She assured me positively that you was but just arrived in Calcutta, madam. But stay—pray, madam, may I be favoured with your name?"

"My name is Fraser, sir," and I permitted Mr Watson to catch a glimpse of the wedding-ring upon my finger. Figure to yourself my alarm, Amelia, when he burst into a great shout of laughter.

"What! the lady over whom Mr Fraser and I have been quarrelling all day?" he cried.

"Oh, dear sir, have I brought Mr Fraser into fresh difficulties?"

"Why, madam, I thought he had taken undue advantage of my easy temper when he confessed he had married the lady I permitted him only to rescue. But I protest I'd have done the same myself on the like provocation."

"But you won't make him suffer, sir, for his generosity to a poor desolate creature that had no friend but him?"

"He has plenty of consolation, madam, if I did. But figure to yourself how the affair appears to his comrades. Lieutenant Fraser, admitted through the Admiral's softness to an indulgence he don't in the least deserve, outstays his leave without permission, and contrives not only to take part in Colonel Clive's battle at Placis but to marry a handsome wife. It's clear he must be punished."

"Oh, pray, dear sir, pray——"

"Now pray, madam, don't cry. I was about to say that for the sake of others I must leave Mr Fraser in his old station, not allowing him to profit by the accidents that have of late advanced so many of our officers to a higher rank, but if he'll carry himself in that situation so as to merit my favour (and with such a lady to inspire him I don't doubt but he will), why, he shall have it!"

Sure I can't tell, my dear girl, whether at the moment I was more grateful for my Charlotte's trick to gain the Admiral's kindness for Mr Fraser, or more ashamed of my jealous misinterpreting of the natural melancholy my spouse had shown on his return from waiting on Mr Watson, seeing his prospects all in danger.

CALCUTTA, *August ye* 19*th*.

How little I imagined, when I closed my last letter to my Amelia, that the truly great and benevolent man whose affable kindness it recorded was shortly to quit the world in which he had obliged so many and displeased none! Three days ago Admiral Watson, the most condescending of patrons, the most skilful of commanders, breathed his last in the hospital here. The disorder from which he suffered had increased continually upon him; but the mournful termination might have been avoided had it not been for a sudden attack of what is called in Bengall a *pucker*[09] fever (which is to say a severe and violent one), of which he expired in four days. There are no words to express the grief and consternation experienced by all in this place, as well Indians as Europeans, on hearing of the shocking event. This excellent person had so endeared himself to all classes by the justness of his sentiments, the politeness of his manners, and the nobility of his disposition, that there's not a creature but feels the loss of a friend. No such funeral procession has ever been seen in Calcutta as that which on Wednesday attended to the burying-ground the remains of one so universally venerated. Not only the officers and seamen of the ships, but the army, the black and Armenian inhabitants, and even the French prisoners, desired to testify their regret for his decease; while Colonel Clive, the only individual that could at all compete with Mr Watson in the public estimation, was present with the rest, and dropped an unfeigned tear. A fortnight back all the talk of the place was of the claim put in by the Admiral for a share in the Muxadavad treasure proportionate to the post he held, and how Colonel Clive, in proposing to deduct for his benefit a certain portion of each person's share, and actually paying over his own part of the sum, had disobliged the Presidency and the army officers; but now there can be few but feel that the Colonel alone has nothing to regret in considering his dealings with the amiable and virtuous person whom we have lost.

Must I confess to my dear friend that in my heart there has been, united with that sense of public loss which could not but make itself felt, a particular grief that the only patron to whom Mr Fraser might reasonably look for advancement in his profession could now oblige him no further?

That this unworthy strain has mingled with my sorrow I can't deny; but my Amelia may judge of the shame with which I contemplated the sentiment when I learned that even on his death-bed Mr Watson remained mindful of the interests of those who had served under him. Yesterday Admiral Pococke, who succeeds the lamented gentleman in the command of his Majesty's naval forces in these waters, having summoned to his presence those officers for whom Mr Watson had been chiefly concerned, promised them his countenance and favour in the future, and made them the most obliging offers of advancement under his own eye. Until that moment, as he confessed to me, Mr Fraser had entertained serious thoughts of quitting the navy and entreating the favour of a commission in the Artillery from Colonel Clive; but finding himself confronted with the same agreeable prospects as before, he is now joyfully resolved to remain in the calling of his choice.

You'll be surprised to hear that we are still residing with Mr and Mrs Hurstwood; but to tell truth we have found it impossible to quit their dwelling. As soon as Mr Fraser proposed seeking a house for ourselves, our friends assured us that theirs was far too large for their wants, and that they would regard it as a favour if we relieved them of a part of it. Now this liberal offer was so great a convenience, considering the huge rents asked here, that we could scarce consent to accept of it; but when my Charlotte painted a moving picture of the solitude I should experience when Mr Fraser was absent on his voyages, and the consolation she might afford me if she needed only to step across the varanda to pay me a visit, my spouse went over to her side at once. Then she sought to compliment me with visions of the assistance I might furnish to her in her household œconomy when she felt vapourish (for indeed she is not strong), and declared at last that if I removed to another part of Calcutta she would compel Mr Hurstwood to remove also and hire the house next to ours, so that I also was brought to consent to remain. But my dear girl must not suppose that we are so poor as to find it difficult to live according to our station. Under the influence of good Mr Holwell and Mr Hurstwood, Captain Bentinck has behaved like a person of honour and probity respecting my dear papa's estate, although his good designs were sorely hindered by his lady; and Captain Colquhoun's gift, of which I can scarce bear to think even now, ensures us a genteel maintenance. With this and Mr Fraser's pay, I'll assure you we find no cause to envy even the wealthiest persons here.

P.S.—Miss Dorman (who is now Miss Dorman no longer, but Mrs Weeks) is come in, and finding me writing, desires her compliments to you, saying that she regards you as a friend of her own. Her humble servant, who was fighting in the Carnatic, came hither with the Madrass detachment, and married her at Fulta, "just in time," says she, "for I had near determined on resigning my pretensions to him and youth together, calling myself Mrs before others tired of calling me Miss,[10] and settling down to cards and scandal as the only old maid in Calcutta, with a cat, an ape, and a poll-parrot to keep me company." But I know my Amelia will rejoice with me that this amiable creature en't compelled to so melancholy a fate.

CALCUTTA, *Sept. ye* 18*th*.

Has my Amelia ever pleased herself with speculations upon the sentiments of mankind after the Deluge? I hope she won't accuse me of irreverence, but I have been wondering whether, when the patriarch and his descendants returned to the scenes with which they had been formerly acquainted, they were at any time wont to spare a compassionate thought for those who had once trod with them the turf of the umbrageous grove, or listened to the murmuring of the brook. Sure they could not have succeeded in forgetting them as completely as though they had never been, and yet our people in Calcutta have contrived to attain to an eminence as uncommon, as inhuman almost, as this. And such a malevolent oblivion is the more astonishing, that those who perished in the miseries of last year were not the worst, but the best, of our community. My papa, Captain Colquhoun, good Padra Bellamy and his son, Mr Eyre, Ensign Piccard, and all the rest—the first two commemorated indeed by the elegant tablets which the pious care of Mr Fraser has had erected in the burying-ground in their honour, but the names of the others allowed to perish unless the excellent Mr Holwell (like your Sylvia a sharer and a survivor of the horrors of those days) should carry out his projected design of raising a suitable monument to their common memory.[11] Is there no pathetic[12] in this strange neglect? 'Tis little wonder, you'll say, that Mr Drake and the Council should desire to shroud in darkness such recollections as could only blacken their own behaviour, but sure it had been but a delicate action on Colonel Clive's part to put them to shame by taking the matter in hand. The Colonel don't think so, however, and Calcutta goes on its way forgetful of the persons in whom it should take most pride. Indeed, my dear, the state of this place now is far worse than when our good Captain Colquhoun used to anticipate a judgment upon it, owing, I fear, to the prodigious sums of money poured into the town as the result of the victory of Placis. True, there was no disputes about the division of the treasure, which was distributed by a committee of the most respectable inhabitants, whose award was received with the greatest complaisance imaginable, but the common men of the army and navy spend their portion of the spoils in the most extravagant folly and wickedness conceivable, and even the gentlemen of the services seem to have lost their senses by reason of this sudden accession of wealth. As I rode through the city this afternoon in my palanqueen, I saw on all sides of me the signs of the most ostentatious luxury, of the most prodigal expenditure of the treasure so unhappily obtained.

Sure I must be vapourish, you'll say, to give vent to these gloomy reflections. Why, so they are gloomy, my dear, but my situation is a melancholy one. Yesterday there arrived in the river the Revenge sloop, which had made an extraordinary quick voyage from Madrass, bringing news of the arrival of a great French fleet on the Choromandel Coast. The season of the year forbids Mr Pococke to take the sea against 'em, but he has thought it well to carry his ships to Ballisore Road, there to keep watch in case of an attempted attack on Bengall, and the vessels dropped down the river to-day. Many friends and relations of the officers were permitted to share the passage as far as Culpee, and Captain Latham complimented me with an invitation on board the Tyger, so that I was able to enjoy Mr Fraser's company for a little longer. But this was not wholly charming, for I could not but see that the dear gentleman was so placed that persons much inferior to him in attainments, and even in age, were entitled to give him their orders. I could not help deploring this to him before we parted, and lamenting that his determined search for me had involved him in such a loss of sea-time and of opportunities for distinction as had brought him into so painful a situation, but he checked me immediately.

"Pray, my dearest girl," he said, "have done once and for all with this talk of obligation between you and me. Sure I had willingly undertook what I did simply to know that my Sylvia was restored to freedom and safety; but when to that is added the honour of possessing her, I am overpaid a thousand times. The favour is all on my side, and if you love me, you'll permit me to rejoice in that thought."

To so affecting an appeal 'twas not possible to return a refusal, although it deprives me of that exercise which is the most charming of all to a generous mind—the consideration of the obligations one owes to one's friends. But my dear Mr Fraser is gone, and what little his Sylvia can do to please him shall be done—although not altogether as my Charlotte desired me just now. Having made me drink a dish of tea on my return from the Gott, and sought in vain to engage me in a cheerful conversation, "Oh, there!" she cried, "go and write to your Fraser. I see you'll take no pleasure in anything until that's done." But I hope I en't so extravagant as Mrs Hurstwood feigns to believe. I will begin a letter to Mr Fraser to-morrow; at present I'll finish that to my Amelia. Do you know, my dear, I fancy this will be the last of my huge pacquets? Letters you'll receive from me in the future, I hope, but scarcely those minute histories which it has so often solaced me to write. These, if I am able to write them at all, must go to my spouse, and my dear girl won't grudge it, knowing that in heart her friend is, as ever, her

SYLVIA FRASER.

APPENDIX.

A.—ON THE SPELLING OF WORDS AND NAMES.

IT will be noticed that the orthography of Indian words in the text differs with each writer, and this is the case in all the writings of the period. That phonetic method of spelling, which has passed into literature in the works of Thackeray and Macaulay, and for a return to which a writer in one of the magazines recently entered a plea, reigned supreme, but with this drawback, that each man expressed differently the sounds he heard. To take one instance, the comparatively simple name Baj-baj appears in various writings as Buz-buzia, Buz-budgee, Busbudgia, Budje Boodjee, and Bougee Bougee, besides the more modern Budge-Budge. The first person that rendered Murshidabad as Muxidavad evidently pronounced the *x* in the Portuguese way, as *sh*, when the name is quite recognisable if the accent be placed on the first syllable, but those who followed him, ignorant of this fact, passed from Muxadavad into Mucksadabad—a terrible example of the dangers of a follow-my-leader policy. Some writers, and notably Holwell, made an effort to obtain uniformity. Aghast at discovering the long *a* sound (as in Khan) variously rendered by *o*, *u*, *au*, and *aw*, they employed *aa* for the purpose, and hence we are confronted with such monstrosities as *Rhaajepoot* for Rajput. Considering the difficulty of rendering Hindustani words by means of English letters, the modern student may be thankful for the Hunterian system, which at least ensures uniformity, even though upon a purely conventional basis. It may be mentioned that the diversity is not confined to Indian words. The name of le Beaume is spelt in four different ways.

B.—THE FAMILY OF ALIVARDI KHAN.

The following table has been compiled from Orme's History and the *Seïr-ul-Mutaqharin* to show the relationship of Alivardi Khan's descendants. The three daughters of Alivardi married the three sons of his brother Hodjee Hamet (Haji Ahmad), while his half-sister Shah-Khanum was married to Mir Jafar, and became the mother of his son Miran.

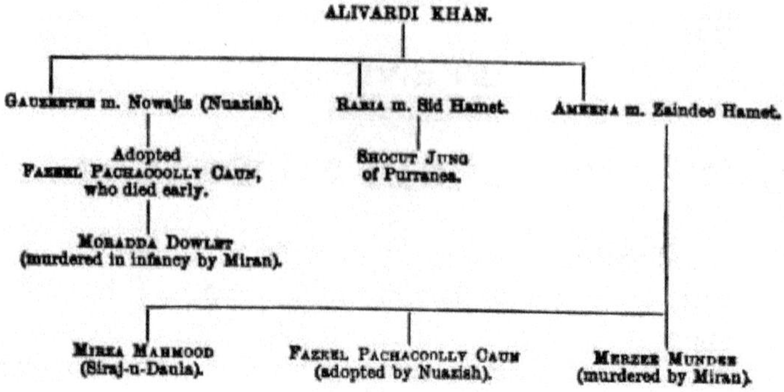

C.—AUTHORITIES FOLLOWED IN THE TEXT.

The period treated in this book is singularly rich in contemporary personal records. Holwell, Watts, and Scrafton have left us lengthy narratives of their experiences, and Ives, Admiral Watson's surgeon and clerk, supplies a detailed account of the campaign of vengeance which terminated at Plassey. Clive's letters give us the military point of view, and in the *Seïr-ul-Mutaqharin* we have that of the natives. Orme's History (1763) appears to have been compiled from other documents still, probably the official letters addressed to the Court of Directors, since his account of Mr Watts' escape from Madhupur, for instance, is far more detailed than that contained in Watts' own 'Memoirs of the Revolution in Bengal.' Orme's account is followed in the text, save that other names have been substituted for those of Messrs Collet and Sykes and Dr Forth, whom the historian mentions as Watts' companions in addition to the Tartar servant. The evidence given before the Parliamentary Committee of 1772 adds many interesting details, and the same may be said of two MSS. in the Hastings Collection, one written by the anonymous junior civilian who is called Mr Dash in the text, the other the *apologia* of Captain Grant, who had fought under Prince Charles Edward at Culloden, and succeeded, when the Jacobite cause was lost, in escaping to Bengal, where ill-fortune still pursued him. I am indebted to Dr Busteed, whose book, 'Echoes from Old Bengal,' is a mine of curious information on eighteenth-century Calcutta, for directing my attention to these writings. The description of Siraj-u-Daula's Durbar is taken from the *Discours Préliminaire* of Anquetil du Perron's translation of the 'Zend-Avesta,' the French traveller having visited Murshidabad during the prince's short reign. For various minor details, the 'Voyages' of Grose and of Mrs Kindersley have been laid under contribution, while Broome's 'History of the Bengal Army' has afforded a standard by which to compare the often varying contemporary authorities.

The variations and discrepancies in these narratives form indeed the great difficulty of the historian, and with these must be joined their omissions, particularly in matters of date. Thus there are no means of knowing the exact time at which Mr Watts' letter of warning as to the Nawab's intentions arrived, or when the Delawar entered the Hugli with the instructions of the Court of Directors, when Siraj-u-Daula was formally proclaimed in Calcutta and the Governor's letter of congratulation forwarded, or when "Fuckeer Tongar" and the Nawab's second messenger arrived, or lastly, when the "first prohibition of provisions" took place, at which time Holwell recommended the seizure of Tanna. I have endeavoured in the text to place these events in their probable order and in a right relation to one another.

D.—THE HISTORICAL PERSONAGES INTRODUCED.

In consequence of the abundant information obtainable, there is little scope for imagination in the treatment of the historical personages brought into the story as secondary characters. Messrs Holwell, Eyre, Bellamy (father and son), Mapletoft, le Beaume, Watts, and Hastings, and Governor Drake and his two friends, stand revealed either in their own writings or those of their contemporaries. The characters of the five captains commanding the Calcutta forces are drawn for us by Holwell, but students of the original narrative will observe that I have substituted the name of Captain Colquhoun for that of Buchanan. So also the brilliant young civilian who survived the Black Hole to become Clive's instrument in the matter of the false treaty is called in the text by the name of Fisherton. It may be objected that the character of Drake and his fellow deserters is drawn too exclusively from the records of those who suffered by their cowardice in forsaking Fort William, but to that I may reply that neither Grant in his MS. defence, nor Manningham in his evidence before the House of Commons Committee, succeeds in shedding any more agreeable light on the disgraceful exploit, while Drake's opinion of the affair is shown by his having, in conjunction with the Council, sentenced Captains Grant and Minchin to be dismissed the Service, for following his own example. Grant, it may be remarked, was afterwards reinstated, in view of his unsuccessful efforts to induce the President to return to the help of those left in the Fort, and he took part in the hostilities which culminated at Plassey.

Admiral Watson's character is described in detail by Ives, and sketched at some length by Watts, while the chance allusions of other writers concur in assuring us of his extreme amiability as a man, and his high qualities as a commander. (His tomb, like that of young William Speke, is still to be seen at the Old Cathedral, Calcutta, and it may be news to some Londoners to learn that there is a monument to him in the north transept of Westminster Abbey.) The remarkable indecision displayed by Clive before the engagement at Plassey is historical, and appears to have been due to one of those fits of depression to which he was subject. The name of Sinzaun will not be found in the records of the period, but we learn from Grant that the Nawab's artillery at the siege of Fort William was under the command of a French renegade, who called himself the Marquis de St Jacques, while the last stand at Plassey was made by a small company of French under a leader called St Frais, whose name was spelt Sinfray by the English and the natives, and who was not killed, as is erroneously stated in the index to Malleson's 'Life of Clive,' but lived to fight another day.

E.—THE TOPOGRAPHY OF CALCUTTA.

One of the chief difficulties in tracing the various localities of old Calcutta is the extent to which the river-bank has altered its shape and position, so that where in Orme's day was water, there are now streets and squares. It is still possible, however, to discover some of the old landmarks, although the Fort William of the text must not be sought for on the site of the present one, for that was built by Clive where the hamlet of Gobindpur had formerly stood. The Post Office marks the spot occupied by the original Fort William, and the site of the Black Hole (the discovery of which in 1883 is recorded by Dr Busteed) is marked by a stone bearing an inscription. The Park or Lal Bagh is the present Tank Square or Dalhousie Square. The site of the church is thought by some to be occupied by St Andrew's Presbyterian Church, while the Old Cathedral (St John's) marks the site of the burying-ground mentioned in the text. The present Government House covers, so far as can be determined, the site of the old Company's House. The gaol, says Broome in 1850, "was about the site of the present Lall Bazar Auction Mart." The present suburb of Hastings stands on the site of Surmans, and the ground between it and the city proper, now occupied by Chauringhi and the Maidan, was still a marshy jungle even at the end of the last century. The Chitpur Road, an old native pilgrim-way, marked the division between the English and native quarters of the town, and the Marhata Ditch followed the course of the present Circular Road. Further information on this interesting subject may be obtained from Dr Busteed's book and Sir William Hunter's 'Gazetteer of India,' art. "Calcutta."

F.—SOME POINTS IN CONNECTION WITH THE FALL OF CALCUTTA.

It is difficult to resist the conclusion that never was a city more thoroughly warned of its impending doom than the Calcutta of 1756, and the fact renders the alternate defiance and cowardice of the Presidency the more unaccountable. That the actual approach of peril took them altogether by surprise appears certain, and Orme blames Mr Watts for not informing them until the danger was close at hand of the anxiety as to their intentions displayed by Alivardi Khan in his death-bed conversation with Dr Forth, which appears to have been considered by Siraj-u-Daula as a justification for his own subsequent proceedings. But without adopting the extreme view of the French, that the siege and its consequences were the outcome of a deliberate plan formed by Drake and his confederates for the destruction of Holwell, there can be little doubt that the President and his two friends were playing a double game, and found themselves defeated only because they met with opponents still less scrupulous than they were. The constitution of the Council was such as to render it extremely easy for them to manipulate public affairs in their own interest. Watts, the accomptant and second in command, was absent at Kasimbazar, and the executive was practically in the hands of the Governor, Manningham the warehouse-keeper, and his "partner" Frankland. The House of Commons Report makes it clear that these three were suspected not only of supporting the claims of Ghasiti Bigam against those of Siraj-u-Daula in the hope of gain, but of accepting a money bribe to allow the admission of Kishen Das into Calcutta. The writer who in the text is called Mr Dash goes further, and asserts roundly that their earlier defiance of the Nawab was intended to alarm the protected merchants and wealthy men of the surrounding districts, and induce them to seek refuge in Calcutta, when the Presidency might levy blackmail on their possessions. After this we are scarcely surprised to learn on the same authority that Drake and his friends were wont to apply to their own use as much as 10,000 rupees a month, which was a part of the sum devoted by the Court of Directors to the payment of the army—an army practically non-existent—nor that the plunder found at Tanna was put on board the Doddalay, the ship which belonged to the three confederates, and transferred to the snow Neptune. Having attained their object in despatching the expedition, the Presidency had no further interest in Tanna, but kept up a show of activity without any real result on the second day, merely in order to cover the passage of the Neptune up to Calcutta. It is some consolation to hear that when Fort William was abandoned, this vessel went ashore near Baj-baj, and the treasure was lost.

Unfortunately for the plans of the Presidency, it can scarcely be doubted that they were overreached from the first. The hollowness of the Nawab's anger against Kishen Das, evidenced not only by the honours showered upon him on the fall of Calcutta, but by the fact that Rajballab, the father, and presumably the more guilty of the two, remained unmolested at the Court from beginning to end of the matter, seems to show that the affair of Kishen Das was nothing but a ruse, intended to bring about the ruin of the English by arousing their cupidity. That it was devised by Amin Chand and his friend Gobind Ram Mitar, as was suspected at the time, in revenge for what they considered the injustice with which they had been treated, is scarcely more doubtful. The double-dyed traitor Amin Chand appears, indeed, to have played both parties false with the greatest impartiality throughout his career, but the special malevolence displayed towards Holwell and the three others by whom he conceived himself to have been particularly injured seems to prove that the overthrow was plotted by him, and this is corroborated by the correspondence discovered between Amin Chand and Manak Chand. In consequence of this unsuspected treachery, the President and his friends, who had counted confidently upon the defeat of the Nawab, first at the hands of Ghasiti Bigam and then at those of his cousin of Parnia, found their confidence futile, and the airy carelessness with which they had been wont to discuss affairs of state, both with casual acquaintances and with the natives, contributed to their downfall by the information it furnished to the enemy. It is interesting to observe that in his examination before the Commons Committee, Manningham observes with the greatest coolness that in his opinion it was not in the power of any man to give a reason for the disaster, and that he knew of no conduct on the part of the Company's servants likely to incense the country government. In regard to their intentions, this is probably true, but it is almost impossible not to believe that their plans for their own aggrandisement recoiled upon them in a way they little expected.

The conduct of the Governor and his friends during the siege appears to have been due merely to pusillanimity, for even Mr "Dash" does not venture to hint at treachery on their part. The incapacity of the engineers prepared a position impossible of defence, and the cowardice of those in command precipitated a defeat which a more resolute resistance might have delayed, and thus averted altogether. The flight of Manningham and Frankland was a natural corollary to the abandonment of the north and south batteries, and the order to the captain of the Doddalay to drop down the river followed easily. In the text I have followed Captain Grant's account of Drake's flight, his own share in which he endeavours to excuse by asserting that the boat in which he accompanied him was the only one left. If this is true, it seems scarcely necessary to have locked the Fort gate to prevent further desertions, as we learn was done, and that others succeeded in getting away is probable from the narrative of Mr "Dash," which ends with a suspicious abruptness after describing the President's escape. Unless the anonymous writer was the Mr Lewis who accompanied Mr Pearkes to the Prince George, and was presumably saved with her crew, he must have found some means of reaching the ships from the Fort, for we know on his own testimony that he was among the refugees at Falta. Le Beaume, who is branded by Broome with the stigma of taking part in the stampede, is shown by Grant's narrative to have been wounded, and by Holwell's to have been sent on board the Diligence on the night of the 18th with Mrs Drake and the three other ladies who had been left behind. I have no authority for identifying these ladies (whose vessel was captured by the enemy off Baj-Baj, and all Holwell's property lost) with those mentioned in the *Seïr-ul-Mutaqharin* as having fallen into the hands of Mir Jafar, and been by him restored to their husbands, but the identification appears probable.

[The End]

FOOTNOTES.

CHAPTER I FOOTNOTES.

[01] **fit** fainting-fit.

[02] **nightgown** the nightgown (a remote ancestor of the tea-gown of to-day) was a semi-fitting flowing robe worn, generally without a hoop, in the morning and on non-ceremonial occasions.

[03] **King's ribbon** the black or scarlet Hanoverian cockade which distinguished the royal forces.

[04] **What will the noble Captain take?** it was customary to address a subaltern as Captain: officers of higher rank, on the contrary, were often spoken of as Mr.

[05] **Colonel Adlercron's regiment of foot** this was the 39th Regiment. The men were to be employed as marines on board the ships.

[06] **Select Piquet** this was composed of cadets waiting for commissions.

[07] **capuchin** a hooded cloak, the usual outdoor garment of the time.

[08] **Gott** *Ghat*, landing-place.

[09] **old Roman** the story is told of Themistocles.

[10] **whisk** whist.

[11] **particular** peculiar.

[12] **Emily** Emily was incorrectly used as the diminutive of Amelia.

CHAPTER II FOOTNOTES.

[01] **Fonchial** Funchal.

[02] **mob** the mob-cap covered the hair almost entirely.

[03] **cuddy** dining-saloon.

[04] **behave with justice and humanity to those serving under him** the brutalities described by Smollett must not be taken as typical of the navy at this time as a whole. There is abundant evidence that many

commanders were the idols of their men, and a private letter from Captain Latham of the Tyger, contributed by its recipient to the 'Gentleman's Magazine' for 1755, shows the gallant officer to have been as full of plans and "fads" for his crew's health and happiness as the most philanthropic captain of to-day.

[05] **island of St Johanne** Johanna, one of the Comoro Islands.

CHAPTER III FOOTNOTES.

[01] **Culpee** Kalpi.

[02] **checks** chiks.

[03] **notch** *nāch.*

[04] **Sawgers** Sagar.

[05] **Gioghis** *Jogis*, also spelt *juggies.*

[06] **Gentoos** Hindus.

[07] **buxies** *bakhshish.*

[08] **Surmans** the southernmost suburb of Calcutta.

[09] **Buzbudgia** Baj-baj.

[10] **Moors** Mohammedans.

[11] **Tanners** Tanna.

[12] **Govindpoor's Reach** the present Fort William occupies the site of Gobindpur.

[13] **near twenty years ago** this was in 1737.

[14] **he should by rights have been born a Quaker** this is the most probable explanation of the statement made by Voltaire and Grose, that Governor Drake was a member of the Society of Friends.

[15] **Dutch baby** doll.

CHAPTER IV FOOTNOTES.

[01] **Beebee** *bibi*=lady. The term *mem-sahib* appears not to have come into use at this date.

[02] **iya** ayah.

[03] **saeb** sahib.

[04] **peculiar** characteristic.

[05] **fly cap** a small cap which allowed the hair to be seen. A dressed suit was a complete dress of one material, with a distinct trimming.

[06] **mohurry, banyan, secar, compidore, kissmagar, consummer, mussall chye, pyke, and harry** it is perhaps scarcely necessary to give the modern spelling of these words: *muhri*, *baniya*, *sarkar*, *comprador* (a Portuguese term), *khitmatgar*, *khansaman*, *masalchi*, *paik*, *hari*.

[07] **Fringys** probably a corruption of Farangi.

[08] **Muxadavad** Murshidabad.

[09] **Cossimbuzar** Kasimbazar.

[10] **Delly** Delhi.

[11] **Morattoes** Marhatas.

[12] **Orixa** Orissa.

[13] **phirmaunds and husbulhookums** *firman*, a charter from the Emperor: *hasbalhukm*, a confirmation of it under the Grand Vizier's seal.

[14] **musnet** masnad.

[15] **dussticks** *dastak*, a permission to trade, given to the servants of the Company, and conferring certain privileges.

[16] **soubahship** *suba*, which is in reality the province or fief governed by a *subadar*, the English took as the ruler's title, and they invented the term *soubahship* to denote his post, which should be *subadari*.

[17] **French necklace** the ribbon with which the neck of the low-cut gown was drawn up.

[18] **Three heads** a *head* was a complete head-dress, including cap and lappets, or pinners.

[19] **facetious** pleasant, obliging.

[20] **Birth-night** the ball on the evening of the king's birth-day.

[21] **shroff** banker. Omy Chund's name is more correctly spelt Amin Chand.

[22] **Train** artillery.

CHAPTER V FOOTNOTES.

[01] **sicca** the sicca rupee was worth 2s. 6d., the ordinary one 2s. 3d.

[02] **bedgown** a loose jacket of coloured cotton.

[03] **molly** malli.

[04] **Moors** Hindustani.

[05] **dufter-conna** daftar-khana.

[06] **Loll Baug** *Lal Bagh*=red garden.

[07] **gwallers** bearers.

[08] **dessert** the ball-supper was called dessert.

[09] **Sucajunk ... Phousdar of Purranea ... Gosseta** Purranea=Parnia. Sucajunk is an ingenious rendering of Shaukat Jang. Gosseta should be spelt Ghasiti, and Phousdar Faujdar.

[10] **Moradda Dowlett** Murad-u-Daula.

[11] **ginanah** zenana.

[12] **Mr Fraser** the name is carefully crossed out in the original.

[13] **Buzars** Bazars.

[14] **Gyria** Gheriah.

[15] **knots** mazes.

CHAPTER VII FOOTNOTES.

[01] **Burraduan** Bardwan.

[02] **Narransing** Narain Sing.

[03] **Jemmautdar** Jemadar.

[04] **chokey** waterside custom-house.

[05] **pycar** native broker.

[06] **Sydabad** Saidabad.

[07] **Someroo** Walter Reinhardt or Reynaud, an Alsatian by birth, known to the French as Sombre, and to the natives as Samru.

CHAPTER IX FOOTNOTES.

[01] **hookers** huqa.

[02] **Sykes** Sikhs.

[03] **make over to you for her use the sum of five thousand pounds** a similar instance of generosity is recorded of an elderly suitor of the beautiful Miss Linley. The lady afterwards became the wife of Richard Brinsley Sheridan.

[04] **buxerries** bakhsharis.

[05] **coffle** *kafila*=caravan.

[06] **Facquier** Fakir.

CHAPTER X FOOTNOTES.

[01] **Rajamaul** Rajmahal.

[02] **Aume-beg** Omar or Emir Beg.

[03] **mounsee** munshi.

[04] **arasdass** arzdasht.

[05] **cossids** kasids.

[06] **tuszaconna** toshakhana.

[07] **Cotwal** *Katwal*, the head of the town police.

[08] **hircara** *harkara*, spy or messenger.

CHAPTER XI FOOTNOTES.

[01] **pawn** *pan*. Miss Freyne's mistake is excusable, for in her day betel was spelt beetle.

[02] **puckery** pagri.

[03] **mulchilca** machalka.

[04] **Esplanade** the open space surrounding the factory.

[05] **petted** piqued; cf. 'in a pet.'

[06] **deloll** dallal.

[07] **top** tope.

[08] **buckshy** *bakhshi*, lit. paymaster.

[09] **Piccard** also spelt Picard, Paccard, and Pischard.

[10] **Bungulo** Bungalow.

[11] **Doddalay** also spelt Doddaly, Dodalay, and Dodley. Is it possible that the ship's name was Dudley?

CHAPTER XII FOOTNOTES.

[01] **shamsingees** probably a kind of blunderbuss fired from a stand.

[02] **bercundauzes** barkandaz.

[03] **seerpaws** apparently *siropa—i.e.*, a robe from head to foot.

[04] **15 feet square** "A cube of about 18 feet" (Holwell); "18 feet long and 14 feet wide" (Cooke).

[05] **a good hundred and fifty** Holwell's final calculation makes the number 146.

CHAPTER XIII FOOTNOTES.

[01] **Mudden** Madan.

[02] **Marrato** Marhata.

[03] **sewaury** *sowari—i.e.*, retinue.

[04] **Buxey** Bakhshi.

[05] **It may be that the Buxey has used Mrs Carey...** Dr Busteed doubts whether Mrs Carey was ever sent to Murshidabad, but her contemporaries were fully persuaded of the fact.

[06] **rain which began on the night of our sufferings** the rains are generally said to have begun on the night of the 21st, but Holwell mentions that on emerging from the Black Hole he lay on the *wet* grass.

[07] **hackery** this, we are told, was a chaise drawn by two trotting oxen, and provided for the Admiral at the public expense.

CHAPTER XIV FOOTNOTES.

[01] **Misery Bye** Misri Bai. *Misri*=sugar-candy.

[02] **louchees** *lutis* (?).

[03] **hallicores** I have been unable to identify this word. It is also spelt *hallachores*. The *harri* or *hallicore* caste is described as the dregs both of *Musselmen* and *Gentoos*, speaking *Pariar* Portuguese.—ED.

[04] **hussy** housewife.

[05] **campaign against the Phousdar of Purranea** the exact date of the beginning of this campaign is not stated.

[06] **Nezmennessa Beebee** probably Nijm-ul-Nissa, *i.e.*, star of women.

CHAPTER XV FOOTNOTES.

[01] **Tannasery** Tenasserim.

[02] **Tellinghy** from Telingana, *i.e.*, the Telugu country, whence most of the Sepoys were recruited at this time.

[03] **French house at Sydabad** the French factory near Murshidabad.

[04] **Captain Coote** afterwards Sir Eyre Coote.

[05] **Adlercron's Regiment** this was the old 39th, the present Dorsetshire Regiment.

[06] **Cossipore** Kasipur.

[07] **Coja Petruce** Khoja Petrus.

[08] **haubitzer** howitzer.

[09] **Siab** sahib.

[10] **tyre** tier.

CHAPTER XVI FOOTNOTES.

[01] **muster** pattern.

[02] **Persic** Persian was the language of the Moguls, or ruling race among the Mohammedans, and therefore that also of Courts and diplomacy.

[03] **milaner** this spelling exhibits the derivation of the word.

[04] **Salabatzing** Salabad Jang.

[05] **our new great fleet under Lally wasn't far off** this fleet did not really arrive until 1758.

[06] **a whisper from Omy Chund** there is no evidence to show who was the real betrayer of Hastings' plot.

CHAPTER XVII FOOTNOTES.

[01] **Augadeep** Aghadip.

[02] **Phousdar Nuncomar** the notorious Nanda Kumar of later days.

[03] **Bawboo** Babu.

[04] **Shaw** Shah.

[05] **Calcapore** the Dutch factory near Murshidabad.

[06] **Pitans and Afguhans** Pathans and Afghans. Possibly Afghaun is the spelling aimed at.

[07] **Kella** Killa.

[08] **Huzzoor Nevees** *Hazur Nawiz—i.e.*, court secretary.

[09] **Sanskerreet** Sanscrit.

[10] **Mr Laws** The French agent at Murshidabad, and nephew of the famous financier. Why Law of Lauriston should have been called Laws is a mystery, but the custom was so well established that the native form of his name was Lāss.

[11] **Terrano** Terraneau.

[12] **Billy Speke ... sustaining an injury that is like to be mortal** Young William Speke died at Calcutta shortly afterwards from the effects of his wound.

[13] **Balagerow** Balaji Rao.

[14] **Armiral Dilleer-jing-behauder** Dilir Jang Bahadar.

[15] **sopha** divan.

[16] **Merzee Mundee** Mirza Mehdi.

[17] **Rajamahol** Rajmahal.

[18] **Palassy** Plassey.

[19] **Moonloll** Mohan Lal.

[20] **Godar Yar Caun Laitty** Khuda Yar Latif Khan.

[21] **Boglipore** Bhagalpur.

[22] **boxwaller** pedlar.

[23] **dussutary** *dasturi*=commission.

[24] **Govindroy** Gobind Rai.

[25] **Badgerow** Baji Rao, a form of Balaji Rao.

[26] **lol coggedge** *lal kaghaz*=red paper.

[27] **Meerum** Miran.

[28] **Maudipore** Madhupur.

CHAPTER XVIII FOOTNOTES.

[01] **loll addama** The English soldiers were so called, either from their sunburnt faces, or, more probably, their red coats.

[02] **Farashdanga ... Zubdatook Toojah** Farashdanga was the native name of Chandernagore, and Zubdatook Toojah that of Renault, its chief.

CHAPTER XIX FOOTNOTES.

[01] **Moneloll** Mohan Lal.

[02] **Saubut Jung Behader** Sabat Jang Bahadar, the name given to Clive.

[03] **The bird of Paradise ... the oak and the primrose** The allusion is evidently to "Obidah and the Hermit," in No. 65 of the 'Rambler.'

CHAPTER XX FOOTNOTES.

[01] **juggies** *jogis*.

[02] **Jelingeer** Jalingi.

[03] **Mr Hastings ... Like Mr Fraser he's a new-married man** the date 1756, usually given for Hastings' first marriage, is impossible if, as is stated by his biographers, the bride was the widow of the Captain Campbell killed at the capture of Baj-baj.

[04] **loll pultun** lal paltan—*i.e.*, red regiment.

[05] **panjammers** paijamas.

[06] **Mr Watts is minded to accompany the army** Malleson, misreading an ambiguous sentence of Broome's, says that Mr Watts remained at Kalna, but his own memoirs state decisively that he was present at Plassey.

[07] **Agey** Ajai.

[08] **Placis** Plassey.

CHAPTER XXI FOOTNOTES.

[01] **the army was to commence its advance at daybreak** Clive's sudden change of plan, which is left unexplained by most writers, is accounted for by Ives and Scrafton as in the text.

[02] **hovitzes** howitzers.

[03] **Modin** Madan.

[04] **Doudpaur** Daûdpur.

[05] **Moraudbaug** Muradbagh.

[06] **nuzzer** nasr.

[07] **Berbohm** Birbaum.

[08] **Nudiah** Nadiya.

[09] **pucker** pakka.

[10] **calling myself Mrs before others tired of calling me Miss** spinster ladies of a certain age were still called Mrs.

[11] **a suitable monument to their common memory** This monument was erected, but was destroyed in 1821, apparently by the vandalism of the Little Englanders of the period.

[12] **pathetic** pathos.

[End of Footnotes]

CPSIA information can be obtained
at www.ICGtesting.com
Printed in the USA
LVHW040938020323
740706LV00007B/487

9 789356 891845